Sacred Text, Secular Times

Proceedings
of the Tenth Annual Symposium
of the Philip M. and Ethel Klutznick
Chair in Jewish Civilization
September 14 & 15, 1997

Studies in Jewish Civilization 10

Sacred Text, Secular Times: The Hebrew Bible in the Modern World

Leonard Jay Greenspoon
Bryan F. LeBeau

Editors

The Klutznick Chair in Jewish Civilization

Creighton University Press
Omaha, Nebraska

Library of Congress Cataloging in Publication Data

Sacred text, secular times : the Hebrew Bible in the modern world /
Leonard Jay Greenspoon & Bryan F. LeBeau, editors.
p. cm. -- (Studies in Jewish civilization. ISSN 1070-8510 ; 10)
"Proceedings of the tenth annual Symposium of the Philip M. and Ethel Klutznick Chair in Jewish Civilization, September 14 & 15, 1997" -- Half t.p.
ISBN 1-881871-32-0 (hard)
1. Bible. O.T.--Criticism, interpretation, etc. Congresses. I. Greenspoon, Leonard J. (Leonard Jay), LeBeau, Bryan F. II. Philip M. and Ethel Klutznick Chair in Jewish Civilization (10th : 1997 : Creighton University) III. Series.
BS1188.S33 2000
221.6--dc21 96-37241
CIP

EDITORIAL
Creighton University Press
2500 California Plaza
Omaha, Nebraska 68178

MARKETING & DISTRIBUTION
Fordham University Press
University Box L
Bronx, New York 10458

Printed in the United States of America

To
Michael J. Proterra, S.J.,
who combines wisdom and virtue
in exemplary fashion

Contents

Acknowledgments

The tenth annual Klutznick Symposium, held on September 14 and 15, 1997, was titled "Sacred Text, Secular Times: The Hebrew Bible in the Modern World." This volume contains printed versions of nine papers presented on that occasion and an additional five solicited papers. The five solicited papers were presented at the annual meeting of the Society of Biblical Literature and the American Academy of Religion, held in San Francisco, in November, 1997. Together these fourteen papers present a rich and varied exploration of the ways in which the Hebrew Bible has influenced the modern world. As we shall see, this influence is not one way, since modern concerns and contemporary perceptions affect the ways in which we read and interpret Sacred Writ.

The tenth Klutznick Symposium featured an exhibit of art related to Genesis 22, the Akedah or Binding of Isaac. Through the efforts and boundless energy of Ori Z. Soltes, then Director of the B'nai B'rith Klutznick National Jewish Museum in Washington, DC, we hosted the premiere of a collection of works by a number of noted artists in a variety of media.

Special thanks also go to Father Ted Bohr, S.J., who directs the gallery at Creighton University's Lied Center, which housed this exhibit. A separate catalogue, " The Binding of Isaac: Genesis XXII and its Progeny," has appeared.

This extra event necessitated more work and more funds than previous Symposia. Fortunately, everyone rose to—and exceeded—the needs of the occasion. First, I express sincere gratitude to the staff responsible for organizing the hundred and one details that all came together in the seemingly effortless public events of the tenth Klutznick Symposium: Kay Replogle, assistant for the Klutznick Chair in Jewish Civilization, and Gloriann Levy, of the Jewish Cultural Arts Council. Next, I thank Bryan Le Beau, then Director of the Creighton Center for the Study of Religion and Society. His fine sense of propriety and proportion, along with his unfailing equanimity in the face of what seemed to me to be an endless string of mini-crises, are rare characteristics that he freely shares. Bryan is also this volume's co-editor, a role he often also filled in the past.

There are numerous individuals and organizations who provided financial support for the tenth Klutznick Symposium. I know that we could not have succeeded without them:

B'nai B'rith Klutznick National Jewish Museum
The College of Arts & Sciences, Creighton University
Dorothy and Henry Riekes
Ike and Roz Friedman Foundation
Jewish Cultural Arts Council
Joseph and Maxine Kirshenbaum
Midwest Express Airlines
The Nebraska Arts Council
The Simon Family of Omaha Steaks

We dedicate this volume to Michael J. Proterra, S. J., Dean of the Creighton College of Arts and Sciences. Michael has been a tireless, eloquent, and generous supporter of our Symposia from their inception. With his retirement in June, 1999, we lose a true friend. Whenever people think of and speak about the Klutznick Chair and its activities, the name of Michael Proterra will be recalled with affection and respect. In acknowledging the service of others, Dean Proterra has often quoted David Starr Johnson: "Wisdom is knowing what to do next. Virtue is doing it." We use it on this occasion to acknowledge Mike's decade of service to us.

Leonard J. Greenspoon, Chairholder
The Klutznick Chair in Jewish Civilization
Creighton University
May, 1999

Editors' Introduction

In many ways, the statistics are startling. In late twentieth century America, in one of history's most secular societies, the Bible continues to be the most purchased, read (or misread), and cited literary work. The Hebrew Bible and the New Testament, generally in translation, are found in almost every home in the United States. Statistics consistently show that almost half of all Americans read the Bible on a regular basis, and Bible study groups are ubiquitous among teens, college students, young adults, the middle-aged, and seniors. Somehow or other and in widely varying ways, this most sacred of texts has managed not only to survive, but to thrive in our secular times. Given the sponsorship of this Symposium by the Klutznick Chair in Jewish Civilization, it seems appropriate to emphasize the Hebrew Bible (often referred to as the Old Testament); naturally, the methods used by scholars to analyze and chart the influence of the Hebrew Bible can also be used to trace the impact of the New Testament.

In organizing the fourteen papers that make up this volume, we were, it seemed, faced with two general organizing principles: either we could, where possible, place the papers in order of the biblical passages they discuss, or we could shape this collection in terms of the type or direction of impact reflected in each paper. We chose the former path; specifically, to organize eleven of the fourteen papers in their "biblical" order, following the order of the Hebrew Bible (rather than that of the Christian Old Testament). The first three defy categorization according to this principle and, moreover, exemplify several overarching themes discernible in the papers that follow. In keeping with this biblical orientation, our brief discussion of each paper begins with and centers on a passage from the Hebrew Bible as rendered in the New Jewish Version (TANAKH: A New Translation of THE HOLY SCRIPTURES According to the Traditional Hebrew Text [Philadelphia: Jewish Publication Society, 1985]).

"See, a time is coming--declares the Lord--when I will make a new covenant with the House of Israel and the House of Judah" (Jeremiah 31:31)

Jeremiah's prophecy provides the source for the terms Old and New Testament (or covenant), which—as is now widely recognized—reflect a Christian perspective. Fred Greenspahn suggests that such a perspective is also responsible for the importation into Judaism of the term Bible, which, although widely used, is at best of ambiguous validity within its new context. Rather, in the quest to understand the nature and function of sacred literature within Judaism, Greenspahn urges reliance on traditional, indigenous Jewish terminology and categories.

"You will proclaim release [or: liberty] throughout the land for all its inhabitants" (Leviticus 25:10)

In a sense, Andrew Skinner and Doris Bergen present opposite sides—one positive, the other decidedly negative—of societal use of the language and imagery of the Hebrew Bible. It is well known that the Liberty Bell in Philadelphia was engraved with this passage from the book of Leviticus. Skinner traces a number of other influences of the Hebrew Bible on the founders of the American Republic. This influence was widespread and profound.

"It is for Your sake that we are slain all day long, that we are regarded as sheep to be slaughtered" (Psalm 44:23 [44:22 in Christian translations])

Equally widespread and profoundly damaging was the misuse or abuse of the Hebrew Bible at the hands of Nazi propagandists, who used the ancient text to demonize German and other European Jews. As Bergen shows, even Christian opponents of Nazism were not immune to anti-Semitism. The quote from Psalm 44 was used by such an opponent to provide a theological understanding for Jewish suffering.

"And God said, 'Let us make man in our image, after our likeness'" (Genesis 1:26)

Richard Middleton's detailed analysis of the first chapters of Genesis, including this verse, seeks to show how these crucial verses should be understood. In the face of numerous attacks by environmentalists and feminists, who can cogently point to the (mis)use of this material to subjugate nature and women, Middleton demonstrates how the divine creation has its roots and fulfillment in love.

"The Lord God formed man from the dust of the earth" (Genesis 2:7)

Eugene Gallagher discusses some of the same material as Middleton, but from a different perspective: how these chapters have been exegeted (or, from traditional perspectives, eisegeted) in support of religious movements outside of mainstream Christianity and Judaism. For example, although the picture of God creating humans from the earth is profoundly meaningful to most Christians and Jews, it is read as a patent falsehood by some religious movements that developed over the past century.

"That same day Noah and Noah's sons, Shem, Ham, and Japheth, went into the ark, with Noah's wife and the three wives of his sons" (Genesis 7:13)

It does not require in-depth analysis to realize that there are some striking omissions of information in the listing of Noah's family: the women are without names, even as their husbands and father are immediately and precisely identified. Within later Jewish and Christian literature, these lacunae are filled, along with the filling out of the personalities of these women, especially Noah's wife. Lesleigh Cushing provides a richly detailed and developed analysis of "Mrs. Noah" from earliest post-biblical times to contemporary novels.

"And he said, 'Do not raise your hand against the boy, or do anything to him. For now I know that you fear God, since you have not withheld your son, your favored one, from Me'" (Genesis 22:12)

Abraham obeys God's command; Isaac is not sacrificed. Is that action (or inaction) heroic? Can this term be applied to any biblical character in the way it was, say, to Achilles, the quintessential hero of ancient Greece? In their analysis Brian Hook and Russell Reno range widely from the biblical period to Greece to early Christianity to the Renaissance to the modern world.

"Sarah died in Kiriath-arba--now Hebron--in the land of Canaan; and Abraham proceeded to mourn for Sarah and to bewail her" (Genesis 23:2)

As noted in the Acknowledgments, Ori Z. Soltes organized an exhibit of artistic works centering on Genesis 22. For his keynote address, which forms the basis for this paper, he broadened his perspective to cover other events and personalities of the Hebrew Bible. But the Akedah and its effects are never far from his concerns, as exemplified by his discussion of works dealing with the domestic consequences—husband and wife (as here), father and son—of Abraham's apparent willingness to sacrifice his son.

"Shechem son of Hamor the Hivite, chief of the country, saw her, and took her and lay with her by force" (Genesis 34:2)

The narrative of Genesis 22 avoids human sacrifice. But violence in many forms nonetheless characterizes much of the book of Genesis. Susanne Scholz provides a suggestive comparative analysis of Genesis 34, where Shechem's violence against Dinah is answered by the violence of the retaliation against Shechem's family engineered by Dinah's brothers. Did Shechem rape Dinah? If she was to any degree "at fault," does that mitigate against the charge of rape? Scholz looks at the parallel answers to these questions provided in the context of nineteenth century Germany by biblical scholars and forensic physicians.

"They saw him from afar, and before he came close to them they conspired to kill him" (Genesis 37:18)

The patriarchal (and matriarchal) families of Genesis not only took violent action against outsiders; they were also capable of inflicting great harm to insiders, as witnessed by the conspiracy against Joseph by his brothers that almost ended in his death. Yes, explains Mark McEntire, the world as narrated in the book of Genesis seems violent—and it was. McEntire brings these concerns to the modern world by noting contemporary interpretations of and reactions to the often violent context in which the Hebrew Bible is set.

"After that, he fell in love with a woman in the Wadi Sorek, named Delilah" (Judges 16:4)

Several papers, including this one by Helen Leneman, analyze the role of female characters in the Hebrew Bible. Delilah (and Samson) and Bathsheba (and David) are among the most famous biblical females. Their narratives, in the books of Judges and Samuel respectively, are rather ambiguous, and later interpreters, using music as well as literature, have variously filled in the blanks left by the biblical text.

"Thus said the Lord to Cyrus, His anointed one--" (Isaiah 45:1)

From at least the first century CE, and probably earlier, individuals have claimed to be the messiah—or the claim was made on their behalf. Typically, "messianic" passages from the Hebrew Bible have been cited as proof texts for such claims. Among such passages is Isaiah 45:1. Harris Lenowitz has uncovered and discussed a nineteenth century Yemenite Jew, who bolstered his claim to messianic status not only by applying biblical passages to himself, but also by creating new "biblical texts" whose prophecies he was fulfilling.

"How can we sing a song of the Lord on alien soil?" (Psalm 137:4)

In modern times, a number of communities have understood themselves in terms derived from the Hebrew Bible. Israel's enslavement in Egypt and its subsequent exodus to freedom form perhaps the most popular of these paradigms. Miguel De La Torre points to another period, the Babylonian exile of the sixth century BCE, as paradigmatic for his fellow Cubans now resident in Miami. He urges his fellow Cubans, both on the island and in Miami, to ask appropriate questions (such as those posed by the author of Psalm 137) and to derive positive responses from the Hebrew Bible, especially the narratives of Ezra and Nehemiah and the prophecies of Jeremiah and Second Isaiah.

"You will listen to the entreaty of the lowly, O Lord, You will make their hearts firm" (Psalm 10:16)

What is it like to read the Hebrew Bible in a non-Western context? Archie Lee provides a fascinating example through his cross-cultural (or cross-textual) reading of laments in classical Chinese sources and the Psalter of the Hebrew Bible, as in Psalm 10. The light shown by this procedure is mutually illuminating and contributes, to use Lee's phrase, to the weaving of a humanistic vision with wide applicability and profound implications.

List of Contributors

Frederick E. Greenspahn	Dept. of Religious Studies University of Denver Denver, Colorado 80208
Andrew C. Skinner	Dept. of Ancient Scripture Brigham Young University Provo, Utah 84602
Doris L. Bergen	Dept. of History University of Notre Dame Notre Dame, Indiana 46556
J. Richard Middleton	Colgate Rochester Divinity School Rochester, New York 14620
Eugene V. Gallagher	Dept. of Religious Studies Connecticut College New London, Connecticut 06320
Lesleigh Cushing	Boston University Boston, Massachusetts 02215
Brian S. Hook	Dept. of Classical and Near Eastern Studies Creighton University Omaha, Nebraska 68178
R. R. Reno	Dept. of Theology Creighton University Omaha, Nebraska 68178
Ori Z. Soltes	Georgetown University Washington, DC 20057

Susanne Scholz	The College of Wooster Wooster, Ohio 44691
Mark McEntire	Dept. of Religion and Philosophy Meredith College Raleigh, North Carolina 27607
Helen Leneman	Rockville, Maryland 20850
Harris Lenowitz	Middle East Center University of Utah Salt Lake City, Utah 84112
Miguel A. De La Torre	Hope College Holland, Michigan 49423
Archie C.C. Lee	Religion Department Chung Chi College Chinese University of Hong Kong

Sacred Text, Secular Times

Proceedings
of the Tenth Annual Symposium
of the Philip M. and Ethel Klutznick
Chair in Jewish Civilization
September 14 & 15, 1997

Does Judaism Have a Bible?

Frederick E. Greenspahn

Several years ago, *The New York Times* reported on its front page what was heralded as the most extensive national study of Americans' religious identity ever conducted under non-denominational auspices. During the last part of 1989 and early 1990, over 100,000 households had been contacted by researchers from the City University of New York's (CUNY) graduate school. On the basis of their findings, they estimated that there were 4.3 million Jews in the United States. Although these data were presented positively, with the Jewish community described as "the largest non-Christian faith represented," "knowledgeable Jews could not help being taken aback, since conventional wisdom has long held that the Jewish population of this country is close to 6 million. What could have happened to a million and a half Jews? Aware of this discrepancy, the newspaper explained that, while a recent estimate by the Council of Jewish Federations put the number of Jews at 5.5 million, the City University researchers did not include those who identify culturally as Jews but not religiously.[1]

The question "Who is a Jew?" is not a new problem for either social scientists or the Jewish community. However, by using religion as their criterion, those conducting the survey chose to disregard nearly a million and a half people who identify themselves as Jews and are, in turn, recognized as such by the Jewish community in all its denominational and political diversity. In other words, the researchers chose to define being Jewish in a way that is quite different from how Jews understand that term. Where, then, did their definition come from? By putting the question in these terms, the answer becomes immediately apparent: Judaism was defined as a religion because that it is how the various Christian denominations whose constituencies make up the vast bulk of those being counted consider themselves. But Judaism does not define itself that way, nor do Jews identify themselves as being

Jewish on that basis. What happened at CUNY is that Judaism (and perhaps other non-Christian traditions as well) was defined in a way that is perceived as natural and appropriate for Christianity, quite apart from how well it suits Jews or others who are also being considered.

Imposing Christian categories on non-Christian traditions is a familiar phenomenon in the study of religion, and examples of the problems which can result are legion. It is this, after all, which accounts for the seemingly endless debate as to whether Buddhism, which has no doctrine of god, is really a religion. A different dimension of the same problem can be seen with the term "Messiah," "which exists as a doctrinal category in Judaism, Christianity, and even Islam, albeit under a different name. It is no wonder, then, that this concept is often used as a basis for comparison, as in the commonplace observation that one of the differences between these traditions is Christianity's belief that the messiah has already come while Jews still await his arrival. Such comparisons are facilitated by the genetic and theological relationships between Judaism and Christianity, which are responsible for the existence of numerous formal parallels. But these concepts often function very differently in their respective traditions. Thus it is noteworthy that the word "messiah," or rather its Greek equivalent *christos*, came to be incorporated in the name of Christianity in a way that is obviously without parallel in either Judaism or Islam.

The same holds true for several other concepts which are ostensibly common to these traditions, including "Sabbath," "Lord," "conversion," "atonement," and possibly even the term "religion" itself, as in the case of Buddhism and now, it would seem, with the New York researchers who used it to identify both Christians and Jews.[2] Despite the similarity of their names and forms, such categories often function quite differently within different traditions, leaving apparent commonalities less similar than is usually recognized.[3]

As the historian Marc Bloch observed, "At the bottom of nearly all criticism there is the problem of comparison."[4] Students of religion must be especially wary of the comparative method, since it so often ends up equating apples and tomatoes simply because they are both red and round. This problem has long been recognized by biblical scholars, who, therefore, emphasize the importance of taking context into consideration before drawing analogies, lest one fall into the trap of what they have come to call "parallelomania."[5]

In spite of these observations, the question posed in the title, whether Judaism has a Bible, still seems patently ridiculous. Obviously Judaism has a

Bible; just ask any Jew. Indeed, where else could Christianity and, ultimately, other traditions have gotten the idea to place a book at the center of revelation?[6] Was it not the existing Jewish Bible that Christianity incorporated into its canon, as acknowledged by the term "*Old* Testament" with which it designates that part of its Scripture that was inherited from the Jews?

Of course, Old Testament is not a term that any Jew could accept, since it automatically alludes to another testament which is not old.[7] However, that problem is hardly restricted to this one phrase. Most of the terms used for the Bible, including several of those now in vogue because of their supposedly neutral tone, are, in fact, "religion bound." For example, First Testament implies another testament every bit as much as Old Testament does.[8] Nor does the widely accepted phrase Hebrew Bible resolve this problem, since the adjective Hebrew (an odd description for a book with major sections in Aramaic) plainly functions to differentiate those sections of the Bible accepted by Jews from others which are not.

One might suppose that the appropriate term from a Jewish point of view would be Bible itself. That, however, raises a somewhat different, but related problem, since it excludes all the books which Christians consider Scripture.[9] However, it is possible to go further and contend that the term "Bible" is inherently problematic for Jews and may be a Christian, and probably Protestant, construct into which the evidence of Judaism is more often forced than appropriately described.

To explore the nuances of this supposedly neutral term, we will use the definition of one eminent modern scholar, whose phrasing reflects what most people understand the word "Bible" to mean. James Barr defines a Bible as "an already existing, defined and delimited, written guide for [a] religion."[10] Each component of this definition contributes an important element to its overall meaning. For example, "already existing" implies that the books included under this rubric were originally written for some other purpose; being Scripture is not, therefore, part of their essence, but the way they came to be used. Books are adopted as Scripture because of the role they play in a particular community. The term "Bible" is, therefore, a functional rather than a formal or essential category.

Second, Barr refers to a Bible as "defined and delimited"; that is to say, it must be a closed and cohesive work, no matter how diverse its various components may once have been. One way in which Judaism accomplished this was by asserting that prophecy had come to an end shortly after the Babylonian exile; anything written later was *ipso facto* non-canonical.[11] Christianity took the same position in response to the heretical movement it called Montanism,[12] as did Islam when it declared Mohammad to have been the "seal of the prophets."[13]

The process of establishing such limits is referred to as canonization. Its significance is nicely illustrated by theologian Avery Dulles' musings as to whether Christianity would accept a newly discovered letter by Paul into its Bible.[14] His conclusion that the answer is not at all certain, even if such a work could pass chronological and authorial muster, confirms what Barr had in mind with his reference to Bibles as being "delimited." That is also why Mormonism's view of an open canon is, in some sense, self-contradictory.[15]

Barr's third criterion, that a Bible must be written, distinguishes it from the broader category of sacred traditions. To be sure, these categories are not always clearly distinct, as in the case of religious traditions *about* biblical characters, such as the assumption of Mary in Roman Catholicism or Abraham's smashing the idols in Judaism. To the extent that these are believed to be grounded in the biblical text, they might be considered to be part of the Bible; however, other sacred traditions are obviously not in the Bible at all.

Barr's reference to being a "guide" suggests that authority is the final criterion for Bibles. This is typically because they are understood as having a divine origin, however that may be expressed. But Bibles are more than *a* guide. The writings of Mary Baker Eddy play a prominent role in Christian Science without in any way displacing what Christian Scientists recognize as the Bible, and the same is true for the Unification Church's *Divine Principle*.[16] Bibles hold a central status in the communities which so honor them. That is why they must be distinguished from the larger category of "sacred books" to which they also belong: All Bibles are sacred, but not every sacred book is a community's Bible. The dangers of ignoring this distinction are well illustrated in the facile comparisons implied by the many works with titles such as *Scriptures of the World Religions* or *The World Bible*.[17] Such collections often mistakenly assume that other traditions impute to all their holy works the characteristics that Christians and Jews ascribe to the Bible alone. But the Bible is more than just a sacred book precisely because of its central role within the religious traditions that revere it.

From this it follows that communities can have only one Bible. That is why Christian theology has devoted so much energy over the centuries to resolving the relationship between the two halves of its own Scripture.[18]

At the same time, religions do not have to have a Bible. Many communities—most notably those with non-literate cultures—have no central book at all. Indeed, the relationship between Scripture and literacy is complex:[19] while Bibles are obviously the product of literate cultures, their existence in turn fosters literacy, at least among some classes, so that their holy words can be given the attention necessary for their role to be fulfilled. Even communities that do have Bibles may be less biblical than we normally think. Within Roman Catholicism, the Bible is not entirely central nor its authority without rival, as is illustrated by the doctrine of papal infallibility, which offers an intriguing parallel to evangelical Protestants' notion of scriptural inerrancy. (Significantly, both received official enactment towards the end of the nineteenth century.)

The case of Roman Catholicism also serves to warn against the seductiveness of assuming that the Bible plays the same role in all the various communities that revere it. Roman Catholics plainly do not regard the Bible or treat it the same way that fundamentalist Protestants do. There is no reason, therefore, to assume that Jews should either. With these considerations in mind, let us ask whether the Jewish Bible meets Barr's criteria.

There is no arguing that the Jewish Bible is written; however, it is not so clear that it is *a* book, with that article's implication of singularity. As much as we may think of the Christian Old Testament as being the Jewish Bible, Judaism itself does not typically conceive of it as a single work. Aside from one exceptional passage in the Talmud,[20] it was not until the tenth century that the constituent books of what is sometimes called the Hebrew Bible (itself a Christian term) were even bound together, and then apparently only as a scribal convenience.[21] Certainly none of the terms which are indigenous to Judaism convey that degree of unity. *Kitvei ha-qodesh* ("holy writings") is plural, while *miqra'* (lit. "recitation") is more generic than singular. Even the growingly popular *TaNaKh* embodies the tripartite structure (Torah, Prophets, Writings) familiar from ancient tradition; moreover, it is not attested until sometime after the Babylonian Talmud was completed — and maybe significantly later.[22]

Nor is what we call the Jewish Bible treated as a unit in Jewish thought or practice. Only the Torah is read completely and without omissions in a regular liturgical cycle.[23] Selections from the Prophets are chosen in a rather haphazard way, while within the Hagiographa only the five scrolls occupy any "scriptural" position at all, although numerous Psalms have been incorporated into the liturgy along with isolated verses from elsewhere. On the basis of Jewish worship, then, it would have to be the Pentateuch which is identified as Scripture. It, indeed, is structured as a book, with all five components bound together in a single scroll which has occupied a place of honor in synagogue architecture (whether in fixed or portable form) since antiquity, a place, moreover, far greater than that given "Bibles" in Jewish custom or law.

This point is supported by the central position accorded the Torah in rabbinic thought and practice. Thus, when Jewish authorities sought (and seek) scriptural justification for laws of uncertain origin, it was invariably to the Pentateuch that they turned, even when its proof texts were reinforced with quotations from the Prophets or the Writings.[24] Indeed, they explicitly state that the Bible's prophetic and hagiographic sections, which in their view merely reiterate what the Pentateuch says,[25] are inherently unnecessary and subject to eventual revocation.[26]

In other words, judged by the criterion of authority, there can be little doubt that it is the Pentateuch—and only the Pentateuch—which is Judaism's Bible. Unlike the Old Testament, it has a title ("Torah") that is both ancient and indigenous to Jewish tradition. Moreover, its centrality can be traced to at least the time of Ezra, with antecedents discernible even earlier.[27]

However, this approach is not without problems. Most difficult is the fact that the Pentateuch is not the real guide for Jewish doctrine and practice. Proof texts often justify already existing practices; the need for scriptural grounding thus tacitly confirms the fact that their real source lies elsewhere.[28] Indeed, for the last several centuries, Ashkenazi Jews have seldom read the Bible directly, but typically with the commentary of Rashi, who provides what amounts to a digest of rabbinic biblical interpretation.[29]

The implications of this observation are supported by the way Judaism confronts contemporary social and technological problems through its responsa literature, in which leading rabbis respond to specific queries. Such works are issued by all the major ideological groupings of contemporary Judaism; and however much their conclusions may differ, their use of the classical tradition to address current dilemmas is fundamentally the same. Moreover, the citations which are used to support these conclusions come overwhelmingly not from the Bible, but from the rabbinic tradition,[30] deriving ultimately from the Talmud, which has consequently become the focus of study within Western Orthodoxy and for religious authority within even liberal communities, including such ostensibly biblicizing movements as Reform Judaism, quite apart from their rhetoric or lay perceptions of how decisions are made.[31] In this respect, Judaism behaves very much like Roman Catholicism, with its reliance on the Church's magisterium rather than the Bible.[32] Thus, the real locus of authority in Judaism lies in the corpus of rabbinic tradition, symbolized by the Babylonian Talmud and systematized in a series of medieval codes, the best known of which (the Shulchan Aruch) was compiled by Joseph Karo in the sixteenth century. To the extent that a community's source of doctrine and practice is its Bible, then, one would have to conclude that it is the Talmud or, perhaps better, the halachic corpus as a whole which plays that role in Judaism.[33]

Unfortunately, such a position is problematic, since the breadth and amorphous nature of these texts can hardly be characterized as "defined and delimited." Nor can the Talmud, which is a specific and coherent piece of work, be given this role, since its discussions do not always reach a clear conclusion,[34] and few Jews of any stripe would recognize the codes or midrashim, which are part of the rabbinic corpus, as holding the same normative status in their tradition as the Bible does for Christianity.

Such problems fade once one turns to indigenous Jewish terminology, which combines all of these sources under the rubric "Oral Torah." It is that Oral Torah to which Judaism ascribes authoritative status, even if it can only be consulted in its written realization, whether in the Talmud or as digested in the various codes.[35] Moreover, this terminology supports both its antiquity—since that name implies that the Oral Torah is as old and authoritative as its written counterpart—and the possibility of a potentially more fruitful approach, one which would treat Torah (Written and Oral together) as Judaism's Bible. For although Judaism is frequently described as holding to a doctrine of two Torahs,[36] there is really only one. Consider the classic mishnaic formulation, according to which Moses received not "the" Torah, but Torah, at Sinai and then handed it down through the generations.[37] According to this view, "the" Torah was (and presumably still is) in heaven, where God used it to create the world and has continued to study it ever since.[38] It is this divine Torah which was revealed to Moses—as a unity, even though parts of it came to be transmitted in two different ways, some written down while other elements were passed on orally, at least until they were collected by the rabbis. Looked at this way, then, one might say that Torah, a generic category like the Hindu Veda, is the Jewish Bible.

Does Judaism, then, have a Bible? Yes, of course; but what is it? Is it the written Scripture (*Tanakh*) or the entire rabbinic corpus, symbolized by the Talmud but including midrashim, codes, and even responsa? More narrowly, one could argue that the Pentateuch, which occupies so central a role in both form (at worship) and substance, is Judaism's Bible, or that all of Torah, in the broadest possible sense, should be considered Bible.

This problem of determining which *one* of these is Judaism's Bible brings us back to the issue with which we began. For just like counting only those who consider Judaism to be their religion as Jews, seeking to identify Judaism's Bible is an exercise in imposing a category taken from one tradition onto another. In this respect, such an undertaking is as absurd as looking for Christian halacha or Hindu eschatology. Bible is a Christian and possibly even a modern Protestant category with inherently Christian features. The only reason the word sounds generic is because our way of seeing the world has been so profoundly affected by Christianity. However, even within Christendom, the Bible is only one type of holy writing or, perhaps better, only one way of transmitting sacred traditions. Judaism has its own ways, which need not conform to those of Christianity, although it is not surprising that they would appear to be similar nor that Christian tradition would believe them to be the same, since it is doctrinally committed to the notion that it absorbed Judaism without making structural or conceptual changes.[39] For purposes of scholarly comparison, however, that assumption cannot be allowed to stand without proof.

Judaism is an independent tradition which must be understood on its own terms, rather than having its unique features forced into the pigeon holes derived from a different culture, however familiar or widespread it may be. In this case, we would do better to try to understand how Jews conceive the nature and function of their sacred literature than to privilege Christianity, in any of its manifestations, by describing how Judaism or any other tradition deviates or conforms.

Notes

[1] *The New York Times*, April 10, 1991, A1 and 18; the results of the National Survey of Religious Identification have since been published in Barry A. Kosmin and Seymour P. Lachman, *One Nation Under God, Religion in Contemporary American Society* (New York: Harmony Books, 1993), where the problem with the Jewish statistics is described on pp. 299-300.

[2] See Wilfred Cantwell Smith, *The Meaning and End of Religion, A New Approach to the Religious Traditions of Mankind* (New York: The Macmillan Co., 1963), chapter 2, 15-50, although Smith's use of the term "faith" may suffer from the same failings.

[3] Thus one might argue that the Torah is more similar to Christianity's Christ than to its New Testament, as Wilfred Cantwell Smith suggests for the Muslim Qur'an (*Religious Diversity* [New York: Harper & Row, 1976], 45).

[4] *The Historian's Craft* (New York: Alfred A. Knopf, 1953), 110.

[5] The term originated with Samuel Sandmel, "Parallelomania," *Journal of Biblical*

Literature 81 (1962):1; for the importance of context, see Shemaryahu Talmon, "The 'Comparative Method' in Biblical Interpretation — Principles and Problems," *Supplements to Vetus Testamentum* 29 (1977): 320-56

[6] This conclusion is implicitly acknowledged by Islam, according to which the Qur'an replaced earlier revelations, which had been found in the Taurat (Old Testament) and Injil (New Testament).

[7] Although the phrase derives from Jeremiah 31:31-33, it was first used for the Hebrew Bible by the Christian authors Irenaeus (*Contra Haereses* 4:28.2), Tertullian (*Adversus Praxeam* 15), and Origen (*Commentary on John* 5:4), and always in tandem with the term New Testament; for translations of these passages, see Lee M. McDonald, *The Formation of the Christian Biblical Canon* (Nashville: Abingdon Press, 1988), 180.

[8] As the second century rhetorician Lucian observed (in a different context), "If there is no other, you are not first; if you are first, then there are others" (*Demonax* [trans. A.M. Harmon, New York: William Heinemann, 1927] 29, Loeb Classical Library, vol. 1, 160-61).

[9] See Franz Rosenzweig, "Zur Encyclopaedia Judaica," *Kleinere Schriften* (Berlin: Schocken Verlag und Jüdischen Buchverlag, 1937), (the review originally appeared in *Morgen* 5 [1929]).

[10] James Barr, *Holy Scripture, Canon, Authority, Criticism* (Philadelphia: Westminster Press, 1983), 1.

[11] Tosefta *Sota* 13:2; Frederick E. Greenspahn, "Why Prophecy Ceased," *Journal of Biblical Literature* 108 (1989): 43.

[12] Irenaeus, *Contra Haereses* 3:11.9 (*Patrologia graeca*, ed. J. Migne, vol. 7:1, 890), Epiphanius, *Adversus Haereses* 1:1 (*Patrologia latina*, ed. J. Migne, vol. 41, 855), and John Chrysostum, *Adversos Judaeos* 6 (*Patrologica graeca*, vol. 48, 910).

[13] Qur'an 33:41.

[14] "The Authority of Scripture: A Catholic Perspective," in *Scripture in the Jewish and Christian Traditions: Authority, Interpretation, Relevance*, ed. Frederick E. Greenspahn (Nashville: Abingdon Press, 1982), 19.

[15] See Kent P. Jackson, "Latter-Day Saints: A Dynamic Scriptural Process," in *The Holy Book in Comparative Perspective*, ed. Frederick M. Denny and Rodney L. Taylor (Columbia, SC: University of South Carolina Press, 1985), 63-4. The "doctrine of continual revelation" asserted in Joseph Smith's ninth Article of Faith ("We believe all that God has revealed, all that He does now reveal; and we believe that He will yet reveal many great and important things pertaining to the kingdom of God" [Joseph Smith, *The Pearl of Great Price* (Salt Lake City: The Church of Jesus Christ of Latter-day Saints, 1972), 60]) is only problematic if one wishes to speak of this revelation (past and future) as constituting a Bible.

[16] See Michel Meslin, "La Bible est-elle un livre à part?," *in Le Christianisme est-il une Religion du Livre*, ed. P. Benoit (Strasbourg, 1984), 131.

[17] E.g., *The Bible of the World*, ed. Robert Ballou (New York: Viking, 1939 and reprinted often, including as recently as 1977 as *The Portable World Bible* [Penguin]); *The*

World's Great Scriptures, ed. Lewis Browne (New York: Macmillan, 1946); *The Scriptures of Mankind, An Introduction*, ed. Charles S. Braden (New York: Macmillan, 1952); and Dwight Goddard, *A Buddhist Bible* (Thretford, VT: 1932, and Boston: Beacon Press, 1994). William Graham's *Beyond the Written Word, Oral Aspects of Scripture* (New York: Cambridge University Press, 1987) and Wilfred Cantwell Smith's *What is Scripture? A Comparative Approach* (Minneapolis: Fortress Press, 1993) come close sometimes to overlooking this same distinction.

[18] Hence the inappropriateness of the current propensity for labeling the New Testament as Christian Scripture, a title which is accurate only for unreconstructed Marcionites; see Jon D. Levenson, "Why Jews Aren't Interested in Biblical Theology," in *The Hebrew Bible, The Old Testament, and Historical Criticism, Jews and Christians in Biblical Studies* (Louisville, KY: Westminister/John Knox, 1993), 33-61.

[19] See Jack Goody, "Introduction" to *Literacy in Traditional Societies*, ed. Jack Goody (Cambridge: University Press, 1968), 2-3 and passim.

[20] Babylonian Talmud, *Bava Batra* 13b.

[21] Moshe Goshen-Gottstein, "The Authenticity of the Aleppo Codex," *Textus* 1 (1960): 1; Gregory A. Robbins, "'Fifty Copies of the Sacred Writings' (VC 4.36): Entire Bibles or Gospel Books?," in *Studia Patristica* 19, ed. Elizabeth A. Livingstone (Leuven: Peeters Press, 1987), 94-95. Alexandrinus includes 2 letters of Clement, Vaticanus is lacking Maccabees, and Sinaiticus includes the epistle of Barnabbas and the Shepherd of Hermes (Brooke F. Westcott, *The Bible in the Church*, 2d edition [London: Macmillan & Co., 1866], 303-308).

[22] Eliezer Ben Yehudah, *Millon ha-Lashon ha-Ivrit ha-Yeshanah veha-Khadashah* (New York: Thomas Yoseloff, 1960), vol. 8, ed. N. Tur-Sinai, 7825. The Aramaic equivalent can be found in masoretic notes, albeit in a somewhat different sense (see Israel Yeivin, *Introduction to the Tiberian Masorah* [Missoula, MT: Scholars Press, 1980], 84; I am grateful to Marc Brettler for drawing this usage to my attention). The tri-partite division itself is first mentioned in Luke 24:44 and the prologue to the Wisdom of Ben Sira by the author's grandson, as well as later rabbinic references.

[23] Contrast James Barr's observation about Christianity: "for purposes of worship, liturgy and preaching rather limited passages have been used since ancient time" (*Holy Scripture*, 91).

[24] For the process of textual justification, see David Weiss Halivni, *Midrash, Mishnah, and Gemara, The Jewish Predilection for Justified Law* (Cambridge, MA: Harvard University Press, 1986).

[25] Babylonian Talmud, *Megillah* 14a, cf. *Exodus Rabbah* 42:8.

[26] Jerusalem Talmud *Megillah* 70d.

[27] Later biblical authors tended to ground various laws and practices in the Mosaic period, just as the Psalter's five-fold structure may be imitative of the Pentateuch.

[28] This is a legacy of Judaism's Pharisaic heritage, which accepted "regulations handed down by former generations and not recorded in the Law of Moses" (Josephus,

Antiquities 13.10.6 [§297]).

[29] Thus also the ancient mandate for including the Targum when reading Scripture (Babylonian Talmud *Berachot* 8a) and contemporary use of Joseph Hertz's commentary, which is now being displaced in Orthodox and Reform congregations by those published by ArtScroll and the Union of American Hebrew Congregations (ed. W. Gunther Plaut) respectively.

[30] For examples, see Peter J. Haas, *Responsa: Literary History of a Rabbinic Genre* (Atlanta: Scholars Press, 1996); a collection of classical examples can be found in Solomon Freehof, *A Treasury of Responsa* (reprinted with *The Responsa* [New York: Ktav Publishing House, 1973]).

[31] Frank Talmage, "Keep Your Sons from Scripture: The Bible in Medieval Jewish Scholarship and Spirituality," in *Understanding Scripture, Explorations of Jewish and Christian Traditions of Interpretation*, ed. Clemens Thoma and Michael Wyschogrod (New York: Paulist Press, 1987), 81-101; and Samuel C. Heilman, *The People of the Book: Drama, Fellowship and Religion* (Chicago: University of Chicago Press, 1983). Note the cover of *The Bible Today* 29:6 (November, 1991), on which a picture of an Orthodox Jew studying the Talmud bears the caption "Torah study in Safed."

[32] Bruce Vawter, C.M., "The Bible in the Roman Catholic Church," in *Scripture in the Jewish and Christian Traditions: Authority, Interpretation, Relevance*, ed. F. E. Greenspahn, 122.

[33] See Jakob J. Petuchowski, *Heirs of the Pharisees* (New York: Basic Books, 1970), 33; and Muslim usage as noted by Camilla Adang, *Muslim Writers on Judaism and the Hebrew Bible: From Ibn Rabban to Ibn Hazm* (Leiden: E.J. Brill, 1996), 17.

[34] See David Kraemer, *The Mind of the Talmud, An Intellectual History of the Bavli* (New York: Oxford University Press, 1990), 92. On p. 106, he cites the biting words of the tenth century Karaite Salmon ben Jeroham: "If the Talmud originated with our master Moses, what profit is there for us in 'another view,' And what can a third and a fourth view teach us, When they tell us first that the interpretation of this problem in law is thus-and-so, and then proceed to explain it with 'another view?'" (from *Sefer Milhamot HaShem*, trans. Leon Nemoy, in *Karaite Anthology* [New Haven: Yale University Press, 1952],78).

[35] On the tradition of not writing down Oral Torah, see Hermann L. Strack, *Introduction to the Talmud and Midrash* (Philadelphia: Jewish Publication Society of America, 1931), 13 and 17-18.

[36] E.g., Ellis Rivkin's reference to the "concept of the twofold Law" (*The Shaping of Jewish History, A Radical New Interpretation* [New York: Charles Scribner's Sons, 1971], 51-53) and Jacob Neusner's to Judaism of the "dual Torah" (e.g., *Torah, From Scroll to Symbol in Formative Judaism* [Philadelphia: Fortress Press, 1985], 74-9, 144-5). Peter Schäfer surveys the history of this terminology in "Das 'Dogma' von der mündlichen Torah im rabbinischen Judentum," in *Studien zur Geschichte und Theologie des rabbinischen Judentums* (Leiden: E.J. Brill, 1978), 153-97.

[37] Mishna *Avot* 1:1; according to some traditions, Moses' Torah includes future questions (midrash *Tanhuma* Buber, Ki Tissa sec. 17), while the Babylonian Talmud *Hagigah* 15b and *Exodus Rabbah* 28:6 trace prophetic and rabbinic teachings back Sinai.

[38] *Genesis Rabbah* 1:1 and Babylonian Talmud *Avoda Zara* 3b; see Qur'an and Gershom Scholem, *The Messianic Idea in Judaism* (New York: Schoken Books, 1971), 294-95, regarding the Ur-Torah *(Torah kelulah)*; according to the rabbis, even fetuses learn Torah in heaven (Babylonian Talmud *Niddah* 30b).

[39] The popular phrase "Judeo-Christian tradition" embodies a contemporary version of this myth, regarding which see Mark Silk, *Spiritual Politics: Religion and American Since World War II* (New York: Simon and Schuster, 1988), 40-53.

The Influence of the Hebrew Bible on the Founders of the American Republic

Andrew C. Skinner

Both the Hebrew scriptures and the Christian New Testament have exerted tremendous influence on American life from the earliest periods of the Republic's history to the present day. However, it seems clear that American political life and culture were, from their earliest beginnings, grounded as much, or more, in the Hebrew scriptures (what Christians call the Old Testament) than in the New Testament—a fact not so self-evident since the American colonies originated as "Christian" colonies. The further back one goes in American history, the more saturated with Hebraic references and allusions one finds American culture to be. Ironically, it is this Hebraic milieu, rather than one grounded in the Christian New Testament, which most fueled the fires of motivation and imagination among American Christian colonists and founders of the Republic. Thus, Cecil Roth could write that were we to "deprive modern Europe and America of [their] Hebraic heritage . . . the result would be barely recognizable."[1]

THE EARLY COLONIAL PERIOD

Many of the early American settlers were good Hebraists and deeply rooted in biblical literature in its original languages. This is true for churchmen, laymen, and political leaders alike.[2] Hebrew was far from being an alien tongue on American Christian soil. Among political figures, William Bradford (1590-1657), one of the original *Mayflower* pilgrims and second governor of the Plymouth Colony, is said to have studied Hebrew more than all other languages because it allowed him to see with his own eyes the ancient oracles of God in their native beauty.[3] Bradford regarded Hebrew as "that most ancient language, and holy tongue, in which the Law and Oracles of God were write [sic]; and in which God, and angels, spake to the holy patriarchs, of old time."[4]

The study of Hebrew is said to have consoled the governor later in his life. Looking back to the landing at Plymouth in the harsh December of 1620 and reviewing the desperate predicament of the colonists, Bradford attributed their sustenance and ultimate success to the spirit and grace of God. He then emphasized his point by citing and drawing parallels to biblical quotations—taken not from the Sermon on the Mount or some other passages from the New Testament, but rather from the Old Testament, specifically Deuteronomy 26:5,7 and the Psalm 107:1-5 and 8.[5] This is all the more significant considering that Bradford regarded the Plymouth colony as an overseas branch of the Congregational Church and conducted it as such whenever possible.

In 1648 Thomas Shepard did a similar thing to Bradford when defending the Bay Colony against charges of cowardice leveled by the Puritans in England, who had stayed at home and fought the Cavaliers. He appealed to Hebrew precedent: "What shall we say of the singular providence of God bringing so many shiploads of His people, through so many dangers, as upon eagles' wings, with so much safety from year to year?" He then supported his thesis with citations from Exodus and Micah.[6]

The first book printed in the colonies was the *Bay Psalm Book*, an English rendition in verse and rhyme of the Psalms from Hebrew by Richard Mather, John Elliot, and Thomas Welde in 1640.[7] And the first Hebrew grammar printed in America was published in 1735 by Judah Monis, a Jewish convert to Christianity and the first full-time instructor of Hebrew at Harvard University.[8]

The first colleges established in colonial America attached particular importance to the teaching of Hebrew.[9] Samuel Johnson, the first president of what was to become Columbia University, said in 1759 that the study of Hebrew was a "gentlemen's accomplishment" and "the mother of all languages." Such a declaration is a far cry from the medieval Christian belief that Hebrew was the language of the diabolical, since the Jews themselves were the children of the devil.[10]

At Harvard, the nation's oldest institution of higher learning (founded in 1636), great value was placed on the study of Hebrew as part of the curriculum. Moreover, an oration in Hebrew was delivered every year at the annual commencement ceremonies until 1817.[11] Lest the significance of this fact be lost, we are to be reminded that Harvard was under church sponsorship at its inception. The university's namesake, John Harvard, was a Puritan minister, and it was his donated library that formed the academic nucleus of the institution.[12]

In 1781, while the American Revolution was in progress, Ezra Stiles, president of Yale University, delivered his public commencement address in Hebrew. He took for a text Ezra 7:10: "For Ezra had set his heart to seek the laws of the Lord, and to do it, and to teach it." According to Charles Seymour, himself a former president of Yale, Stiles was fluent in Hebrew, which he spoke with an unusual grace.[13] When he became president of the university in 1777, Stiles assigned Hebrew study to a prominent place in the college curriculum. Naturally, the best collection of readings for the Hebrew language class was to be found in the Hebrew Bible. Little wonder, then, that the official seal of Yale University is engraved with the words *urim ve-tumim* (the Urim and the Thummim) from Exodus 28:30 and elsewhere.

WHY THE INTEREST

One reason colonists were so interested in the Hebrew scriptures has to do with the fact that Hebrew itself was regarded as a most ancient, sacred language. But another, perhaps paramount, reason for early American interest in the Hebrew scriptures concerns the Exodus theme. American colonial founders thought and spoke of themselves as the Chosen People. Not only did they call America the new Promised Land, but, in the words of one scholar, "they grew to regard themselves as so like the Jews that every anecdote of tribal history seemed like a part of their own recollection."[14] From Benjamin Franklin's grandfather, Peter Folger of Rhode Island, came a little ditty coined in 1676:

New England they are like the Jews, as like as like can be.[15]

It followed that the colonial settlers regarded the Old Testament as a rule of life and the source of instruction in difficult political times. The Hebrew scriptures constituted for them an important guide in most aspects of faith and political practice: "They identified themselves and their destiny within the focus of biblical history: King James I was their Pharaoh, America was Canaan, and the Atlantic Ocean was the Red Sea."[16] The cornerstone of the "New Jerusalem" which the Puritans yearned to establish in the wilderness of America was the Hebrew Bible.[17] They named their communities after towns mentioned in Hebrew scripture, and they chose biblical names for their children. An examination of place names in modern America reveals that half the states contain a Bethel, around twenty states have a Goshen or a Hebron, and there are at present about thirty Jerusalems or its derivative, Salem.[18] Other common biblical place names include Sharon, Damascus, Moriah, Jordan, Canaan, Lebanon, and Carmel. On the other hand, the name Nazareth, which seems specifically Christian since it does not appear anywhere in the Old Testament, the Talmud, or Josephus, is not so common in America.[19]

Hebraic influence on colonial education, both formal and informal, was tremendous. Professor Randall Stewart's assertion, which has become almost axiomatic, is instructive: "The Bible has been the greatest single influence on our literature."[20] But more to the point, it was not the New Testament which formed the foundation of this influence educationally, but the Hebrew scriptures. Carlos Baker, in a brilliant essay entitled "The Place of the Bible in American Fiction," confirms our observation:

> Well into the early national period, when our prose fiction began, the New England mind was saturated with the Old Testament rather than the New. All children were raised on the Bible from the cradle, and writers could assume, as we can no longer do, that the stories of Moses in the bulrushes, or Lot's wife, or Ruth amid the alien corn, or Abraham's sacrifice, were known to them as our children know the complex lore of missiles and moon-conquest. Professor Miller has observed that "there are hundreds of Edens, Josephs, Elijahs for every rare crucifixion or still more rare recreation of the Manger, while Madonnas, are, of course, non-existent."[21]

The influence of the Hebraic literary environment was long lasting. The mood created and promoted by the colonial educators and leaders became so well entrenched in American life that one twentieth-century American author would declare that New England itself was also a "holy land."[22] The effects of the slavery-deliverance-promised land metaphor on every aspect of American political life were profound. This metaphor originated in a thorough knowledge of history presented in the pages of the Hebrew scriptures, and it is nowhere better demonstrated than in Revolutionary-period political commentary.

POLITICAL SATIRE

Political satire in the form of biblical parodies became especially popular in

New England prior to the Revolution, owing to American awareness of a deep-seated trend in English political literature of the eighteenth century. Bernard Bailyn tells us that no fear, no accusations, no warnings were more common among the voices of political opposition in Great Britain during the eighteenth century than those which spoke of tyranny and attempted enslavement on the part of the government. This was picked up in Boston, whose Committee of Correspondence condemned the Coercive Acts as "glaring evidence of a fixed plan of the British administration to bring the whole continent into the most humiliating bondage."[23] Other British actions were similarly viewed as "the attempts of a wicked administration to enslave America."[24] The First Continental Congress, in a formal address to the people of Great Britain, expounded on "the ministerial plan for enslaving us"; and the Second Continental Congress justified its activity by reference to "the rapid progress of a tyrannical ministry."[25]

Such denouncements had a special resonance in the colonies, where people generally were acquainted with the biblical Book of Esther. Here they possessed a ready-made model for a wicked and tyrannical ministerial conspiracy attempting to usurp sacred rights and enslave an entire people — namely, the bloodthirsty Haman at the court of Ahasuerus. In 1775, a Newbury, Massachusetts minister, Oliver Noble, made specific reference to:

> Haman the Premier, and his junto of court favorites, flatterers, and dependents in the royal city, together with governors of provinces, councilors, board of trade, commissioners and their creatures, officers and collectors of revenue, solicitors, assistants, searchers, and inspectors, down to tide-waiters and their scribes, and the good Lord knows whom and how many of them, together with the coachman and servants of the whole. <footnote: Not that I am certain the Persian state had all these officers . . . or that the under-officers of state rode in coaches or chariots.... But as the Persian monarchy was despotic... it is highly probable.> Now behold the decree obtained! The bloody plan ripened! [The] cruel perpetrators of the horrid plot and a banditti of ministerial tools through the provinces [had everything in readiness] But behold!... A merciful God heard the cries of this oppressed people.[26]

Reverend Noble drew close parallels. Haman was Lord North; Esther and the Jews were the colonists; and Mordecai was Benjamin Franklin.[27]

This was not the first time a British leader had been associated with the Esther story. As early as 1747 Cadwallader Colden, acting governor of New York, had been described as New York's Haman by an angry patriot, Philip Livingston.[28]

Colonial propaganda often took the form of biblical imitation to review and criticize specific enactments of the British government. In what has been described as the "the most ambitious and nearly successful of half a dozen Biblical imitations which appeared in the Revolutionary period," *The First Book of the American Chronicles of the Times* reviewed the six-month period following the passage of the Port Bill, catching "the accent of the Old Testament chronicle books."[29] It was published serially in Philadelphia during the winter of 1774-1775 and is so clever and complete in its characterization that identification of the intended protagonists becomes an engaging exercise, as the following paragraphs demonstrate.

When the men of Boston learn that the "great Sanhedrim"[30] (British government) had passed "a decree that their harbours be blocked up" and that Rehoboam the king had sent Thomas the Gageite to enforce it, they "entered into a solemn league and covenant, that they would obey the book of the law, and none other."[31] The allusions to Old Testament figures as well as the use of "biblical" language are so obvious as to need little comment, except to say that the covenant-style phraseology is reminiscent of passages like 2 Kings 23:3, which describes King Josiah's experience. It reads:

> And the King stood by a pillar, and made a covenant before the Lord . . . to perform the words of this covenant that were written in this book. And all the people stood to the covenant.

As the parody continues, the other American "tribes" take pity on the Bostonites:

> And they got ready their camels and their asses, their mules and their oxen, and laded them with their meat, their fine wheaten flour, their rice, their corn, their beeves and their sheep, and their figs and their tobacco abundantly, and six thousand shekels of silver, and threescore talents of gold, and sent them, by the hands of the Levites, to their brethren, and there was joy in the land.

In letters to King Rehoboam, Thomas the Gageite complains that the Americanites are "giants, men of great stature, and we seem but as caterpillars in their sight." Rehoboam replies that his grandfather corrected them with rods, "but I will chastise them with scourges." When Thomas lays siege to Boston, one of the citizens of the town says that they do not mean to sell their birthright "for a dish of TEA," and Jedediah (Samuel Adams) reads to the men of Boston certain letters that the Congress has addressed to Rehoboam:

> Hast thou not sent forth a decree, that all the world should be taxed for the God of the TEA CHEST?...Would we not all to a man (were it the laws of our own land) rather sooner agree voluntarily to burn our throats with a ladle of hot mush, our own country produce and manufacture, than have the nosle of a tea pot crammed down our throats, and scalded with the abominable and baneful exotic, without our own consent?
>
> And moreover, O king, hast thou not made a Jesuitical decree, that our half brethren the Canadians and Quebeckites fall down and worship graven images? And peradventure, we and our children be commanded to fall down and worship them also....We cannot apostatise, we will not, though Belzebub himself should be belwether to his holiness, and stand at our gate with all his bald pated fryars, and imps of hell at his elbow.

The king is then advised to revoke the "ill advised commandments." "Otherwise," continues the *Chronicles*:

> we do most firmly resolve, that we will have no farther dealings with thy people; and that in the space of sixty days we will not traffick with them for their TEA, their tea cups, their saucers, nor their slop bowls. . . . And whereas thou pridest thyself, our raiment will wax old, and we shall go naked and barefooted, knowest thou not O king, the Lord our God clothed our forefathers in the wilderness, and their garments waxed not old, neither did their feet swell?

In the end, Mordecai the Benjamite (Ben Franklin) laments, "Wo unto the land whose king is a child, whose counsellors are madmen, and whose nobles are tyrants, that devise wicked counsel, for they shall be broken like potters clay." It was reported by the *North Carolina Gazette* that *The First Book of American Chronicles of the Times* sold upwards of three thousand copies in just a few months.[32]

DURING THE WAR

Cecil Roth has pointed out that the Hebraic conception of the tripartite agreement between God, his people, and their earthly ruler formed the basis of support for constitutional government in England. This was taken over by colonial leaders and, in turn, "by the fathers of the American Revolution, who were inspired at every turn by the ideas of the Bible." Professor Roth continues:

> The "Pilgrim Code" of Plymouth Colony (1636) and the "Body of Liberties" of Massachusetts (1647) were confessedly based on the Hebrew scriptures, and the leaders of the American Revolution, from Benjamin Franklin downwards, were imbued with Hebrew conceptions. It was Hebraic mortar . . . that cemented the foundations of the republic.[33]

In the same vain, Gabriel Sivan has written:

> Over 2,000 years after the Covenant of Deuteronomy (27:14-16), when the Israelites signified their consent ("Amen") to the theocratic system of Moses, the Pilgrim Fathers rediscovered and transmitted the Bible's social contract in their Mayflower Compact (1620): "We...doe by these presents solemnly and mutually in ye presence of God, and of one another, covenant and combine our selves togeather into a civill body politick" in order to frame "just and equall lawes." Since these refugee Puritans saw their new religious society as a "continuation and extension of the Jewish church." they held their responsibility to be not to kings or bishops but to God Himself. These "new Israelites" had been led into their Promised Land from Egyptian bondage in England and they firmly believed that the Prophets spoke as much to them as they had to the Hebrews of old. Their first Thanksgiving celebration (1621) was more a Jewish fast and day of prayer than the traditional festivity of modern times; in the nature of his authority their elder or minister was more like a Rabbi than an Anglican priest; and their Sabbath observance

and church practice found a model in what they knew of Jewish ceremonial from the Bible. In civil and ecclesiastical government the will of the majority was law, and even trial by jury was rejected as having no Scriptural basis and precedent. The Mosaic Law was adopted in the Connecticut Code of 1650 and half of the statutes in the Code of the New Haven Colony (1655) refer to the "Old" Testament.[34]

Without question, the slavery-deliverance-promised land motif remained an effective metaphor during the Revolution and was prominent in the minds of its leaders as well as common supporters. On July 4, 1776, the Liberty Bell was rung to signal the Continental Congress's adoption of the Declaration of Independence. Commissioned in 1751 by the Pennsylvania Provincial Assembly to hang in the new State House (renamed Independence Hall) in Philadelphia, the Liberty Bell was inscribed with the words of Leviticus 25:10: "And proclaim liberty throughout the land unto all the inhabitants thereof." It is significant that this potent symbol of the nation's freedom bore a verse from the Hebrew scriptures and not something from one of the sayings of Jesus or Paul on freedom and liberty.

On the same day that the Declaration of Independence was adopted, Thomas Jefferson, John Adams, and Benjamin Franklin were assigned the task of formulating an official seal for the new nation.[35] They and other national founders, including the Reverend Thomas Hooker (who wrote the constitution for Connecticut in 1649), came to believe that the most substantive and appropriate image to display on the Great Seal of the new Republic, because it symbolized the ideals of the new nation, was a reflection of the message found in Exodus 14:8-30 and Numbers 14:14. Here is Franklin's description of the way he thought it should be portrayed:

> Moses standing on the Shore, and extending his Hand over the Sea, thereby causing the same to overwhelm Pharoah who is sitting in an open Chariot, a Crown on his Head and a Sword in his Hand. Rays from a Pillar of Fire in the Clouds, reaching to Moses, to express that he acts by Command of the Deity. Motto, *Rebellion to Tyrants is Obedience to God.*[36]

Jefferson's proposal was very similar:

> Pharaoh sitting in an open chariot, a crown on his head and a sword in his hand passing thro' the divided waters of the Red sea in pursuit of the Israelites: rays from a pillar of fire in the cloud, expressive of the divine presence, and command, reaching to Moses who stands on the shore and, extending his hand over the sea, causes it to overwhelm Pharaoh. Motto. Rebellion to tyrants is obedience to god.[37]

Jefferson's scheme seems to have derived from Franklin's, but was not the future president's only proposal, at least not according to John Adams, who presents us with added insight. In writing to his wife, Abigail, on August 14, 1776, Adams reported that for the image of the Great Seal:

> Mr. Jefferson proposed the children of Israel in the wilderness, led by a cloud by day and a pillar of fire by night; and on the other side, Hengist and Horsa, the Saxon chiefs from whom we claim the honor of being descended, and whose political principles and form of government we have assumed.[38]

Professor Gilbert Chinard, distinguished biographer of Jefferson, wrote that "Jefferson's great ambition at that time was to promote a renaissance of Anglo-Saxon primitive institutions on the new continent."[39] According to another scholar, Jefferson, who had studied the institutes of Anglo-Saxon government, believed that they were very close to, and an extension of, those principles of representative government practiced by ancient Israel under the leadership of Moses.[40]

THOMAS JEFFERSON

It is instructive to note that Jefferson was not a biblical man, by which we mean that his was an overwhelmingly rationalist approach to life. He once counseled that all issues, even religious matters, should be submitted to the rigorous test of reason: "Fix reason firmly in her seat, and call to her tribunal every fact, every opinion."[41] In fact, Jefferson even saw this overriding loyalty to reason as a *religious* duty. "For the use of reason," he noted, "everyone is responsible to the God who planted it in his breast, as a light for his guidance."[42]

Jefferson, like John Adams, did not possess a very high regard for reliance on revelation. If God had spoken literally to humankind at one time, "the vagaries of centuries of translation and transmission had left the contemporary reader of the Bible with imperfect texts, meaningless phrases, corrupted manuscripts."[43] Jefferson's counsel was to read the Bible as one would read the ancient historians Livy or Tacitus. Those ideas which contradicted the laws of nature must be examined much more closely and skeptically. Both the Old and New Testaments contained sections of purely human composition, and, he added, "parts are of the fabric of very inferior minds." Jefferson cited the famous story of Joshua commanding the sun to stand still (contained in chapter ten of the book of Joshua) as a case in point. As anyone could plainly discern, such an event would be contrary to natural law. Examine all the circumstances, Jefferson advised, and then ask which is more probable: an error in reporting or a violation of nature's law?[44]

Nevertheless, for all of Jefferson's cautions, he was still greatly influenced by the Bible, as his proposal for the Great Seal of the new nation testifies. And with regard to the ideological foundations of the new nation, we find him making more direct references to the Hebrew scriptures than to the New Testament. For example, he unhesitatingly rejected the atheism of some of the French philosophes, finding such a position illogical and untenable. For him, creation necessitated "a first cause, possessing intelligence and power; power in the production, and intelligence in the design and constant preservation of the system."[45]

For Jefferson, the opening phrases of the Declaration of Independence were neither idle nor rhetorical: under "the Laws of Nature and of Nature's God all men are created equal . . . they are endowed by their creator with certain unalienable rights." Thus Jefferson exulted in the words of Psalm 148 — recommending them to John Adams "as an excellent portrayal of Nature's God":

> Praise the Lord!
> Praise the Lord from the heavens, praise him in the heights!
> Praise him all his angels, praise him, all his host!
> Praise him, sun and moon, praise him, all you shining stars!
> Praise him, you highest heavens, and you waters above the heavens!
> Let them praise the name of the Lord!
> For he commanded and they were created.
> And he established them for ever and ever;
> He set a law which cannot pass away.

Jefferson was also fond of Psalm 18:9-10 because the words of that passage spoke of Nature, which itself spoke the language of God.

Scholars have spent considerable time trying to understand where Jefferson got the phrase, "pursuit of happiness," that he also included in the Declaration. And commensurate effort has been expended in determining what he meant. As Pauline Maier explains, the Hebrew scriptures tremendously influenced colonial thinking on this point:

> For Jefferson and his contemporaries, happiness no doubt demanded safety or security, which would have been in keeping with the biblical phrase one colonist after another used to describe the good life — to sit at peace under their vine and fig tree with none to make them afraid (Micah 4:4).[46]

In short, even though Jefferson was not a biblical literalist and did not accept every verse as inspired, he was, without question, deeply influenced by the texts of the Hebrew scriptures. They were, so to speak, in the very air he breathed. In a letter to one of his associates, written after the new federal government was firmly in place, Jefferson complained about the ongoing oppression of liberties and the betrayal of the spirit of the Revolution by the new aristocracy. He used a biblical analogy to describe American patriots "who once were Samsons but who now 'have had their heads shorn by the harlot England.'"[47] Later, in his Second Inaugural address, Jefferson called for "the favor of that Being in whose hands we are, who led our fathers, as Israel of old, from their native land and planted them in a country flowing with all the necessaries and comforts of life."[48]

In the words of one of Jefferson's biographers: "Jefferson not only knew his Bible, he also knew when it seemed most appropriate to evoke its imagery."[49] That imagery most relevant to colonial America's circumstances came largely from the Hebrew scriptures. In fact, in at least one of his writings, Jefferson seems to distinguish the Old Testament from the New Testament by referring to the former as *the* Bible, while the New Testament was simply called the "Testament." Both, he said, are part of the common law.[50]

THE VIEW OF OTHERS

Others who shared the views of Jefferson and Adams regarding the excellence of reason over revelation also demonstrated their familiarity with the Hebrew scriptures. Ethan Allen of Vermont, who published *Reason the Only Oracle of Man* in 1784, acknowledged that scripture implied that "none by searching can find out God," quoting from Job 11:7. But, he went on to say, mankind should exercise their reason on divine topics in order to rid themselves of blindness and superstition. It is instructive to point out that Allen's appeal was to a text found in the Old Testament rather than the New.

From among the undated papers of Alexander Hamilton we read his following incomplete comment about the Jewish people:

> . . . progress of the Jews and their [lacuna] from their earliest history to the present time has been & is, intirely out of the ordinary course of human affairs. Is it not then a fair conclusion that the cause also is an extraordinary one—in other words that it is the effect of some great providential plan? The man who will draw this Conclusion will look for the solution in the Bible. He who will not draw it ought to give us another fair solution.[51]

Such a reference can only be to the Hebrew scriptures, which presents the destiny of Israel, specifically the Jews, as following a divinely appointed or providential plan.

BENJAMIN FRANKLIN

Not only does Benjamin Franklin's proposal for the Great Seal of the United States reflect a significant understanding and application of the slavery-deliverance-promised land motif as found in the Hebrew scriptures, but several of his other papers and letters also convey a sense of Franklin's thorough knowledge of the Old Testament and its influence upon him as well as his contemporaries. One of the more interesting examples is a letter to Samuel Cooper, dated May 15, 1781, wherein Franklin extolled the virtues of a sermon which Cooper had preached to celebrate the inauguration of the new government. Franklin then noted:

> Nothing could be happier than your choice of a text, and your application of it. It was not necessary in New England, where everybody reads the Bible, and is acquainted with scripture phrases, that you should note the texts from which you took them; but I have observed in England, as well as in France, that Verses and expressions taken from the sacred writings, and not known to be such, appear very strange and awkward to some readers.[52]

Since the text was taken from Jeremiah 30:20-21 ("Their Congregation shall be established before me: and their Nobles shall be of themselves, and their Governor shall proceed from the midst of them"), one wonders how accurate Franklin's comment would be in our day: namely, that since everybody reads the Bible, it would not be necessary to cite the references for passages quoted. However, one also wonders if Franklin isn't really telling us that in his day New Englanders knew the biblical references to every passage of scripture which applied to their situation as a new nation in the context of the slavery-deliverance-promised land motif.

During the Revolution, references to ancient Israel as a symbol of the American colonies were constant, especially in New England. A typical communication in the *Boston Gazette,* for example, dated May 6, 1782, begins: "My dear countrymen, my sincere wish and prayer to God is, that our Israel may be saved from the rapacious jaws of a tyrant."[53]

The slavery-deliverance-promised land experience of ancient Israel remained a powerful metaphor for Franklin throughout his life. In a letter to the editor of the Federal Gazette, dating from 1788, Franklin unequivocally applied the circumstances of ancient Israel to those of the American colonists. The introductory paragraph of the letter sets the stage for what turns out to be a comparison of the ancient Israelites and the anti-federalists in America:

> A zealous advocate for the proposed federal Constitution, in a certain public assembly, said, that "the repugnance of a great part of mankind to good government was such, that he believed, that, if an angel from Heaven was to bring down a Constitution formed there for our use, it would nevertheless meet with violent opposition." He was reproved for the supposed extravagance of the sentiment; and he did not justify it. Probably it might not have immediately occurred to him, that the experiment had been tried, and that the event was recorded in the most faithful of all histories, the Holy Bible; otherwise he might, as it seems to me, have supported his opinion by that unexceptional authority.[54]

Franklin went on to explain how God chose and nourished a single family until it became a great people, a people God delivered from bondage through a great leader—Moses—through whom he also provided a divinely sanctioned Constitution with ministers to head the new government (Moses, Aaron, and his sons). "One would have thought," said Franklin:

> that this appointment of men, who had distinguished themselves in procuring the liberty of their nation, and hazarded their lives in openly opposing the will of a powerful monarch, who would have retained that nation in slavery, might have been an appointment acceptable to a grateful people; and that a constitution framed for them by the Deity himself might, on that account, have been secure of a universal welcome reception. Yet there were in every one of the thirteen tribes some discontented, restless spirits, who were continually exciting them to reject the proposed new government, and this from various motives. Many still retained an affection for Egypt, the land of their nativity; and these, whenever they felt any inconvenience or hardship, though the natural and unavoidable effect of their change of situation, exclaimed against their leaders as the authors of their trouble; and were not only for returning into Egypt, but for stoning their deliverers.[55]

The parallels between the ancient Israelites and the American colonists are crystal clear: a new nation seeking to secure liberty from a powerful monarch, a new constitution framed with God's help, and the disaffected of the new nation seeking to return to the land of their nativity and captivity. Franklin concluded his letter by affirming his belief in the divinely inspired nature of the federal Constitution and the influence of Providence upon the General Convention. He could hardly conceive of such a momentous transaction as was undertaken by the Constitutional Convention being left to chance.

AFTER THE WAR

After the War was over, the stories and themes of the Hebrew scriptures continued to be used by many as vehicles to inform and teach the public about historical events and political issues. Thomas Jefferson, who made explicit reference to certain passages in the Hebrew scriptures, was himself referred to symbolically in the context of those scriptures. Medford, Massachusetts, pastor David Osgood employed bitter invective against Jefferson as president: if George Washington was the nation's King David, said Osgood, Jefferson was the rebellious son Absalom.[56]

In 1801, the Reverend Nathanael Emmons preached a fast-day sermon on the radical and regrettable change of leadership in Israel—but of course everyone understood that he meant President Thomas Jefferson of the United States. Emmons drew his own analogy, not to Absalom, but to King Jeroboam who replaced his two wise and righteous predecessors, David and Solomon (Washington and Adams). Jeroboam employed "every artifice to prejudice the people against the former administration," causing great disaffection "by basely misrepresenting the wise measures of that wise and excellent ruler." Jeroboam and his administration, being "artful and designing politicians," were responsible for bringing their nation to its sorry state, Emmons declared, as a direct result of their "depravity of the heart" more than their "weakness of understanding."[57]

Perhaps the most impressive presentation of national history cast in the guise of Hebrew narrative was published in 1785 by Timothy Dwight. Entitled *The Conquest of Canaan*, this American epic poem, written in eleven books of rhymed pentameters, retells the story of Joshua's leadership of Israel during their conquest of the promised land. But, in fact, it is a colossal and symbolic account of Washington's conquest of the British and the establishment of America. Dwight wanted to give the New World an epic poem of its own, such as the *Iliad* was to Greece, or the *Aeneid* was to Rome. And though he was a rigid Calvinist, as well as a "Yankee Christian gentleman,"[58] he chose an episode from the Hebrew scriptures as the pattern for his own composition.

As the poem opens, the reader understands that Joshua is the hero, "Chief," and "Leader" of the action, divinely appointed:

> The chief, whose arm to Israel's chosen band
> Gave the fair empire of the promis'd land,
> Ordain'd by Heaven to hold the sacred sway,
> Demands my voice and animates the lay.

THE
CONQUEST
OF
CANÄAN;
A POEM, IN ELEVEN BOOKS.
BY TIMOTHY DWIGHT.

Fired, at firſt ſight, with what the Muſe imparts,
In fearleſs youth we tempt the height of arts.
POPE.

HARTFORD:
PRINTED BY ELISHA BABCOCK.
M,DCC,LXXXV.

The Israelites, in accord with sacred history outlined in the Book of Joshua, are represented in circumstances of extreme distress. Jabin, the Canaanite king of Hazor, has sent an army to afflict Israel. Hanniel presents a defeatist oration, rehearsing the Israelites' misery, the impossibility of their success because of the strength, skill, and numerous allies of their enemy's armies. Even if they are able to conquer Canaan, they will be ruined in the process.

Joshua tries to reply that Providence is with them, but is interrupted by Hanniel who openly accuses Joshua of trying to usurp kingly authority. However, Joshua's rebuttal carries the hour. He points out the misery of their experience under the King of Egypt and declares the certainty of their success, the favor and revealed designs of Heaven. He then exults in the future glory of their own kingdom.

This epic is sufficiently full of noble speech and deeds, on the one hand, and gore and savage battle, on the other, to satisfy any reader of the Hebrew scriptures:

> Now where the Chief terrific swept the field,
> And, clothes in terror, ranks on ranks repelled;
> Whilst a red deluge o'er his footsteps spread
> And countless torrents sprouted from the dead.
> (Book XI, lines 881-884)

Ultimately, Joshua and Israel's armies are successful. As the poem ends, Israel expresses gratitude to God, the one who gave them both victory and their great mortal leader, Joshua:

> The storm retir'd; the ensigns gave command,
> And round their Leader throng'd the conquering band.
> . . . While Joshua's thoughts mount upward to the skies,
> And fear, and wonder, in his bosom rise. . . .
> And songs rose grateful to the Eternal Name---
> Blessed be the Power divine—rejoiced they sung---
> The green vales echoed, and the forest rung---
> Blessed be the hand, that clave the conscious sea,
> And robbed in thunder, swept on foes away!
> Let endless blessings round our nation rise
> Cheer all our lives, and waft us to the skies!
> (Book XI, lines 1113-1114, 1119-1120, 1124-1130)

Throughout the poem, Dwight emphasizes the connection between ancient Israel's situation and the new American nation, which, having just defeated the British, owes it gratitude to God and to General Washington, a leader in the mold of Joshua. In fact, the work is explicitly "Dedicated to George Washington, Esquire":

> Commander in Chief of the American Armies
> The Savior of his Country
> The Supporter of Freedom
> And Benefactor of Mankind

The Conquest of Canaan is an epic of considerable emotion and power, made more poignant by an appreciation for the original story in the Hebrew scriptures. It undoubtedly had an impact on contemporary times, as did other symbolic presentations connecting the new nation with events described in the Hebrew Bible. For the first president's inauguration in 1789, a Hebrew prayer was written in which the name of Washington appears as an acrostic. The prayer invokes God's blessing on the father of our country as well as on the vice president, senators, and representatives of the United States.[59]

To his EXCELLENCY,
GEORGE WASHINGTON, ESQUIRE,
Commander in chief of the American Armies,
The Saviour of his Country,
The Supporter of Freedom,
And the Benefactor of Mankind;

This Poem is inſcribed,
with the higheſt reſpect for his character, the moſt ardent wiſhes for his happineſs, and the moſt grateful ſenſe of the bleſſings, ſecured, by his generous efforts, to the United States of North America,

by his moſt humble,

and moſt obedient ſervant,

TIMOTHY DWIGHT.

Greenfield, in Connecticut,
March 1, 1785.

CONCLUSION

The Hebrew scriptures had an enormous and profound impact on American colonial life. Of this period Perry Miller has said: "The remarkable aspect about . . . such daily conversation as we find reliably recorded, is that the Biblical vision out of which these particular examples comes was so predominantly, almost exclusively, confined to the Old Testament."[60] This Hebraic influence on the found*ers* and found*ing* of the American Republic is especially keen. Though we often think of the American Revolution as being under the direct influence of rationalists and rationalism, images and even language drawn from the pages of the Hebrew Bible were at least as powerful a force in shaping the new nation as John Locke or Thomas Paine.

Ironically, in the early decades of the nineteenth century, when Protestant piety was turning away from the Old Testament towards the New (as Jefferson seems to have done in his later life), there was a cultural flowering or efflorescence of Hebraic feeling and imagery in art and popular literature. It came from the political sphere; it continues to infuse our national ethos today. Echoes of the words of Herman Melville, writing in 1850, seem still to reverberate in the collective unconscious of the American nation: "We Americans are the peculiar, chosen people — the Israel of our time; we bear the ark of the liberties of the world."[61]

Notes

[1] Cecil Roth, *The Jewish Contribution to Civilization* (New York: Harper and Brothers Publishers, 1940), 21.

[2] See the partial but extensive list of colonial Hebraists in Robert H. Pfeiffer, "The Teaching of Hebrew in Colonial America," *Jewish Quarterly Review* 45 (1955): 365-66.

[3] William Chomsky, *Hebrew: The Eternal Language* (Philadelphia: The Jewish Publication Society of America, 1975), 249.

[4] Allen Johnson, ed., *Dictionary of American Biography* (New York: Charles Scribner's Sons, 1937), 1:562.

[5] William Bradford, *Of Plymouth Plantation* (New York: Alfred A. Knopf, 1959), 62-63. See also Perry Miller, "The Garden of Eden and the Deacon's Medow," *American Heritage* 7 (December, 1955): 59.

[6] Miller, "The Garden of Eden and the Deacon's Meadow," 59.

[7] Chomsky, *Hebrew: The Eternal Language,* 248.

[8] Pfeiffer, "The Teaching of Hebrew," 369.

[9] Pfeiffer, "The Teaching of Hebrew," 363.

[10] Joshua Trachtenberg, *The Devil and the Jews* (Philadelphia: Jewish Publication Society of America, 1983), 61-63.

[11] Chomsky, *Hebrew: The Eternal Language,* 248.

[12] Gabriel Sivan, *The Bible and Civilization* (Jerusalem: Keter Publishing House, 1973), 236.

The effects of this linguistic and literary Hebraic involvement on colonial politics were noteworthy. The break with England in 1776 apparently even prompted a few revolutionaries to suggest that Hebrew, the original language of the Bible, be adopted as the official language of the new-born country.

[13] Chomsky, *Hebrew: The Eternal Language*, 248.

[14] Miller, "The Garden of Eden and the Deacon's Meadow," 60.

[15] Miller, "The Garden of Eden and the Deacon's Meadow," 60.

[16] Chomsky, *Hebrew*, 249.

[17] Sivan, *The Bible and Civilization*, 236.

[18] Timothy P. Weber, "Mapping the American Zion," *Textures-Hadassah National Jewish Studies Bulletin*, Vol. 13, No. 2 (May, 1995): 3.

[19] The place name Nazareth is to be found eight times in countries around the world, four of those are in the United States: Colorado, Kentucky, Pennsylvania, and Texas.

[20] Randall Stewart, *American Literature and Christian Doctrine* (Baton Rouge, 1958), 3.

[21] Carlos Baker, "The Place of the Bible in American Fiction, " in *Religious Perspectives in American Culture*, ed. Ward and Jamison, (Princeton: Princeton University Press, 1961), 247.

[22] Howard A. Bridgman, *New England in the Life of the World* (Boston: Pilgrim Press, 1920), 5.

[23] Quoted in Bernard Bailyn, *The Ideological Origins of the American Revolution* (Cambridge, Massachussetts: Harvard University Press, 1967), 126.

[24] Bailyn, *Ideological Origins*, 126.

[25] Bailyn, *Ideological Origins*, 126.

[26] Quoted in Bailyn, *Ideological Origins*, 127

[27] Bailyn, *Ideological Origins*, 127.

[28] Quoted in Milton Klein, *William and Mary Quarterly*, third series, 17 (1960): 445.

Other examples of biblically patterned political satire from prewar years demonstrate a familiarity with many other stories from the Hebrew scriptures. A work attributed to Stephen Hopkins was entitled *The Fall of Samuel the Squomicutite, and the Overthrow of the Sons of Gideon*. The allusion to two Old Testament figures is unmistakable, but they merely represented two of Hopkins' political adversaries, Samuel Ward and Gideon Wanton.

Hopkins, Ward, and Wanton hailed from Rhode Island, where the former became embroiled in something not unlike a tribal feud against the other two. Based on political differences as well as sectional rivalry, the hostility broke out when Ward defeated Hopkins for political office. The feud raged between 1757 and 1768. It was finally resolved when both men were chosen as delegates to the First Continental Congress in 1774. See Dumas Malone, ed., *Dictionary of American Biography* (New York: Charles Scribner's Sons, 1958), 10:437.

[29] Bruce I. Granger, *Political Satire in the American Revolution*, 1763-1783 (Ithaca: Cornell University Press, 1960), 70.

[30] The New testament form of the word appears as Sanhedrin, while the form *Sanhedrim* in *The First Book of the American Chronicles of the Times* seems to reflect the normal masculine Hebrew plural ending "im."

[31] Quoted in Granger, *Political Satire*, 68.

[32] Granger, *Political Satire*, 69, note 45.

[33] Roth, *Jewish Contribution to Civilization*, 15.

[34] Sivan, *The Bible and Civilization*, 174-175.

[35] Richard S. Patterson and Richardson Dougall, *The Eagle and the Shield — A History of the Great Seal of the United States* (Washington: U.S. Government Printing Office, 1978), 6.

[36] Julian P. Boyd, ed., *Papers of Thomas Jefferson* (Princeton: Princeton University Press, 1950), 1:494.

[37] Boyd, *Papers of Thomas Jefferson*, 1:495.

[38] Boyd, *Papers of Thomas Jefferson*, 1:495.

[39] Quoted in W. Cleon Skousen, *The Making of America* (Washington: The National Center for Constitutional Studies, 1985), 32.

[40] Skousen, *Making of America*, 32.

[41] Edwin S. Gaustad, *Sworn on the Altar of God: a Religious Biography of Thomas Jefferson* (Grand Rapids, Michigan: William B. Eerdmans Publishing Company, 1996), 27.

[42] Quoted in Gaustad, *Sworn on the Altar of God*, 29.

[43] Quoted in Gaustad, *Sworn on the Altar of God*, 28.

[44] Andrew A. Lipscomb, ed., *The Writings of Thomas Jefferson*, Monticello Edition (Washington: The Thomas Jefferson Memorial Association, 1904), 6:258-259, 14:72.

[45] Quoted in Gaustad, *Sworn on the Altar of God*, 37.

[46] Pauline Maier, *American Scripture: Making the Declaration of Independence* (New York: Alfred A. Knopf, 1997), 134.

[47] Quoted in Gaustad, *Sworn on the Altar of God*, 88.

[48] Quoted in Gaustad, *Sworn on the Altar of God*, 100.

[49] Gaustad, *Sworn on the Altar of God*, 100.

[50] Lipscomb, *The Writings of Thomas Jefferson*, 14:75.

[51] Harold C. Syrett, ed., *The Papers of Alexander Hamilton* (New York: Colunbia University Press, 1979), 26:774.

[52] Albert Henry Smyth, ed., *The Writings of Benjamin Franklin* (New York: Haskell House Publishers Ltd., 1970), 8:257.

[53] Quoted in Miller, "The Garden of Eden and the Deacon's Meadow," 58.

[54] Smyth, *The Writings of Benjamin Franklin*, 9:698. For the entire text, see 9:698-703.

[55] Smyth, *The Writings of Benjamin Franklin*, 9:699.

[56] Quoted in Gaustad, *Sworn on the Altar of God*, 108.

[57] Quoted in Gaustad, *Sworn on the Altar of God*, 108.

[58] Johnson, *Dictionary of American Biography*, 1:576.

[59] Jacob Kabakoff, "The Use of Hebrew by American Jews During the Colonial Period," in *Hebrew and the Bible in America: The First Two Centuries*, ed. Shalom Goldman (Hanover, New Hampshire: University Press of New England, 1993), 193.

[60] Miller, "The Garden of Eden and the Deacon's Meadow," 55.

[61] Quoted in Miller, "The Garden of Eden and the Deacon's Meadow," 61.

Old Testament, New Hatreds: The Hebrew Bible and Antisemitism in Nazi Germany

Doris L. Bergen

The role of antisemitism in the Holocaust is more contested than ever these days. On the one hand, Daniel Goldhagen insists on a specifically German, "eliminationist" variety of antisemitism that motivated the perpetrators and caused the Holocaust.[1] At the same time, Henry Friedlander's work on the origins of Nazi genocide and the murder of those deemed handicapped pushes antisemitism to the margins.[2] When viewed in the context of what Sybil Milton has called "the Nazi quest for a biologically homogeneous society," "Jewish suffering appears as just one part of an assault that targeted people considered handicapped, Gypsies, and Jews for sterilization, deportation, and annihilation."[3] Is there a way to reconcile key aspects of these positions? Is it possible to acknowledge, as Goldhagen does, the particular zeal with which the Nazis and their accomplices pursued Jews and at the same time to recognize, as Friedlander and Milton do, that murdering Jews was part of a larger program in which the Nazis' victims were connected in significant ways?

The answer, I believe, is yes. But to find the common ground, it is necessary to pay more attention to religion than is often the case in studies of the Holocaust. It is not religion in the narrow, doctrinal sense that is crucial here, but religion in its varied cultural manifestations. Some recent works emphasize the importance of Christian prejudices against Jews in laying the foundations for the Shoah.[4] Donald Niewyk and others have shown how, in the nineteenth and twentieth centuries, "new" racial forms of hatred built on top of and drew from "old" religious hostilities.[5] But exactly how did Christian anti-Jewishness and secular, genocidal hatreds connect? After all, many top Nazis like Hitler and Martin Bormann, ideologues like Alfred Rosenberg, and "ordinary" German perpetrators among the SS, Einsatzgruppen, and camp guards were not practicing Christians; indeed, some were openly hostile and perceived Christianity as a devious extension of Judaism.[6]

Paradoxically, one link between the old religious anti-Judaism and the new "racial" anti-semitism was the Bible. Even secular, anti-Christian ideologues in Germany belonged to a culture steeped in the stories, language, and images of the Christian Bible, Old and New Testaments. Biblical allusions, sometimes distorted and watered down but nevertheless identifiable, formed part of the shared legacy to which Nazi propaganda appealed and part of the culture with which its specific stereotypes resonated. Attention to biblical influences points to something unique about the Nazi murder of the Jews. Of the groups targeted by the Nazis for persecution and destruction, only Jews could be linked so closely to the force of religious tradition. Only in the case of Jews could religious distinctions masquerade as racial ones, which they did in the Nuremberg Laws. In Nazi Germany, it was the religion of one's grandparents, not some putatively racial distinctions of blood or physical appearance, that determined who counted as a Jew.[7]

But if attention to biblical echoes lends credence to claims of uniqueness, it also suggests ways that the murder of Jews was linked to the Nazis' broader genocidal project. Popular sources for stereotypes of Jews, Gypsies, and people considered handicapped differed, but in each case attacks drew on established hatreds and used familiar cultural codes. And those prejudices connected and reinforced each other in vicious ways. European folklore did not accuse Gypsies of killing Jesus, but it charged them with forging the nails that pierced his flesh.[8] Images of deformity and parasitism served propagandistic purposes against the handicapped, but they could also be transferred to purported racial enemies: Gypsies and Jews.[9] And the centuries-old paranoia about homeless, predatory outsiders could be mobilized against both those groups as well.[10]

So a look at biblical allusions in Nazi anti-semitism can help us identify what was unique to the Shoah while recognizing its place in the wider Nazi program of race, space, and murder. It can also alert us to both the cultural rootedness and the arbitrariness of the process by which ideologues and practitioners of genocide selected and defined their victims. Nazi Germans may have "constructed" their targets as outsiders, but they did so with the tools that their culture—their religion, education, literature, folklore, and history—placed at their disposal.

Where do we see biblical traces in the Nazi assault on Jews and what functions did such references serve? One key use of the Bible was in defining Jews, giving names and content to what turned out to be a rather abstract category. Nazi propaganda notwithstanding, it was not possible to identify Jews by their physical properties, attitudes, or even necessarily their names. The project of identification and isolation needed new markers. Accordingly, a 1938 German regulation required those defined by the Nuremberg Laws as Jews to take on another name if their given names were not sufficiently "Jewish." Women were to add Sara, men Israel.[11]

Why those names? Drawn from the Old Testament stories of matriarchs and patriarchs, they were familiar to German gentiles with even the most rudimentary religious education. Presumably, unlike some Old Testament names, they were not common among Christians in Germany.[12] But why choose biblical names at all? The authorities might simply have imposed "names" like "Jew" and "Jewess." Such an approach, however, would have lacked the legitimacy that biblical names implied. Non-Jewish Germans could imagine that they were merely asserting historical and religious truths rather than creating arbitrary lines of demarcation between themselves and their neighbors. Moreover, in the context of Nazi measures against Jews, those biblical names took on a brutal irony: Sara, mother of a people? Israel, founder of a nation? Indeed. Hitler's repeated references in *Mein Kampf* to Jews as the "Chosen People" echo that mockery.[13]

In a situation where many German gentiles had limited contact with Jews or where those Jews they did know bore little resemblance to the images Nazi propaganda disseminated, biblical characters may have seemed more real than actual Jews. Thus biblical terms could serve as labels for Jews as a whole: "Hebrews" or "Judah" functioned as synonyms for "the Jew";[14] Frankfurt am Main and Berlin became "little Jerusalems."[15] In turn, enterprising anti-semites could express their hatred through attacks on Old Testament names and symbols as well as through aggression against living Jews. Jürgen Stroop, the SS commander who crushed the Warsaw Ghetto uprising in 1943 and oversaw the deportation and murder of those Jews remaining there, began his career as Joseph Stroop, a member of the *Volksdeutsche Selbstschutz* (the ethnic German militia) in Poland. He changed his name because Joseph sounded "too Jewish."[16] Members of the pro-Nazi German Christian movement within Protestant church equated their attack on the Old Testament with an assault on Jews in their own society. Established in 1939, their Institute for Investigation and Eradication of Jewish Influence on German Church Life offered a theological pillar to the genocidal project.[17] Even pastors could be heroes in a battle where the enemy was a passage from the Old Testament.

Whether the context was secular or religious, biblical allusions in the Third Reich were rarely neutral. They bound Jews to negative stereotypes based on accounts, retold and retooled, from the Bible. In the hands of German gentiles, the stories of the golden calf and the money changers in the temple turned into illustrations of "Jewish materialism."[18] Cain became the accursed, wandering Jew.[19] The gospels, especially John, provided antisemitic vocabulary and images that were by no means reserved for professing Christians. Secular Nazis and neopagans too called Jews "whitewashed sepulchers," "vipers,"and "Pharisees."[20]

Use of such images joined decidedly anti-Christian voices with others from within the churches. Alfred Rosenberg dubbed the Old Testament a collection of "stories of pimps and cattle traders";[21] but the high school religion teacher and German Christian agitator Reinhold Krause earned "sustained applause" in November, 1933, when he repeated that phrase at a rally of twenty thousand people. Like Rosenberg, Krause viewed "liberation from the Old Testament" as part of the current assault on Jews in Germany: "If we National Socialists are ashamed to buy a tie from a Jew," he told his audience, "how much more should we be ashamed to accept from the Jew anything that speaks to our soul, to our most intimate religious essence?"[22]

In Nazi Germany, the story of Jesus's crucifixion provided a meeting point for all kinds of hatreds, religious and secular. Germans from Martin Niemöller to Hitler and Bormann pointed to the gospel accounts as evidence of Jewish perfidy in their own times.[23] A 1939 flyer of the German Christian movement numbered "destructive Jews" in their own age among "the same Jewish criminal people who nailed Christ to the cross!"[24] As an example they pointed to Herschel Grynszpan, a young Jew who shot a German consular official in Paris to protest the deportation of his parents and other Polish Jews living in Germany in the fall of 1938. Goebbels seized on Grynszpan's action to launch the November, 1938, "Kristallnacht" pogrom. In the hands of antisemites, the Oberammergau Passion Play became a propaganda pageant with no need even to change the text.[25] A noble Jesus, villainous Pharisees, and treacherous Judas fitted perfectly into an allegory of modern-day "Aryans" and Jews.

Biblical images were powerful weapons because they were so deeply embedded in German culture. But that same familiarity also led German gentiles to appropriate Bible stories in asserting their own claims to superiority. In doing so, they often showed resentment that the Jews had been God's first favorites, that they had occupied the center of a story whose focus Christian Germans longed to be. Thus Hitler's derision of the Jewish "Chosen People" revealed a claim that it was the "Aryan" Germans who really merited that title. And by the end of *Mein Kampf*, Hitler had seized the role. He and his people, he wrote, "have been chosen by Fate to be the witnesses of a catastrophe which will be the most powerful substantiation of the correctness of the folkish theory of race."[26]

Biblical appropriations were as likely to cast Christian Germany in Jewish as in gentile roles. In the 1930s, enthusiastic Protestant publicists likened Hitler's "deliverance" of Germany to the exodus from Egypt.[27] A Nazi educational slide set included an image called "David and Goliath." It showed a stereotypically drawn "Jewish" David crouched naked and Neanderthal-like behind a bush. His opponent, the giant Goliath, loomed in Aryan splendor before him.[28] And in one of the most famous speeches of his career, his address of 30 January 1939 to the German Reichstag, Hitler assumed the role of a Hebrew prophet, calling down destruction on a sinful Jewish people.[29] His words echoed a theme common in anti-Jewish Christian literature of the 1930s and 1940s. The Old Testament, some of its defenders argued, was to be salvaged, not because it honored or glorified the Jews, but precisely because its prophets and punishments proved God's displeasure with those "hard-necked" people.[30]

Of course German culture had no monopoly on the Bible. A study of other European societies would doubtless reveal similar uses and abuses of biblical texts. Nevertheless, attention to biblical references suggests some ways that German anti-semitism may have been unique. Probably no other culture shared the particular combination of a popular tradition steeped in biblical images and a theological legacy of scriptural liberalism. The Bible was a vital part of popular culture in some other communities as well, for example, among the Calvinists of the Netherlands and the Huguenots of France. But in those cases, fierce loyalty to the text and its authority could serve as a check on anti-Jewish (re)interpretations. In fact, associating the Old Testament with Jews could inspire rescue operations as it did for the Huguenots of Le Chambon-sur-Lignon in southern France. Pierre Sauvage's film, *Weapons of the Spirit,* shows how some of the villagers even referred to the Jews they sheltered as "Old Testaments."[31] Like Nazi

Germans, those French Protestants perceived a link between the Hebrew Bible and living Jews. But in contrast to the Germans, they understood that connection as a call to solidarity. Would they have done the same for Gypsies?

In Germany one finds little if any evidence of rescue impulses based on attachment to the Old Testament. Indeed many Christians in Germany seemed willing to abandon or at least pick and choose from their scriptures. Those tendencies had roots in German theological traditions. Martin Luther, Friedrich Schleiermacher, and Adolf von Harnack, arguably the most influential Protestant theologians in Germany before Karl Barth, had all contributed to that end.[32] German revisionists of the Old Testament often cited Luther as an authority on how to separate its "gold and jewels" from the "litter, stubble, and straw" it contained.[33] Christian defenders of the Old Testament argued its merits as an anti-Jewish text.[34] Leaders of the Confessing Church, the camp within German Protestantism committed to preserving some sphere of ecclesiastical independence from encroachment of Nazi state power, also practiced biblical anti-Judaism and, as Uriel Tal has shown, criticized the pro-Nazi German Christians and racist neopagans by comparing them to Jews.[35] Even Christians engaged in helping Jews and so-called non-Aryans retained anti-Jewish readings of biblical texts. In *After Auschwitz*, Richard Rubenstein describes his 1961 meeting with Heinrich Gruber, a prominent Protestant churchman whose work on behalf of German Jews and Christians of Jewish background had landed him in Dachau. When Rubenstein asked whether the murder of the Jews had been God's will, Gruber read from Psalm 44:22: "For Thy sake are we slaughtered every day." Like Nebuchadnezzar and other "rods" of divine anger, he insisted, Hitler had been sent by God to smite His people.[36]

Biblical references resonated in Germany because they were familiar. Germans heard them taught at home and preached from the pulpit. As late as 1940, after years of Nazi propaganda deriding Christian institutions, over ninety-five percent of Germans still remained taxpaying members of a church.[37] Proverbs and sayings brought the Bible into everyday language,[38] and children learned Bible stories in school. In fact, one German worker's memoir from 1918 complained that he had been taught little else. His education, he contended, had equipped him only to "join a nomadic tribe of the ancient Hebraic sort."[39] Biblical notions reconciled easily with popular stereotypes of Jews.[40] The idea of the chosen people connected to paranoia about a Jewish world conspiracy; Jacob's purchase of his brother's birthright for "a mess of pottage" fit in with notions of Jewish trickery; accusations that

Jews had crucified Jesus dovetailed with the popular stab-in-the-back myth that blamed treacherous Jews for the loss of the war in 1918.[41] Bible stories helped make the fantastic and often contradictory claims of Nazi propaganda against Jews seem familiar.

What can we conclude from this look at the uses of the Bible in German anti-semitism? The legacy of Christian anti-Judaism, as well as its residue in the form of anti-Jewish biblical images, made Jews even more vulnerable than racial ideology alone would have. Within Germany, church leaders spearheaded a protest to the killing of those deemed handicapped. Many of those same men remained silent on the subject of the Jews.[42] Biblical allusions and religious prejudices gave a metaphysical dimension to Jew-hatred. In Nazi eyes, Jews were devils, the embodiment of evil. Already in the 1940s, Joshua Trachtenberg explored the powerful parallels between Nazi stereotypes and medieval religious visions of Jews.[43] Wolfgang Gerlach and others have pointed out the challenge to Christian theology of an analysis of Nazi anti-semitism that takes seriously its religious components.[44]

A focus on the Bible reveals some significant meshing of religious anti-Jewishness and secular anti-semitism in the Third Reich. But attention to biblical references also hints at commonalities between the Nazi attack on Jews and other genocides. All drew on the culture around them, mobilizing and manipulating old and new tools in the service of murder. Anti-Gypsy images in poetry and folklore dated back to the middle ages; superstitious as well as scientific stereotypes haunted those considered deformed; popular literary, religious, and scholarly sources underpinned homophobia, anti-Slavism, and racism against Afro-Europeans. Awareness of the shared and distinct sources of prejudice allows us to see Nazi crimes as an interlocking system of specific assaults. Perhaps it can also alert us to cultural factors in contemporary hatreds. The tradition of warrior ballads in the Balkans is just one example. The ubiquitousness of cultural references suggests that even mass killers need to rationalize their actions, to cast them in familiar terms. Even murderers and brutes want God—or at least tradition—on their side.

Any study of the cultural contexts of genocide reveals how little we understand about the actual causes of intergroup hostility. Too often our explanations extend only as far as identifying some purported racial, ethnic, or religious difference. In doing so, as Gavin Langmuir has pointed out, we risk committing the "fallacy of misplaced concreteness, the error of mistaking a very abstract construction for a concrete fact or phenomenon of nature."[45] That is, if we are not careful, we buy into the same arbitrary distinctions that fueled the perpetrators' own endeavors.

Notes

[1] Daniel Jonah Goldhagen, *Hitler's Willing Executioners* (New York: Alfred A. Knopf, 1996).

[2] Henry Friedlander, *The Origins of Nazi Genocide: From Euthanasia to the Final Solution* (Chapel Hill and London: University of North Carolina Press, 1995).

[3] Sybil Milton, "The Context of the Holocaust," *German Studies Review* 13 (no. 2, 1990): 269-83.

[4] See, for example, Gavin I. Langmuir, *History, Religion, and Antisemitism* (Berkeley: University of California Press, 1990); and John Weiss, *Ideology of Death: Why the Holocaust Happened in Germany* (Chicago: Ivan R. Dee, 1996).

[5] Donald Niewyk, "Solving the 'Jewish Problem' — Continuity and Change in German Antisemitism, 1871-1945, *Leo Baeck Yearbook* (1990): 369; see also Yehuda Bauer, "Vom christlichen Judenhaß zum modernen Antisemitismus — Ein Erklärungsversuch," in *Jahrbuch für Antisemitismusforschung* 1, ed. Wolfgang Benz (Frankfurt and New York: Campus Verlag, 1992): 77-90.

[6] Even members of the staunchly pro-Nazi "German Christian" movement complained about anti-Christian attitudes in the SA, SS, and army. See, for example, Walter Schultz to Hitler, 30 April 1941, and attached, untitled report, relevant sections entitled "Bekämpfung und Verächtlichmachung des Christentums und der Kirche,"and "Angriffe auf Geistliche," Bundesarchiv Koblenz (hereafter BA Koblenz) R 43 II/172/fiche 1. For neopagan logic that denounced Christianity as disguised Judaism, see Friedrich Oberschilp, "Meine Antwort an Herrn Pfarrer Brökelschen," *Drehscheibe. Das Blatt der denkenden Menschen*, no. 42 (13. Gilbhard [Sept.] 1935): 165-67, Archiv der Evangelischen Kirche im Rheinland, Düsseldorf (hereafter AEKR Düsseldorf), Nachlaß Superintendent Dr. Wilhelm Ewald Schmidt, no. 17.

[7] Raul Hilberg discusses development of a definition of "Jews" in Nazi Germany in *The Destruction of the European Jews,* revised ed., vol. 1 (New York: Holmes and Meier, 1985), 65-80. A first step was the Interior Ministry regulation of 11 April 1933 that defined as of "non-Aryan descent" anyone with a parent or grandparent of the Jewish religion. As Hilberg, p. 67, points out, that definition was "in no sense based on racial criteria." A definition of "Jews" followed two years later, in the First Regulation to the Reich Citizenship Law, 14 November 1935 (RGBl I 1333). The basis of distinction remained the religious status of the grandparents.

[8] This point was made by Ian F. Hancock in his address to the Annual Scholars' Conference on the Holocaust and the Churches, Minneapolis, March 1996. See also Charles Godfrey Leland, *Gypsy Sorcery and Fortune Telling* (New York: University Books, 1962), ix; and the poem, "The Gypsy and the Jew," referring

to accusations that the two groups shared a part in the crucifixion of Jesus, quoted in Dennis Reinhartz, "Damnation of the Outsider: The Gypsies of Croatia and Serbia in the Balkan Holocaust, 1941-1945," in *The Gypsies of Eastern Europe,* ed. David Crowe and John Kolsti (Armonk, NY: M.E. Sharpe, 1991), 82.

[9] For example, one public speaker warned that a future Germany infiltrated by Judaism and its offspring, Christianity, would be a nation of "epileptics and idiots, bred through incest." See Pastor Kittmann to Public Prosecutor, Tilsit, 1 April 1937, 1. Bundesarchiv Potsdam, Deutsche Glaubensbewegung files, DG III 1937-39, 345. These materials have been re-catalogued since I first used them in what was then the Zentrale Staatsarchiv Potsdam.

[10] For an example of anti-Gypsy propaganda based on the idea of the wandering people, see "Fahrendes Volk: Die Bekämpfung der Zigeunerplage auf neuen Wegen," in *NS-Rechtsspiegel,* Munich (21 Feb. 1939), in *Archives of the Holocaust: An International_Collection of Selected Documents,* ed. Henry Friedlander and Sybil Milton, vol. 1, *Bildarchiv Preussischer Kulturbesitz, Berlin,* part 1: 1933-1939, ed. Sybil Milton and Roland Klemig, fig. 151.

[11] Regulation Requiring Jews to Change Their Names, August 1938, signed by Dr. Stuckart for the Reich Minister of the Interior and Dr. Gürtler, Reich Minister of Justice, in *Documents of the Holocaust: Selected Sources on the Destruction of the Jews of Germany and Austria, Poland, and the Soviet Union,* ed. Yitzhak Arad, Yisrael Gutman, and Abraham Margaliot (New York: Yad Vashem/Pergamon Press, 1981), 98-99.

[12] For a discussion of the issue of "Jewish" and "Christian" first names in an earlier period of German history, see Dietz Bering, *The Stigma of Names: Antisemitism in German Daily Life, 1812-1933,* trans. Neville Plaice (Ann Arbor: University of Michigan Press, 1992), 44-75.

[13] Adolf Hitler, *Mein Kampf,* ed. John Chamberlain et al (New York: Reynal and Hitchcock, 1940) e.g.: 75, 251, 412.

[14] See Hitler, *Mein Kampf,* 196, equating "the Mosaic religion" with the "doctrine of the preservation of the Jewish race"; or headline "Judas Greuelhetze," *Der Stürmer,* Nuremberg, no. 23 (June 1933), in Friedlander and Milton, vol. 1, fig. 121.

[13] For example, see reference to Frankfurt am Main as the "new Jerusalem" in handwritten account, Pastor Otto Koch, "Meine Erlebnisse als `Deutscher Christ,'"[1954], 3, in uncatalogued collection of the Kirchengeschichtliche Arbeitsgemeinschaft, no. 17, Kommunalarchiv Minden.

[16] Christian Jansen and Arno Weckbecker, *Der "Volksdeutsche Selbstschutz" in Polen 1939/40,* vol. 64, *Schriftenreihe der Vierteljahrshefte für Zeitgeschichte,* ed. Karl Dietrich Bracher et al (Munich: R. Oldenbourg, 1992), 69.

[17] See "Eröffnung des 'Instituts zur Erforschung und Beseitigung des jüdischen Einflusses auf das deutsche kirchliche Leben,' *Die Nationalkirche,* no. 19 (Weimar, 7 May 1939): 213, Evangelisches Zentralarchiv Berlin 1/C3/174. A

considerable amount of information on the Institute is included in the files of the Provinzialsynodalrat der Rheinprovinz A VI, 2, AEKR Düsseldorf; see also Susannah Heschel, "Nazifying Christian Theology: Walter Grundmann and the Institute for the Study and Eradication of Jewish Influence on German Church Life," *Church History* 63 (1994): 587-605.

[18] For example, in a speech of 21 October 1941, Hitler claimed that "The Jew ... worshipped and continues to worship ... nothing but the golden calf." *Hitler's Secret Conversations, 1941-44,* trans. Norman Cameron and R.H. Stevens (New York: Octagon Books, 1953), 63. For a 1930s version of the story of Jesus and the money-changers in the temple, see *Das Evangelium Johannes deutsch,* Heinz Weidemann and "ein Bremer Kreis" (Bremen: H.M. Hauschild, 1936), 7.

[19] Pamphlet by Pastor Hans Volkenborn, *Das Reich der Christen ohne Kirche Christi?* (Herten [Westphalia]: Kniffla, [1937]), 7, in Kommunalarchiv Minden DCS.O.

[20] Hitler's description of Jesus's attack on the traders in the temple with a reference to Jews as vipers was quoted in the *Völkischer Beobachter,* Munich (12 April 1922), in *Hitler's Words: Two Decades of National Socialism, 1923-1943,* ed. Gordon W. Prange (Washington, D.C.: American Council on Public Affairs, 1944), 71.

[21] Alfred Rosenberg, *Der Mythus des 20. Jahrhunderts: Eine Wertung der seelisch-geistigen Gestaltenkämpfe unserer Zeit* (Munich: Hoheneichen Verlag, 1935), 614.

[22] Reinhold Krause, "Rede des Gauobmannes der Glaubensbewegung 'Deutsche Christen' im Groß-Berlin, gehalten im Sportpalast am 13. Nov. 1933 (nach doppelten Stenographischem Bericht)," 6-7, Landeskirchenarchiv Bielefeld (hereafter LKA Bielefeld) 5,1/289,2.

[23] See for examples the following: Martin Niemöller's explanation in a sermon of the "manifest penal judgment" against the Jews: "The Jews have caused the crucifixion of God's Christ.... They bear the curse, and because they rejected the forgiveness, they drag with them as a fearsome burden the unforgiven blood-guilt of their fathers." Quoted in Ruth Zerner, "German Protestant Responses to Nazi Persecution of the Jews," *Perspectives on the Holocaust,* ed. Randolph L. Braham (Boston: Kluwer-Nijhoff, 1983), 63; Bormann's reference to the Jews crucifying Jesus in note to Hitler, conversation, Werwolf, evening 25 July 1942, in *Hitlers Tischgespräche im Führerhauptquartier 1941-1942,* ed. Henry Picker (Stuttgart: Seewald, 1965), 475; Hitler's reference to the crucifixion in *Hitler's Words,* 72.

[24] See flyer, "Juda in der Kirche!," 13 May 1939, no signature [Thuringian German Christians], United States Holocaust Memorial Museum Archive, RG 11.001M.11, Reel 80, Fond 1240, Opis 1, Folder 55.

[25] Saul S. Friedman, *The Oberammergau Passion Play: A Lance Against Civilization* (Carbondale and Edwardsville: Southern Illinois University Press, 1984), esp. 114-130.

[26] Hitler, *Mein Kampf,* 952.

[27] Pfenningsdorf, "Schicksalsfrage an die Kirche!." *Die Nationalkirche,* Hesse-Nassau edition, no. 6 (5 Feb. 1939): 55, LKA Bielefeld 5,1/293.

[28] "David und Goliath," Antisemitic caricatures for educational slide set, "Jews, Freemasons, and Communists," n.p., n.d., in Friedlander and Milton, vol. 1, fig. 106.

[29] "Speech before the Reichstag," 30 January 1939, quoted from the *Völkischer Beobachter,* 31 Jan. 1939, in *Hitler's Words,* 82

[30] For example, in 1935, a German Christian leader in Merseburg identified the psalms, poetic books, and prophets as worthy of preservation. Asked why the prophets, he responded, "the prophets are ... downright anti-Semitic in their focus." Pastor Ziehen, "Wir Deutsche Christen und das Alte Testament," *Kirche im Aufbruch. Mitteilungsblatt der Deutschen Christen im Gau Halle-Merseburg,* no. 11/12 (July 1935): 7-8, LKA Bielefeld 5,1/291,2.

[31] Pierre Sauvage, "Weapons of the Spirit," (New York: First Run/Icarus Films, 1986). See also Philip P. Hallie, *Lest Innocent Blood Be Shed: The Story of the Village of Le Chambon and How Goodness Happened There* (New York: Harper and Row, 1979), esp. reference to Deuteronomy 19:7-10 on 109.

[32] For example, Luther denounced the Book of Esther as a favorite of Jews, "beautifully attuned to their bloodthirsty, vengeful, murderous yearning and hope." "On the Jews and Their Lies," trans. Martin H. Bertram, in *Luther's Works, ed.* Helmut T. Lehmann, vol. 47, *The Christian in Society,* part 4, ed. Franklin Sherman (Philadelphia: Fortress, 1971), 157. He said the Epistle of James "doesn't amount to much," and maintained "that some Jew wrote it who probably heard about Christian people but never encountered any." "Table Talk Recorded By Caspar Heydenreich, 1542-1543," no. 5443, summer or fall 1542, in *Luther's Works,* vol. 54, ed. and trans. Theodore G. Tappert (Philadelphia: Fortress, 1967), 424. Schleiermacher dismissed most of the Old Testament as nothing "but the husk or wrapping of its prophecy," and added that "whatever is most definitely Jewish has least value." Even the "utterances of the noble and purer Heathenism" might be as "near and accordant" to "Christian usage." Schleiermacher, *The Christian Faith,* ed. H.R. Mackintosh and J.S. Stewart (Philadelphia: Fortress, 1928, rep. 1976), 62. Adolf von Harnack questioned retention of the Old Testament in the Protestant canon, characterizing it at times as archaic and outmoded. Important works include *Lehrbuch der Dogmengeschichte* (1885-89); *Das Wesen des Christentums* (1899-1900), a series of lectures; and *Geschichte der_altchristliche Literature* (1893-1904).

[33] See *Das Ringen der deutschen Christen um die Kirche,* no author, no. 5, *Deutsche Christen im Kampf — Schriften zur allgemeinen Unterrichtung,* ed. League for German Christianity (Weimar: Verlag Deutsche Christen, 1937), 4, LKA Bielefeld 5,1/292,1.

[34] One Protestant author offered Luther as an example of how it was possible to hate Jews but accept the Old Testament. Pamphlet, "Das Alte Testament ein 'Judenbuch'?," no author, no date, responsible: Protestant Parish Service (Ev.

Gemeindedienst) for Württemberg, Stuttgart, 1-4.

[35] Uriel Tal, "On Modern Lutheranism and the Jews," *Leo Baeck Yearbook* (1985): 204.

[36] Richard Rubenstein, *After Auschwitz: History, Theology, and Contemporary Judaism,* second edition (Baltimore: Johns Hopkins University, 1992), 8-10.

[37] See data from the Ministry of Church Affairs, "Zusammenstellung über Kirchenaustritte und Kirchenrücktritte bezw. Übertritte, ermittelt nach den von den Kirchen veröffentlichten Zusammenstellungen," no author, [1940] in BA Koblenz R 79/19.

[38] On biblical allusions in German proverbs, see Wolfgang Mieder, *Deutsche Sprichwörter in Literatur, Politik, Presse, und Werbung* (Hamburg: Helmut Buske, 1983). Mieder says that Hitler used biblical quotations to give his speeches "eine volkssprachliche Bildlichkeit," 7. See also Carl Schulze, *Did Biblischen Sprichwörter der deutschen Sprache,* ed. Mieder vol. 8, *Sprichwörterforschung,* ed. Mieder (Bern: Peter Lang, 1987). Schulze's book was first published in 1860.

[39] Alwin Ger quoted in Mary Jo Maynes, *Taking the Hard Road: Life Course in French and German Workers' Autobiographies in the Era of Industrialization* (Chapel Hill and London: University of North Carolina Press, 1995), 87-88.

[40] As David Bankier put it, "Nazi antisemitism was successful ... because large sectors of German society were predisposed to be antisemitic." David Bankier, *The Germans and the Final Solution: Public Opinion under Nazism* (Oxford and Cambridge, Mass: Blackwell, 1992), 155.

[41] For example, a 1932 publication's outline of common criticisms against the Old Testament hinted at parallel stereotypes of Jews: it was a "Jewish book"; it was ethically a poor example for children — "Jacob was a cheat, Abraham a liar, David an adulterer." See Ernst Kalle, *Hat das Alte Testament noch Bedeutung für den Christen?,* no. 12, *Der Kampf-Bund,* ed. Evang. Provinzialamt für Apologetik (Gütersloh: C. Bertelsmann, 1932), 3.

[42] On church leaders' attitudes toward the Jews, see Wolfgang Gerlach, *Als die Zeugen Schwiegen: Bekennende Kirche und die Juden* (Berlin: Institut Kirche und Judentum, 1987).

[43] Joshua Trachtenberg, *The Devil and the Jews: The Medieval Conception of the Jew and Its Relation to Modern Antisemitism* (New Haven: Yale University Press, 1943).

[44] Gerlach, *Als die Zeugen Schwiegen.*

[45] Gavin I. Langmuir, "Prolegomena to Any Present Analysis of Hostility Against Jews," in *The Nazi Holocaust: Historical Articles on the Destruction of the European Jews,* vol. 2, *The Origins of the Holocaust,* ed. Michael R. Marrus (Westport and London: Meckler, 1989).

Creation Founded in Love: Breaking Rhetorical Expectations in Genesis 1:1-2:3[1]

J. Richard Middleton

Genesis 1:1-2:3 is a paradigmatic text. Here we find a portrayal of God's founding creative act "in the beginning," at the outset of the biblical canon, as the preface or overture to the entirety of Scripture. This placement alone would require those who take the Bible as normative to treat this portrayal as paradigmatic for the character of the God disclosed in the rest of the Bible.

But, beyond its canonical placement, the text is paradigmatic in another sense, since it plainly asserts in 1:26-27 that humanity is created to be God's "image" (*tzelem*) and "likeness" (*d^emût*). Although the meaning of this assertion has been widely disputed over the millennia, it suggests minimally that the human vocation is somehow modelled on the nature and actions of the God rhetorically portrayed in Genesis 1.[2]

But Genesis 1 is paradigmatic in yet a third sense, in terms of the impact it has had historically on Western civilization. Even before modern times, this text has had a significant role in shaping Jewish and Christian understandings of God as Creator and the world as an ordered universe subject to the Creator's will. Indeed, many historians argue that it was the worldview embodied in the Genesis 1 creation story which shaped the development of modern western science.[3] With the onset of modernity in sixteenth and seventeenth century Europe, Genesis 1 became a crucial text for those involved in articulating the growing consciousness of progress and the scientific conquest of nature. Thus the philosopher Francis Bacon (who did more than anyone else singlehandedly to popularize the growing scientific worldview in his native England) utilized the notion of humanity made in

God's image with a mandate to have dominion over the animals and subdue the earth (Genesis 1:26-28) as explicit legitimation for the scientific project.[4]

Today, in a context many have designated "postmodern," when the ideals and achievements of modernity are being subjected to serious critique, the Baconian notion of a divinely ordained human conquest of nature is held in deep suspicion. Not only that, but the larger background picture of God's relation to the created order as portrayed in Genesis 1 is less and less believed (and often openly questioned). But this should come as no surprise. Paradigms are "pharmacological," to use a phrase derived from Jacques Derrida's commentary on Plato's *Phaedrus*. Like the value of writing, which Socrates compares to a "drug" (*pharmakon*) in the *Phaedrus*, the Genesis 1 creation story (and the understanding of God, world, and humanity contained therein) may function as either remedy or poison.[5] While clearly paradigmatic, the biblical text may, in principle, be either positive or negative in its influence. And significant ethical objections have recently been raised against Genesis 1. In what follows, I cite two broad sets of objections to the text. While both sets of objections constitute important ethical challenges which should not be ignored, neither is based on a careful reading of the biblical text. It will thus be my task to address these objections by a close rhetorical reading of Genesis 1:1-2:3 as a coherent literary unit.

CREATION AS A VIOLENT ACT

One of the most basic challenges to the normative value of Genesis 1 is Catherine Keller's important book, *From a Broken Web*, in which she claims to discern a creation-by-combat theme in the text.[6] Even before she examines Genesis 1 specifically, however, Keller reads the traditional conception of the God-creation relationship in Judaism and Christianity as essentially patriarchal, encoding the "separable," heroic male ego as the divine element in a religious worldview. Noting that women are often associated with nature and matter in Western history (hence the *double entendre* of "matrix"), she argues that the traditional model of God's transcendent, sovereign relationship to the world serves to legitimate male/God domination of female/nature.[7]

But Keller goes considerably further than that general indictment. Analyzing the oppressive patriarchal social structures of ancient Greece and Mesopotamia, she claims to find their ideological roots in paradigmatic Greek and Mesopotamian myths of a heroic male god's primordial slaying and dismemberment of a female monster (whether Greek Medusa or Babylonian

Tiamat, to give two of the most famous examples). Keller then posits a similar (though more submerged) *Chaoskampf* theme in the Genesis text and claims this as the chief paradigmatic legitimation of patriarchy in both Judaism and Christianity.[8]

Keller's analysis here draws on Herman Gunkel's classic 1895 book, *Schöpfung und Chaos in Urzeit und Endzeit,* which compared Genesis 1 with the Babylonian creation story known as the *Enuma Elish* (then only recently discovered in 1873).[9] Among the similarities between the two texts, Gunkel noted the etymological relationship between *t^e^hôm* (the Hebrew word in Genesis 1:2 for the "deep," the primordial ocean over which God's Spirit moves) and *ti' amat* (an Akkadian word meaning "ocean" or "sea,"which functions as the name of the divinized primordial ocean, also portrayed as a sea monster, in the *Enuma Elish*).[10] Beyond the etymological connection (and feminine gender) of both words, Gunkel pointed out the remarkable thematic similarity of Marduk's mode of creating in the *Enuma Elish* with that of the biblical God in Genesis 1. Whereas Marduk (in order to gain ascendancy as head of the most recent generation of gods in the Babylonian pantheon) conquers Tiamat (the new pantheon's primordial enemy and leader of the olden gods) and splits her dead carcass in half in order to construct heaven and earth, two of God's creative acts in Genesis 1 involve separating or dividing the waters (on both the second and third days of creation).[11]

The presence, thus, of a primordial watery soup or ocean which is separated and bounded to produce the differentiation of a complex world (along with a number of other parallels) has caused many biblical scholars over the years to view Genesis 1 as influenced by the ideas of the *Enuma Elish* (if not by the text itself). Indeed, the widespread scholarly opinion that Genesis 1 originated in priestly circles during the Babylonian exile lends credence to the notion of *some* sort of relationship between Genesis 1 and the Babylonian text. Yet scholars have disagreed about the precise nature of the relationship between the two. Many since Gunkel have viewed Genesis 1 as merely a reflex of the *Enuma Elish*, while as others, more recently, have understood the biblical text to intentionally polemicize against the *Enuma Elish*. A few even question the notion of any relationship and posit instead Egyptian or Ugaritic parallels for Genesis 1.[12]

Keller clearly opts for the first of these positions.[13] She admits that on a "surface" reading the Genesis text seems to breathe quite a different atmosphere from the Babylonian combat myth and is characterized not by violence, but by "austere imagery."[14] Yet, drawing on depth psychological categories, she claims to "see a subtle belligerence at work behind the serene transcendence of the priestly scenario" and goes so far as to suggest that "the brutal cosmocrat Marduk bequeaths his patrimony to the Hebrew creator."[15] "Huge pieces of history begin to fall into place: it is the heroic-matricidal impulse that provides the common denominator of the misogyny of Greece and of the Near and Middle East."[16]

The relevant point for our purposes is that Keller reads Genesis 1 in accordance with the rhetorical expectations of the *Enuma Elish*. That is, because of similarities between the two texts, she simply assumes Genesis 1 harbors a notion of creation founded in violence.[17] This portrayal of God as divine Warrior subjugating primordial chaos (personified as feminine) has, she argues, contributed historically (and continues to contribute) to the legitimation of violence and oppression, especially against women, in cultures influenced by the Bible.

Whereas Keller may be influenced by Gunkel's work on the relationship between the biblical and Babylonian texts, her evaluation of the ethical implications of the combat myth draws on the analysis of Paul Ricoeur in his celebrated book, *The Symbolism of Evil*. Ricoeur argues — correctly, I believe — that the *Enuma Elish* paradigmatically legitimated a theology of holy war, where the Babylonian king represented Marduk in vanquishing Babylon's enemies as historical embodiments of the primal chaos monster.[18] Ricoeur explains:

> It will be seen that human violence is thus justified by the primordial violence. Creation is a victory over an Enemy older than the creator; that Enemy, immanent in the divine, will be represented in history by all the enemies whom the king in his turn, as servant of the god, will have as his mission to destroy. Thus Violence is inscribed in the origin of things, in the principle that establishes while it destroys.[19]

While utilizing Ricoeur's insight into the connection between a violent myth of origins and continuing historical violence, Keller critiques Ricoeur for conveniently ignoring "that the primordial enemy is a woman and that the cosmos established by her destruction is not accidentally a patriarchy."[20]

Catherine Keller represents a particularly important feminist voice today. Her indictment of the biblical text is not at all idiosyncratic, but is rooted in a reputable tradition of biblical scholarship that is attuned to the ancient Near Eastern theme of the divine conquest of primordial "watery" evil as the basis for establishing cosmic order. This indictment is also rooted in an undeniable history of women's experience of suffering within patriarchal religious traditions, and must therefore be taken with utmost seriousness.[21] In the end, however, I believe that Keller's suspicious reading of Genesis 1 is rhetorically unwarranted. There are, in fact, three crucial dimensions of the Genesis 1 creation account that directly contradict the *Chaoskampf* theme.

THE ABSENCE OF THE COMBAT MYTH IN GENESIS 1

The first is the role given to *tᵉhôm*, the primordial ocean in Genesis 1:2, and to *hammayim*, "the waters" (on the second and third days of creation), and especially the status of *hattannînim haggᵉdolîm*, "the great beasts" of the sea in verse 21. The deep in Genesis 1 is just that—water. It is neither divine nor demonic. It is no threat and so God does not need to fight it,[22] though God does separate or divide the waters for various cosmic structures to emerge (a theme typically found in Sumerian creation myths, with no reference whatsoever to combat).[23] Thus George Barton (writing even before Herman Gunkel) notes that, despite all the similarities between the *Enuma Elish* and Genesis 1, "The waters in the Hebrew narrative are not in conflict with God during the creative process, but are gently brooded over by the *rûa* and easily influenced by it."[24]

But not only are the waters thoroughly demythologized in Genesis 1, so are the sea monsters. Although *tannîn* (or the plural *tannînim*) in biblical poetic texts is often translated "dragon" (or "dragons")[25] since the word can stand in apposition (as a roughly parallel term) to Rahab the sea monster (as in Isaiah 51:19 or Psalm 89:11 [Eng 89:10]) or to Leviathan the many-headed twisting sea serpent (as in Isaiah 27:1 or Psalm 74:13-14), both of whom are pictured as YHWH's adversaries,[26] this is certainly not the meaning of the term in Genesis 1. On the contrary, here the *tannînim* are, to use Gunkel's words, "transformed into a remarkable sort of fish, which is to be included among other created beings."[27] In Genesis 1 even the dragons are part of God's peaceable kingdom. Thus Psalm 104, a creation psalm with many affinities to Genesis 1, says that YHWH formed Leviathan to "sport" with (Psalm 104:26). As Jon Levenson puts it, the feared primordial sea monster of ancient Near Eastern mythology is the biblical God's "rubber duckey"![28]

The second dimension of the Genesis text which clearly distinguishes it from creation-by-combat is the decided ease with which God creates, in contrast to Marduk's bloody struggle against a primordial enemy. This ease is suggested by the immediate and unproblematic response of creatures to God's commanding fiats. The typical pattern of divine command (for example, "let there be light" or "let the waters be separated") followed by an execution report ("and there was light," or "and it was so") pictures God as encountering no resistance in creating the world. God commands and creation obeys his every word. To put it differently, God rules willing subjects, who do not have to be coerced or subdued to his will.

Indeed, this is a ruler who does not command, so much as invite creatures to respond to his will. This invitational character of God's creative fiats is indicated by the fact that they are not technically imperatives at all, but jussives (which have no exact counterpart in English). As Eugene Roop explains, the force of the Hebrew jussive can range "from the very strong (almost a command) to the very soft (almost a wish)" and "always possesses a voluntary element."[29] Whether we read these jussives rhetorically as God's commands (to which there is no resistance), on analogy with the sovereign decrees of a king, or, following Walter Brueggemann, as God's gracious "summons" or "permission" for creatures to exist,[30] we are certainly very far removed from the *Chaoskampf* motif. In Roop's words: "Creation comes by divine direction, not by a dictator's demand."[31] The ease of creation — indicated both by the jussives and by the immediate compliance of creatures — is a prominent rhetorical feature of Genesis 1, reflected even in the gentle, repetitive cadences of the text, which progressively builds to a climax, but unlike a genuine narrative contains not a trace of plot tension or resolution (that is, there is no evil to be resisted or overcome).

The third rhetorical indicator which differentiates Genesis 1 from the combat myth is God's evaluation of each stage of the creative process as "good" (*tôb*) and in verse 31 of the entire finished product as "very good" (*tôb m*^{e}*'od*). The word *tôb* has here at least a twofold connotation, aesthetic and ethical. The cosmos is thus "good" in two senses: it is both pleasing to God, as a beautiful, well-constructed world, and it is evaluated positively since it is enacts God's will (and is not recalcitrant or rebellious).[32] On this point, nothing could be further removed from the *Enuma Elish*, which is filled with bloody battles between the gods (culminating in Marduk's dismembering of Tiamat). The prominence of the creation-by-combat theme in the *Enuma Elish* represents primal evil as a constitutive dimension of the cosmos, which has always to be violently repressed that it might not overwhelm the fragile cosmic order imposed by the gods.

If a theology of holy war (with disastrous implications for human oppression) grows naturally out of the worldview exemplified by the *Enuma Elish* (that is, evil is primordial chaos, while goodness, represented by cosmic order, is later, founded by the vanquishing of chaos), it becomes evident that a creation which is originally "very good" would sustain an entirely different sort of historical action.[33]

This means that one of Keller's assumptions is simply wrong. There is no creation-by-combat in Genesis 1, so it cannot (legitimately) function as a paradigmatic model of divine/male violence against women. Even Gunkel, upon whom Keller is dependent and who certainly *did* portray both Genesis 1 and the *Enuma Elish* as different versions of one basic Semitic combat myth (a questionable notion at best),[34] nevertheless described Genesis 1 as an essentially *faded* version of the myth, one which had been fully demythologized and transformed in accordance with Israel's monotheistic faith.[35] Today, it is even common for interpreters of Genesis 1 to understand the creation story as intentionally polemicizing against either ancient Near Eastern theological and cosmogonic ideas in general or specifically against those ideas found in the *Enuma Elish*.[36] Although there is some debate as to whether the text is intentionally polemical (I believe it is),[37] it is now widely agreed among biblical scholars that Genesis 1 embodies a quite distinctive understanding of divine creative power when compared with the *Enuma Elish*.[38] Minimally, we could say that the text breaks with the rhetorical expectations of ancient (particularly, Babylonian) readers regarding the nature of divine creative power.

Even John Day, who rejects a Babylonian background for Genesis 1 and posits instead the influence of Ugaritic ideas for the undeniable presence of the combat myth in the Bible, does not find that myth in Genesis 1.[39] In contrast to a primordial battle, creation in Genesis 1 is simply, in his own words, "a job of work."[40] God is pictured here not as warrior, but as craftsman or artisan. Or, in Jon Levenson's terms, which he applies to both Genesis 1 and Psalm 104, this is "creation without opposition."[41] And if you read Levenson's extraordinary book, *Creation and the Persistence of Evil*, you would realize what a concession this statement is, for Levenson (like Day) finds creation-by-combat in many poetic texts of the Hebrew Bible (in considerably more texts than I would admit), but goes on to say of Genesis 1 that this creation story (without opposition) "now serves as the overture to the entire Bible, dramatically relativizing the other cosmogonies."[42] That is, its canonical placement makes its portrayal of God's founding creative act paradigmatic in a way that the other cosmogonies are not.

CREATION AS THE IMPOSITION OF TRANSCENDENT WILL

But Catherine Keller is not the only recent voice raising ethical objections to

Genesis 1. As a parallel to Keller's claim that patriarchy and the systemic oppression of women may be traced back to the Genesis text, we find the widespread contemporary notion that Genesis 1 is the ultimate root of the environmental crisis. The popularity of this claim stems primarily from the famous 1967 article of Christian historian Lynn White, Jr., titled "The Historical Roots of Our Ecologic Crisis."[43] Similar critiques have, however, been widely proposed, most notably by historian Arnold Toynbee, Buddhist philosopher Daisetz T. Suzuki, cultural critic Theodore Roszak, and scientists Ian MacHarg and David Suzuki (among many others).[44] It has now become popular wisdom to make the historical claim that the modern environmental crisis, which is the direct result of the exploitative stance toward nature characteristic of modern Western science, can be traced back to the culture of Western Christianity in which modern science arose. This culture, notes White, was informed paradigmatically by the creation story in Genesis 1.

White (and those who follow him) do not typically appeal to the presence of the combat myth in Genesis 1 in marshalling their critique. There are, however, two dimensions of the critique that are especially relevant for our consideration. First, White and company claim that "nature" (the nonhuman creation) is devalued and descralized as an inert object, related to God only extrinsically in the Bible (and especially in Genesis 1), which thus makes it available for human manipulation and exploitation. According to White, the biblical worldview not only understood God as absolutely transcendent, but effectively exorcised all spiritual or divine powers from the natural realm, with the result that "the old inhibitions to the exploitation of nature crumbled."[45] Thus Ronald Reagan, then governor of California, is cited by White as a latter-day inheritor of this worldview, when he reduces nature to mere physical facticity in his famous comment: "when you've seen one redwood tree, you've seen them all."[46]

Secondly, White claims that this reductive "denaturing" of creation is compounded by the creation of humans in the "image" and "likeness" of God, granted a mandate of limitless dominion over the nonhuman creatures, charged to subdue the earth in God's name. Thus humans "share, in great measure, God's transcendence of nature," says White, and the biblical creation account teaches that "no item in the physical creation had any purpose save to serve man's purposes."[47] Together, this picture of a desacralized cosmos, a transcendent God, and an elevated human status reveals a hierarchical dualism of God and humans on the one side and nature on the other, thus legitimating human coercive domination of nature, in imitation of God's primordial coercive relation to the natural world.[48] What is perhaps most crucial for our discussion is that God's extrinsic, over-against relationship to the world (a relationship characterized by the unilateral exercise of absolute power over, on God's part) gives humans (in the divine image) license to appropriate and exploit the world as the "masters and possessors of nature" (to use René Descartes' famous phrase).[49]

This ecological critique is combined with feminist concerns about the traditional picture of God in the writings of Sallie McFague. In her widely read book, *Models of God: Theology for an Ecological, Nuclear Age*, McFague utilizes a nuanced version of the ecological critique to call into question the model of God's sovereign relationship to the world which is presupposed in the Genesis text.[50] Admitting (perhaps with an eye to White) that it is "simplistic to blame the Judeo-Christian tradition for the ecological crisis, as some have done, on the grounds that Genesis instructs human beings to have 'dominion' over nature,"[51] McFague nevertheless indicts what she describes as "royalist, triumphalist images for God — God as king, lord, ruler, patriarch" — that is, the classical Jewish and Christian "monarchial" model of divine transcendence and sovereignty over the cosmos.[52]

McFague indicts such images because she understands this model of God to have functioned historically as an exemplar or paradigm for human violence (as humans, particularly men, have imitated their divine monarch). But beyond this violence, McFague intimates at a different (disempowering) function of the monarchial model, which is perhaps more characteristic of women's experience. According to McFague, this model of God fosters, at worst, "militarism and destruction" (if we—typically men—*imitate* God's sovereignty) and, at best, "attitudes of passivity and escape from responsibility" (if we—usually women—understand ourselves in *contrast* to God, who has all power).[53] McFague thus proposes alternative, non-violent, and empowering models of God for this "ecological, nuclear age," namely God's embodiment in the world, God as Mother who births the universe, or God as Lover and Friend of the earth.[54]

Unfortunately, the model of divine creative power represented in the objections of White and McFague finds unwitting support in the comments of many biblical scholars concerning Genesis 1. These comments come especially to the fore in comparisons between the creation accounts in Genesis 1 and 2. The obvious differences in content, sequence, style, and emphasis of the two accounts are typically portrayed in the literature in terms of two central contrasts, namely 1) between God's transcendence and immanence, and 2) between the orderliness and unpredictability of creation.

As an example of the first contrast, James Crenshaw distinguishes the portrayals of God in the two creation accounts as follows: "In the first account the Deity is transcendent, removed from any contact [with the world] except verbal, whereas the second story emphasizes divine nearness in very concrete ways."[55] Tamara Cohen Eskenazi likewise explains that the creation accounts portray "God as both magisterially remote (Genesis 1) and intimately engaged with creation (Genesis 2)."[56]

The second contrast is illustrated by Robert Alter's depiction of creation in Genesis 1 as essentially a harmonious "balancing of opposites" in contrast to the concern evident in Genesis 2 with "the complicated and difficult facts of human life in civilization."[57] And Crenshaw, in a similar manner, states that whereas "within the Priestly creation account there is complete symmetry,"[58] Genesis 2 portrays reality as "unpredictable."[59]

Both sets of contrasts are brought together in an important rhetorical study of Genesis 1-2 by Dale Patrick and Allen Scult titled "Genesis and Power."[60] Like Crenshaw, Alter, and Eskenazi, these authors attempt not to sever, but to creatively juxtapose (as complementary), the portrayals of God in the two creation accounts. For Patrick and Scult, Genesis 1 and 2 portray two necessary, but fundamentally different, types of power, which they name divine *authorship* (Genesis 1) and divine *authority* (Genesis 2), respectively. Whereas *authorship* refers to "a circumscribing force" extrinsic to that over which power is exercised and which is able unilaterally to "determine the outcome" (much as an author transcends and is able to control what he writes), *authority* refers to a form of power that is more relational and engaged, indeed is "embroiled in the indeterminacy of conflict."[61]

Whatever the good intentions of Patrick and Scult (and others) who desire to keep both portrayals of divine power in creative tension, if Genesis 1 does indeed portray God as extrinsic, transcendent force or will unilaterally imposing order upon creation as an inert object, then I would have to agree in principle with White and McFague. Given the notion of humanity as *imago Dei*, this picture of divine creative power (upon which humans are to model their actions) could very well serve to legitimate aggressive control and limitless exploitation of the natural world, or possibly passivity and disempowerment in some cases (as McFague intimates).[62] Whereas the portrayal of God as divine Warrior which Catherine Keller discerns in Genesis 1 would constitute the text's endorsement of explicit violence from the beginning of the world, White's and McFague's critical (and even Patrick and Scult's more sanguine) discernment of an extrinsic divine transcendence deterministically ordering creation (a form of a primordial coercion) might constitute the endorsement of an *implicit* violence at the human level.

These feminist and ecological objections to the notion of human and divine power in Genesis 1 make the paradigmatic character of the text in question immensely problematic, especially for those, like myself, interested in what sort of ethics the text might authorize. But they also make the text worthy of further study. These objections thus require us, minimally, to investigate whether a responsible reading of the text discloses an oppressive ideology or whether this ideology is more a function of the text's later effective history, that is, how it has been received by successive communities of interpretation throughout the ages.

While this essay does not claim to be any sort of definitive answer to these important ethical objections, it does constitute an attempt to explore what sort of creative power Genesis 1 rhetorically depicts God as exercising, specifically with the above objections in mind. On my reading, the text depicts God's founding exercise of creative power in such a way that we might appropriately describe it as an act of *love*. This depiction arises from a number of rhetorical features of the text.

VARIATIONS IN THE LITERARY PATTERN OF GENESIS 1

The first feature is the curious occurrence of non-predictable variations in the literary patterning of Genesis 1. These variations fly in the face of the well-worn characterization of the rhetorical world of Genesis 1, by numerous commentators, as a world *par excellence* of ordered regularity.

First, there are variations in what I call the "fiat" pattern of the text. This is the pattern, recognized by many scholars, of 1) God's *fiat* ("let there be"), followed by 2) an *execution report* ("and it was so"), and 3) an *evaluation report* ("God saw that it was good").

Yet this pattern (repeated for each of God's eight creative acts, over six days of creation) is inexplicably broken at a number of points. Thus the *execution report* ("and it was so") is missing from God's sixth creative act (fish and birds) on day 5 and from God's eighth creative act (humanity) on day 6. Likewise, the *evaluation report* ("God saw that it was good") is missing from God's second creative act (separation of the waters) on day 2 and from God's eighth creative act (humanity) on day 6. Actually, it is not quite accurate to say that the execution report or the evaluation report is simply missing from God's eighth creative act. That would be too simple. Technically, they are not missing, but *displaced*, the execution report to 1:29, where it serves to conclude God's assignment of food to both humans and animals, and the evaluation report to 1:31 where it functions to summarize God's evaluation of the entire creative process ("God saw all that he had made, and behold it was very good").

To make things even more complicated, however, the text contains two quite different sets of execution reports. Whereas the first type reports in summary fashion that "it was so" (or, in the first case, that "there was light"), the second type is more extended and reports some specific action of God (making, creating or separating).[63] The second type occurs either in lieu of the first type (in one instance, on day 5) or more typically it supplements the first type, though in one case (God's third creative act, the separation of land from water) it is simply absent.

Furthermore, the order of the elements in the fiat pattern is not always the same for each of the eight creative acts (SEE FIGURE 1, page 68). If we number the elements according to their first occurrence (such that 1 stands for God's fiat, 2 for the summary execution report, 3 for the evaluation report, and 4 for the more extended execution report), with x any missing element in the pattern, the order could be represented as follows. For God's first creative act, the order is 1, 2, 3, 4; for the second act, it is 1, 4, 2, x; for the third act, it is 1, 2, 3, x; for the fourth act it is 1, 2, 4a, 3; for the fifth act, 1, 2, 4b, 3; for the sixth act, 1, 4, 3, x; for the seventh act, 1, 2, 4, 3; and for the eighth act, 1, 4, 2x, 3x (the combination of x with 2 and 3 here symbolizes a displaced—not *quite* missing—element).[64]

Even the fourth, fifth, and seventh creative acts, which, on the surface, seem to follow an identical pattern (1, 2, 4, 3), harbor a further variation in the form that the extended execution report takes, indicated above by the addition of the letters a and b to 4 in two of the cases. In the fourth act, the extended execution report does not report God's action at all, but that of a creature (the earth), while in the fifth act, the report is doubled, reporting first that God made the great lights and secondly that God placed them in the dome of the heavens. Furthermore, this execution report is so expanded that it has become an extended purpose statement for the creation of the heavenly bodies. That is, even when item 4 (the extended execution report) appears in the same relative position in the fiat pattern, there are internal variations in the nature and function of the item.

A further, equally non-predictable variation in the fiat pattern is the fact that half of the fiats (numbers 1, 2, 3 and 5) simply call a particular creature to exist (or to be separated, as in number 3), without specifying how that will come to be (e.g., "let there be light" or "let the waters be gathered"), while the other half (numbers 4, 6, 7 and 8) name a creature God has previously created and invite that creature actively to participate in the creative process (e.g., "let the land produce vegetation").[65] All of this suggests that although there is a discernible pattern to each of God's eight creative acts, this pattern is by no means simple, obvious, or predictable. It is, on the contrary, highly complex.

A second set of important literary variations concerns what I call the pattern of "panels" in the text. Since at least the eighteenth century, biblical scholars have noted that God's creative days may be divided into two symmetrical triads or corresponding panels of three days each.[66] The first panel (days 1-3) has to do largely with God engaging in acts of *division* or *separation*, by which God brings into being the various regions or spaces or realms of the created order; while the second panel (days 4-6) has to do with God *filling* these regions he has previously separated with living (or at least mobile) beings. It has even been suggested that these two panels (of regions and occupants) correspond to the introductory statement in verse 2 that the earth was "formless" (*tohû*) and "empty" (*bohû*).[67] The act of creation would then consist in God bringing form and structure to that which was formless (panel 1) and filling with living or mobile creatures that which was empty (panel 2).[68] Genesis 2:1 would thus provide a fitting conclusion (an inclusion, perhaps) to the creation story in its summary statement that "the heavens and the earth were created" (panel 1) "and all their host" (panel 2).[69]

Whether or not Genesis 1:2 and 2:1 can be made to bear this particular interpretation, the division into two triadic panels seems quite secure (SEE FIGURE 2, page 69). Thus, on days 1-3, God separates light from darkness and names them "day" and "night" (day 1), then separates the waters above from the waters below by a firmament or transparent dome and names this dome "sky" (day 2), then separates the waters below from dry ground and names them "seas" and "earth" (or "land") respectively (day 3). Corresponding to days 1-3, we have days 4-6, on which God fills precisely the static spaces he has just created with the mobile creatures that appropriately inhabit them. Hence, on day 4, corresponding to the separation of light and darkness on day 1, God sets sun, moon, and stars (which are mobile, though not living, creatures) in the sky; corresponding to the separation of sky and waters on day 2, God fills the waters with fish and the sky with birds on day 5; and corresponding to the separation of dry land from the waters on day 3, God fills this land with land animals of all sorts, including humans, on day 6. And running through the correspondences, there is an observable progression, repeated in each panel, from heaven (days 1 and 4) to waters (days 2 and 5) to earth (days 3 and 6).[70]

But this beautifully simple pattern of correspondences is complicated (beautifully) by the fact that whereas days 1-2 and days 4-5 contain one single act of creation each, days 3 and 6 (at the bottom of each panel) contain two acts each. So we have eight creative acts, each introduced by a divine decree or fiat, spread over six days. Thus, on day 3, we find both the separation of dry land from the waters and the growthvegetation on the dry land. And on day 6, corresponding to these two acts of creation on day 3, we have the creation first of land animals and then of humans, a special kind of land animal. This is certainly beautiful symmetry and it seems—at first blush—to corroborate the judgment of many biblical scholars concerning the prominence of balance and order in the text.

Yet note two anomalies in this pattern. First of all, God's fourth creative act (on day 3) is the creation of vegetation (plants and trees) on the land. But this is technically an act of *filling* (not forming) which seems out of place in terms of the literary structure of the chapter.[71] Yet it could be said that plants and trees are not mobile creatures (in the same sense that fish, birds, animals, humans and the heavenly bodies are) and so they fit in the first panel, which describes the creation of static realms.

The second anomaly in the literary pattern of the panels is God's fifth creative act (the heavenly bodies) on day 4. Although this is certainly an act of filling (which fits days 4-6), it might appropriately have been placed in the first panel (days 1-3) since the stated purpose of the sun and moon is to *separate* day from night or light from dark (this is, however, temporal, not spatial separation).[72] So we have the interesting phenomenon of two sets of borderline creatures (vegetation and the heavenly bodies) that overlap from one panel to the next. Would it be appropriate to say that although the text is clearly concerned with ordered categories of creation, these categories have "fuzzy" boundaries?[73]

Beyond these, there are other non-predictable variations in the text relevant for our consideration. Thus, the text uses a cardinal number in the "evening and morning" formula concluding the first day of creation ("day one") and ordinals for the rest ("second day," "third day" etc.). Then, we find the presence of the Hebrew definite article in the formula for day 6 ("and there was evening and morning, *the* sixth day") and in the references to day 7 ("*the* seventh day"), in contrast to the lack of the article in the first five occurrences of the formula.[74]

We might further cite the distribution of God's acts of "creating" (*bara'*) versus "making" or "doing" (*`asah*) throughout the text (*bara'* in 1:1, 21, 27 [three times], 2:3; *`asah* in 1:7, 16, 25, 26 and 31, 2:2 [twice], 2:3). While the words do have slightly different semantic ranges, there is no unequivocally clear rationale for their distribution in Genesis 1:1-2:3.

I could go on, for example, by citing God's *mode* of creation/making in the text. While the majority of God's creative acts in Genesis 1 presuppose the existence of the *tohû wabohû* (the earth in its initial watery or chaotic state) and represent God shaping or developing this primordial "stuff" into more complex creatures, three exceptions seem to be light (on day 1), the firmament (on day 2), and humanity (on day 6). These three creative acts are all portrayed rhetorically as *ex nihilo* or *de novo*, without the mention of any prior matter used in their construction.

While none of these literary variations is strictly predictable, some of them do make sense in terms of the architectonic scheme of the text, perhaps highlighting rhetorically some important point. Many of the variations, however, seem on the face of it random (and it is not an easy task to determine which are which).[75]

But more than that, the sheer number of variations in the patterning of the text can be multiplied almost infinitely (I have barely scratched the surface). There are even nuanced sub-variations within the variations. Although I have already indicated some of these, there are others. Thus we find the intriguing fact that of the four times that a creature is invited to participate in the creative process, only once is it actually reported that a creature acted on the invitation (the land brought forth vegetation); in the other cases, the creature is called to act, but *God's* action is reported.[76] And there is the further variation that while the first seven of God's fiats are jussives, the eighth is a cohortative (let us make"), where the subject of the action is God together with the (implied) heavenly court.[77]

This complexity reminds me of nothing so much as "fractals" in contemporary chaos theory, the phenomenon whereby complex, non-Euclidian shapes (like a coastline or the edge of a leaf) remain equally complex no matter what level of magnification is used to observe them. No matter how deep you go with a fractal, you never reach a straight line; there is always more complexity to be found. The literary variations of Genesis 1:1-2:3 are, I submit, analogous to fractals in this respect.

But these literary variations are like fractals also in being fundamentally non-predicable. That is, whereas the world rhetorically depicted in Genesis 1 is certainly ordered, patterned, and purposive (a point often noted by commentators), this world is not mechanistically determined, as if it were governed by ineluctable ironclad Newtonian laws. The literary variations suggest that creation is neither random (stochastic) nor strictly predictable (deterministic). There is a certain (if I might dare to say it) incipient subjectivity or freedom granted to the cosmos by God, by which it is allowed, in response to the Creator's call, to find its own pattern.[78] The God who is artisan and maker, reflected rhetorically in the literary artistry of the text, does not over-determine the order of the cosmos.

There is a helpful analogy here to what chaos theorists call a "strange attractor" (SEE FIGURE 3, page 70). The notion of a "strange attractor" is an attempt to describe the stabilizing factor in systems of turbulence (such as a waterfall, the stock market, or the human brain). As such, it is an alternative to the two main types of attractors previously known in physics, namely fixed points (in steady-state systems) and limit cycles (in continuously repetitive dynamic systems).[79] Although the path of motion around a strange attractor looks, on the surface, random, it is actually fractal, exhibiting (paradoxically) infinity and unpredictability within a closed, finite system. This is very like the literary pattern of Genesis 1, which combines a repetitive order with unpredictable variations. Thus, to follow up on the analogy from chaos mathematics, not only does Genesis 1 depict a fractal universe, but it depicts a Creator less like a Newtonian lawgiver and more like a strange attractor (SEE FIGURE 4, page 71).

GOD SHARES POWER WITH CREATURES

While this non-coercive freedom God grants to creation is not exactly synonymous with "love" (on most understandings of the term), it is a move in that direction. A much clearer move, however, is the text's depiction of the process of creation as God sharing power with creatures, inviting them to participate (as they are able) in the creative process itself.[80] Thus, among the many purpose statements given for the creation of sun and moon is the statement that they are to *govern* the day and the night (1:16, 18). If we think about it, this correlates perfectly with their purpose (also stated) to *separate* day from night (1:14, 18). Both governing (or ruling) and separating are paradigmatically divine acts not only in the ancient Near East (especially in Sumerian and Akkadian creation accounts), but also in Genesis 1, where God's sovereign creative activity on days 1-3 consists precisely in three acts of separation by which the major spaces or realms of the created order are demarcated. Likewise, the "expanse" or "firmament" (*raqîa`*) which God created (on day 2) is granted the god-like function of separating the waters above from the waters below (1:6), in imitation of God's own separation of light from darkness on day 1. Rhetorically, this implies that sun, moon, and firmament, like humans in God's image, participate in (or imitate) God's own creative actions. God grants these royal tasks to creatures willingly, allowing them a share of his power and rule.

But these are by no means the only "divine" actions that creatures participate in. On days 3, 5 and 6 (in vv. 11-12, 20, and 24), God commands or (better) invites the earth (twice) and the waters (once) to participate in creation by bringing forth living creatures. Whereas the earth is invited to produce first vegetation (v. 11) and later land animals (v. 24), the waters are invited to teem with water creatures (v. 20).[81] They are invited, in other words, to exercise their God-given fertility and thus to imitate God's own creative actions in filling the world with living things. Actually, God takes quite a risk in calling for the earth to produce vegetation since up to that point in the story God has not yet engaged in the act of filling (it is not until days 4-6 that God fills with mobile beings the regions or spaces demarcated on days 1-3). So, on day 3, the earth literally has no model or exemplar to follow. Indeed, on the next day, it is *God* who imitates the *earth's* creative action by filling the sky with heavenly bodies which, in the literary structure of Genesis 1, is a derivative action.[82] God is, rhetorically speaking, pre-empted by the earth.[83]

But beyond the invitation to the earth and the waters, God "blesses" the fish and the birds on day 5, and humans on day 6, with fertility, and invites them to multiply and *fill* the waters and the earth, (again) in imitation of God's own creative acts of filling. In this connection, there is a notable asymmetry between God's acts of separation (acts 1-3, on days 1-3) and filling (acts 4-8, on days 3-6), which also suggests a willingness to share royal power on God's part. The asymmetry consists in the intriguing detail that while God names the various realms or spaces that have been separated, God does not name any of the inhabitants of those realms.[84] Why does God refrain from naming these creatures? Perhaps because the Creator does not want to hoard this prerogative, but, on the contrary, wishes to give space for humanity to complete this privileged task. And indeed in Genesis 2 *'adam* names the animals, thus exhibiting his rule over them.[85]

While these are not dimensions of the Genesis 1 creation story that are often noticed, attention to these rhetorical features points us to a God who does not hoard divine creative power, with some desperate need to control, but rather to a God who is generous with power, sharing it with creatures, that they might make their own contribution to the harmony and beauty of the world.[86]

THE HUMAN CONTRIBUTION

But the contribution of creatures, which God not only allows but indeed encourages, is clearest and most decisive in the case of humanity, to whom God explicitly grants the status and role of *tzelem 'elohîm* (the image of God) and the commission to extend God's royal administration of the world as authorized representatives on earth.[87]

What is paradoxical is that precisely at this point my reading of the text is in significant tension with a previously mentioned rhetorical study of Genesis 1 by Dale Patrick and Allen Scult. Patrick and Scult claim that God is depicted in the text with such absolute power that humans are rendered powerless objects of divine will (a depiction, at least implicitly, of God as tyrant, and certainly in conflict with my claim regarding love). God's power, according to Patrick and Scult, is literally "authorial," indicated by (among other things) creation by the word. It is the power of an author over a composition or inert piece of work. Humans, by contrast, they *correctly* note, are the subjects of no actions in the text. Humans quite literally do nothing in Genesis 1.[88] This portrayal of God vis-à-vis humans in Genesis 1 is "balanced," they argue, by the more "parental" image of God in Genesis 2, where humans are depicted as agents in their own right, conversing with, even resisting, their Creator/Parent.[89]

Now there is some truth to this reading. While *'adam* is the (implicit) grammatical subject of *radah* (rule) and *kabaš* (subdue) in Genesis 1:26, this language occurs in God's commissioning of the human creature, and not in any reported action performed by humans in the chapter. The trouble is that Patrick and Scult draw the wrong conclusion from this important point. Not only do they ignore the text's clear and explicit assertion that humans are created *like* this "authorial" God, commissioned to rule the animals and subdue the earth (which they would be hard put to explain), but more importantly their reading misrepresents the rhetorical (indeed, canonical) relationship between Genesis 1:1-2:3 and what follows. Whereas God grants humans the power of agency on the sixth day of creation, setting the stage, so to speak, for the drama of human history-making, the actual exercise of human agency does not begin until the paradise/fall story of Genesis 2-3.

There are two important rhetorical clues for understanding Genesis 1 not as an alternative creation story to Genesis 2 (which it either contradicts or balances), but as a prelude to the rest of the Genesis narrative, setting up the normative conditions for what follows. The first clue is the highly significant absence of the concluding "evening and morning" formula on the seventh day, an absence which Augustine noted sixteen centuries ago.[90] Each day of creation is concluded by the line "and there was evening and there was morning," day one, second day, third day, etc., until the sixth day. But when creation is complete and we would expect a final formula, "There was evening and there was morning, the seventh day," there is none, rhetorically indicating that the seventh day is open-ended or unfinished. In the literary structure of the book of Genesis, the seventh day has no conclusion since God continues to "rest" from creating, having entrusted care of the earth to human beings.[91] Thus the paradise/fall story of chapters 2-3 takes place (as do all the events narrated in the book of Genesis and, by extension, in the rest of the Bible) on the seventh day, when God "rests," having delegated post-creation rule of the earth to humanity.[92]

This leads to the other rhetorical clue for the relationship of Genesis 1:1-2:3 with what follows, namely the *tôlᵉdôt* formula, found in Genesis 2:4a, which introduces the "generations" of the heavens and the earth, in the sense of what developed out of them.[93] Throughout the book of Genesis the phrase "these are the *tôlᵉdôt* of" Terah, Noah's sons, Ishmael, etc., introduces either a list of progeny descended from the one named (their genealogy) or an ensuing narrative involving prominent members of the named person's progeny. But in Genesis 2:4a the formula is distinct in that it serves to introduce the first episode of human history (the paradise/fall story), as that which developed out of "the heavens and the earth" which God has just finished creating.[94] The fact that Genesis 1:1-2:3 does not begin with a *tôlᵉdôt* formula suggests it functions as a prologue to the rest of the book, constituting a description of the initial conditions which (ought to) hold for the rest of the story. It is for this reason — and not because it portrays God as having all power — that no human activity is reported in the Genesis 1 creation story.

Genesis 1:1-2:3 thus portrays God as taking the risk, first of blessing human beings with fertility and entrusting them with power over the earth and the animals, and then of stepping back, withdrawing, to allow humans to exercise this newly granted power, to see what develops. Contrary to Patrick and Scult's analysis, Genesis 1 depicts what is precisely a loving, parental exercise of power on God's part. Indeed, God in Genesis 1 is like no one as much as a Mother, who gives life to her children, blesses them, and enhances their power and agency, and then takes the parental risk of allowing her progeny to take their first steps, to attempt to use their power, to develop towards maturity.[95]

That this maturity is radically different from the unlimited exploitation of the world that Lynn White and others are so worried about is indicated by the central fact which has been staring us in the face: the text itself states that God's action and rule are paradigmatic for human action. This is indicated both by the notion of humanity created in God's image and likeness and by the text's canonical placement at the beginning of Scripture. Given my rhetorical reading of Genesis 1, this suggests, minimally, that the sort of power or rule that humans are to exercise is loving power. It is power used to nurture, enhance, and empower others, non-coercively, for *their* benefit, not for the self-aggrandizement of the one exercising power.[96] In its canonical place in the book of Genesis, the creation story in 1:1-2:3 thus serves as a normative limit and judgment on the violence which pervades the primeval history, indeed the rest of the Bible, and human history generally.[97]

In pointed contrast to this violence (especially as portrayed in Genesis 3-6), a beautiful example of the loving exercise of power is found in the actions of Noah in the context of the Flood story. In Genesis 3, the primeval human pair rebel against God and then Adam begins to rule the woman (a rule which is not reciprocated) and names her "Eve" (thus treating her as he did the animals).[98] In Genesis 4, Cain impulsively murders his brother Abel out of resentment, while he-man Lamech boasts to his two wives (the first reference to polygamy in the Bible) that he has in vengeance killed a youth for daring to injure him. And this violent propensity spirals out of control until in Genesis 6 humans fill the earth with their violence or bloodshed (*chamas*), and the earth, which God created good, becomes corrupt and God is "grieved"(*`atzab*) in her heart that she ever raised such an ungrateful brood of children (6:5-6). And then comes the flood. But while humans in the primeval history typically use their power autonomously and so violently, Noah is a righteous man (6:9) and so exercises power in a different manner. It is significant, I believe, that the one righteous person exercises rule over the animals by taking them on the ark and thus preserving their life in a time of threat.[99] Noah in the Flood story is an example of someone imitating God's paradigmatic life-enhancing use of power as depicted in Genesis 1.

CREATION FOUNDED IN LOVE

Like every reading of any text, this one is contestable, subject to dispute at various points and (admittedly) dependent on the preunderstanding and commitments of the interpreter. Nevertheless, in view of what is ethically at stake here, I have taken the risk of offering my reading of Genesis 1:1-2:3.

I have argued that the objections of Keller, White, McFague, while representing important ethical concerns (which I largely share), are simply misguided in the case of Genesis 1. Although it is undeniable that the text has historically been read through the lens of the *Enuma Elish* and the Western aspiration of the scientific conquest of nature, with resulting violence against women and the environment, Genesis 1 is by no means locked into this economy of meaning. On the contrary, a close reading of the text depicts God neither as a warrior creating by violence nor as an extrinsic transcendence unilaterally imposing order on the world. Rather, Genesis 1 artfully shatters both ancient and modern rhetorical expectations and, instead, depicts God as a generous Creator, sharing power with a variety of creatures, inviting them (and trusting them — at some risk) to participate in the creative (and historical) process.[100]

I, of course, harbor no illusions that one alternative reading of a single biblical text can change by fiat an ingrained mindset or habitual praxis concerning the use of power. Nevertheless, given the long modern history of misreading (which constitutes an act of violence against the text), perhaps it is time to begin a pattern of reading differently, respecting the alterity of the text, listening for its word to us, attending to its disclosure of God and the human calling. Perhaps, then, our practice of reading (which we might call a hermeneutic of love) would model in advance the new ethic of inter-human relationships and ecological practice that we are aiming for and which is rooted in this very text.

In the end, the theological claim (which connects the textual reading to the ethical praxis) amounts to the thesis that we ought not to separate our redemptive vision of God's love from God's creative power. Speaking out of my own (Christian) tradition, I would say that—without theological contradiction—Genesis 1:1-2:3 converges on John 3:16. In both creation and redemption, "God so loved the world that he gave ...."

Figure 1 Variations in the Fiat Pattern of Genesis 1

I	II	III	IV	V	VI	VII	VIII
1	1	1	1	1	1	1	1
2	4	2	2	2	4	2	4
3	2	3	4a	4b	3	4	2x
4	x	x	3	3	x	3	3x

Legend:
1 = fiat ("let there be")
2 = summary execution report ("and it was so")
3 = evaluation report ("and God saw that it was good")
4 = extended execution report (specific creative action of God noted)
x = missing or displaced element
a, b = internal variation within an element of the pattern
Roman numerals (I, II, etc.) represent God's eight creative acts over six days

Figure 2 The Structure of Literary Panels in Genesis 1:1-2:3

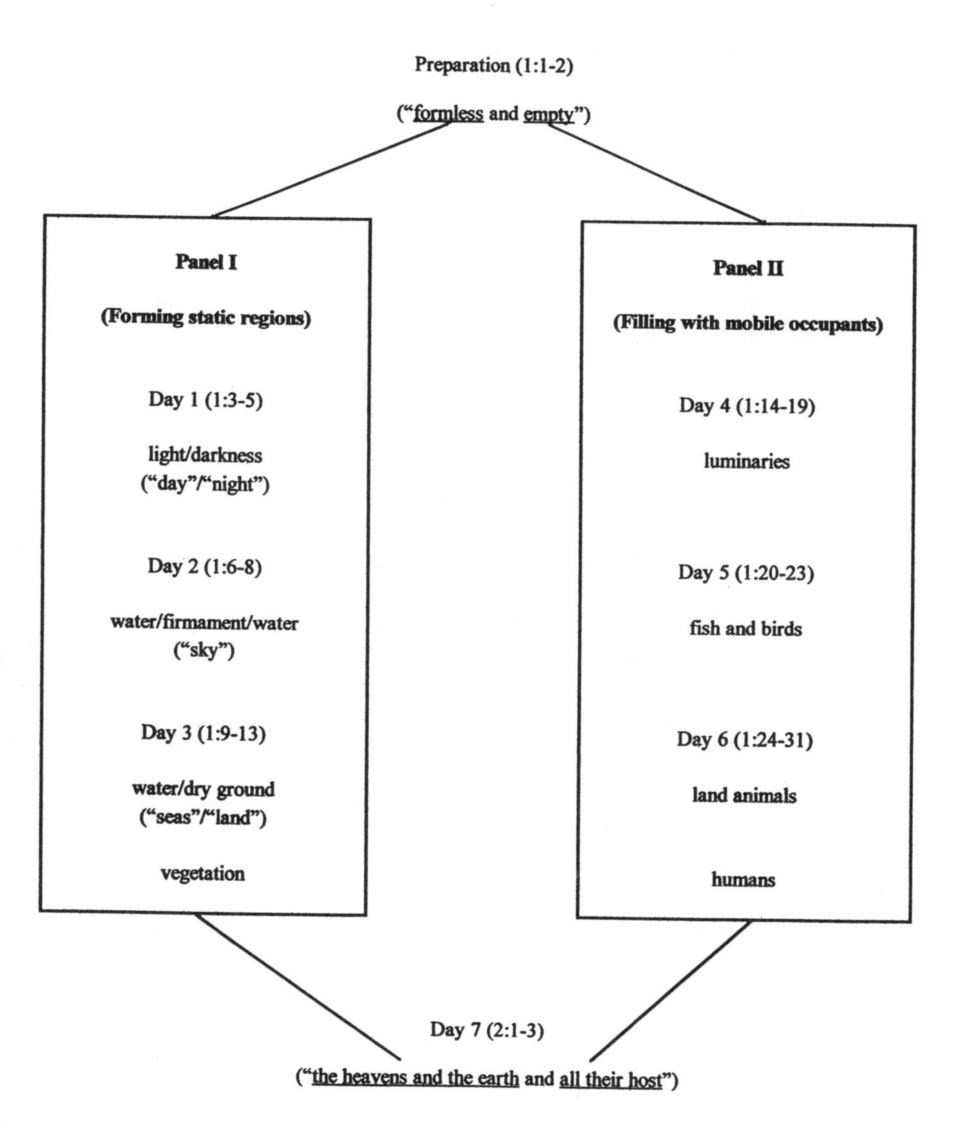

Figure 3 The Lorenz Strange Attractor

The Lorenz attractor is a butterfly-shaped chaotic system that contains an infinite number of trajectories that never intersect one another within a bounded space. By plotting the trajectories over time in three-dimensional space, the strange attractor, which governs the chaotic system, can be discerned. The upper left hand graph shows a non-fractal attempt to plot the variables, resulting in no discernable pattern whatsoever.

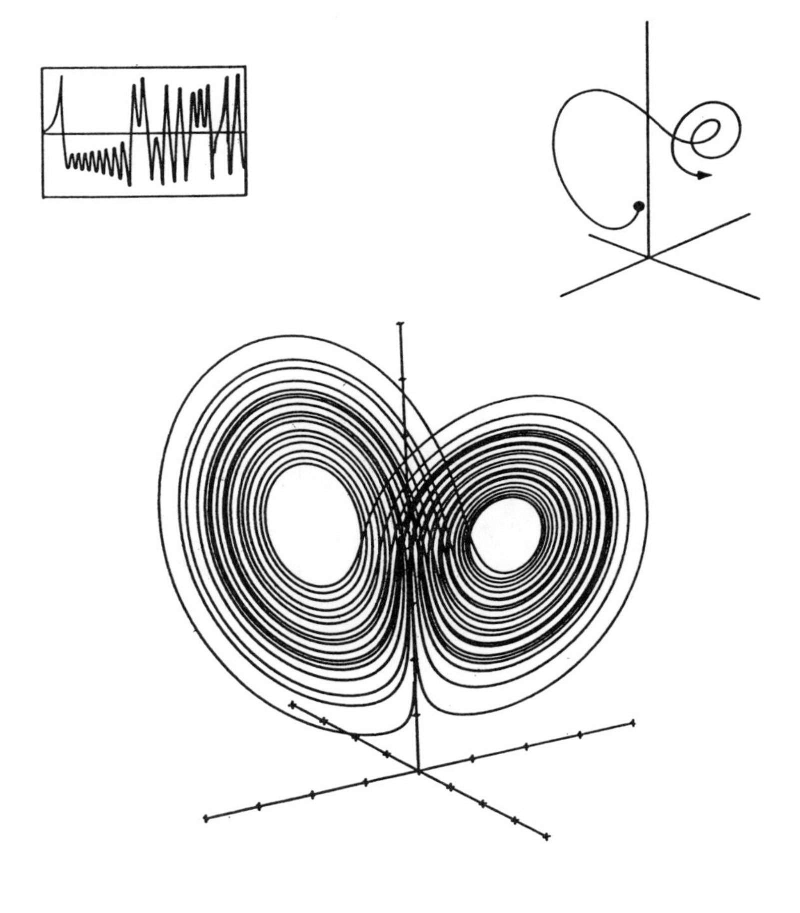

Figure 4 The Winged Bird Attractor

A famous chaotic pattern, the winged bird attractor reveals the inherent order discernable over time in what initially seem to be random variations.

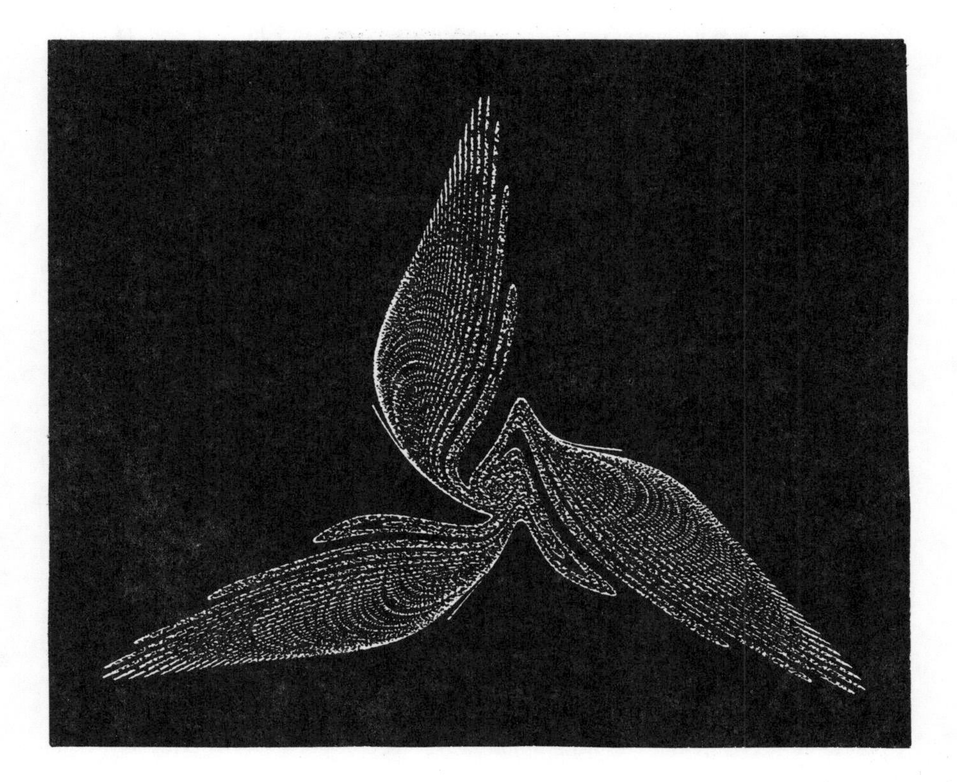

Notes

[1] Earlier versions of this paper were presented at a conference on Love in Jewish, Christian and Islamic Traditions, hosted by the Brock Philosophical Society at Brock University, St. Catharines, ON, February, 1995, and in the Exegesis of Biblical Texts on Ethical Themes Group at the annual meeting of the Society of Biblical Literature in Philadelphia, PA, November, 1995.

[2] For a preliminary attempt to elucidate the meaning of humanity as *imago Dei*, without however engaging in extensive rhetorical analysis of the creation story, see my essay "The Liberating Image? Interpreting the *Imago Dei* in Context," *Christian Scholar's Review* 24/1 (1994): 8-25; and also J. Richard Middleton and Brian J. Walsh, *Truth Is Stranger Than It Used to Be: Biblical Faith in a Postmodern Age* (Downers Grove, IL: InterVarsity; London: SPCK, 1995), 111-125.

[3] For example, R. Hooykaas, *Religion and the Rise of Modern Science* (Grand Rapids, MI: Eerdmans, 1972); Eugene M. Klaaren, *Religious Origins of Modern Science: Belief in Seventeenth-Century Thought* (Grand Rapids, MI: Eerdmans, 1977); M. B. Foster, "The Christian Doctrine of Creation and the Rise of Modern Natural Science," *Mind* 43 (1934): 446-468; and Francis Oakley, "Christian Theology and the Newtonian Science: The Rise of the Concept of the Laws of Nature," *Church History* 30 (1961): 433-457.

[4] Bacon's role in the development of modern science is addressed in Richard Foster Jones, *Ancients and Moderns: A Study in the Rise of the Scientific Movement in Seventeenth Century England* (New York: Dover Publications, 1982). Even before Bacon, Renaissance humanists in fifteenth century Italy (like Ficino, Morandi, and Pico della Mirandola) developed an interpretation of the *imago Dei* as the creative, transformative, energy by which humans (in imitation of God's own creative activity) shape earthly life through cultural-historical action, whether in city-building, alchemy, politics, scholarship or the arts. On the Renaissance humanists and the *imago Dei*, see the massive study by Charles Trinkaus, *In Our Image and Likeness: Humanity and Divinity in Italian Humanist Thought*, 2 vols. (Chicago: University of Chicago Press, 1970). For an analysis of modernity as an historical epoch with its own distinctive ideals and worldview, see Brian J. Walsh and J. Richard Middleton, *The Transforming Vision: Shaping a Christian World View* (Downers Grove, IL: InterVarsity, 1984), chaps. 8 and 9; and Middleton and Walsh, *Truth Is Stranger Than It Used to Be*, chap. 1.

[5] Jacques Derrida, "Plato's Pharmacy," chap. 1 of *Dissemination*, trans. Barbara Johnson (Chicago: University of Chicago Press, 1981). Derrida's point that writing (and all of life) is *intrinsically* (always already) *both* remedy and poison (see esp. p. 70) is somewhat different from the point I am making here, namely that texts *may* be used in different ways, some healthy, some not. I am concerned, in other words, to note that the "effective history" (*Wirkungsgeschichte*) or interpretive reception of texts (Genesis 1 included) is not predetermined in advance,

but often develops in ways (negative or positive) that contravene "authorial intent."

[6] Catherine Keller, *From a Broken Web: Separation, Sexism, and Self* (Boston: Beacon Press, 1986). Although I ultimately dissent from Keller's reading of Genesis 1, I am sympathetic to a great deal (though not all) of the overall argument of this superb book.

[7] On the relationship between the oppression of women and the environmental crisis, see Susan Griffin, *Woman and Nature: The Roaring Inside Her* (New York: Harper & Row, 1978).

[8] This is the burden of Keller's argument in *From a Broken Web*, chap. 2: "Of Men and Monsters"(pp. 47-92).

[9] Herman Gunkel, *Schöpfung und Chaos in Urzeit und Endzeit: Eine religionsgeschichtliche Untersuchung über Gen 1 und Ap Joh 12* (Göttingen: Vandenhoeck & Ruprecht, 1895). Charles A. Muenchow's abridged English translation of pp. 3-120 has been published as "The Influence of Babylonian Mythology Upon the Biblical Creation Story," chap. 1 in *Creation in the Old Testament*, ed. Bernhard W. Anderson, Issues in Religion and Theology 6 (Philadelphia: Fortress, 1984), 25-52.

[10] Note that whereas Gunkel (followed by Keller) thought that *tᵉhôm* was derived from *ti'amat*, most Old Testament scholars have followed Alexander Heidel's argument that this is morphologically impossible and that both words probably have a common (proto-) Semitic root (Heidel, *The Babylonian Genesis: The Story of Creation,* 2nd ed. (Chicago and London: University of Chicago Press, 1951; "Phoenix Books," 1963), 100.

[11] The *Enuma Elish* actually contains a double combat motif. Early on in the myth, before Marduk vanquishes Tiamat (who represents the salt water ocean), Ea (Marduk's father) vanquishes Tiamat's consort Apsu (who represents the fresh waters). For English translations of the *Enuma Elish*, see E.A. Speiser, "Akkadian Myths and Epics," pp. 60-72, in James B. Pritchard, ed., *Ancient Near Eastern Texts Relating to the Old Testament*, 3rd ed. with *Supplement* (Princeton: Princeton University Press, 1969); Alexander Heidel, *The Babylonian Genesis*, chap. 1: "Enuma Elish"; and Stephanie Dalley, *Myths from Mesopotamia: Creation, the Flood, Gilgamesh and Others* (Oxford: Oxford University Press, 1989), "The Epic of Creation," 228-277.

[12] Among the minority who posit an Egyptian background for Genesis 1, see James K. Hoffmeier, "Some Thoughts on Genesis 1 & 2 and Egyptian Cosmology," *Journal of the Ancient Near Eastern Society* 15 (1983): 39-49; and A. S. Yahuda, *The Language of the Pentateuch in Its Relation to Egyptian Literature and History,* vol. 1 (London: Oxford University Press, 1933), esp. chaps. 2 and 3. For references to the other positions taken on the matter, see *infra*, nn. 36 and 39.

[13] Her comparison of the *Enuma Elish* with Genesis 1 is found in *From a Broken Web*, 73-92.

[14] Ibid, 80, 85.

[15] Ibid., 86, 87. She especially appeals to James Hillman.

[16] Ibid., 86.

[17] One of the problems with this approach to reading texts is that it looks for similarities of underlying themes and genres, but tends to ignore the particularity or "actuality" (to use James Muilenburg's term), that is, the actual rhetorical assertions of the text under consideration. To put it differently, although two texts may utilize a similar motif or theme, what is crucial is not simply pointing out this similarity, but discerning how each text distinctively uses the theme in question. Part of the problem goes back to Gunkel himself, who pioneered the discipline of "form criticism," which was based on the comparison of literary genres and motifs in the Bible and the ancient Near East. For an important critique of this comparative approach by a leading form critic who was at the time President of the Society of Biblical Literature, see James Muilenburg's now classic 1968 presidential address, published as "Form Criticism and Beyond," *Journal of Biblical Literature* 88/1 (March 1969): 1-18. Muilenburg is widely credited with inaugurating the discipline of rhetorical criticism of the Hebrew Bible, a discipline to which I am indebted in this essay. For a brilliant analysis of the significance of *differences* in the use of a common motif, see Robert Alter, *The Art of Biblical Narrative* (New York: Basic Books, 1981), chap. 3, which examines five betrothal type-scenes in the Hebrew Bible.

[18] See Paul Ricoeur, *The Symbolism of Evil*, trans. Emerson Buchanan (Boston: Beacon, 1969), 194-198. Ricoeur's extensive analysis of the *Enuma Elish* occurs in part II, chap 1: "The Drama of Creation and the 'Ritual' Vision of the World." Ricoeur's analysis of the function of the combat myth may be applicable also in other ancient Near Eastern cultures outside of Babylon. For example, the Egyptian combat myth known as "The Repulsing of the Dragon" was interpreted in ancient times as a mythic account to be historically enacted in military campaigns of the pharaoh against the enemies of the empire. For various versions of "The Repulsing of the Dragon," see Pritchard, ed., *Ancient Near Eastern Texts Relating to the Old Testament*, 7, 11-12, and 367 (this myth portrays the nightly struggle of the sun god Re with Apophis the serpent who tries to swallow him in the underworld, followed by Re's victory resulting in the birth of the new day). Although we have no evidence concerning the political implications of the Ugaritic combat myths, in which Ba'al conquers watery enemies, it is likely they had a similar function. On the political implications of the combat myth in Israel, see Patrick D. Miller, Jr., *Holy War and Cosmic War in Early Israel* (unpublished doctoral dissertation, Harvard Divinity School, 1963).

[19] *The Symbolism of Evil*, 182-183. Another author who discerns the violent implications of the combat myth for human life is liberation theologian Pedro Trigo. Trigo addresses the function of the modern worldview (which he thinks is modeled on the ancient combat myth) in fostering geopolitical violence (especially in the

Third World) in his *Creation and History* (Maryknoll, NY: Orbis, 1991), part 2, entitled "From Chaos and Cosmos to Faith in Creation" (pp. 69-108). The significance of the combat myth can, however, be read differently. Thus Jon Levenson (in *Creation and the Persistence of Evil: The Jewish Drama of Omnipotence* [San Francisco: Harper & Row, 1988]) can celebrate what he takes to be the positive psychological value of the myth, whether found in the ancient Near East, the Bible, or later Jewish writings. Although I find Levenson's analysis of the existential sense of fragility that results from the combat myth quite profound (esp. chap. 2: "The Survival of Chaos After the Victory of God," pp. 14-25), by and large he does not adequately address the negative ethical and political implications of the *Chaoskampf* theme, particularly its function to legitimate violence on the human plane.

[20] Keller, *From a Broken Web*, 77.

[21] Likewise worthy of sustained interaction is Keller's more recent book, *Apocalypse Now and Then: A Feminist Guide to the End of the World* (Boston: Beacon, 1996), which continues the argument of *From a Broken Web* in challenging religious expectations of a violent end to evil. Some of her argument from the more recent book is distilled in "Power Lines," chap. 4 in *Power, Powerlessness, and the Divine: New Inquires in Bible and Theology*, ed. Cynthia L. Rigby (Atlanta, GA: Scholars Press, 1997).

[22] This is not to say that the theme of God doing battle with the sea or the waters is absent from the Hebrew Bible. On the contrary, it is quite common in poetic texts, though rarely, in my opinion, denoting creation. More usually, the mythological waters allude to historical enemies whom God has vanquished or will vanquish (as in Psalms 18:15-17, 65:7, 144:7; and Isaiah 17:12-13) or to the Red Sea through which the Israelites passed at the exodus (as in Psalms 77:16-20, 106:9, 114:3, 5; and Isaiah 51:10; cf. Habakkuk 3:8). The background of such texts is, however, to be found not in the *Enuma Elish*, but in Ugaritic mythology where Ba'al vanquishes an enemy known variously as Prince Yam (Sea) or Judge Nahar (River). In the Hebrew Bible, Sea and River (or Jordan) occur as parallels in the context of the combat myth in Psalm 114:3, 5; and Nahum 1:4.

[23] The theme of creation by separation (the splitting of heaven from earth) is found, for example, in the Sumerian myths *The Creation of the Pick-Ax* and *Gilgamesh, Enkidu, and the Netherworld*. See W. G. Lambert, "The Cosmology of Sumer and Babylon," chap. 2 in *Ancient Cosmologies*, ed. Carmen Blacker and Michael Loewe (London: George Allen & Unwin, 1975), 42-62.

[24] George A. Barton, "Tiamat," *Journal of the American Oriental Society* 15 (1893): 18. Note that Barton's article was published even before Gunkel's more famous study (Gunkel cites it in "The Influence of Babylonian Mythology," p. 51, n. 31). Yet, even in this first exhilarating flush of noting similarities between the two accounts, Barton (like Gunkel) was also aware the divergences between them.

[25] See, for example, the occurrence of *tannîn* (singular) as a mythological adversary or enemy of YHWH (though often representing a historical or political

enemy) in Job 7:12; Psalms 44:20 (Eng 44:19); Isaiah 27:1, 51:19; Ezekiel 29:3 and 32:2. The plural *tannînim* also occurs in Psalm 74:13 and Psalm 89:11 (Eng 98:10).

[26] Leviathan (Hebrew *liwyatan*) is described in Isaiah 27:1 as a twisted and crooked serpent, and is mentioned also in Psalms 74:14, 104:26; Job 3:8 and 40:25-41:26 (Eng 41:1-34). Leviathan is the Hebrew version of the seven-headed water serpent known in the Ba'al myths as *ltn* (usually vocalized as *lôtan* since William F. Albright's proposal in "New Light on Early Canaanite Language and Literature," *Bulletin of the American Schools of Oriental Research* 46 [1932]: 19). This is evident not only from the fact that both names are philologically equivalent, but also from the description of *lôtan* as a "twisted" and "crooked" serpent in both the Ba'al myth and Isaiah 27:1 (the Ugaritic and Hebrew words used in these texts are precise cognates). Rahab, which clearly designates a serpent in Job 26:12 (but which so far has no known parallel in ancient Near Eastern literature), is mentioned also in Job 9:13; Isaiah 30:7, 51:19; Psalms 87:4, 89:11 (Eng 89:10); and in the plural in Psalm 40:5 (Eng 40:4).

[27] Gunkel, "The Influence of Babylonian Mythology Upon the Biblical Creation Story," 49.

[28] Jon Levenson, *Creation and the Persistence of Evil*, 17, citing one of his students. Levenson goes on to suggest that the sport or play of God with Leviathan in Psalm 104:26 may not be quite so harmless and may in fact represent (as in Job 40:25-26) "catching the great sea beast with a hook and line" (p. 17). However, in his later, more extensive analysis of Psalm 104 (in chap. 5), Levenson refers to Leviathan as God's "toy" and is careful to distinguish this account from creation-by-combat.

[29] Eugene F. Roop, *Genesis* (Believers Bible Commentary; Scottdale, PA and Kitchner, ON: Herald, 1987), 27.

[30] Brueggemann, *Genesis* (Interpretation; Atlanta: John Knox, 1982), 30; cf. 32. Note that Brueggemann does not oppose command to permission, and thus speaks of God's "lordly permit" (p. 30) which enables creatures to be.

[31] Roop, *Genesis*, 27.

[32] On the various senses of Hebrew *tôb*, see Douglas A. Knight, "Cosmogony and Order in the Hebrew Tradition," chap. 5 in *Cosmogony and Ethical Order: New Studies in Comparative Ethics*, ed. Robin W. Lovin and Frank E. Reynolds (Chicago and London: University of Chicago Press, 1985), 145.

[33] This is not to claim that the worldview of Genesis 1 is found consistently throughout Scripture. On the contrary, the Hebrew Bible contains at least three rather clear creation-by-combat texts (Job 26:7-14; Psalms 74:12-17 and 89:5-14) and is full of difficult (perhaps contradictory) ethical tensions, including a theology of holy war (especially in the Deuteronomistic literature).

[34] Gunkel speaks either of the "Marduk-Yahweh myth" in the singular ("The Influence of Babylonian Mythology Upon the Biblical Creation Story," p. 43) or of "one and the same myth which is preserved in two different but related versions" (p. 44). He repeatedly calls them "recensions" of the same myth (pp. 46-49).

[35] Gunkel notes "the unmistakably huge difference between the Babylonian and the biblical creation accounts. . . . Genesis 1 is essentially a faded myth" (ibid., 46).

[36] On Genesis 1 as polemic or critique of ancient Near Eastern ideas, see Gerhard F. Hasel "The Significance of the Cosmology in Genesis 1 in Relation to Ancient Near Eastern Parallels," *Andrews University Seminary Studies* 10/1 (1972): 1-20; Hasel, "The Polemic Nature of the Genesis Cosmology," *Evangelical Quarterly* 46 (1974): 81-102; J. A. Sanders, *The Old Testament in the Cross* (New York: Harper & Brothers, 1961), chap. 2: "Creation and the Creator," 37-55 (esp. pp. 44-45); Nahum M. Sarna, *Understanding Genesis* (New York: Schocken Books, 1970; reprint of 1966 ed.), 1-36; Flemming Hvidberg, "The Canaanitic Background of Gen. I-III," *Vetus Testamentum* 10 (1960): 285-294; James L. Crenshaw, "The Human Dilemma and the Literature of Dissent," chap. 10 in *Tradition and Theology in the Old Testament*, ed. Douglas A. Knight (Philadelphia: Fortress, 1977), 235; Norman C. Habel, *Literary Criticism of the Old Testament* (Philadelphia: Fortress, 1971), 26; Umberto Cassuto, *A Commentary on the Book of Genesis*, Part I: *From Adam to Noah*, trans. Israel Abrahams (Jerusalem: The Magnes Press, 1961), 7, 39, 49; Everett Fox, *The Five Books of Moses* (New York: Schocken Books, 1995), 12; J. Albertson, "Genesis 1 and the Babylonian Creation Myth," *Thought* 37 (1962): 226-244; and John H. Stek, "What Says the Scripture?" chap. 7 in *Portraits of Creation: Biblical and Scientific Perspectives on the World's Formation*, ed. Howard Van Till et al (Grand Rapids: Eerdmans, 1990), esp. 229-232.

[37] This would, however, require reconstructing the original social context of the creation story. For an attempted reconstruction see Middleton and Walsh, *Truth Is Stranger Than It Used to Be*, chap. 6.

[38] This is admitted even by scholars who do not posit an explicit or intentional polemic in the text. See, for example, Alexander Heidel, *The Babylonian Genesis*, chap. 3: "Old Testament Parallels," 82-140.

[39] For his argument concerning a Canaanite (as opposed to a Mesopotamian) background to biblical cosmogonies, see John Day, *God's Conflict With the Dragon and the Sea: Echoes of a Canaanite Myth in the Old Testament,* University of Cambridge Oriental Publications (Cambridge: Cambridge University Press, 1985), 1-18.

[40] Day, 49, 52, 61. Other creation texts that Day groups with Genesis 1, in that they are characterized by God's non-conflictual containment of the waters, include Psalm 33:7-8; Proverbs 8:24, 27-29; Jeremiah 5:22 and 31:35.

[41] This is the title of Levenson's chapter on Psalm 104 in *Creation and the Persistence of Evil* (pp. 53-65), a phrase he also uses to characterize the cosmogony of Genesis 1 (p. 127).

[42] Levenson, *Creation and the Persistence of Evil*, 100. Whereas Levenson thinks that creation-by-combat characterizes all biblical cosmogonies except Psalm 104 and Genesis 1, John Day thinks it characterizes even the cosmogony in Psalm 104. Bernard F. Batto is, however, the only contemporary biblical scholar I have

been able to find who continues to think it characterizes Genesis 1 as well. While Batto admits that the *tannînim* have been demythologized in Genesis 1, he critiques Levenson's reading of the demythologization of the waters as follows: "But this fails to reckon with 'the Abyss' (*tehôm*) itself as P's primary symbol for the primordial arch-foe of the Creator in Genesis 1." See Batto, *Slaying the Dragon: Mythmaking in the Biblical Tradition* (Louisville, KY: Westminster/John Knox, 1992), 213, n. 19.

[43] Lynn White, Jr., "The Historical Roots of Our Ecologic Crisis," *Science* 155 (March 10, 1967): 1203-1207. Reprinted as Appendix I (pp. 125-[44] Arnold Toynbee, in *The Toynbee-Ikeda Dialogue* (Tokyo: Kodansha International, 1976); Daisetz T. Suzuki, "The Role of Nature in Zen Buddhism," *Eranos-Jahrbuch* 22 (1953): 292; Theodore Roszak, *Where the Wasteland Ends* (Garden City, NY: Doubleday, 1972); Ian MacHarg, "The Plight," in *The Environmental Crisis: Man's Struggle to Live with Himself*, ed. Harold Helfrich (New Haven, CT: Yale University Press, 1970); and David Suzuki, *Subdue the Earth*, the third video in *A Planet for the Taking*, an eight-part series produced by the Canadian Broadcasting Corporation (1986). For a wide survey of this critique in recent literature, see Cameron Wybrow's excellent study, *The Bible, Baconianism, and Mastery over Nature: The Old Testament and Its modern Misreading* (New York: Peter Lang, 1991), esp. "Introduction: The Mastery Hypothesis" (pp. 3-35).

[45] White, 133.

[46] Ibid., 135.

[47] Ibid., 132.

[48] Both dimensions of the charge are lucidly addressed by Wybrow in *The Bible, Baconianism, and Mastery over Nature*. His careful examination of the understanding of "nature" and "dominion" in pagan antiquity (chaps. 1 and 2), in the Bible (chaps. 3 and 4), and at the start of the modern scientific era (chap. 5) serves as perhaps the most comprehensive rebuttal of the ecological objections in the literature. Wybrow, however, unwisely follows the idiosyncratic opinion of biblical scholar James Barr in disassociating the *imago Dei* from the mandate to dominion in Genesis 1.

[49] From the *Discourse on Method*, part 6. In René Descartes, *Discourse on the Method of Rightly Conducting One's Reason and Seeking Truth in the Sciences*, trans. Donald A. Cress (Indianapolis and Cambridge: Hackett Publishing Co., 1980), 33.

[50] See Sallie McFague, *Models of God: Theology for an Ecological, Nuclear Age* (Philadelphia: Fortress, 1987), chap. 3: "God and the World" (esp. pp. 63-78 on the monarchial model of God). A similar argument is articulated in McFague, "Models of God for an Ecological, Evolutionary Era: God as Mother of the Universe," in *Physics, Philosophy, and Theology: A Common Quest for Understanding*, ed. Robert J. Russell et al (Vatican City State: Vatican City Observatory; Notre Dame, IL: University of Notre Dame Press, 1988), 249-271.

[51] McFague, *Models of God*, 68.

[52] Ibid., 61.

[53] Ibid., 69. McFague herself does not distinguish these as typically male and female experiences of God. But this distinction would be consistent with her argument.

[54] Ibid., 69-87. For God as Mother giving birth to the universe, see McFague, "Models of God for an Ecological, Evolutionary Era: God as Mother of the Universe," esp. 255-262.

[55] James L. Crenshaw, *Story and Faith: A Guide to the Old Testament* (New York: Macmillian; London: Collier Macmillian, 1986), 39.

[56] Tamara Cohen Eskenazi, "Torah as Narrative and Narrative as Torah," in *Old Testament Interpretation: Past, Present, and Future*, ed. James Luther Mays, David L. Petersen, and Kent Harold Richards (Nashville: Abingdon, 1995), 17.

[57] Alter, *The Art of Biblical Narrative*, 143, 145.

[58] Crenshaw, 61.

[59] Ibid., 60. It is difficult to understand the persistence of this portrayal of God or the widespread assumption that it characterizes the creation account in Genesis 1. Apart from the fact that this assumption may be rooted in the notion of the combat myth, which involves the imposition of order on recalcitrant "chaos," the perception of the priestly creation story as one of invariant order *par excellence* may go back to a peculiarity of the history of critical biblical scholarship. In this scholarship, the literary style of the so-called "Priestly" document (of which Genesis 1 is a part) has historically been contrasted with that of the so-called "Yahwist" document (which includes the Genesis 2 creation story). Sean McEvenue's survey of scholarly evaluations of the narrative style of the priestly writer notes the frequency with which terms like "pedantic," "stereotyped," and "monotonous" arise in the works of prominent scholars like Julius Wellhausen, S. R. Driver, Gerhard von Rad, and Claus Westermann (see Sean E. McEvenue, *The Narrative Style of the Priestly Writer* [Rome: Biblical Institute Press, 1971], 5-8). Although McEvenue does not deal explicitly with Genesis 1, it is a short step from the assumption of a pedantic, monotonous, and artificial literary style for the priestly writing in general to the claim that the priestly creation story is characterized by repetitive order and imposed symmetry. But this is, of course, merely a supposition on my part.

[60] Dale Patrick and Allen Scult, *Rhetoric and Biblical Interpretation* (Sheffield, UK: JSOT Press, 1987; Almond Press, 1990), chap. 6: "Genesis and Pow r: An Analysis of the Biblical Story of Creation," 103-125.

[61] Ibid., 117.

[62] It is intriguing that apart from biblical scholars who often claim to find in Genesis 1 the very model of divine power that White and McFague decry, many — if not most — Christian theologians unproblematically assume this same model for their understanding of God as Creator and the world as created. Michael Welker has helpfully described this theological model as a generalized hierarchical picture

of production, causation, and dependence (Welker, "What is Creation? Rereading Genesis 1 and 2," *Theology Today* 48/1 [April 1991]: 56-71). Citing a number of prominent theological definitions of "creation," Welker demonstrates that there is widespread consensus in the Christian tradition that creation (whether act or product) consists in a simple "pattern of power" (p. 59). As *act* or *process*, creation involves being unilaterally caused or produced by a transcendent reality, while as *product*, it involves absolute dependence on this transcendent reality. Not only is this a remarkably thin and abstract notion of creation, but as Welker points out, it is widely assumed that such a notion of the God-creature relationship adequately characterizes the biblical creation account in Genesis. Like Welker, I argue that this is simply false. The biblical picture is significantly more complex.

[63] Ever since the original proposals of Bernhard Stade (*Biblische Theologie des Alten Testaments*, 2 vols. [Tübingen: Mohr, 1905-11], 1:349) and Friedrich Schwally ("Die biblischen Schöpfungsberichte," *Archiv für Religionswissenschaft* 9 [1906]: 159-175), it is sometimes claimed by biblical scholars (especially those oriented to tradition criticism) that the Genesis 1:1-2:3 creation story derives from an older *Tatbericht* or deed-oriented report of creation (which described God's actions in creating) edited together with a later *Wortbericht* or word-oriented report (which introduced the notion of God speaking creation into being). One possible evidence for this is the two types of execution reports in the text. Perhaps the first type is derived from the *Wortbericht*, while the second is derived from the *Tatbericht*.

[64] Although this variety is characteristic of the Hebrew text, it is not always evident in the LXX. Indeed, the LXX of Genesis 1 often harmonizes and systematizes the variations of the MT, sometimes supplying missing items or arranging them in a more consistent pattern.

[65] We could say that the first type of fiat names only the object and not the subject of the action (as the second does). This would, however, be a comment about the force of the text's *meaning*, and not technically a comment on the grammar of the Hebrew text. Grammatically, the difference is that the first type has the creature in question as the subject of the verb *to be* (and in one case as the subject of a passive verb, "be gathered"), whereas the second type has the creature as subject of some other (active) verb, which implies that creature's participation in creative activity.

[66] Henri Blocher traces the observation of this symmetry or correspondence back to Johann Gottfried von Herder. See Blocher, *In the Beginning: The Opening Chapters of Genesis*, trans. David G. Peterson (Downers Grove, IL: InterVarsity, 1984), 51.

[67] First suggested by M. J. Larange, "Hexameron (Genese 1 a 2,4)," *Revue Biblique* 5 (1896): 382. Cited in Blocher, *In the Beginning*, 51, n. 45.

[68] This is not to deny that *tohû wabohû* may also function as a hendiadys, meaning something like "an empty wasteland" and certainly has an onomatopoeic sense (which might be conveyed by expressions like "hurly burly" or "helter

skelter"). The phrase may well function on multiple levels.

[69] This reading of Genesis 2:1 is prefigured in the famous medieval distinction between God's work of separation (*opus distinctionis*) on days 1-3 and his work of adornment or embellishment (*opus ornatus*) on days 4-6. (See, for example, Thomas Aquinas, *Summa Theologiae*, I, Q.65, a. answer to objection 1). The medieval distinction, however, is between separation and adornment (as opposed to filling) and seems to be based on the Vulgate's mistranslation (following the LXX) of Hebrew *saba'* (actually *s^eba'am*, "their host") by the Latin *ornatus*. It seems that the translators of the LXX misread *saba'* ("host," "company," or "army") as *sebî* ("beauty," "glory," or "adornment"). The NIV tries to capture something of both senses in its translation of *saba'* in Genesis 2:1 as "vast array."

[70] Bernard W. Anderson observed this progression in his excellent essay, "The Priestly Creation Story: A Stylistic Study," chap. 3 in his *From Creation to New Creation: Old Testament Perspectives,* Overtures to Biblical Theology (Minneapolis: Fortress Press, 1994). It should be noted that Anderson uses the word "panel" in his essay (which was first published with a slightly different title in 1977) to refer to each of God's eight creative acts (pp. 45-46), while I have used "panel" to refer to the two corresponding triads of days.

[71] Yet the (unexpected) creation of vegetation at this point makes perfect sense (in retrospect) as a necessary preparation to God granting this vegetation as food to animals and humans on day 6 (note that days 3 and 6 are parallel in terms of the architectonic scheme of the chapter).

[72] Thus both the last creative act on the first "panel" (days 1-3) and the first creative act on the second "panel" (days 4-6) overlap the panels in a symmetrical asymmetry.

[73] Another case of literary variation that involves overlap of boundaries is the threefold occurrence of "blessing" in the text. Twice God blesses living, organic creatures with fertility, the flying creatures and water dwellers on day 5 and humanity on day 6, but there is surprisingly no blessing mentioned for land animals. Instead, we find that the seventh day is blessed, though this is blessing for sanctification, not for fertility. Not only is the blessing of the seventh day an unexpected variation, but it serves rhetorically to connect the seventh day with the prior six days of God's creative activity, even though it stands structurally outside the two panels of six creative days.

[74] This literary variation probably serves rhetorically to emphasize the special, climactic character of days 6 and 7, highlighting (respectively) the creation of humanity in God's image and the completion of God's creative work.

[75] This is because so many conflicting (ad hoc) explanations for particular variations have been suggested by commentators. It is thus hard to know whether the explanations really explain the variations or exist primarily in the mind of the commentators.

[76] Presumably primary and secondary agency are compatible. There have,

however, been other explanations, for example, that the creature in question was unable to act, since it did not possess the requisite generative powers. This interpretation goes back to Rabbinic sources. See Wybrow, *The Bible, Baconianism, and Mastery over Nature*, 122.

[77] Without intending to bore the reader (since the variations could be multiplied indefinitely), we could note further that in three of the four cases that God's fiat does *not* invite a creature to actively participate in creation, the verb *to be* is used (God invites a creature to exist), whereas in one case (God's third creative act) a different verb is use (God calls the waters to *be gathered* to one place).

[78] There are many biblical passages which describe the subjectivity or responsiveness of creation to God. For a discussion of these passages, see Brian J. Walsh, Marianne B. Karsh and Nik Ansell, "Trees, Forestry, and the Responsiveness of Creation," *Cross Currents* 44/2 (1994): 149-162; Wybrow, *The Bible, Baconianism, and Mastery over Nature*, chap. 3: "Nature in the Old Testament: Desacralized but Not De-animated" (pp. 109-134); Terence E. Fretheim, "Nature's Praise of God in the Psalms," *Ex Auditu* 3 (1987): 16-30; and Middleton and Walsh, *Truth Is Stranger Than It Used to Be*, 147-152.

[79] The term "strange attractor" was coined by David Ruelle and Floris Takens in a 1971 paper called "On the Nature of Turbulence," in *Communications in Mathematical Physics* 20 (1971): 167-192. Good introductions to chaos theory include James Gleick, *Chaos: Making a New Science* (New York: Viking, 1987); and Ian Stewart, *Does God Play Dice? The Mathematics of Chaos* (Cambridge, MA and Oxford, UK: Blackwell, 1989). George Lakhoff's marvelous book, *Women, Fire, and Dangerous Things: What Categories Reveal about the Mind* (Chicago and London: University of California Press, 1987) goes well beyond mathematics and chaos theory to show connections between the findings of a large number of disciplines on what he calls "motivated" (p. 96) patterning, distinct from the traditional false alternatives of either random/stochastic or predictable/deterministic patterns. By articulating examples of such "motivated" patterning in the world studied by biology (see chapter 11: "Species"), Lakhoff implicitly reopens the old question, long laid to rest by deterministic science, of intelligent design in nature (see esp. chaps. 4-8 in Part I: "Categories and Cognitive Models").

[80] Beside myself, Terence E. Fretheim is the only other biblical scholar I know of who has *foregrounded* the risk-taking, power-sharing character of God in Genesis 1, thus challenging traditional readings of the text. See both his comments on Genesis 1 in *The New Interpreter's Bible*, Vol. 1, ed. David L. Petersen (Nashville, TN: Abingdon, 1994), "The Book of Genesis: Introduction, Commentary and Reflections," and his beautiful little-known essay called "Creator, Creature, and Co-Creation in Genesis 1-2," in *All Things New: Essays in Honor of Roy A. Harrisville*, ed. Arland J. Hultgren, Donald H. Juel and Jack D. Kingbury, Word and World Supplement Series (St. Paul, MN: Word and World, 1992), 11-20. Although the rhetorical reading of Genesis 1 presented in this paper was developed before I read either of Freitheim's works cited above, I was already fundamentally indebted

to his classic *The Suffering of God: An Old Testament Perspective* (Overtures to Biblical Theology; Philadelphia: Fortress, 1984) for his insightful elucidation of the biblical portrayal of God as passionately involved with the created order.

[81] The first two of these three commands/invitations are rhetorically distinguished by a cognate accusative construction in the Hebrew, involving an assonance between the verb and its object in each case (thus v. 11 says literally "let the earth green with greenery" or "let the earth vegetate vegetation"). William P. Brown ("Divine Act and the Art of Persuasion in Genesis 1." in *History and Interpretation: Essays in Honour of John H. Hayes*, ed. M. Patrick Graham, William P. Brown and Jeffrey K. Kuan [Sheffield, UK: JSOT Press, 1993], 24, 27) calls this feature *figura etymologica* and detects it at two other places in Genesis 1. The first is 1:15 ("let them be *for lights* in the expanse of the sky *to give light*") and the second (based on his reconstruction of a lost consonant from the Hebrew *Vorlage*, suggested by the LXX) is 1:20, which would make two occurrences in this verse ("let the waters *cause swarms of living creatures to swarm* and *cause flyers to fly about* in the expanse of the sky"). Brown defends his reconstruction of the *Vorlage* of Genesis 1 at greater length in *Structure, Role, Ideology in the Hebrew and Greek Texts of Genesis 1:1-2:3* (Atlanta: Scholars Press, 1993), 139-140, n. 29.

[82] Indeed, all God's acts of filling (the sky and sea with birds and fish on day 5 and the land with animals and humans on day 6) are derivative in this sense, coming as they do after the earth's creative activity.

[83] I am not claiming that the text assigns any autonomy (ontological or otherwise) to creatures, since all the "divine" or "god-like" functions of creatures that I have enumerated are God-given and delegated. Yet I want to take the rhetoric of the text seriously in its portrayal of creaturely power.

[84] This asymmetry could be counted as another variation in the "fiat" pattern. And, like fractals, there is further variation *within* this variation. Thus, on days 1 and 3, God names that which has been separated (light and darkness are named "day" and "night" in 1:5; the dry land and the waters are named "earth" and "seas" in 1:10). On day 2, however, God does not name that which has been separated, but the separator itself (the expanse that divides the waters is named "sky" in 1:8). A further variation is that the naming itself occurs at different places within the fiat pattern (twice after and once before the evaluation report). This is simply further evidence that the text's "order" is highly complex and flexible.

[85] Here I follow Phyllis Trible regarding the significance of naming in Genesis 2-3 (*God and the Rhetoric of Sexuality* [Philadelphia: Fortress, 1980], chap. 4: "A Love Story Gone Awry," esp. 133-134). My one disagreement with Trible would be that I do not think the power involved in naming inevitably involves subjugation. It does, however, involve a power differential between the one naming and the one named.

[86] This reading certainly contravenes any interpretation of Genesis 1 that claims that humans are absolutely unique among creatures in imaging God. The

picture given in the text is considerably more nuanced than that.

[87] Apart from the fact that the Genesis text itself associates humanity as "image of God" with the mandate to rule (in 1:26-28), there is a significant literature in ancient Egypt and Mesopotamia which applies the term primarily to *kings* (and to a lesser degree to *priests*). In other words, the term "image of God" with the mandate to rule (in 1:26-28), there is a significant literature in ancient Egypt and Mesopotamia which applies the term primarily to *kings* (and to a lesser degree to *priests*). In other words, the term "image of God" designates those who are called to represent the divine on earth, a usage which clearly suggests power and privilege. See Phyllis A. Bird, "'Male and Female He Created Them': Gen 1:27b in the Context of the Priestly Account of Creation," *Harvard Theological Review* 74 (1981):129-159; D. J. A. Clines, "The Image of God in Man," *Tyndale Bulletin* 19 (1968): 53-103; and Jeffrey H. Tigay, "The Image of God and the Flood: Some New Developments," in *Studies in Jewish Education and Judaica in Honor of Louis Newman*, ed. Alexander M. Shapiro and Burton I. Cohen (New York: KTAV, 1984), 169-182.

[88] Patrick and Scult actually claim that there are no creaturely actors at all (human or otherwise) in the Genesis 1 creation account, whereas the text itself clearly represents the earth (or land) as an active participant in creation (1:22).

[89] To illustrate the range of interpretations possible on this point, note that Francis Watson (in *Text, Church and World: Biblical Interpretation in Theological Perspective* [Edinburgh: T. & T. Clark; Grand Rapids: Eerdmans, 1994], 150) argues for a fundamental *congruence* (rather than contrast) between Genesis 2 (the quest for a human dialogue partner for *'adam*) and Genesis 1 (God's quest for a human dialogue partner). My understanding of the relationship between these two chapters is more complex than either of these options.

[90] Augustine, *Confessions*, Book XIII, chap. 36. This absence has been noted by many biblical scholars, though few draw the requisite conclusions from it.

[91] Contra Watson (*Text, Church and World*, 143; 313, n. 3) who claims that God's rest is necessitated by the labor implicated in the metaphor of God as artisan constructing the cosmos. I would argue that God's "rest" follows naturally on the heels of God's (royal/parental) delegation of responsible stewardship to humanity.

[92] God's "rest" does not here mean cessation of action, only that the initial conditions of a meaningful world are completed. Indeed, God continues to act, upholding the universe by divine power and effecting deliverance from bondage and sin. Thus in the New Testament, Jesus defends healing on the Sabbath because the Father also works (salvifically) on the Sabbath (John 5:19). Comments Blocher: "God's sabbath, which marks the end of creation, but does not tie God's hands, is therefore coextensive with history." (Blocher, *In the Beginning*, 57.) Sometimes Christian theologians have referred to the era of human history as the *eighth* day of creation, but this is unnecessary in the context of the Genesis narrative which knows no conclusion to the seventh day.

[93] Although it has often been traditional for biblical scholars to treat these *tôl^{e}dôt* headings as conclusions (and one still finds such treatment today), a careful reading shows that not all of them could plausibly function as conclusions, whereas they all function very well as headings or superscriptions. The classic argument for this is found in Frank Moore Cross, *Canaanite Myth and Hebrew Epic: Essays in the History of the Religion of Israel* (Cambridge: Harvard University Press, 1973), 301-305 (from chap. 11: "The Priestly Work," 293-325).

[94] Note Francis Watson's similar claim that the Genesis 1 creation story "must determine the theme and scope of the story that follows. The 'beginning' referred to at the outset is *also* the beginning of a book, and engenders in the reader's mind the expectation . . . of a coherent plot" (Watson, *Text, Church and World*, 153).

[95] Even the nuances of *tôl^{e}dôt* contribute to this picture. A plural noun formed from the verb *yalad*, "to bear," "to beget," *tôl^{e}dôt* is a developmental, birthing word, and its placement in Genesis 2:4a suggests by its connotations a parental, nurturing picture of God.

[96] A theological analysis of divine power quite congenial to my own is found in Kyle A. Pasewark, *A Theology of Power: Being beyond Domination* (Minneapolis: Fortress, 1993), esp. chap. 4: "Power and Communication of Efficacy" (pp. 186-235). It is interesting that Pasewark traces the notion of power as the "communication of efficacy" (a non-zero sum notion) back to Martin Luther's description of God's creative power in Genesis 1.

[97] For a discussion of the normative character of Genesis 1 in relation to the violence which pervades Scripture, see Middleton and Walsh, *Truth Is Stranger Than It Used to Be*, chap. 6, esp. 127-140.

[98] Again, I follow Phyllis Trible (see supra, n. 85). George W. Ramsey disputes Trible's interpretation of this verse (and her claims concerning the significance of naming, in general) in "Is Name-Giving an Act of Domination in Genesis 2:23 and Elsewhere?" *Catholic Biblical Quarterly* 50 (1988): 24-35. While Ramsey is certainly correct that naming does not necessarily imply domination or control in the Bible (as Trible seems to say), this does not address a nuanced variant of Trible's point (which I would like to advance), namely that naming is typically an act involving asymmetrical power (that is, one with superior power usually does the naming). Whether that power will be used for domination or not is a separate issue. Genesis 1 certainly suggests that it need not be so used.

[99] This point is also noted in Richard J. Clifford, "Creation in the Hebrew Bible," in *Physics, Philosophy, and Theology: A Common Quest for Understanding*, ed. Robert J. Russell et al (Vatican City State: Vatican City Observatory/ Notre Dame, IL: University of Notre Dame Press, 1988), 165.

[100] Perhaps the interpretive process is also at its best an act of loving power, an attempt to image God, characterized also by risk.

"Not Yours, But Ours:" Transformations of the Hebrew Bible in New Religious Movements

Eugene V. Gallagher

The Bible has long played a central role in new or alternative religious communities.[1] In their efforts to establish themselves, many new religions both challenge and capitalize upon the broad cultural legitimacy that the biblical tradition enjoys throughout the world. In fact, the persistent appearance of new religious movements throughout history occurs in part because the Bible itself has provided powerful paradigms of both reform and innovation.[2] Frequently, new religious movements create texts that imitate, interpret, supplement, or intend to supplant the Bible. They find their essential inspiration, record their sacred history, locate their ritual paradigms, inscribe their ethical imperatives, and express their theological convictions in scriptural texts of their own making. Through using, interpreting, and re-making the Bible, new religious movements lay claim to an authoritative past that they hope will bestow contemporary legitimacy, even in cases of radical innovation. As Jan Shipps has observed, "the past is a matter of fundamental importance to new religious movements. The assertions on which they rest inevitably alter the prevailing understanding of what has gone before, creating situations in which past and future must both be made new."[3]

IMITATING A BIBLICAL MODEL: *THE HOLY PIBY*

One example of the adoption of biblical models for an innovative message comes from a striking religious text produced in the 1920s by a devoted admirer of Marcus Garvey's message of dignity and self-empowerment for the African diaspora. *The Holy Piby*, which identifies itself as "a book founded by the Holy Spirit to deliver the gospel commanded by the Almighty

God for the full salvation of Ethiopia's posterities,"[4] contains a number of passages that are directly modeled on biblical texts.[5] It begins with an account of a seven day creation, includes a story of a divine commissioning of a prophet, describes the prophetic communication of God's law to human beings, provides historical accounts of the doings of God's chosen people, records prayers and creedal affirmations, and even gives an account of the "facts of the apostles." The entire book is saturated with "biblical" idioms. The ends to which it deploys its biblical language, however, reaffirm Shipps' observation that new religions strive to re-create both the past and the future.

The Holy Piby reveres Marcus Garvey as "God's foremost apostle"[6] and shares his passion for self-determination and self-sufficiency for Africans at home and abroad. Its espousal of those values, however, is not expressed simply in the rhetoric of social justice or political interests. Instead, it employs a language of divine command, explicitly according to Garveyite virtues the religious status of the ten commandments delivered to Moses on Mount Sinai. In preparation for receiving God's commands, the prophet Athlyi receives a call that parallels that of Moses. In the words of *The Holy Piby*:

> And it came to pass that the mighty angel robed in four colors descended from among the great heavenly host. When Athlyi saw the angel descending he feared with great fear and hid behind the root of a tree. But the angel of the Lord came up unto him and said, Athlyi, come forth for the Lord has made thee shepherd of his anointed children of Ethiopia.

The angel of the Lord robed Athlyi in four colors and commanded him to put forth his right hand and the messenger presented in his right hand a staff and in his left hand the Holy Law, saying:

> Go and administer this law through thine apostles unto the children of Ethiopia and command them to rise from the feet of their oppressors . . . . The angel of the Lord hesitated, then said to Athlyi, swear before the Lord God that thou wilt administer the law unto the children; then Athlyi lifted his eyes to the heaven and said, the heaven and earth bear witness to my saying I will.[7]

The law that Athlyi swears to administer is in the form of twelve commandments, which emphasize the building and maintaining of community among the Ethiopian race. As *The Holy Piby* claims in its distinctive style, the purpose of the new religion is "to set up a real religious and material brotherhood among the children of Ethiopia."[8] Implying that the Ethiopians are now to be considered God's chosen people, the text draws an explicit parallel between the law that Moses received and that more recently given to Athlyi. To facilitate comprehension, the points are expressed in a question and answer format:

> Q11. What is God's holy law to the children of Ethiopia?
> A. A written document handed to Athlyi by an angel of the Lord whose name was Douglas.
> Q12. What is the difference between God's holy law to the children of Israel and God's holy law to the children of Ethiopia?
> A. There is much difference, the holy law to the Israelites was given to Moses, but God's holy law given to the children of Ethiopia was handed to Athlyi by a messenger of the Lord our God, notwithstanding in the law given to the Israelites there are ten commandments but in the law given to the children of Ethiopia there are twelve.[9]

In those passages, the trials of Moses and the Hebrews in Egypt are explicitly appropriated as a model for understanding the difficulties of the African diaspora. Like the Hebrews, the Africans abroad have also been favored by divine intervention; like the God of the Hebrews, the God of the children of Ethiopia provides explicit instructions for the establishment and maintenance of community life. Although *The Holy Piby* remains reticent about the location of the "promised land" in which the community will dwell, it is easily harmonized with Garvey's message of a return to Africa.[10] Wherever God's chosen will reside, however, they will need to follow a very explicit set of laws, designed to build and maintain communal solidarity before God.

The first commandment accurately captures the focus of that program: "Love ye one another O children of Ethiopia, for by no other way can ye love the Lord your God."[11] The commandments then take a decidedly practical turn as they recommend industriousness, thrift, hard work, cleanliness, punctuality, honesty, and truthfulness. In fact, *The Holy Piby* traces the current plight of the African diaspora directly to the neglect of such practical virtues. The text observes that "for as much as the children of Ethiopia, God's favorite people of old, have drifted away from his divine majesty, neglecting life economic, believing they should on spiritual wings fly to the kingdom of god, consequently [they] became a convenient for the welfare of others. Therefore the whole heaven was grieved and there was a great lamentation in the Kingdom of God."[12] Becoming "a convenient for the welfare of others" refers to the catastrophic effects of slavery on Africans both at home and abroad. Another oblique reference occurs in the seventh commandment: "Let no people take away that which the Lord thy God giveth thee."[13] The antidote to slavery's devastation is to build a self-sufficient society for the children of Ethiopia. The eighth and ninth commandments express both positive and negative dimensions of that general theme:

> 8. Thou shalt first bind up the wound of thy brother and correct the mistakes in thine own household before ye can see the sore on the body of your friend, or the error in the household of thy neighbor.
> 9. O generation of Ethiopia, shed not the blood of thine own for the welfare of others, for such is the way to destruction and contempt.[14]

Only at the end of its list of twelve does *The Holy Piby* offer a strong verbal parallel to the first commandment of the ten in the Hebrew Bible, stating, "O generation of Ethiopia, thou shalt have no other God but the Creator of heaven and earth and the things thereof."[15] *The Holy Piby's* placement of the strongest parallel to the Hebrew Bible's first commandment at the end of its list effects a change in emphasis and indicates that solidarity and mutual support among the children of Ethiopia are most urgently commanded.

Both the archaic, "biblical" language and the form of a list of commandments are clearly designed to lend legitimacy to *The Holy Piby's* Garveyite message among those who are familiar with the biblical narratives. Those devices are reinforced by the brief opening description of the creation of the world in seven days, which occupies only six verses and omits much of the detail of the Genesis account.[16] The creation story is followed by an intriguing designation of Elijah as the only God, perhaps conflating the name of the ancient prophet with the divine name "El."[17] Throughout *The Holy Piby* there also runs a persistent identification of Ethiopia as an oppressed nation in need of redemption.[18]

Along with Athlyi's reception of the twelve commandments, those passages indicate how thoroughly *The Holy Piby* is grounded in the narratives of the Hebrew Bible. In *The Holy Piby* the sufferers of the African diaspora become the new Hebrews, an oppressed nation whose plea is heard by a God who raises up for them a prophet who delivers the divine law. The Hebrew Bible thus becomes the primary legitimating factor for a new religion. Its connection to the Bible, and its title and contents, are intended to lend *The Holy Piby's* innovative religious message a legitimacy and authority that it otherwise would not have. The adoption of biblical models, themes, and messages is precisely what allows *The Holy Piby* to remake the past and envision a new future in continuity with that past.

Although the Afro Athlican Constructive Church, which published *The Holy Piby*, did not flourish and seems not to have left many traces, the text did play a prominent role in the origins of another new religion, the Rastafarian movement in Jamaica in the 1920s and 1930s.[19] To this day, Rastafarian thinkers continue to view their own situation through the lenses provided by the Hebrew Bible. While they yearn for Zion, they see themselves as captives in Babylon. They look for a prophet like Moses to lead them on their Exodus. They live in and through models provided by the Hebrew Bible.[20]

DRAWING THE NEW OUT OF THE OLD: MARY BAKER EDDY'S COMMENTARY ON GENESIS

Although *The Holy Piby* devoted only cursory attention to the creation narrative in Genesis, other new religious movements have subjected it to much more searching inquiries. The treatment in Mary Baker Eddy's *Science and Health with Key to the Scriptures* (1875) is a good example of how radically innovative ideas can be drawn out of familiar texts through the application of consistent interpretive principles. The preface of *Science and Health* documents Eddy's focus on the Bible, noting that "as early as 1862 she began to write down and give to friends the results of her Scriptural study, for the Bible was her sole teacher."[21] Accordingly, a summary of the religious tenets of Christian Science affirms that "as adherents of Truth, we take the inspired Word of the Bible as our sufficient guide to eternal Life."[22] In seeking the truth, Eddy's Christian Science brings a distinctive hermeneutic to bear upon the biblical text. A literal reading is completely ruled out;[23] instead, Christian Science asserts that "our aim must be to have them [the scriptures] understood spiritually, for only by this understanding can truth be gained. The true theory of the universe, including man, is not in material history but in spiritual development."[24] The primacy of spiritual understanding is simply posited rather than demonstrated; it is the rock bottom given from which any reading of the Bible must proceed. Interpretation thus becomes a process of separating truth from error, discerning the metaphorical meaning of the text, and uncovering the divine message that has been "so smothered by the immediate context as to require explication."[25] When those hermeneutical principles are applied to Genesis 1:1-4:16 in a verse-by-verse commentary, they produce a reading that finds both support and sanction for the distinctive ideas of Christian Science in the creation narrative.[26]

Eddy begins with the provocative assertion that "the book of Genesis is the history of the untrue image of God"[27] in so far as it portrays God as involved in any way with materiality. Eddy, however, does not intend to overthrow the authoritative status of Genesis, but to correct all previous misreadings of it. She strives to maintain the authority but re-define the meaning of the biblical book. To support her position, Eddy capitalizes on nineteenth century scholarly insights into the dual creation stories of Genesis.[28] When understood properly, Gen. 1:1-2:3 does in fact "reflect" the true image of God, but the narrative of Gen. 2:4-4:16 is "a picture of error throughout."[29] What Eddy adds, then, is the theological conviction that the first story alone communicates divine truth.

In Genesis Eddy discovers how "Infinite Mind creates and governs all, from the mental molecule to infinity. This divine Principle of all expresses Science and Art throughout His creation, and immortality of man and the universe....Mind is the Soul of all. Mind is Life, Truth, and Love which governs all."[30] In keeping with those theological assertions, all references to land, waters, plants, animals, and humans must be subjected to a transformative metaphorical interpretation. For example, Eddy interprets the separation of the land and waters in Genesis 1:9 as describing how "Spirit, God, gathers unformed thoughts into their proper channels, and unfolds these thoughts."[31] Having established the nature of the creator God as an incorporeal "divine Mind," Eddy extends her interpretation to include the nature of human beings, who, as Genesis 1:26-27 reports, are made in the image and likeness of God. In her reading, "Man is the family name for all ideas — the sons and daughters of God."[32] Eddy appeals to the reader to recognize in Genesis an account of true human nature as revealed by Christian Science:

> Now compare man before the mirror to his divine Principle, God. Call the mirror divine Science, and call man the reflection. Then note how true, according to Christian Science, is the reflection to its original. As the reflection of yourself appears in the mirror, so you, being spiritual, are the reflection of God. The substance, Life,

> Intelligence, Truth, and Love which constitute Deity are reflected by His creation; and when we subordinate the false testimony of the corporeal senses to the facts of Science, we shall see this true likeness and reflection everywhere.[33]

She finds further support for that view in the King James Version translation of Genesis 2:4-5 that she uses. Commenting on the phrase that God "made the earth and the heavens, and every plant of the field before it was in the earth," Eddy seizes on the apparently temporal reference, "before," concluding that "here is the emphatic declaration that God creates all through Mind, not through matter—that the plant grows, not because of seed or soil, but because growth is the eternal mandate of Mind."[34] Eddy thus finds in the first creation story in Genesis an authoritative description of how a wholly incorporeal God created through mind alone a universe of ideas, including immortal humans, all without the slightest taint of materiality. The truth unveiled by Christian Science about God and human beings offers the only escape from sin, sickness, and death.[35]

Given Eddy's reading of the first creation account in Genesis, it is not at all surprising that she would find Adam's formation out of dust and the breath of God in Genesis 2:7 to be a massive affront to truth. In fact, Eddy baldly states that "it must be a lie."[36] In her view, "the Science of the first record proves the falsity of the second. If one is true, the other is false; for they are antagonistic."[37] Yet the thorough going wrong headedness of the second creation story still serves Eddy well. Without explaining why such diametrically opposed stories could be included in the same text, Eddy nonetheless portrays the second creation story as an inverse image of the truth. At virtually every turn it is mistaken, confused, misleading, contradictory, or just plain wrong. It has the sole virtue of pointing out the truth through its consistent dedication to error. As Eddy asserts, "no one can reasonably doubt that the purpose of this allegory—this second account in Genesis—is to depict the falsity of error and the effects of error."[38]

Ultimately, then, the two creation accounts in Genesis teach the same thing, one positively, once its spiritual sense is properly discerned, and the other negatively, as a cautionary tale of error. The two approaches to the disclosure of the truth reinforce the fundamental convictions of Christian Science that "there is no life, truth, intelligence, nor substance in matter. All is infinite Mind and its infinite manifestations, for God is All-in-all. Spirit is immortal Truth; matter is mortal error. . . . Therefore, man is not material; he is spiritual."[39]

Unlike the Afro Athlican Constructive Church that first published *The Holy Piby*, Christian Science has remained a vital religious organization since its founding in the late nineteenth century. Its fortunes have ebbed and flowed, and its beliefs, particularly about modern medicine, have sometimes brought it into sharp conflict with the government. But its distinctive reading of the Bible, including the creation stories of Genesis, has continued to nourish the minds and hearts of individual believers. Although one might argue that the interpretation of Genesis in *Science and Health* departs so far from the details of the text as to constitute a reading *against* the text rather than *of* it, *Science and Health* repeatedly asserts that it is not only in continuity with the biblical tradition but also the most accurate interpretation of it.

Science and Health's primary interest, however, lies in the widely recognized and historically attested authority of the Bible rather than in any particular narrative or legal paradigms that it may offer. By reading her teachings out of the Bible, Mary Baker Eddy was able to clothe a dramatic innovation in familiar garments. By so doing, she also made the entrance into Christian Science easier for anyone familiar with the biblical tradition. Her biblical interpretations also gave the theology of Christian Science a timeless quality, locating its roots deep in antiquity; it became much less something that Eddy concocted on her own and more something that had been there all along, only waiting to be discovered.

To accept Eddy's teachings is not only to accept her interpretation of the Bible. It is also to remake the Bible itself into something new, a document that speaks in a new voice and communicates an unanticipated and surprising message for the modern world. Additionally, it urges on those who can read the Bible according to the hermeneutical principles of Christian Science a new understanding of all other religious groups who have read and claimed to find truth in the biblical texts. From the perspective of Christian Science, their misreadings of the text become part of the history of error. Thus Eddy's reading of Genesis not only reveals significant dimensions of Christian Science's self-understanding, but also indicates how complete the transformation of the Hebrew Bible may be in a new religious tradition.

A NEW TRUTH FOR THE LAST DAYS: GENESIS IN UNIFICATIONIST THOUGHT

Like many other new religions, the Unification Church of Reverend Sun Myung Moon has produced its own authoritative texts. Most prominent among them is the *Divine Principle*.[40] Although the *Divine Principle* itself functions in many ways within the Unification Church as a scriptural text,[41] it neither closely models itself on the Bible or individual books or passages nor does it constitute a formal commentary on the Bible or any section of it. It might best be understood as an organized series of theological and philosophical reflections on prominent biblical themes, among them the creation story of Genesis. Although the *Divine Principle* shares with *The Holy Piby* and *Science and Health* an interest in the creation stories of Genesis 1:1-4:16, it focuses on the account of the "Fall." In its treatment of the Fall the *Divine Principle* reveals the central preoccupations of Unification theology.

Like *Science and Health*, the *Divine Principle* brings a distinctive hermeneutic to the interpretation of the Bible. Like Christian Science, the Unification Church rules out the possibility of any simple or literal reading of the text. Acknowledging that "truth, of course, is unique, eternal, unchangeable, and absolute," the *Divine Principle* asserts that "the Bible, however, is not the truth itself, but a textbook teaching the truth. . . . Therefore, we must not regard the textbook as absolute in every detail."[42] Nonetheless, the Bible speaks with a single voice because "God is eternal absolute, and one. Therefore, His will is one and the Bible, which is an expression of His will, is also one."[43]

According to the Unification Church, all human interpretations of the Bible have failed to grasp its meaning, and what we all need now "is not another human interpretation of the Bible, but God's interpretation."[44] The *Divine Principle* contains God's interpretation of the Bible because it stems from Rev. Moon's visionary encounter with Jesus himself. As a hagiographic pamphlet based on recollections of his earliest followers, it laconically describes the divine commissioning of a young Sun Myung Moon in 1936:

> It wasn't until the age of sixteen . . . that his mission was fully made known to him. It was at sunrise on Easter morning while he was in deep prayer that a great vision came to him. Jesus appeared to him and told him that he was chosen to complete the mission Jesus had begun 2,000 years ago.[45]

Unificationists believe that Moon's call to his prophetic mission came at a crucial juncture for humankind. The *Divine Principle* asserts that "today's religions have failed to lead the present generation out of the dark valley of death into the radiance of life, so there must now come a new truth that can shed a new light."[46] That new truth will have widespread transformative effects on human life. It will ensure the triumph of democracy over communism, unite everyone into a single, harmonious human family under the parental guidance of God, and bring into existence the Kingdom of God on earth.[47] The new truth revealed in *Divine Principle* also confirms, rather than challenges, discoveries in other realms of human knowledge. For example, "the process of creation as it is written in the Bible is in accord with the evolutionary sequence of creation known to modern scientists."[48] The *Divine Principle* thus stands as nothing less than the clearest expression ever presented of God's will for human beings, of the previously obscured and overlooked meaning of the biblical texts, and of the unity of human knowledge.

One of the most distinctive messages of the *Divine Principle* concerns the nature of the Fall. The text observes that:

> when God created Adam and Eve, He gave them three great blessings: to be fruitful, to multiply and fill the earth, and to subdue it and have dominion (Gen. 1:28). Had man followed the words of this blessing and become happy in the Heavenly Kingdom of God, God also would have felt much happiness.[49]

The first humans, however failed to observe God's command, with the consequences that "man was cut off from having a give and take relationship with God, thus failing to unite into one body with Him. Instead, man entered into a give and take relationship with Satan, forming a reciprocal base with him."[50] The *Divine Principle* also makes the singular assertion that the Fall was precipitated by Eve's adulterous sexual relations with Satan. That reading of the creation story depends upon a symbolic interpretation in which :

> the Tree of the Knowledge of Good and Evil symbolized Eve, the fruit of the tree was the symbol of Eve's love. The fact that Eve ate of the Tree of the Knowledge of Good and Evil means that she had an illicit love relationship with Satan, and the fact that Eve gave Adam the same fruit implies that she seduced Adam to fall in the same way.[51]

The *Divine Principle* thus identifies two separate dimensions of the Fall: "the fall through the blood relationship between the angel and Eve was the spiritual fall, while that through the blood relationship between Eve and Adam was the physical fall."[52] The first humans' adulterous liaisons prevented Eve, Adam, and all of their offspring, because of their genetic inheritance of the effects of original sin, from reaching the state of perfection that God had intended for them. Their actions separated them from God and created "a false family" devoid of God's presence.[53] Ever since, it has been God's strongest desire to restore humankind to its original state.[54] Jesus of Nazareth's attempt to effect that restoration was cut short by his death on the cross, and it is now the awesome responsibility of Reverend Moon, as the "Lord of the Second Advent," to initiate the restoration of humankind through his preaching of the Principle.

The Unificationist reading of Genesis is based on an understanding of the Bible as a historically conditioned expression of divine truth. Because the Bible is a product of its times, new revelation is not only possible but necessary, and the Unification Church officially holds that even the *Divine Principle* does not exhaust the possibilities of God's revelation. Because the Reverend Moon has for the first time clearly disclosed God's true purpose in creating the world, as well as what really went wrong with the original creation, his unveiling of the Divine Principle at work in human life and history necessarily leads to a new interpretation of the creation stories in Genesis. But where Mary Baker Eddy found the key to understanding the scriptures in the first creation story, the *Divine Principle* dwells instead on the interactions between Eve and the serpent and Eve and Adam. The assertion that Eve's and Adam's sins were sexual in nature triggers a new reading of subsequent human history. In that history God's desire for men and women to form loving families by uniting with each other and with God is continually undermined by the aftershocks of the Fall. God's attempts to restore the original, pre-Fall state of humanity by raising up prophets and potential messiahs, particularly Jesus of Nazareth, have met with only limited success. Thus the stage is set for the mission of Reverend Moon, who in these last days brings a new revelation that offers humankind the opportunity to return to an Edenic state.

The Unification Church's understanding of God, human nature, history, eschatology, revelation, family, and many other fundamental topics stems directly from its reading of Genesis. Although the Unification Church explicitly accepts the Bible as a testimony to truth, through consistent application of its distinctive interpretive principles and axioms it is able to read out of the Bible extensive confirmation of its particular view of the world. Its interpretation of Genesis remakes the past, especially the interactions of Eve, Adam, and the serpent, in order to prepare for a present and near future in which Reverend Moon, Unificationists devoutly hope, will usher in the restoration of the world. The *Divine Principle's* interpretation of the creation accounts in Genesis, which occupies nearly a fifth of the entire text, anchors the Unification Church's innovative theology in a religious past that has broad legitimacy. Further, it implies that the Reverend Moon's message is to be accepted as the latest and clearest development of that religious heritage rather than as a radical departure from it.

As in the cases of *Science and Health* and *The Holy Piby*, the *Divine Principle* transforms the Hebrew Bible into a foundational text for a new religious movement. The identification of a new religious message with an ancient authoritative text is designed to innoculate the new religion against charges that it is merely and solely new, and therefore easily dismissed as an ephemeral invention. But even as the appropriation of the Hebrew Bible grounds and legitimizes often radical religious innovation, it does not leave the Bible itself unaltered. The very act of appropriation makes of the Bible a Unificationist text, or a Christian Science text, or a text of the Afro Athlican Constructive Church. Within those religious traditions the Bible takes on an indelible new meaning as it is read through the lenses provided by the distinctive new revelation of a founder like the author of *The Holy Piby*, Mary Baker Eddy, or Sun Myung Moon.

The dynamic processes by which the Bible is incorporated into new religious movements are themselves, of course, not new at all. In few places have they been evoked so vividly as in the brief exchange between the early Christian philosopher Justin and his (fictional) Jewish interlocutor Trypho in the second century CE *Dialogue with Trypho*. At one point, when Justin is trying to convince Trypho of the correctness of his position on a specific issue, he decides to appeal to a commonly recognized authority. Concerning certain prophecies Justin asks Trypho, "aren't you acquainted with them. You should be, for they are contained in your Scriptures," but then Justin appears to catch himself and adds a very significant coda, "rather not yours, but ours."[55] With those last few words Justin reveals a great deal about the dynamic process of scriptural appropriation in new religious movements. He concedes the authoritative nature of a specific text, the Hebrew Bible, but he also corrects himself about whose religious possession it really is.

The early Christian readings of the Hebrew Bible made it as much a Christian text, the "Old Testament," as the *Divine Principle's* reading of the same Bible makes it a Unificationist text. In attempts by new religious movements to appropriate pre-existing scriptures for their own uses, there is a persistent tension between the need to acknowledge the established authority of the Bible and the desire to make it over in the image of the new religion. In effect, each new religion that attempts to appropriate the Hebrew Bible as an authoritative text proclaims to all other religious traditions that make claims on the same text that it is "not yours, but ours." The legitimacy of such claims is easily enough addressed within a specific religious tradition, but it is much more difficult to adjudicate across religious traditions. Thus one of the fates of the Hebrew Bible in the modern world is to be a highly contested object not only within various streams of Judaism or Christianity but in broader circles as well.

CONCLUSIONS

In many ways the appropriation of the Hebrew Bible by various contemporary new religious movements simply echoes the transformations of biblical themes, characters, literary forms, and topics in the Christian New Testament and the Quran. The Hebrew Bible has continually been subjected to interpretation and re-interpretation not only within Judaism but in other religious traditions as well. From that perspective, the closing of the canon of scripture has primarily served to focus the ingenuity of various exegetes on a limited number of books. But while the choice of books might have been limited, the range of possible interpretations certainly has not. As Jonathan Z. Smith has observed, "where there is a canon we can predict the necessary occurrence of a hermeneute, of an interpreter whose task it is to continually extend the domain of the closed canon over everything that is known or everything that is."[56]

The author of *The Holy Piby*, Mary Baker Eddy, and the Reverend Sun Myung Moon all endeavored to extend the domain of the Hebrew Bible to address issues, such as the plight of the African diaspora, the nature of material and immaterial reality, and the fallen nature of humankind, that were most important to them. Further, by addressing those issues through their use of the Hebrew Bible, they were able to claim for their innovative ideas a legitimacy and potential audience that they might otherwise not have had. By presenting their thoughts in the form of imitations of, interpretations of, or meditations upon the Hebrew Bible, they placed themselves squarely within the broad stream of religious traditions that have grown out of that Bible. Far from being the idiosyncratic musings of a few religious eccentrics, their theological doctrines assumed a borrowed air of legitimacy. In the cases of the Afro Athlican Constructive Church, Christian Science, and the Unification Church, the Hebrew Bible provides a precious connection to an authoritative religious past, a powerful legitimation for innovative religious ideas, and a well-traveled path of entry for converts from mainstream religious communities. Without their foundation on the Hebrew Bible, neither the self-understanding of those religious communities nor their relationship to other more mainstream traditions would be the same.

Notes

[1] There is substantial controversy about terminology in the study of contemporary new religious movements. Most academic observers reject "cult" as an unhelpful pejorative and prefer to describe the objects of their study as new, alternative, or emergent religions. See the discussions in Rodney Stark and William Sims Bainbridge, *The Future of Religion: Secularization, Revival, and Cult Formation* (University of California Press, 1985); Timothy Miller, ed., *America's Alternative Religions* (Albany: SUNY Press, 1995); and James A. Beckford, *Cult Controversies: The Societal Response to the New Religious Movements* (London: Tavistock, 1985).

[2] See, for example, Morton Smith's treatment of the prophetic literature and the rise of Judaism in *Palestinian Parties and Politics That Shaped the Old Testament* (New York: Columbia University Press, 1971).

[3] Jan Shipps, *Mormonism: The Story of a New Religious Tradition* (Urbana: University of Illinois Press, 1985), 53.

[4] *The Holy Piby* (Woodbridge, NJ: Athlican Strong Arm Company, 1924), I. I will follow internal divisions, giving references to chapter and verse where possible and to pages where chapters and verses are not indicated.

[5] The text draws from the Christian Scriptures as well as the Hebrew Bible. It contains a catechetical introduction, a creedal statement, a "Shepherd's Prayer," and a section on the "facts of the apostles" that obviously draw on Christian models.

[6] *The Holy Piby*, "The Facts of the Apostles," 1.4.

[7] Ibid., "Aggregation," 2.1-3, 6, 7.

[8] Ibid., "Questions and Answers," 1.

[9] Ibid., 2-3.

[10] On Garvey and his message see Judith Stein, *The World of Marcus Garvey: Race and Class in Modern Society* (Baton Rouge: Louisiana State University Press, 1966); for a collection of recent scholarly essays on Garvey, see Rupert Lewis and Patrick Bryan, eds., *Marcus Garvey: His Work and Impact* (Trenton, NJ: Africa World Press, 1991).

[11] The Holy Piby, "Aggregation," 3.1.

[12] Ibid., 1.1-2.

[13] Ibid., 3.7.

[14] Ibid., 3. 8-9.

[15] Ibid., 3.12.

[16] See ibid., "Athlyi," 1.1-6. The brevity of the creation story suggests that its importance is carried as much by its form and placement at the beginning of the text as it is by its specific details.

[17] See ibid., 2.8: "For Elijah do the heavenly host worship as god of the universe and in him do I, Athlyi, believe as the only God."

[18] See "Aggregation," 1.3-4, and 1.5: "There is a great convention in heaven, saith the angels of the Lord, unto you this day we are sent by the Lord to felicitate, for thou art appointed shepherd to lead Ethiopia's generations from the oppressive feet of the nations, and there are appointed also prophets to prepare the way before thee."

[19] See Robert A. Hill, "Dread History: Leonard P. Howell and Millenarian Visions in Early Rastafari Religions in Jamaica," *Epochae* 9 (1981): 30-71, esp. 34-35; and Barry Chevannes, *Rastafari: Roots and Ideology* (Syracuse: Syracuse University Press, 1994), 42.

[20] On biblical themes in Rastafarian thought, see Chevannes, *Rastafari*, 114-118, 235-239; Leonard Barrett, *The Rastafarians* (Boston: Beacon Press, 1988), 68-78 83, 103-113, 125-130, 137. No one has done more to spread the Rastafarian message throughout the world than the late Bob Marley; on Marley, see Timothy White, *Catch a Fire: The Life of Bob Marley*. On reggae music and its relations to Rastafarian themes, see Kevin O'Brien Chang and Wayne Chen, *Reggae Routes: The Story of Jamaican Music* (Philadelphia: Temple University Press, 1998).

[21] Mary Baker Eddy, *Science and Health with Key to the Scriptures* (Boston: The First Church of Christ, Scientist, 1875 [1994 printing]), viii; see 126. On *Science and Health,* see Robert Peel, "Science and Health with Keyto the Scriptures," in Ernest S. Frerichs, ed., *The Bible and Bibles in America* (Atlanta: Scholars Press, 1988) 193-213. For a brief overview of Christian Science see John K. Simmons, "Christian Science and American Culture," in Miller, ed., *America's Alternative Religions*, 61-68; for more detail, see Stephen Gottschalk, *The Emergence of Christian Science in American Religious Life* (Berkeley: University of California Press, 1973).

[22] *Science and Health,* 497.

[23] See ibid., 537.

[24] Ibid., 547.

[25] Ibid., 501 (quotation); see 505, 506, 511, 548.

[26] On the use of both the Bible and *Science and Health* in Christian Science, see Peel, "Science and Health," 205-206.

[27] *Science and Health,* 502.

[28] See ibid., 523.

[29] Ibid., 526.

[30] Ibid., 507-508.

[31] Ibid., 506.

[32] Ibid., 515.

[33] Ibid., 515-516.

[34] Ibid., 520.

[35] See ibid., 472, 492, 536.

[36] Ibid., 524.

[37] Ibid., 522.

[38] Ibid., 537.

[39] Ibid., 468.

[40] On the authorship of the *Divine Principle* see George D. Chryssides, *The Advent of Sun Myung Moon: The Origins, Beliefs and Practices of the Unification Church* (London: Macmillan, 1991), 23-24.

[41] For a functional definition of what constitutes "scripture," see Wilfrid Cantwell Smith, *What is Scripture?* (Philadelphia: Fortress Press, 1993).

[42] *Divine Principle* (New York: The Holy Spirit Association for the Unification of World Christianity, 1973), 9.

[43] "Divine Principle: Two Hour Lecture," in Michael Mickler, ed., *The Unification Church II: Inner Life* (New York: Garland Publishing, 1990), 3. Page references are given to the pagination of the book as printed in bold-faced type, although it also reproduces the original pagination of the pamphlet.

[44] Ibid.

[45] "Sun Myung Moon," in Mickler, ed., *The Unification Church II*, 108.

[46] *Divine Principle* , 10.

[47] See ibid., 11, 12, 13.

[48] Ibid., 51.

[49] Ibid., 41.

[50] Ibid., 30. On the Unificationist concept of 'give and take action" see Chryssides, *The Advent of Sun Myung Moon*, 25, 35.

[51] Divine Principle: Six Hour Lecture," in Mickler, ed., *The Unification Church II*, 64.

[52] *Divine Principle*, 77.

[53] "Divine Principle: Four Hour Lecture" in Mickler, ed., *The Unification Church II*, 27.

[54] See "Divine Principle: Six Hour Lecture," in Mickler, ed., *The Unification Church II*, 51.

[55] See Justin, *Dialogue with Trypho*, 29. I follow the English translation in Thomas B. Falls, trans., *Writings of Justin Martyr,* Fathers of the Church, Vol. 6 (New York: Christian Heritage, 1948), quotation from 191.

[56] Jonathan Z. Smith, "Sacred Persistence: Towards a Redescription of Canon," in William Scott Green, ed., *Approaches to Ancient Judaism: Theory and Practice* (Missoula, MT: Scholars Press, 1978), 11-28, quotation from 23.

The Missing Missus

Lesleigh Cushing

The Book of Genesis brims over with rich characters: heroes and their foes, parents and their children, husbands and their wives. And yet there is a marked absence in the cast: Noah, who dominates the book for four chapters, has an all but nonexistent wife. She is mentioned explicitly five times, and her appearance in each case is formulaic. Three times she appears third in the catalogue of "Noah, his sons, and his wife and his sons' wives" (6:18[1] 7:7, 8:18). Once, the order is slightly altered, as God says to Noah, "Go out of the ark, you and your wife and your sons and your sons' wives" (8:16). And once the roll is elaborated as "Noah with his sons, Shem and Ham and Japheth, and Noah's wife and the three wives of his sons entered the ark" (7:13). The only two other references to her are indirect; she is part of the collective "all [Noah's] household" (7:1) and of "those that were with [Noah] in the Ark" (7:23). She is unique among the matriarchs of Genesis in that her personality, lineage, and even her name remain a mystery. Unlike Eve, Sarah, Hagar, Rebekah, Rachel, and Leah—the other women in Genesis whose husbands have covenants with God—she never speaks. Virtually everything about her is left to speculation: What was she like? Did she get along with her husband? How did she respond when the waters of the flood receded? Did she even alight from the ark?

To some, it may be surprising to find that the character of this matriarch, who is virtually forgotten in the Bible, is explored at length in later writing. Over time, through diverse traditions, there develops a considerable corpus of literature surrounding Mrs. Noah. The earliest texts treating Noah's wife are concerned not with inventing a new character, but simply with identifying who she was and where she came from. In this endeavor, early writers take their cues almost exclusively from the biblical text, venturing little into other sources. Consequently, early identifications of Mrs. Noah reveal much about the interpretive methods of an era. The early writers' occupation with inner-biblical exegesis reflects a concern for the integrity of the biblical text and a belief that clarification for any scriptural ambiguity may be found within the Bible itself. Slowly, however, textual interpretation yielded to literary imagination, and popular views of Mrs. Noah began to emerge. On the one hand, these portraits reveal a substantial knowledge of earlier legend; on the other, they reflect popular conceptions of women. Finally, in the twentieth century, treatments of Mrs. Noah serve as a barometer for the modern, secular view of the Bible. The more Noah and God are read as patriarchal, the more prominent Mrs. Noah becomes.

Through the centuries from the Bible to the present, there has been an ongoing interest in the missing missus, in the matriarch the Bible forgot. We can read across the years — through the rabbinical literature and the medieval mystery plays and contemporary feminist literature, to name but a few examples — and we can trace a movement in the recasting of Mrs. Noah. Over time, accounts of her become more detailed, more elaborate. Where in the early centuries after the close of the biblical canon Mrs. Noah occupied only fragments of thoughts in the interpretive imagination, where the fleshing out of her person was handled not in full sentences but in mere phrases, later writers and interpreters take an increasing interest in her, to the point that she becomes not only the heroine of full novels, but the new author of history in one modern account. We can trace, across time and tradition, a movement of Mrs. Noah from nought to aught to other to author to authority.

FROM NOUGHT TO AUGHT: EARLY IDENTITIES

Both the rabbis and the pseudepigraphical[2] writers were troubled by the enigma of Noah's wife. They contrived to fill in the gaps left by her absence, determining her lineage, assigning her names, and in some instances even fleshing out her character and developing her personality.

The Book of Tobit, found in the Catholic deuterocanon and the Protestant Apocrypha, does provide information about her stock. The book, which is set in eighth-century BCE Nineveh, but likely written before the second-century BCE, tells the story of Tobit, an exile from the tribe of Naphtali, and his family. Tobit's son Tobias is to marry, and Tobit instructs him to "beware of every kind of fornication, [and to] marry a woman from among the descendants of [his] ancestors," reminding him that "Noah, Abraham, Isaac and Jacob, our ancestors of old, all took wives from among their kindred" (Tobit 4:12).[3] From as early as the sixth century, the rabbis refer to her as Naamah,[4] a name taken from the Cainite genealogy in Genesis 4:22 — "the sister of Tubal-cain was Naamah."[5] The only one of the four antediluvian women named[6] whose husband is not mentioned, and approximately Noah's contemporary, Naamah was considered by the rabbis to be a natural match for the patriarch. This marriage of Noah and Naamah would have settled one textual problem for the rabbis, while presenting another: How could Noah, who "walked with God" (6:9) consort with the descendant of Cain, "a man cursed from the ground" (4:11)? By way of answer, later Jewish tradition has the righteous Noah marry another Naamah, a descendant of Seth,[7] as the Cainish woman mentioned above "was too wicked a personage to be a fitting consort for him."[8] This other Naamah was a daughter of Enoch, and in the *Sefer Ha-Yashar*, a thirteenth century book of Jewish ethics, Noah is reported to have married her when he was 498 years old.[9] *The Book of the Cave of Treasures,* a history of Israel from the creation to the crucifixion of Jesus, reportedly written by the fourth century church leader Ephraim the Syrian, preserves another tradition:

> When Noah saw that sin had increased in his generation, he preserved himself in virginity for five hundred years. Then God spake unto him and said unto him, "Take unto thee to wife Haykêl, the daughter of Namûs (or Namûs Haykêl), the daughter of Enoch, the brother of Meth-uselah." [10]

Haykêl is also the name given her in *The Book of Adam*, a Syriac work which predates, but is closely related to, *The Book of the Cave of Treasures*, but there she is "the daughter of Abaraz, who was one of the children of the family of Enos."[11] In *The Book of Jubilees,* a second century BCE work purporting to be a revelation to Moses on his second ascent to Mount Sinai, she is the "daughter of Rake'el, daughter of his father's brother,"[12] and her name is 'Emzara.[13]

This recurring concern with ensuring that Mrs. Noah was of a respectable pedigree, and not a descendant of Cain, reflects one trend in post-biblical thought: to depict her as a good woman, a suitable match for the only righteous man in his generation. There are a number of extra-biblical stories which emphasize her goodness. In Bereshit Rabba 23:3, an aggadic Midrash on the book of Genesis, the rabbis ask themselves why her name is Naamah and answer that it is because her deeds were pleasing (in Hebrew *ne'emim*). In the Talmud,[14] as in *The Book of Adam and Eve,* she is the loyal wife who informs Noah that Ham has shamed him by mocking his nakedness.

This concern with casting her in a favourable light was by no means universal; in many instances, she is cast as a trouble maker, even as an associate of the devil. Francis Lee Utley remarks that "rabbinical commentators...developed a romance between her and the fallen angel Azazel, of which the offspring was the demon Asmodeus."[15] In his *Legends of the Jews*, Louis Ginzberg records that Noah's wife "received the names Noema, lovely one, from the sounds she made with cymbals as she called on the idolators to worship."[16] Further, Utley notes that "in the Asatir [edited by] Gaster,[17] Naamah is a witch like her daughter Gifna, and was the inventress of the art of music."[18] According to Epiphanius,[19] as recorded in M. R. James' *Lost Apocrypha of the Old Testament*, the Gnostics[20] held that Mrs. Noah:

> often tried to be with Noah in the ark and was not permitted, for the Archon who created the world wished to destroy her with all the rest in the flood; and she, they say, seated herself on the ark and set fire to it, not once or twice, but often, even a first, second and third time. Hence the making of Noe's ark dragged on for many years, because it was so often burned by her.[21]

In the Qu'ran[22] "Noah's wife, known as Wailu, tries to persuade the people that her husband is mad";[23] she is cast in Moslem tradition as an unbeliever and damned to hell as a result.[24]

That there is such a great disparity in the post-biblical accounts of Mrs. Noah may be explained by the fact that post-biblical tradition concerning Noah is also contradictory. The biblical narrative is ambivalent about him: he is both the sole righteous man in a generation of sinners and a senseless drunkard. Consequently, post-biblical accounts reflect the polarity in his portrait.

The midrashic literature preserves an ongoing debate about Noah's righteousness.[25] Ginzberg records one legend that traces Noah's righteousness back to his birth:

> The body of the babe [Noah] was white as snow and red as a blooming rose, and the hair of his head and his long lochs were white wool, and his eyes like the rays of the sun. When he opened his eyes, he lighted up the whole house, like the sun, and the whole house was very full of light. And when he was taken from the hand of the midwife, he opened his mouth and praised the Lord of righteousness.

> His father Lamech was afraid of him [as he explained], "it seems to me that he [Noah] is not sprung from me, but from the angels."[26]

Some rabbis contend that "had he lived in another generation, his righteousness would have been still more strongly marked."[27] Conversely, others consider him to be righteous relative only to his generation (in such instances the latter part of the verse "Noah was a righteous man; he was blameless *in his age*" is read as a qualifier). Others "go still further and assert that Noah himself was included in the divine decree of destruction, but that he found grace in the eyes of the Lord for the sake of his descendants."[28]

Our initial response to the abundance of mutually contradictory traditions about Noah's wife might not be one of surprise; given the ambivalence toward the patriarch, it is to be expected that the matriarch also generate a mixed response. And yet, we should step back from the depictions of Noah, and register some amazement that a woman who scarcely appears at all in the Bible becomes a figure at all in later literature. She begins to command the attention of biblical interpreters and commentators, and so begins to assume an identity, making the transition from absent to present, from nought to aught. She gains a lineage and a personal history, if not yet a persona. She becomes the skeleton of a character, alternately the attractive woman and the detracting wife.

FROM AUGHT TO OTHER: THE CONTRARY WIFE

Perhaps more alarming than the divergent early depictions of Mrs. Noah is that out of the mass of conflicting legends about her there emerged a consistent characterization of her in the Middle Ages in England. A shrew and an abusive wife, she was a very popular dramatic figure, known and loved not for being righteous but for being difficult.

From the ninth century on, there is evidence that biblical plays—called "mystery plays"[29]—were performed, usually out of doors, for the general public. By the twelfth century, the loose form of these plays had been tightened up. Performed about eight weeks after Easter, when the days were long, they comprised a parade in which a bishop or priest carrying the host would proceed through the town, moving from church to church, followed by churchmen and, later, by guilds men. Biblical episodes spanning the Creation to the resurrection were dramatized. Eventually, wagons acting as stages would make stops along the route, with guilds men acting out a biblical story at each post. In time, in some of the towns it was the shipbuilders who came to perform the flood sequences. Of the extant mystery plays, the story of Noah and his wife appears in the Newcastle fragment and in the York, Chester, and Wakefield (also known as Towneley[30]) flood plays.[31]

In these plays the character of Mrs. Noah, generally called Uxor,[32] began to take shape. One critic of Medieval literature notes that "although [Mrs. Noah] is mentioned in all other versions from the Bible on, she is never known to utter a word until the dramatists of the Middle Ages make her an important member of their *dramatis personae*."[33] The literary persona that developed is quite distinct from the English "orthodox medieval theologian['s view that] Uxor was the meek and virtuous woman of the French *Mistere*, the Old Testament prototype of Mary."[34] Before the mystery plays gained widespread popularity, "mainstream medieval writers saw Noah's wife as a compliant follower of her husband's and God's wishes. Theologians even [averred] 'Noe significat Christum, uxor eius beatam Mariam.'"[35] However, throughout these plays, the character once understood to prefigure Mary becomes associated almost exclusively with Eve.[36] Consider the following descriptions of the extant plays which feature Noah's wife.[37]

The most positive depiction of Mrs. Noah in the English dramas is in the York play. Though stubborn and slightly abusive, she is on the whole a sympathetic character here. We first encounter her once Noah has completed the building of the ark and sent his eldest son to "goos call youre modir and comes neare."[38] After initially refusing to come, Uxor is compelled by curiosity to have a look. When she sees what Noah has built, she bids everyone to "come downe and go do somwhat ellis."[39] She declares that the ark is silly and turns to go home. When her sons attempt again to persuade her to come aboard, she puts them off by insisting she must go home and pack her belongings. Noah is frustrated and asks her, "Woman, why dois thou thus? To make us more myscheve?"[40] She replies that she is upset at having been left alone unawares, while he went off to build. Noah apologizes, explaining that "it was Goddis wille withowten doutte."[41] She hits him in response. Finally, Uxor declares that if she is to board, she wants her "commodrys and cosynes bathe — That wolde I wente with us in feere,"[42] but he says it cannot be done. She boards the ark nonetheless, and once there grieves and laments the loss of her friends. Her daughters-in-law rally round her and offer comfort. What we discern in this depiction is a woman defined by her relationships to those around her. She is hurt when her husband abandons her to build the ark, despondent when she must abandon her friends to board it, and comforted and cheered by her relatives. Frequently accused[43] of being petty or materialistic for wanting to return for her belongings, the York Uxor may equally well be understood simply as afraid of the unknown and wary of the possibility that she may be separated from those for whom she cares.

In the "Processus Noe" of the Wakefield play, Uxor is the most developed character. She spans the poles, moving from recalcitrant to repentant. At the outset of the play, she is a violent woman whom Noah fears and abuses. When God reveals his plan to Noah, Noah is faced with the considerable task of winning his wife over to the idea of living aboard an ark. A henpecked husband, he dreads telling her the divine plan. When he does, she levels a tirade against husbands in general and Noah in particular: "we women may wary all ill husbandis; I have oone bi Mary."[44] Noah tells her to be quiet, she refuses, he strikes her, and she strikes him back.

When we next see Uxor, Noah is attempting to coax her onto the ark, stating urgently, "tent hedir tydely, wife, and consider, hens must us fle, all sam togeder, in hast."[45] When she tells him he should run if something scares him, Noah realizes that she has not grasped the import of the boat. He stops to explain the flood, and the audience is made aware that *she* is the one who is afraid. The ark frightens her because she cannot tell its front from its back. "I dase and I dedir"[46] for fear, she tells Noah and runs off, claiming she has some spinning to do.[47] One of her daughters-in-law suggests that "if ye like ye may spyn, moder, in the ship,"[48] but she will not be persuaded. Noah threatens her with force, and they beat each other until they board the ark together and are reproached by their sons who accuse them of being "spitus" (spiteful).

By the last episodes of the play, Noah and his wife are reconciled, and her feistiness has been tempered. When the storm at sea is rough, Uxor calls out to God: "This is a perlous case: Help, God, when we call."[49] When Noah plumbs the depth to see whether the flood is abating, he asks her to "tent the stere-tre," to which she replies, "That I do ful wysely."[50] The truculent wife has become complicit; the sparring couple, partners. When Noah consults her "Dame, thi counsell me what fowll best myght and cowth with flight of wyng bryng, without tarryng, of mercy som tokynyng ayther bi north or southe,"[51] she suggests that they send out a raven, which they do, with 'doofys oone or two' just to be sure. It is a fitting closure to the play that she is the one who spots the dove returning to the ark, reminding us that she has made peace not only with her husband but with the ark and the future to which it bears them.

In the Chester mystery cycle, we find the most obstreperous Uxor. Historically, the waterleaders and drawers of Dee presented the third pageant of Noah's flood,[52] in which Noah's declaration to his wife that "in this vessell wee shal be kepte, my children and thou, I would in yee lepte" is met by her staunch refusal to board the ark. She tells him that she "will not doe after thy reade," and when he insists, counters that "By Christe, not or I see more neede, though tho stand all daye and stare."[53] Noah dispatches Shem to fetch his tenacious mother, but she sends her son back to her husband with the message that "I will not come therin todaye."[54] She prefers to remain drinking with her "gosseppes all" and will not board unless they do. As Noah will not allow them to, she encourages him to "rowe forthe" with another wife. Shem finally gets her on board, presumably by force, as he warns her "in fayth, mother, yett thou shall [board], whether thou will or nought."[55] When Noah welcomes her onto the "boote," she retaliates by hitting him, at which point her role in the drama ends.

The most menacing and dangerous Uxor appears in the Newcastle play. In this rendition, an angel visits Noah and instructs him to build an ark, the construction of which he conceals from his wife. Like Eve before her, she is sought out by the devil, who hopes to use her to gain insight into her husband's activity. The devil convinces her that Noah's secret scheming will certainly harm her and her children, and encourages her to give her husband an elixir which causes him to reveal that he is fulfilling God's command and building an ark. When Noah realizes that he has divulged the divine plan, he asks God whether he will be able to continue the task, and the angel replies that he will. Ultimately, Uxor's affiliation with the devil does not hinder God's plan, but the potential for real wickedness is greatest here.

The insistence in Medieval literature upon a contrary Mrs. Noah who frustrates her husband's designs raises two questions: Whence came the tradition of the truculent wife? And, why was it so popular during this period?

Millicent Carey, who in 1930 published a book-length "study to determine the conventional and original elements in four plays commonly ascribed to the Wakefield author," reports that a large body of literature concerning Noah arose in England between the seventh and fifteenth centuries. Intrigued by the recurring appearance of a shrewish, obdurate Mrs. Noah, she asks: "How did the idea of a stubborn uxor evolve? Is her refusal to go into the ark the result of a gradual development of her character, or were the dramatists here following a tradition handed down to them from non-dramatic sources? Is she a purely English product?"[56] Carey's subsequent survey of English sources, French recounting of Old Testament tales, Cornish plays, and Jewish legends yields no roots of the stubborn wife tradition. Consequently, she devises a seven-part schema which reconstructs elements that she believes aided in the development of the medieval Uxor character. These may be summarized thus: 1) in the Bible, Noah's wife is an inhabitant of the Ark; 2) the *Cursor Mundi*[57] and Cornish *Creation*[58] reflect an established tradition that Noah's relatives mocked his building of an ark; 3) Noah's wife becomes a speaking character in the medieval cycle plays; 4) the introduction of the devil as a tempter of Uxor in the Newcastle Noah's ark echoes the story of Adam and Eve; 5) the playwrights are familiar with the widespread tradition of the shrewish wife and know of the marital discord expressed in popular literature; 6) the author of the Cornish *Creation* explores the "dramatic possibilities" of Uxor's desire to save her household goods: she is depicted as hesitant to follow Noah; and 7) the "trouble-motif" of the Newcastle play and the "hesitation-motif" of the Cornish one were combined with the popular "shrew-motif."[59] Hence the emergence of the recalcitrant wife.

In the decade following the publication of Carey's book, there were two responses to her hypothesis. In the first, "A Note on Noah's Wife," Katherine Garvin notes that "in the illustration on p.66 of the Caedmonian MS Junius XI,[60] there is a portrayal of the ark which gives details that are not in the text of the Caedmonian *Genesis*."[61] In the illustration to which she refers, "one of the women, whom we may assume to be Noah's wife, seems to be unwilling to mount the ladder, and is expostulating with one of the three sons."[62] Garvin suggests that these details evidence a tradition of the stubbornness of Noah's wife that predates even the Cornish or French plays. Garvin concludes: "It does not seem fanciful to assume the legend [of the stubborn wife] is known to the artist, who is consistent in his addition of apocryphal and other material to the Biblical text."[63]

Anna Mill, who published the second response to Carey's work, traces Noah's wife's relationship with the devil, going back through the apocryphal literature treating Noah's wife as far as the lost *Book of Noria*:

> As early as the fourth century... a development of the character had taken shape among the heretical sects. Thus, according to Epiphanius, Heresy xxvi, the Gnostic *Book of Noria* seems to have registered a certain truculence on the part of Uxor, an alliance with the powers of evil, and a desire to thwart her husband in his heaven-

> sent mission through setting fire to the Ark repeatedly, so that the building dragged on for many years. [64]

It is a theme which appears in a substantial body of literature which begins with the Gnostic book mentioned here and includes Moslem legends; Wogul folk-tales; Russian, Magyar, and Roumanian accounts; and a Viennese chronicle from the last quarter of the thirteenth century.[65] The primary elements (seen to some degree in the Newcastle fragment) which "reappear again and again attached to popular versions of the Noah legend [are] the corruption of the wife by the evil one, the use of an intoxicating potion for the discovery of Noah's secret,[66] the devil-naming trick[67] by which he enters the ship."[68]

That there are no known English redactions of a recalcitrant wife before the Middle Ages is surprising to Mill, as it had been to Carey. She notes that "among the many Medieval English representations of the flood in illuminated manuscripts, sculpture, or other forms of art,[69] I know of no other instance of this apocryphal Noah material"[70] treating Mrs. Noah's reluctance to board the ark.[71] There is no literary antecedent, and no one can pinpoint when the story gained currency in English, yet it has captured the imagination of numerous tellers.

Thus the medieval literature presents a new development: Mrs. Noah is nearly always depicted as opposing her husband. Her stance against him and her workings against God's plan for salvation set her apart as the other. Noah alternately attempts to win her over or to silence her. Even in the instances where she does succumb, however, her acquiescence is less noteworthy than her truculence.

THE OTHER: MRS. NOAH IN TWENTIETH CENTURY REVISION OF SCRIPTURES

With the mystery plays begins a trend in English literature toward the demythification of the flood story. In the medieval drama, Mrs. Noah was utterly stripped of pretension: cast as the shrewish wife of popular culture, she loses all the pomp one expects of a biblical character. In these plays Noah has lost some of his stature; suddenly he appears to be a lot like everyone else. He has an exhausting job, disobedient children, and a difficult wife, whom he even strikes from time to time. The blameless man, righteous in his generation, is no longer beyond reproach. And yet, because of his relationship with God—the only character in the medieval flood play to retain his scriptural splendor—he is afforded credence and respectability, and is able to maintain a degree of grandeur.

The medieval playwrights' tendency to render the Bible in mostly human terms is picked up by a number of twentieth century writers. Generally, their works reflect a trend which began with the mystery plays, that is, a turn towards "the visualiz[ation of] scenes realistically in terms of the modern world. "[72] Characters speak the vernacular of the region and behave according to the customs of the day. Where Mrs. Noah was the best evidence of this conceit in the medieval drama, in the modern literature even God may bear striking resemblance to the writers' contemporaries. Where the medieval plays may provide an index of popular conceptions of women,[73] one can read the twentieth century works as a reflection of modern views of the Bible. The most recent ones, in particular, display a tension about the rewriting of Biblical narratives. On the one hand, to rewrite the text is to suggest that in some way the original falls short in its telling, that it no longer communicates adequately with a modern audience. On the other, to rewrite is to assert that the story itself is *worth* telling, that there is something in it that needs to be communicated.

The reworking of the flood story has been a popular undertaking for this century's writers, who have employed the biblical narrative as a vehicle for their pacifism, socialism, feminism, and egalitarianism, to cite but a few examples. In the grand tradition of the biblical text, however, many of these writers do not include a Mrs. Noah.[74] Nonetheless we can find a number of works in which the character of Mrs. Noah is developed.

Zora Neale Hurston's one act play, *The First One*, written in 1926 and published a year later in Charles Johnson's anthology of Harlem Renaissance writing *(Ebony and Topaz)*, marks the author's first revision of a biblical story.[75] The play is set in the valley of Ararat, one morning three years after the flood. Noah has awoken early to make sacrifices to commemorate the cessation of the flood and to "give thanks to Jehovah that he hath spared us."[76] He calls his sons to join him, but Ham and his wife, Eve, are not to be found. To the consternation of Ham's brothers and their wives, the couple arrives late, with Ham announcing: "We ring flowers and music to offer up. I shall dance before Jehovah and sing joyfully upon the harp that I made of the thews of rams."[77] Mrs. Shem is disgusted by Ham and his wife, and accuses them of "bawling and prancing all during the year [while] Shem and Japheth work always in the fields and vineyards and you do not but tend the flock and sing."[78] Noah quells the argument and proceeds with the ceremony. At the conclusion of the sacrificial service, Noah evokes the destruction of the earth and his family's salvation. Mrs. Noah recalls ("feelingly"as the stage direction indicates): "Yes, three years ago, all was water, *water,* WATER! The deeps howled as one beast to another. <She shudders.> In my sleep, even now, I am in that Ark again being borne here, there on the great bosom."[79] Ambivalent toward her salvation from the flood, Hurston's Mrs. Noah, who is moved by the memory of those who were not aboard the ark, recalls the Uxor of the York plays, who was concerned about those who were left behind.

Mrs. Ham ("wide-eyed") adds: "And the dead! Floating, floating all about us — We were one little speck of life in a world of death!...And there, close beside the Ark, close with her face upturned as if begging for shelter— my *mother*!"Mrs. Shem, unsympathetic to her sister-in-law's grief, chews on a piece of meat from the altar, as she replies simply: "[Your mother] would not repent. Thou art as thy mother was—a seeker after beauty of raiment and laughter. God is just. She would not repent."[80] Mrs. Shem's contempt for Ham and his wife is shared by Mrs. Japheth; together these two women are ultimately responsible for the cursing of Ham. As the celebration continues, Noah becomes drunk. His boisterous drunken state, in which he sings about being "a young ram in the spring," spirals into melancholy and horror as he recalls the death and destruction wrought by the waters of the flood. Miserable and delusional, he creeps into his tent, from which he calls out to Mrs. Ham, who has been filling his cup through the course of his drunkenness: "Eve, wine, quickly! I'm sinking down in the WATER! Come drown the WATER with wine."[81] Ham arises drunkenly, slurring the same song his father had been singing, and follows his wife into the tent, from which his raucous laughter soon emanates. Ham emerges, laughing still and announcing to his sisters-in-law: "Our father has stripped himself, showing all his wrinkles. Ha! Ha! He's no young goat in the spring. Ha! Ha! The old Ram, Ha! Ha! Ha! He has had no spring for years!"

Mrs. Shem and Mrs. Japheth rally their husbands to vindicate their father-in-law, insisting that they cover their elder. The sons do so and, at their wives' prompting, inform their father that he has been "wickedly shamed"by Ham. Noah, "struggling drunkenly to his feet," apprehends what is being told to him and announces that the perpetrator "shall be accursed. His skin shall be black! Black as the night, when the waters brooded over the Earth!"[82] Mrs. Noah re-enters, rushes toward her husband, and attempts to stop his mouth with her hand, but Noah continues: "Black! He and his seed forever. He shall serve his brothers and they shall rule over him."[83]

Throughout the play, Hurston has "assig[ned] so-called black characteristics to Ham":[84] he is the dancer, the music-maker, the reveler, where his brothers are the diligent workers, the responsible sons, the staid religionists. However, when Ham actually becomes black, and not simply "acts" so, the rest of the family understands that a great tragedy has happened. The sisters-in-law, who precipitated the curse, beg their father-in-law to unsay what he has done. Filled with grief and remorse, they are awed and terrified that a drunken curse was heard and enacted by Jehovah. Mrs. Shem and Mrs. Japheth, who in their pettiness and shrewishness of the opening sequences resemble the Mrs. Noah of the mystery plays, are stupefied by the consequence of their vindictiveness. Mrs. Shem, the instigator, declares: "Black! He could not mean *black.* It is enough that he should lose his vineyards,"at which:

> There is absolute silence for a while. Then realization comes to all. Mrs. Noah rushes in the tent to her husband, shaking him violently. "Noah! Arise! Thou art no lord of the Earth, but a drunkard! Thou hast cursed my son.... Thou must awake and unsay thy curse. Thou must!"
> <She is sobbing and rousing him.... Mrs. Noah wails and the other women join in. They beat their breasts.>[85]

Here Mrs. Noah displays an affinity toward her son that is not apparent in any of the preceding literature. In the medieval plays, Noah uses his sons as a means of enticing his wife to board the boat. They are linked with the father, while the daughters-in-law relate to Uxor.

This is but one of a number of reversals Hurston has effected in her short piece. First, Ham's wife is Eve. Where in the Medieval literature the Eve figure (Uxor) was fraught with negative connotation, the allusion here seems to be positive, stressing her position as the mother of the black race. Second, the sons' wives are the shrews, where they had previously been benevolent. Third, Mrs. Noah is a compassionate woman, a sympathetic character. At the outset, she appears as a humane woman deeply disturbed by the flood ordeal; as the play closes, she is a mother deeply disturbed by her son's burden. She is the mother who cannot look at her black son, though she loves him. Where Shem recoils from Ham's touch, Noah exiles his accursed son, instructing him: "Arise, Ham. Thou art black. Arise and go out from among us that we may see thy face no more, lest by lingering the curse of thy blackness come upon my seed forever." Mrs. Noah averts her face when he approaches, "so that [her] baby may not see the flood that hath broken the windows of my soul and loosed the fountains of my heart."[86] Apart from his wife, she is the only character in the play who is not repulsed and frightened by Ham's blackness. In this respect, she is once again connected with Eve.

What has been identified as the American "demythologizing of the Bible by means of homely realism" is "closely paralleled"[87] in Andre Obey's *Noah* (1929), a French play whose English translation was very popular in the thirties. In Obey's telling, the patriarch is a modest man, who speaks simply and treats his God as a friend. We hear him calling up to the unseen Lord, apologizing for disturbing him, and inquiring whether or not he should include a rudder on the ark. While this Noah is very close to his God and understands him to be a tired old man, worn down by the wickedness of mankind, his family is suspicious of Him. Ham, who eventually leads his brothers and the younger women to a mutiny against Noah, is particularly skeptical about God's plan.

Mama, the Mrs. Noah of the play, is caught between Noah's faith and Ham's doubt. On the one hand, she tells Noah, "[I] love you very much. It isn't hard to love a man like you."[88] On the other, she is a protective mother who tells her kids to bundle up well, to watch out for big waves, and to take care not to slip on the ark's deck. The lengthy confinement on the ark causes her to fall prey to doubt. In defending her children, who with Ham's encouragement become increasingly difficult after they have fought with their father, she tells Noah ("in a choking voice"): "It's — it's long for them, you know — this trip."[89] In truth, the trip is wearing her down, and Noah knows it. He laments to the animals about his wife:

> It's the children, you see, the children. And there's Mama. She's weakening too. Mama's beginning to fail me! I never though I'd live to see that. It's breaking me up — it's killing me. Here I am in the middle of six of seven question marks — I have to know all the answers. But I'm only an old farmer — All these things that are happening to me — they — you know — flatten me, bowl me over, don't you see?[90]

All that is happening begins to flatten Mama, too. When Ham suggests that Noah is a fraud who did not release the dove but has hidden it in order to procure it later and pronounce it a miracle, Mama is concerned about how the children's lack of faith will affect their father. Ultimately, she begins to doubt him too. However, as Ham taunts his father, she suddenly comes around, realizing that Noah is not a trickster. She is mortified to see her son mocking her husband, and mutters to herself, "My God, let me die rather than see this."[91] The dove flies into her hands, recalling the Wakefield story, but the children remain convinced that their father is a sham.

Despite Mama's best intentions to support Noah and remain loyal to him, she cannot conceal her disappointment about the postdeluvian world. She comes down from the ark, surveys the surroundings, and complains, "Look, this isn't home. What a wilderness! It's so cold. So bare! And that horrible damp smell."[92] She longs to return to the ark, momentarily forgetting how hard life during the flood had been. She curses her husband, who is building an altar in the distance:

> Wicked man! Mystery man! Weakling! Dolt! You think you can lead men, and you let everything lead you. You're a traitor! That's what you are! Traitor! Oh! <She turns, wild-eyed, towards the deck.> Oh I was busy setting a basket ready for the cat — Kitty! Kitty! Come here. You're all I have left.[93]

Her anger spirals into dementia. In the final scene of the play she is completely disoriented. She asks Noah why their friends don't come by any longer; she wonders why no one has welcomed them back from their big trip. She then answers herself, believing that God has forbidden them visitors. She is angry with God and terribly, terribly sad.

While the wives of Noah we have seen thus far have been types, the Mama of Obey's *Noah* is very real. She is an old woman whose ill health is a cause of worry to her family. They discourage her from walking quickly, from dancing, from drinking too much coffee. She is beloved by her husband, her sons, and the three orphan girls from next door who join them on the ark. These last call her Mother, while her husband is Mr. Noah. She is a loyal wife who gets frustrated; a loving mother who knows her children's faults. And she is a fallible woman: an emotionally strong character who becomes mentally weak. The fleshing out of Mrs. Noah as a complex character is purely Obey's invention.

We have in Obey's play a theme that has not been touched on by any of the writers we have surveyed thus far: the unfeasability of the venture. Ham raises practical questions about the structure of an ark large enough to support those spared, about where in the desert all the flood waters will come from. He also raises profound questions about his father: Is he a trickster who relies on sleight of hand, or is he an agent of God?

The play itself raises the biggest question of all: What would the toll of the flood be? There are two levels to the answer Noah gives. On a small scale, the toll is the collapse of familial harmony. The mother who held the family together could not withstand the pressures of the voyage and the restoration of the world. On a larger scale, the answer is the same: the collapse of harmony. Obey has the three sons alight from the ark squabbling and calling each other racist names. Despite the appearance of the rainbow just as Noah loses all hope, Obey seems to suggest that the new world will be as discordant as the old.

In H. G. Wells' *All Aboard for Ararat,* a visitor who claims to be "God Almighty, Maker of the Universe" appears on the doorstop of Noah Lammock, a writer who has begun to suspect that the collapse of humanity has come. God, who has picked Noah from the phonebook on account of his biblical name, proposes that they make an ark and restore civilization: "What I propose is that with my help and under my instruction you should construct an Ark, an Ark that this time will be a success. Into the Ark we will put reproductive samples of every good thing that is in the world, beasts, birds, arts and crafts, inventions and discoveries, literature. Carefully chosen and carefully vetted."[94]

Two things are going on here. The biblical text is being affirmed. God acknowledges the first Noah, the first Ark, and even his own ability to alter the course of history. And yet, even in this affirmation, there is an undermining. A new text is being written that is not Scripture: it is on one level Lammock's books and on another the very H. G. Wells text the reader holds. The suggestion is that the Bible somehow no longer stands. The new Noah is not a righteous man chosen for any of his own qualities, but a man selected nearly at random to construct an Ark that "this time will be a success." God, the infallible, concedes that His prior decisions were inadequate, that his previous plans had failed. God even calls into question his own authority, admitting that he has "recently been detained as — as an Incomprehensible, shall we say? — in a private lunatic asylum."[95]

Wells' is the first account which explicitly makes reference to the biblical text. In the Medieval literature, the plays tow the line of Scripture; they conceive of themselves as relating what was in the Bible. In some respects, this is true too of the twentieth century plays seen here: they present the usual Scriptural story, but as told from another perspective. Certainly, they may add details that were not in the text, but they essentially retell the standard story. Wells, however, is conscious of writing a *new* testament. He is doing again what the Bible did before, trying to correct its failings, to improve upon the first attempt. Hence he refers frequently back to the Book of Genesis, a text that both God and Noah Lammock know well.

When God announces: "when this inundation of foul warfare is over and the stench has subsided, the Ark will rest again on another Ararat, and out you will come, all of you, to a cleansed, renascent world," Lammock interrupts him with a question. Lammock, a childless divorced writer who lives alone, cannot fathom who "all of you" might be. God elaborates:

> "You and your seed. You and your family. Your wife whom I have found for you, your sons, Shem, Ham and Japhet, and their wives and little ones. For the strange thing is that, under very slightly different names, practically all the family of your prototype are to be found on earth again. The coincidence is so remarkable that the temptation to see how far the parallelism will go is in itself enough to justify—" "*No,*" interrupted Noah, with an emphasis that seemed to startle even God himself, "*you don't. No!*" "I don't?" "You don't put that over on me. No! If you bring back that infernal woman, you may count your Ark *off*. I won't have anything to do with it."[96]

After this outburst and an accusation that God knows practically nothing about women, Noah Lammock reveals much about his ex-wife. He states that "of the original Mrs. Noah, of course, I have nothing to say. She has remained nameless and blameless down the ages,"[97] but of the second Mrs. Noah, he has nothing *good* to say. He calls her "a vain, restless, jealous exhibitionist, a dishonest and consuming woman. She was — temperamental to an extreme degree.... There was no satisfying her and no pacifying her. [He concludes] she went off at last and I was able to divorce her. She made marriage so horrible to me that I have never tempted Fortune again."[98]

And yet God is insistent that because she is a intelligent woman, a writer too, she should naturally become Noah's companion again. Noah objects strongly, listing numerous faults of hers, ranging from instability to shallowness, from literary pretention to promiscuity, at which point God interrupts with a startling revelation: "All this increases the parallelism [with the original Noah] remarkably."[99] Noah, understandably, is taken aback. One of the few of his generation at all versed in Scripture, he states, "But in the Bible — Mrs Noah never says a word or does a thing."[100] What follows is a striking instance in which the God of the new Scripture explicates to his chosen Noah the old Scripture account of the chosen Noah:

> "The character of the former Mrs Noah," said God, speaking with a judicious slowness and pitting the finger-tips of one open hand against the finger-tips of the other, "has remained above suspicion for four thousand, two hundred and eighty-nine years, precisely. Yes. In the toy Arks given to children, I observe, she is represented by an extremely upright figure with a conspicuous, serviceable-looking bust and a costume devoid of the slightest hint of feminine coquetry. She wears the sort of hat a charity school girl might wear. Her cheeks display an unmitigated shining glow of health, as though powder was unknown to her. That, I may tell you frankly, does her no sort of justice, either way. My Book states certain facts and makes no comments. The Patriarchs and Prophets were sufficiently scandalous to supply whatever human interest was needed without putting in superfluous gossip. Still — Mrs Noah....I thought you understood....I gave certain facts about this lady. They seem to me to speak for themselves. Have you never noted their implications? Consider what those facts were. She had three sons. One was an extremely dark, if not absolutely black, boy, Ham. The other was sallow with dark curly hair and what one calls nowadays an Armenoid profile, Shem. The third, Japeth, was what the Germans would consider a Nordic type, all milk and roses. Samples in fact of the chief varieties of mankind. Now Noah, like yourself, was a quiet righteous man. He had great gifts, yes — but I put it to you; *was he capable of that much versatility?*"[101]

The assumptions are cast aside: the Bible is shown to be a partial account and God is revealed to be the only reliable transmitter of history. This does not, however, mean that the new Noah has any faith in him. Despite the fact that God is insistent that the ex-Mrs. Noah Lammock would like nothing more than to reform her ways somewhat and to reunite with Noah, to act as his housekeeper, kennel-maid, secretary, typist, amanuensis, and exponent,[102] Noah Lammock is adamant that he have nothing further to do with this woman, who taunted and insulted him and made his life unpleasant for many years.

Noah eventually turns to the biblical text to support his conviction that he need not have female accompaniment in his nursing the world back to health: he points to the drunkenness of Noah and the havoc which it wrought, and promises God that should he have to contend with his ex-wife, he will without doubt also take to drink.

God ultimately concedes that Noah has provided considerable scriptural evidence to suggest that the idea of a woman on board might not necessarily be a good one. From this point, God turns to Noah for suggestions, and Noah dissects all His preconceptions about the second Ark:

> Let us be clear, first of all, whom we will *not* take. When we get out of our Ark on Ararat this time, we certainly won't have any Shem, any Ham or any Japhet; we'll have clear-headed, back-boned, clean-minded people. We won't have any nonsense about the seed of Abraham and the Chosen People. We won't have any Messiahs or Saviours or Leaders to lead them to do what they ought to do of themselves. Let us wipe out all of these blunders from the human now and for ever. If it is going to be a New Deal, let it be a new deal. That, Sir, is how I see it. I can no other.[103]

And so begins the blueprint for a second ark. This one is devised almost exclusively by Lammock. God has relinquished His authority. A new covenant for all mankind is being written, and for the first time, it is man, not God, who prepares it.

If we can discern the beginning of a trend toward the demythologisation of biblical characters with the mystery plays, the first half of the twentieth century reflects the demythologisation of entire stories. Hurston, Obey, and Wells all call into question the reliability of the biblical version, telling tales that not only flesh out but also undermine the scant scriptural account. Furthermore, all present us with postdeluvian discord, with the failure, on some level, of the new society. In each account, Noah's family is the microcosm of the new world gone wrong, epitomised in the tension between Noah and his wife.

FROM OTHER TO AUTHOR(ITY)

The question of preparing a new account brings us to the final two texts we will treat: Timothy Findley's *Not Wanted on the Voyage*[104] and Jeanette Winterson's *Boating for Beginners*.[105] These two late twentieth century novels differ from the other stories treated here in two respects. They purport to tell the flood story as it happened, and not as it was misrecorded in scripture, and they tell the accurate tale from an expressly female perspective. The Other becomes not only the Author, but also the Authority.

Though the historical setting of these works is radically different, the two share many profound similarities. Both authors reevaluate the primacy given to the male figures in the biblical account. With the exception of the postdiluvian episode of the drunkenness of Noah, the narrative in Genesis centers on one man and his god, to whom all other characters are subordinated. Winterson and Findley both attempt to bring the background characters, the marginalized figures, into the fore and to give them voices.

In Canadian novelist Timothy Findley's *Not Wanted on the Voyage,* we have the story of Noah, a very old man, who lives in a primitive rural setting with his wife, his three sons, and their three wives, as indicated in the Bible. Findley's Noah is a righteous man, and, unlike his heathen contemporaries, he heeds the word of the Lord Yaweh.[106] Thus when Yaweh, frustrated by the state of creation and exhausted by his role in it, arrives to recuperate at Noah's home and instructs Noah to build an ark, Noah complies. The frame in the modern telling is much the same as in the biblical account. The perspective of the story has changed, however: Findley gives us Noah as seen through the eyes of his wife and of the animals gathered on the ark. Most of the tale takes place on the ark, to which the biblical story scarcely ventures, where Noah's family and the animals consider themselves to be held captive. None of these characters chose their destinies; they were corralled by force or fear to leave their homes and their antediluvian lives "to be saved." They are characters who see Noah not as "a righteous man, blameless in his age," but as a patriarch, a tyrant, and even, ultimately, a murderer.

Findley's account of the flood begins with a quotation from Genesis 7:7—"and Noah went in, and his sons, and his wife, and his sons' wives with him into the ark, because of the waters of the flood"— immediately undermined by the assertion: "Everyone knows it wasn't like that."[107] In Findley's account, the way it was is far darker than in any of the accounts we have seen thus far. Any romanticising of the voyage is stripped away, as the events are rendered starkly real: "the whole world has been reduced to...four storeys of earth and heaven rounded by the stinking yellow walls and sticky pitch of a leaking gopher wood ark."[108] Findley leads us to understand that while the skeleton of a story given in the Bible may be accurate, the details are too sparse to be believed, to be capable of relaying the truth. Consequently, he presents the whole story, as told by a more or less reliable narrator, one of Noah's unwilling accomplices trapped within these stinking walls.

The dominant perspective in *Not Wanted on the Voyage* is Mrs. Noyes'. She is the sensitive and stubborn wife of Noah, the woman whose voice is altogether written out of the biblical account. The novel is the report of her rebellion against her husband's fanaticism, of her quest to find a space in a situation which has not only silenced her, but robbed her of her power to decide for herself. Findley's Noah is abusive to his family and particulary to his wife. Mrs. Noyes presents her antediluvian husband as a scientist entirely lacking in compassion, a man so driven by his pursuits that he loses respect for life. Before the flood, the animals on his farm lived in fear that he would steal their babies for deadly experiments. At sea, he spirals toward greater barbarism. When the adolescent Emma, Japheth's virgin wife, refuses to have sex with her husband, Noah rips her hymen with the horn of the fragile and magical unicorn. In the process, the unicorn's horn is severed from its head, and it bleeds to death. Similarly, Noah obliterates another species aboard the ark in his throwing the demons overboard. The worst of his butchery is his killing three small children — children who more resemble apes than humans and who, it becomes clear, are all Noah's offspring.

Where Noah is the abusive tyrant, Mrs. Noyes is the nurturing rebel. She labours to save one of the ape children from the waters of the flood. She smuggles cats aboard the ark. Where her husband lacks regard for the captive animals, she is able to hear their voices, able to sense their suffering. While her husband holds no life sacred but his own, Mrs. Noyes values even the least of the beings aboard the ark. So sensitive is she to the suffering of those around her, and so abused by her husband, that she takes to drink in an effort to numb herself to the pain that surrounds her.

Findley's wife is a culmination of the trend begun with the early interpreters and fleshed out in the mystery plays; the theme of the recalcitrant wife. In keeping with the tradition of dissent, she initially refuses to board the ark. When at last she is corralled into coming, she rebels fiercely against her being constricted with the animals in the lower reaches of the ark, and devises plans for mutiny. Ultimately, she becomes the central figure in the story, assuming the voice of both authority and reason. Noah's exploits are seen through the lens of her anger and disbelief; his brutality is seen as even more savage in light of her sensitivity. She has a rapport with the animals, almost all of whom speak to her, and a respect for her children despite their foibles. She is a stubborn character, weakened only slightly by her propensity for drink, and she provides a strong foil of justice and righteousness to Noah's corruption. While Mrs. Noyes becomes the teller of Findley's tale, the voyeur of atrocity and the relayer of the truth, Jeanette Winterson, a contemporary British author, writes Noah's wife, Grace, out of her telling. We are presented only with her faded memory, as kept alive by the widowed Noah; this may be read as a direct counter to the Biblical story, which makes no effort to preserve the memory of the matriarch.

Where Winterson writes Noah's wife out, she replaces her with a consort for Noah, a Bunny Mix, romance novelist. Noah opts to save her from the flood because "she's useful, and she'll be able to help with the books." Winterson's Noah is a chronicler; he has taken it upon himself (or mostly upon himself) to record the history of the world. This history of the world is far more radical than the one we have preserved in Genesis. While most of the writers we have considered here remain essentially faithful to the structure of the biblical narrative, Winterson plays with it. She denies the chronology in Genesis, which asserts a specific order of events and a situation of the story in the mythological past, and concocts a new setting. Her Noah does not make his home in a primitive farming community. Rather he runs a pleasure boat company in Ur, during an era remarkably similar to the late twentieth century. This world is one where frozen food and romance novels are consumed *en masse*, where Northrop Frye and Martin Amis are prominent literary figures, where evangelism is rampant, and where God has only recently begun to exist. He appears to Noah as a huge hand poking down from the sky; he holds a yellow and black sign proclaiming, "I AM THAT I AM, YAHWEH THE UNPRONOUNCEABLE."[109] Noah announces the revelation at a press conference, confounding a public who cannot understand why Yahweh has not made himself known previously. Thus Noah becomes The Unpronounceable's publicity agent: together the two script a bestseller called *Genesis, or How I Did It,* which is "a kind of global history from the beginnings of time showing how the Lord had always been there, always would be there, and what a good thing this was."[110] They follow this up with a second installment — *Exodus, or Your Way Lies There* — which, like the first, sold out over and over again.

Noah enlists Bunny Mix to liven up his stories, as he recognises that "even [Yahweh's] autobiography [was] going to need a bit of romantic interest, and [Noah did]n't want to have to write those bits."[111] She becomes one of Noah's co-conspirators and, like Mrs. Noyes, is given a voice, although not much of a personality. However, there is a marked distinction between the authorial voices given to the two women by these contemporary authors. Findley's Mrs. Noyes is responsible for transmitting the truth, the grisly detail of a story intentionally misrecorded and misremembered. The biblical story is the cover-up; *Not Wanted on the Voyage* is the expose. By contrast, Bunny Mix, as partner of Noah, becomes the hand behind the biblical text. Once again, the Bible is a cover-up, a story created expressly to mislead, but in this instance it is the woman who is complicit in the miscreation.

In Winterson, the truth, the actual happenings, are preserved by Gloria Munde, the young woman hired to round up animals for a movie Noah is ostensibly filming. Gloria soon learns that Noah is actually collecting species with which to repopulate the world, which Yahweh has arbitrarily decided to flood. The Almighty, we learn, is "fed up of this world and its whingeing, scrounging pop-art people,"[112] and seeks to begin anew. After considerable whingeing of his own, Noah complies with Yahweh's scheme. He alerts only his sons to the forthcoming annihilation, leaving the rest of the world, for whom he has become a spiritual guru, ignorant.

With a band of misfits including Marlene, a transsexual; Doris, a woman cast as a crone in Noah's film; and Desi, Shem's wife and the woman who uncovered the plan to drown the world, Gloria takes on the questionable task of enlightening the masses. The unlikelihood of their assemblage causes Marlene to remark: "We can do our best to warn people as soon as we can prove it, but what makes you think anyone is going to believe a zoo keeper, a transsexual and a member of the rich middle class?"[113] Adam, Noah, Abraham — it is men like these who are afforded glimpses into the workings of God. Women, and particularly such a motley crew of them as Gloria's, are not among the privileged. All the same, they are given a mission, with a demon appearing to them and informing them that:

> God *will* flood the world, Noah *will* float away, and unless you lot do your best to stay alive there won't be anyone left to spread the word about what really happened. It doesn't even matter if you forget what really happened; if you need to, invent something else. The vital thing is to have an alternative so that people will realise there's no such thing as a true story.[114]

Given this option, the women choose to live, to build themselves life rafts and to the make the best go at survival that they can. They realise that "given the will, no flood myth would destroy them. Gloria loved the world; and many waters cannot quench love, neither can floods drown it."[115] So, in the interest of an alternate telling, and out of a quest for continuous prose, these four women toast a new world and shut themselves away in their waterproof containers. The alternate telling they lived to perpetuate is, of course, Winterson's *Boating for Beginners*, and the role of the women in this story becomes the same as the role of Noah in the Biblical one: to make known the past and thereby the truth.

It is hardly surprising that the late twentieth century yields us feminist retellings of the flood story. The account given in the Bible seems to demand a retelling; the suspicion it invokes in the postmodern reader is too great to be dismissed. The voice is too unilateral, too authoritative; there is no possibility for dissent. We are skeptical of an account that suggests unanimousness. We suspect there must have been those who did not toe the line, those whose were pushed into the background and silenced. The mention of four women — of Noah's wife, and his sons' three wives — without a single detail to identify them causes the reader to wonder who were these figures, where had they gone, what had they thought. And so modern writers take up the pen and invent an alternate version, a version as told by the silent onlooker, reminding us yet again that "there are no true stories."

The feminist reader of Genesis knows that it could not be a woman's account. Woman is written out of the story. Noah has the only voice, and he speaks instead of, and not necessarily for, the other characters. God is vengeful and wrathful and, like his human friend, patriarchal. He is male, he addresses only males, he demotes the female characters to the rank of appendage to their males. Winterson attributes the tone of Genesis to a conscious decision made in a moment of frustration: "An idea occurred to Noah...: when he sat down to redraft *Genesis*, he'd make sure everyone knew where the blame lay. Women; they're all the same."[116] Winterson chooses therefore to write her story from the woman's point of view, to present a story with an alternate truth, one which demythifies the righteous Noah and his omnipotent God.

In *Not Wanted on the Voyage*, by contrast, there is more going on than simply a giving of voice. There is also a taking away. In Findley's telling, the antediluvian animals are able to speak. The sheep sing in a choir conducted by Mrs. Noyes, the cats converse with their mistress, the fairies whisper her their secrets. When the ark alights, however, the capacity for speech has disappeared. When Mrs. Noyes assembles her flock to sing, she is greeted by "silence. Not a word. Only baaa. The sheep would never sing again."[117] The trauma of the voyage has robbed the animals of their voice and simultaneously the world of its innocence. Suddenly only human beings can speak; suddenly we are the sole preservers of truth and likewise of falsehood. In their sadness and horror, in the shock of what has transpired, Findley's women recoil from the task of presenting an authoritative account. They cannot tell a tale that glorifies that God who drowned the world and stole its words. Nor can they perpetuate the myth of Noah's blamelessness. The wickedness of man is so great that they can fathom no response. Mrs Noyes knows this. So does her daughter-in-law, Hannah, who was raped by her husband's father, who writes in her journal: "By God...if women had writen stories, they would have writen of men more wikkednesse than all the sex of Adam may redresse."[118] Rather than make the horrifying palatable, the incredible tenable, the atrocity bearable, the women opt for silence. And the men choose glosses and lies. So, the employment of a hermeneutic of suspicion, a distrust in the biblical account, leads Findley to attempt to recapture the female voice. He is motivated if not by a quest for truth then by one for balance. There must be a new author, a new authority. A female voice must stand alongside the dominant male one. This voice belongs to Noah's wife.

CONCLUSION

We have traced a trajectory through time and traditions, one which attempts to reassert the identity of a character written out of the Bible. Noah's wife, mentioned in Genesis only in relation to her husband, begins with early postbiblical interpretation to take on an identity. The nought becomes aught. Over time, she becomes not simply an appendage to her husband — Noah's wife — but something other. Initially this otherness is manifested in her identity and lineage; she is given a history that sets her apart from her husband's family. But soon, her otherness is exemplified in her becoming unlike her husband. She questions him, she defies him, she even hits him. The tradition of the truculent wife is born. It is a tradition prevalent in English mystery plays, and it maintains currency even through the early twentieth century. The literary imagination persists in conceiving of our heroine as a rebel. Simultaneously, the literary world resists the gospel truth and begins to question the authority of the biblical text. The flood story is farfetched, fantastical. It is patriarchal, patronising. And lo, there springs up a tradition of Noah's wife not simply as other but as author, as the keeper of the truth of the biblical story. That she tells her story, from her perspective, affords her the status of authority; the original telling is rendered suspect, the new one legitimate. Mrs. Noah is the new hero, the new voice, the bearer of a new tradition.

In a rite of passage that took millennia to complete, Mrs. Noah has emerged from the background. From the scant skeleton offered in Genesis, a person is born. The details of her development vary through time and place; her biography is hardly consistent and by no means verifiable. And yet, through the centuries, and through Jewish, Christian, Muslim, and secular literature, Noah's wife evolves. Hers is the story of an ongoing transition, of a movement from nought to aught to other to author, and even to authority.

Notes

[1]Unless otherwise noted, all Biblical citations refer to the book of Genesis in the Jewish Publication Society *Tanakh* (Philadelphia,1985).

[2] The pseudepigrapha are documents written between the third century BCE and the second century CE by both Jewish and Christian writers. These writings, so-named because many of them were falsely attributed (often to biblical figures), comprise reflections on and expansions of Scripture.

[3] *The Apocrypha,* trans. Edgar Goodspeed (New York: Vintage, 1989), 114

[4] Bereshit Rabba 22.4. See Francis Lee Utley, "The One Hundred and Three Names of Noah's Wife," *Speculum* 16 (1941): 432.

[5] Only five times in the book of Genesis does a woman's name appear in a genealogy: Naamah (4:22), Milcah and Iscah (11:29), Rebekah (12:23), and Dinah (30:21). The biblical narrative provides details about three of them, but of the exceptions, Naamah and Iscah, we know almost nothing.

[6] The other three are Eve (2:18ff), Adah, and Zillah (4:19ff).

[7] In light of the confusion and overlap in the Cainite (4:17ff) and Sethite (5:6ff) genealogies, such an adjustment of Naamah's lineage is not necessarily a stretch. It is plausible that extra-biblical tradition might place her as a descendant of Seth.

[8] Utley, "Noah's Wife,"445.

[9] This late-life wedding accounts for the fact that Noah did not have sons until he was five hundred years old.

[10] Sir E. A. Wallis Budge, *The Book of the Cave of Treasures* (London: The Religious Tract Society, 1927), 99.

[11] Budge, 99. By this account, Noah married a woman from the Cainite genealogy.

[12] R. H. Charles, *The Book of Jubilees* (Oxford: Clarendon Press, 1912), vs.5:33.

[13] Utley, "Noah's Wife," 427. Jack P. Lewis in *A Study of the Interpretation of Noah in Jewish and Christian Literature* (Leiden: E.J. Brill, 1978),14, notes that a variation of this name is found in a Syriac fragment cited by R. H. Charles.

[14] Sanhedrin 70a.

[15] Utley, "Noah's Wife," 451.

[16] Louis Ginzberg, *Legends of the Jews* (Philadelphia: Jewish publication Society, 1913), Vol. I, 117-8; vol. V, 147-8.

[17] Moses Gaster (1856-1939) was a rabbi, scholar, and Zionist leader whose bailiwick included Romanian literature, comparative and Jewish folklore, Samaritan studies, liturgy, and Anglo-Jewish history. He translated the fourth century CE Samaritan *Asatir*, an Arabic version of the book of Joshua.

[18] Utley "Noah's Wife," 433.

[19] Epiphanius (b. c. 315, Palestine—d. 403) was a bishop of the early Christian Church, noted for his struggle against beliefs he considered heretical (including Jews and Gnostics).

[20] Members of philosophical and religious movement prominent in the Greco-Roman world in the second century CE. Gnostic sects appear to have shared an emphasis on the redemptive power of esoteric knowledge, acquired not by learning or empirical observation but by divine revelation.

[21] M. R. James, *The Lost Apocrypha of the Old Testament* (London: Society for Promoting Christian Knowledge, 1920), 13.

[22] 71:11.

[23] "Noah," *Benet's Reader's Encyclopedia*, 3rd edition (New York: Harper & Row, 1987), 698.

[24] Anna Jean Mill, "Noah's Wife Again," *PMLA* 56 (1941): 615. In Moslem legend, Lot's wife was also condemned to hell.

[25] See, for instance, Gen. R. 30:7, Sanhedrin 108a.

[26] Louis Ginzberg, *Legends of the Bible* (New York: Jewish Publication Society, 1992), 66.

[27] Sanhedrin 108a, Gen. R. xxx.10.

[28] "Noah," *The Jewish Encyclopedia*, 319.

[29] The mystery plays (or mysteries) were one of three principal kinds of vernacular drama of the European Middle Ages, along with the miracle play and the morality play. Originally the term mystery play was used only to designate plays based on the Old and New Testaments and the Apocrypha; it is now used interchangeably with "miracle play" (a term originally used to refer exclusively to plays based on the lives of saints).

[30] The plays are named for the towns in which they were performed.

[31] "Mystery play," Britannica Online. <http://www.eb.com:180/cgi-bin/g?DocF=micro/412/91.html>.

[32] Literally "wife" in Latin.

[33] Millicent Carey, *The Wakefield Group in the Towneley Cycle* (Baltimore: Johns Hopkins Press, 1930), 66.

[34] Mill, "Noah's Wife Again," 615.

[35] Michael Foley, "Noah's Wife's Rebellion: Timothy Findley's Use of the Mystery Plays of Noah in *Not Wanted on the Voyage*," *Essays on Canadian Writing* (Summer 1991): 175-182.

[36] In the mystery plays, prominent women are generally portrayed as either a Mary or an Eve. This dichotomization of women was popular in contemporary sermons, with preachers warning that women were contrary, wild, and even tools of the devil — all characteristics of our Mrs. Noah.

[37] The order in which they appear best illustrates the emphatic departure from the "seek and virtuous" forerunner.

[38] Richard Beadle, ed., *The York Plays* (London : E. Arnold, 1982), 84.

[39] Beadle, 85.

[40] Beadle, 85.

[41] Beadle, 85.

[42] Beadle, 86.

[43] See Melvin Storm, "Uxor and Alison: Noah's Wife in the Flood Plays and Chaucer's Wife of Bath," *Modern Language Quarterly* 48 (December 1987): 303-319, as well as articles by Garvin and Utley cited elsewhere in these notes.

[44] Happe, *English Mystery Plays: A Selection* (Baltimore : Penguin Books, 1975), 107.

[45] Happe, 108.

[46] Happe, 109.

[47] See Laura F. Hodges, "Noe's Wife: Type of Eve and Wakefield Spinner," in *Equally in God's Image: Women in the Middle Ages* (New York: Peter Lang, 1990),30-39, on the cultural significance of spinning in the Middle Ages and on the association of spinning with Eve, and thereby of the Wakefield Uxor with Eve.

[48] Happe, 110.

[49] Happe, 113.

[50] Happe, 113.

[51] Happe, 114.

[52] See introduction to R. M. Lumiansky and David Mill, *The Chester Mystery Cycle* (London: Oxford University Press, 1986).

[53] Lumiansky, 46.

[54] Lumiansky, 51.

[55] Lumiansky, 52.

[56] Carey, 76.

[57] One of the earlier extant English biblical paraphrases, the *Cursor Mundi* is a long Middle English poem, written c. 1300, which attempts to recount the whole history of the world.

[58] A medieval Cornish play, *The Creation of the World* (*Gwreans an Bys*), is the last example of a tradition in Cornwall of composing and performing secular plays side by side with religious plays. The earliest extant manuscript of the Cornish *Creation* was written by William Jordan of Helston in 1611, and was reprinted with an English translation in 1864.

[59] Carey, *The Wakefield Group,* 77.

[60] Caedmon (c. 658-680) was allegedly an illiterate herdsman inspired in a dream to utter verses about the beginning of time, thus becoming the first Old English Christian poet. His fragmentary hymn, the Caedmonian *Genesis*, remains a symbol of the adaptation of the aristocratic-heroic Anglo-Saxon verse tradition to the expression of Christian themes. ("Caedmon" Britannica Online <http://www.eb.com:180/cgi-bin/g?DocF=micro/96/91.html>)

The Junius manuscript, to which Garvin refers, contains Old English paraphrases of Genesis, Exodus, Daniel, and stories of Christ and Satan, copied about 1000 CE, and given in 1651 to the scholar Franciscus Junius by Archbishop James Ussher of Armagh. Although originally attributed to Caedmon, the attribution is doubtful as the poems seem to have been written at different periods and by more than one author. ("Caedmon manuscript" Britannica Online,<http://www.eb.com:180/cgi-bin/g?DocF=micro/96/92.html>)

[61]Katherine Garvin, "A Note on Noah's Wife," *Modern Language Notes* 49 (1934): 89.

[62] Garvin, 90. Sir Israel Gollancz, who wrote the introduction to the British Academy's edition of the Caedmon manuscript, dates this illustration to approximately 1000 CE.

[63] Garvin, 89-90.

[64] Mill, "Noah's Wife Again," 615.

[65] Mill, 619.

[66] In a good number of the revisions of the flood story, God urges Noah not to reveal his shipbuilding activity to anyone, including his wife.

[67] The devil instructs Mrs. Noah not to enter the ark, despite her husband's continued directions to do so. Noah grows increasingly perturbed, until he ultimately curses "Come aboard you devil you," or a similar variant, thereby unwittingly giving the devil license to board the ark. A number of stories recount that, once aboard, the devil made holes in the ark in an attempt to frustrate God's plan for salvation.

[68] Mill, "Noah's Wife Again," 616.

[69] Mill does acknowledge the correlation between the Caedmonian *Genesis* and the legend, and points also to the Queen Mary Psalter, an early 14th century work agreed to be by an English illustrator (Mill, p.620), wherein Gabriel instructs Noah to build an ark. In this telling, "the necessity for secrecy is explicitly stated, as well as the devil's temptation of Uxor and the potion to make him betray his secret" (Mill, p.621). The psalter, however, deviates from the medieval plays in that Uxor is not reluctant to enter the ark: she is depicted standing at the foot of the ladder behind two of her sons, while Noah hoists the third one on board.

[70] Mill, 622.

[71] Adelaide Bennett, with "The Recalcitrant Wife in the Ramsey Abbey Psalter," in *Equally in God's Image: Women in the Middle Ages* (New York: Peter Lang, 1990), 40-42, brings to the discussion, a half century later, a third illustrated manuscript depicting the story. She cites the Ramsey Abbey Psalter (c. 1300), which "illustrates Noah alone in the ark filled with creatures and his spouse still standing in the rising water filled with submerged bodies. At this last crucial moment, he grabs his wife's left wrist and, and with his left hand raised, commands her to come on board. Meanwhile a winged devil clings to her back, dissuading her from boarding"(Bennett, p.40).

[72] Murray Roston, *Biblical Drama in England* (Evanston: Northwestern UP,1968), 264.

[73] Consider the introduction to the Towneley play in Happe's *Mystery Plays* (written as late as 1975), which notes that "Theologically [Noah's wife's] rebelliousness is an example of the inferiority and corruptibility of woman (cf. Eve in *Paradise Lost*)." Happe, 97.

[74] In Cecil Day-Lewis' *Noah and the Waters* (New York: Transatlantic Arts, 1947), Rumer Godden's *In Noah's Ark* (New York: The Viking Press, 1949), and William Golding's *The Spire* (New York: Harcourt, Brace & World, 1964), for instance, she is non-existent.

[75] Robert Hemenway, *Zora Neale Hurston: A Literary Biography* (Urbana: U. Illinois Press, 1977), 68, points out that Hurston's playing with the biblical flood narrative "revealed to [her] the possibilities of presenting a black version of the Old Testament, a revelation which would reach fruition in [her] novel about Moses as a hoodoo man, *Moses, Man of the Mountain* (1939)."

[76] Zora Neale Hurston, "The First One: A Play in One Act," in *Ebony and Topaz,* ed. Charles S. Johnson (New York: Books for Libraries Press, 1927), 53.

[77] Hurston, 54.

[78] Hurston, 54.

[79] Hurston, 54.

[80] Hurston, 54.

[81] Hurston, 55.

[82] Hurston, 55.

[83] Hurston, 55.

[84] Hemenway, 68.

[85] Hurston, 56.

[86] Hurston, 57.

[87] Roston, *Biblical Drama*, 283.

[88] Andre Obey, *Noah*, trans. Arthur Wilmurt (New York: Samuel French, 1935), 17.

[89] Obey, 45.

[90] Obey, 46.

[91] Obey, 57.

[92] Obey, 64.

[93] Obey, 64.

[94] H. G. Wells, *All Aboard for Ararat* (New York: Alliance Book Corp., 1941), 25.

[95] Wells, 13.

[96] Wells, 26.

[97] Wells, 27.

[98] Wells, 27.

[99] Wells, 28.

[100] Wells, 28.

[101] Wells, 28-29.

[102] Wells, 30.

[103] Wells, 32.

[104] Jeanette Winterson, *Boating for Beginners* (London: Minerva, 1990).

[105] Timothy Findley, *Not Wanted on the Voyage* (Toronto: Penguin, 1984).

[106] Throughout *Not Wanted on the Voyage,* Findley spells out the tetragramaton as Yaweh, where scholars generally use Yahweh.

[107] Findley, 1.

[108] Findley, 280.

[109] Winterson, 13.

[110] Winterson, 14.

[111] Winterson, 114.

[112] Winterson, 90.

[113] Winterson, 96.

[114] Winterson, 123-4.

[115] Winterson, 146.

[116] Winterson, 117.

[117] Findley, 348.

[118] Findley, 288.

Abraham and the Problems of Modern Heroism

Brian S. Hook and R. R. Reno

Does the Judaeo-Christian tradition of story-telling have a vision of the heroic which presents human excellence with sufficient clarity and force to render it visible and compelling? Answering this question turns out to be perplexing. To be sure, the Bible can be read as an ancient document which reveals examples of human excellence: men and women who are exceptionally faithful, brave, strong, or devoted. However, if we read the Bible under the guidance of either Jewish or Christian traditions of interpretation, then the text is first and foremost about God: what he does and demands, promises and delivers. The piety of both Judaism and Christianity presses toward a recognition of divine deeds rather than human accomplishments. God, in short, is the hero of the Bible.[1]

The dominance of the divine leads to questions about human participation. To the extent that the Bible is a story about God, how do we fit in? If we find our fulfillment in a story about God's actions, then what is our place? If God is the hero, then can we aspire to more than a supporting role, a spiritual attendant to the great divine warrior? Or, even more troubling, are we simply part of an anonymous chorus dedicated to praising divine triumphs? These questions cluster around a central problem, the problem of recognizing distinctively human achievement and presenting it for imitation in a cosmos suffused with uniquely divine glory.

Neither Judaism nor Christianity has viewed this as a difficult practical problem. We participate in God's greatness and glory by being chosen by Him and by inhabiting that chosenness in obedience and faith. And, as a matter of fact, people *are* shaped and formed by the biblical vision of divinely governed life. Their commitments of faith and obedience are not spectral but quite real, so however we might conceive of the problem of participation, we should not allow ourselves to question whether or not it is possible. The collection of writings called the Bible and the interpretive traditions of Judaism and Christianity which treat these writings as authoritative seem quite capable of making people into participants. The faithful can become exceptional participants in God's greatness. Nonetheless, what so obviously happens is not always easily understood.

Two difficulties emerge when we think about the traditional claim that human beings participate in divine glory through obedience and faith. One difficulty focuses on the way in which God is the dominant actor or hero of the biblical story. In the Christian theological tradition, this takes the form of an ongoing debate about grace and free will. Surely, reasons the advocate of free will, a predetermined blessing can be possessed only as an extrinsic gift. Our true participation requires us to choose, accomplish, or in some way enter into the blessing as one worthy of the gift. Otherwise, we are mere automata. Let us call this the problem of possession: at root, the grace and free will debate concerns our ability to possess the blessings and excellences promised by God as genuine, personal attributes rather than as divine declarations and imputed qualities.

The second difficulty concerns the specific form of our possession of God's blessings through obedience and faith. Can we really say that doing the will of another, even God, can lead to us to participate in the glory or greatness of the other? Should we not say, instead, that obedience and faith involve giving up our very selves, so instead of participating, we are allowing ourselves to be absorbed and even annihilated? Or, to paraphrase Friedrich Nietzsche, is the way of obedience and faith anything other than a prolonged act of self-destruction?[2] Let us call this the problem of personal significance or distinctiveness, for Nietzsche points to the way in which the raw ambition of the biblical tradition on behalf of the glory and holiness of God can consume rather than elevate the merely human participants.[3]

These two problems—possession and personal significance—are quite relevant to modernity. Alienation and domination are, perhaps, the two afflictions which most preoccupy the modern mind. In our terms, alienation is a problem of possession. We feel somehow distant from the most important and time-consuming aspects of our lives. Work, family, leisure, as well as our inner lives of conscience, self-image, desires, are fragmented. We seem unable to see ourselves as full and undivided participants in any of these facets of life. Domination, in turn, is a problem of personal significance. We feel the demands of culture, the workplace, and relationships as constraining limitations upon the fullness of our personalities. Rules, bosses, and peer pressure reduce us to our roles, preventing us from realizing our individuality.

To be sure, these few lines about alienation and domination are inadequate both to the phenomena and the rich literature of diagnosis. Our project, however, is not to address modernity, at least not on its favored terms. Instead, our claim is that these problems are embedded within the biblical vision of human life. Moreover, these problems are not simply present in the biblical account of human life as latent and unexamined; they are recognized and addressed by the canonical text, as well as by those who have accepted its authority. Indeed, the tradition of writing and reflection which constitutes both Judaism and Christianity works strenuously to understand how obedience yields a fullness of character which is both visible and compelling, a character which is, in a word, heroic.

THE GREATNESS OF ABRAHAM

Let us offer an example in order to bring into focus the difficulties of possession and personal significance. Consider a contrast between Abraham and the archetypal hero of classical literature, Achilles. Of course, these two figures, the one central to the literature of Greek culture and the other to the biblical narrative, are different. Achilles is a warrior, swift-footed, efficient, and triumphant on the plains of Troy. As he is presented in Homer's great epic, the *Iliad*, Achilles faces a fateful choice: either a long life in anonymity or a brief life of glory. He chooses glory, and this choice requires him to be present on the battlefield as the dominant figure. Even though his glory is, in some sense, already known and guaranteed by the gods, the dramatic action of the *Iliad* moves toward the enactment of his greatness. His absence from the battle with the Trojans is crucial. The Greeks are pushed back to their ships, and disaster is imminent as Hector, the greatest of the Trojan warriors, sets fire to the first of the Greek ships beached on the shore. At that moment, everyone knows how utterly indispensable Achilles is. Without his sword, the Greeks face defeat and destruction. When he returns, however, the Trojans are forced into full retreat; before the gates of Troy itself Achilles kills Hector, securing the ultimate defeat and destruction of Troy. The greatness of Achilles is now manifest for all to see.

As readers of the *Iliad,* we face a number of enigmas and puzzles. What is the true nature of Achilles' conflict with the Greek leader, Agamemnon? Why does Achilles allow his best friend, Patroclus, to enter battle, only to be killed? How does the intervention of the gods influence the action? All these questions and many more are important for a full reading of that great epic, but one thing is crystal clear: the struggle between Greeks and Trojans turns on the person of Achilles. Even in his absence, Achilles controls events. The Greeks fall from defeat to defeat. When he returns, the Greeks rise from victory to victory. As the epic draws to a close and Achilles is honored by friend and foe as the greatest warrior, the reader can find no reason to withhold his or her admiration. However much the gods might influence events, the glory which he chose by returning to battle was earned and is rightfully his. One can hardly imagine saying that Achilles does not participate in the glory and greatness of victory.

When we frame the difference between Achilles and Abraham in terms of possession, the contrast is extreme. Unlike the *Iliad* which develops amidst a compound of human and divine intentions and actions, the Genesis narrative turns on God's choices and commandments. God says to Abraham, "Go from your country and your kindred and your father's house to the land that I will show you. I will make you a great nation, and I will bless you, and make your name great" (Genesis 12:1-2).[4] Like Achilles, Abraham shall be remembered and honored, but unlike Achilles that honor stems not from his own great deeds. His glory as father of a chosen people, a glory that outstrips Achilles', is a gift rather than an achievement. Herein lies the problem of possession in the biblical depiction of human greatness. The greatness of Abraham is tremendous, beyond that envisioned by the author of the *Iliad*, but that greatness is imputed rather than earned, alien rather than intrinsic.[5]

Abraham's two famous deceptions illustrate the way in which the man Abraham is separated from the power and glory of his chosenness. During a famine, Abraham travels to Egypt and, fearing for his life, he tells his wife, Sarah, to say that she is his sister (Gen. 12:10-20). Here, we certainly are not dealing with a man of Achillean courage and martial prowess! Nor, for that matter, is Abraham exemplifying an Odyessian cleverness. The text tells us of no plan or subterfuge by which Abraham will take advantage of the Egyptians in their ignorance. Abraham is simply a vulnerable nomad. Yet, because he is chosen by God, Abraham shall be honored rather than humiliated. Pharaoh takes Sarah into his household, the LORD afflicts and conquers with great plagues. With God as the active agent, the defeated Pharaoh returns Sarah and sends Abraham on his way.

The same pattern is repeated with King Abimelech (Gen. 20:1-18). This time, Abraham himself tells the king that Sarah is his sister, and Sarah is taken by the king into his household. But a dream informs King Abimelech that should he sleep with Sarah, he will die, and he hastily returns her to Abraham, asking why he resorted to deception. Abraham's reply is telling. "I did it," Abraham says, "because I thought, there is no fear of God at all in this place, and they will kill me because of my wife" (Genesis 20:11). This is an extraordinary passage, not because the patriarch has lied, but because King Abimelech assesses Abraham's power far more highly than does Abraham himself. To propitiate this power, King Abimelech makes great gifts to Abraham. He wishes to win his favor, for he recognizes that far from being vulnerable, Abraham has the power of life itself. And indeed, upon receipt of the gifts, Abraham prays to God on behalf of Abimelech and his people, "and," the Genesis story concludes, "God healed Abimelech, and also healed his wife and female slaves so that they bore children. For the LORD had closed fast all the wombs of the house of Abimelech because of Sarah, Abraham's wife" (20:17-18). The honor of God is vested in Abraham, so however weak he may be in the affairs of men, perhaps justifiably worried that he will be killed by a greater worldly force, Abraham is in fact to be feared.

With both Pharoah and King Abimelech, Abraham is weak and strong at the same time. He is powerless as a human force, so vulnerable that he resorts to deceptions which have tried both Jewish and Christian commentators who would like to present Abraham as a hero worthy of our admiration. Yet in both cases Abraham triumphs, or, more accurately, God triumphs on Abraham's behalf, making good the promise He made when He called Abraham out of the land of his fathers. Both scenes portray a weak man. Abraham is weak in the kind of strength necessary to prevent potentially hostile forces from taking away his wife and possessions, even his life. The deceptions also carry connotations of a weakness of character. It is almost as if the Genesis narrator deliberately tells these tales in order to accentuate just how little Abraham contributes to his greatness. Nothing could be further from the ambiance of heroic action which dominates the *Iliad.* Unlike Achilles, when we look at Abraham in these stories of deception, we do not say, "Ah yes, a man worthy of the glory bestowed upon him by God." Abraham receives the promise, but he seems not to possess any qualities or excellences which might make him a fitting participant in work which God intends to do through him. Abraham is not chosen because worthy; he is worthy simply because chosen.

The Genesis narrative does not leave Abraham an empty vessel of divine favor. Although Abraham is not a warrior like Achilles whose greatness is manifested in the test of arms, he does undergo the famous test of faith told in Genesis 22, the binding of Isaac. The dramatic dynamic of trial or test is important, for just such a scene yields insight into the character of the contestants. A race reveals who is the fastest runner; a fight reveals the fiercest warrior. In Abraham's test, we have just such a moment of discernment. However, the test does more than manifest or reveal Abraham's worthiness. The test also allows Abraham to fully enact his excellence. A race not only reveals the fastest runner. Under the full strain of competition, the race often induces a runner to run even faster. In the heat of battle, the warrior outdoes himself. In a similar fashion, the stark conditions of Abraham's test allow him to bring whatever excellence he might possess to full form and expression. Here, Abraham comes to inhabit his worthiness in action. In the test, we see the excellence which Abraham possesses and which makes him a fitting participant in God's great work.[6]

In both respects, as a manifestation of what Abraham possesses and as a full enactment of that possession, the trial is decisive for our view of Abraham's participation in the drama of God's greatness and glory. Indeed, the test comes upon the reader with such urgency because the question of Abraham's worthiness is so close to the surface of the preceeding narrative. It is as if the Genesis narrator were quite sensible that, up to this point, the story of Abraham has been much more a story of God than of a man, and he now wishes us to bring the qualities of this human covenant partner more fully into view with the clarifying scene of trial or test. In this way, we will be reassured that Abraham possesses real qualities of character which signal a genuine participation in the unquestionable greatness of God.[7]

Not only does Genesis 22 seem to fill the reader's desire for insight into that aspect of Abraham's character, but the trial also takes up the preceding form of Abraham's participation in God's promise. The extensive material on the birth of Isaac suggests that the main form of Abraham's participation in that promise of greatness has been through patrimony. However much Abraham might fail to possess military might or even moral character, at least he possesses a son after his flesh and, through this son, the greatness which is promised. What is so striking about the trial of Abraham, and what has made it so appealing to Christian interpreters, is that the dynamics of the test run contrary to this genealogical form of participation in divine greatness established earlier in the narrative and instead place emphasis on a quality distinctive to Abraham: his obedience. The test reveals to us why Isaac is not an extrinsic gift, but is an entirely fitting blessing which God has bestowed upon Abraham.[8]

Clearly, then, the setting of Genesis 22 encourages us to focus on Abraham and the question of how he participates in God's blessing. How, we find ourselves asking, does Abraham live up to the promise of chosenness? How does Abraham receive and retain the embodiment of the promise, his son Isaac? And by posing these questions in the context of a test, the narrative brings us toward clear answers. Yet, in so clearly answering the question of possession, the question of what virtue or excellence characterizes Abraham, the biblical narrative brings us directly to the problem of personal distinctiveness. We now turn to the famous story of Abraham's test to see how the excellence in Abraham's character is revealed and how that excellence is a problem.

The story begins as a poignant reversal of the preceding narrative. In Genesis 12, God calls Abraham out of the land of his fathers to a place, says the LORD, that "I will show you." In that land he has received a promise and a son in that promise. Now, at the end of his active career, the test begins with God calling Abraham to a new place, echoing the formula, "that I shall show you" (see Gen 12:1 and 22:2). But this is not a new start, but rather a macabre reversal of events. Where before events unfolded toward the birth of Isaac, now, in the compressed period of three days, events flow toward the sacrifice of Isaac. What the LORD has given, the LORD shall take away. And what does Abraham do? He obeys. Strikingly, this story neither hints of the Abraham who would bargain with God nor suggests the man who despaired of God's promises and resorted to subterfuge and deception. Both of these moments in the earlier Genesis material give Abraham a distinct personality. But now, in the context of his trial, Abraham is almost mechanical in his speech and behavior, obedient without hesitation. "Stay here with the donkey; the boy and I will go over there; we will worship, and then we will come back to you," says Abraham, speaking to his servants with the strictest economy of words, revealing absolutely nothing of the pathos of the moment. Indeed, only the voice of God speaks of that pathos. "Take your son, your only son Isaac, whom you love," says God. Only God, it seems, can speak of the emotions which swirl around the scene—the "only son" in whom Abraham has placed so much hope, and whom he loves. In contrast, Abraham's character is portrayed with striking one-dimensionality. God calls and commands: Abraham answers and obeys.

The Genesis account of Abraham's trial leaves nothing to chance. Abraham's obedience carries him to the point of raising his knife to slay his son, but an angel of the LORD calls out, giving us as readers the moral of the story: "Do not lay your hand on the boy or do anything to him; for now I know that you fear God, since you have not withheld your son, your only son, from me" (22:12). The test has revealed that quality of Abraham which makes him great—he withholds nothing from the LORD. This quality, variously described as faith, zealous obedience, steadfast piety, makes Abraham the worthy participant in God's great works. Indeed, with this quality so clearly manifested by the trial, Isaac is returned to Abraham. Throughout, Abraham participates in God's greatness through Isaac. But where God had previously given Isaac purely through the promise, now, at the conclusion of the test, Abraham possesses Isaac through his obedience as well. Abraham's outward possession of the promise in Isaac is now paired with an inward possession of faith.

Interpreted in this way, the trial of Abraham provides a rather tidy solution to the problem of possession. Abraham's chosenness does not rest upon him as an external and extrinsic fact, as it seems to do in the stories of deception. Abraham is a full participant in God's blessings through a quality distinctive to his character, that is to say, through his obedience. However, just at the point where the story of Abraham seems to move toward clarity about what, exactly, Abraham possesses which makes him genuinely part of the greatness which God has promised him, we find ourselves running head on into the problem of personal distinctiveness. How can the kind of obedience given stark form in Genesis 22 allow room for Abraham to have any personal significance? To be sure, in his test Abraham leaves behind those character traits which made him seem an inadequate covenant partner fear of worldly power and anxiety about his patrimony—but he manifests a quality which makes him seem an inhumanly focused fanatic, a single-minded madman who is willing to sacrifice his son. The story seems to say that Abraham, and by extension the reader as well, must empty himself in obedience in order to be the kind of person who can fully participate in God's blessing. But, we might legitimately ask, as has Nietzsche, whether there is an identifiable person left to enjoy God's blessing if the very quality we must possess is an obedience which is willing to sacrifice all that we love and hold dear.

This second difficulty can have an immediate intuitive purchase on our minds, but lacks clear shape and form. Yes, we might find ourselves saying, there is something very troubling about the Abraham of Genesis 22, but what, exactly, is the problem? We can make some headway by comparing the canonical account of Abraham's test and the version recounted by the Jewish historian Josephus in his *Jewish Antiquities* (I.13.1-4).[9] Where the Abraham of Genesis is laconic and devoid of any suggestion of reason or emotion, for Josephus, Abraham is a fully drawn character. In the canonical story, a single phrase uttered by the divine voice is freighted with the full weight of Abraham's relation to Isaac: "Take your son, your only son, whom you love" (22:2). In contrast, Josephus describes the beloved Isaac as devoted in filial obedience and excellent in the practice of virtue. What parent would not love such a son? Further, as the two journey to Moriah, Josephus is concerned to explain why Abraham is so brief with his servants, revealing nothing of either his plans or his emotions. According to Josephus, Abraham's zeal for obedience was married with a wisdom about human nature. Should he say more, his servants might try to prevent him from doing God's will.

In Josephus' account, Abraham anticipates this difficulty and tells his servants nothing of his plans so as to avoid their resistance to God's will. Most importantly, when the altar is prepared, Josephus composes a speech in Abraham's voice, and in that speech Abraham gives his reasons for his obedience to the divine commandment. Each of these additions—the elaboration of Abraham's relationship to Isaac, the interpolation of Abraham's motives for saying so little, and the entire speech of self-justification—has the effect of filling out the character of Abraham. What Genesis 22 presents as a remarkably thin human figure with no hint of passion, analysis, or deliberation, Josephus transforms into a person with commitments, plans, and reasons.

The contrast between Josephus' Abraham and the Abraham of Genesis 22 is telling. Where the canonical Abraham is empty, Josephus rushes to fill in the blanks. By filling in the blanks, Josephus creates a very different picture of how we participate in God's greatness and glory. Obedience of the sort described by Josephus allows for an independent character. Abraham possesses reasons for obeying. He has thought his way through the commandment to sacrifice his son and he sees its justice, even its beauty.[10] We can see the Abraham of Josephus' account as a multi-faceted individual with particular and justifiable attachments to his son, a wisdom about human nature, and a reasoned theological understanding of God's plans and purposes. In contrast, the Abraham of Genesis 22 possesses nothing other than obedience. He withholds nothing, he is willing to give everything in his obedience to God's commands. However, this attribute is very odd indeed: the more one is like Abraham, the more one possesses that which makes one a worthy partner in God's great works, the less one can claim to possess or to hold something which is distinctively one's own.

The ambiance of trial and test makes it crystal clear that obedience is the key, and we do in fact know what obedience entails. If commanded to take, go, and sacrifice, then one must take, go, and sacrifice. Yet, even though we see the figure of Abraham in this trial with exemplary clarity, what is there in him to grasp? How, exactly, might we understand Abraham so that we can begin the process of disciplining ourselves to be like him? With Josephus, the reader might quarrel with Abraham's reasoning, but with Genesis 22, is there anything there which even allows us to enter into Abraham's personality? Is he, finally, a recognizable person at all or does his obedience make him an extension of God's will? Should we conclude, then, that far from explaining how we might participate in something so great as God's promise of blessing, the solution proposed by Genesis 22 actually compounds the difficulties? The recognizably human Abraham of the deceptions seems unable to inhabit his chosenness, yet the worthy Abraham we encounter in the story of the binding of Isaac seems unrecognizable as a human being.

HEROISM IN HELLENISTIC JUDAISM

Although the trial of Abraham brings the quality and difficulty of obedience into stunningly sharp focus, the problem it presents is not unique. The biblical text offers a number of historical summaries which draw attention to important events and characters in the career of the nation of Israel (e.g., Joshua 24, Ezekiel 20, Nehemiah 9, Psalms 78, 105, 135 and 136).[11] Yet, when we turn to any of these summaries, the emphasis falls exclusively on God's actions.[12] Abraham and Isaac, Moses and Aaron, are important, but only because they are the recipients of God's steadfast love and beneficiaries of His righteous anger. Clearly, within the ambit of the canonical texts of the Hebrew Bible, extraordinary efforts are made to render the significance of ancestors as players in the unfolding drama of the covenant, a drama in which God is the initiating and sustaining agent. Yet, in spite of these efforts, precisely because the emphasis consistently falls upon God, the human actors tend to fade into pale and slender recipients of the promise of chosenness.

Yet, across the relentless scriptural emphasis upon the role of God, human endeavor often flashes up with importance. For example, in the deutero-canonical writings of the Hellenistic period, the Maccabean revolt looms large as a historical trial of faith in which human actors are portrayed as embodying significant and indispensible virtues. The revolt against Seleucid oppression of Temple worship began in 167 BCE. In an effort to evoke and adequately portray the heroism of those who rebelled, ancestors are recalled. The texts use these ancestors to invite us to see and imitate a distinctively human excellence. For example, 1 Maccabees 2:51-64 contains a catalogue of heroes. "Remember the deeds of the ancestors," we are told, and those ancestors are Abraham and Joseph, Pinehas and Joshua, Caleb and David, Elijah and Daniel. Each has done deeds of faithfulness which are worthy of honor. A similar list occurs in 4 Maccabees 16:20-21, emphasizing the steadfastness of Abraham and Isaac on Mount Moriah, Daniel among the lions, Hananiah, Azariah and Mishael in the fiery furnace.[13]

Both lists draw our attention to figures who exemplify an excellence. In this sense, the human figures of the earlier historical summaries come out from the background of the drama of the covenant and stand as actors with their own distinctive contribution. Yet even here we find that the passive element predominates. For what is the excellence which is pressed upon us, to be recognized and cherished? In 4 Maccabees, steadfast endurance and zealous obedience are the admirable traits of the ancestors. The author of 4 Maccabees emphasizes both when he evokes Abraham's trial: "Abraham was zealous to sacrifice his son Isaac, the ancestor of our nation; and when Isaac saw his father's hand wielding a knife and descending upon him, he did not cower" (4 Maccabees 16:20). The moral of the story is clear: "Fight zealously for our ancestral law" (16:16) with the zeal of Abraham, and endure pain and death with the courage of Isaac. Abraham's obedience to God's commandments endures even to the extreme of sacrificing his son. Isaac's trust in the Lord extends even to the acceptance of death. In both cases, the excellence highlighted points beyond itself. Both Abraham's zeal and Isaac's courage make them exemplary vehicles for divine action. In this sense, the Hellenistic texts arising out of the Maccabean revolt differ from the historical summary in Joshua 24 only by specifying the way in which the human actor participates in the divine drama. In both cases, however, the larger theme is the same: God is the hero. Moreover, neither diverges from the stark outlines of Genesis 22. The human heroism is to stand and obey. In this way, the faithful and zealous person participates in the unconquerable greatness and glory of God.

This absorption of human heroism into divine heroism, or, perhaps more accurately, this characterization of human heroism as a disposition of willingness to be taken up into divine heroism, is reinforced by the immediate context of the list of ancestral heroes found in 1 Maccabees. The excellence of these heroes has more to do with the strength of God than with the strength of their characters. "So observe," the author counsels, "from generation to generation, that none of those who put their trust in him will lack strength," concluding with the exhortation, "be courageous and grow strong in the law, *for by it you will gain honor*" (1 Maccabees 2:61,64). The final clause is crucial. Honor flows from the law, from the strength and honor of God, and not from the heroic characters. Steadfast endurance and zealous obedience are certainly attributes of the ancestors, attributes to be imitated and honored in the troubled times of the Maccabean revolt, but those qualities are exemplary because of the law. It and not heroic action is the source of honor. Here again we confront the enigma of biblical heroism. How can the zeal of Abraham and the courage of Isaac become anything more than transparent vessels of God's greatness? How can they be presented to us as worthy of attention and admiration when, in fact, our eyes should be on God? How can these exemplary figures possess or embody the honor which is, finally, God's? And, like Genesis 22, the answer is the same. We participate in God's greatness through obedience and faith, qualities especially manifest and most fully enacted in times of trial. But this solution is itself fraught with questions. Are the qualities of obedience and faith, however human they might be, thinning rather than thickening? Is zeal in obedience, even to the point of sacrificing our most intimate loves, a virtue which tends toward absorption into God rather than partnership with God?

TRAILS OF FAITH IN EARLY CHRISTIANITY

Within the Christian frame of reference, the way in which Abraham participates in God's greatness by giving himself and all he has entirely in obedience comes into sharp focus in the person of Jesus of Nazareth. Indeed, one can read the Christian account of Jesus' death as an intensification of the trial of Abraham. Not surprisingly, then, one of Paul's most famous and influential summaries of the significance of Jesus draws out exactly the same theme of obedient giving which characterizes the trial of Abraham. In the Letter to the Philippians, Paul writes that Jesus, who participates fully and completely in the greatness and glory of God, "emptied himself, taking the form of a servant, being born in the likeness of men. And being found in a human form he humbled himself and became obedient unto death, even death upon the cross" (Philippians 2:7-8). For Paul, we might say that Jesus is both Abraham and Isaac rolled into one, offering himself in sacrifice.[14] And Paul is quite clear that this self-emptying, humiliation, and sacrifice constitute the glory and greatness of Jesus. Precisely because of these things, "God has highly exalted him and bestowed on him the name which is above every name...."(Philippians 2:9). Like Abraham, Jesus's achievement is that he has withheld nothing.[15] Somehow, for the biblical hero of Genesis 22 and for the New Testament as a whole, giving up everything is the fullest possible form of our participation in divine greatness and glory.

Just as certain texts in Hellenistic Judaism highlighted the effectiveness of zealous faith, early Christianity insisted that there is an achievement and greatness in giving up everything, including oneself. Accounts of sainthood accent this power by narrating the saint's progress through the obstacles that stand in the way. Hagiographies usually take a perspective from which the power is located with the saint at least as much as with God, something acquired gradually,[16] not given instantaneously. The gradual possession of God's power is part of the process of development, and the mechanism is the test. The test is the focal point, and is as formative for the saint as it is revealing to the audience. Therefore, accounts of martyrdom and monastic discipline emphasize the agonistic nature of these lives. The faithful are tested by Satan directly, through deception, through persecution, even through their own appetites. But the faithful own their own successes: even if God provides the Spirit of discernment and the strength to endure, there is no mistaking that the faithful themselves are actively doing the discerning and the enduring. When the progressive development is emphasized, the characters become "thicker" and more recognizable as humans, and more imitable. They possess God's power *and* qualities or virtues worthy of that power.

The Life of St. Antony[17] provides an excellent case in point. Athanasius casts Antony in the patterns of several biblical characters, among them Job, Jesus, and Paul. In the desert, where Antony has gone to perfect his spiritual discipline, Satan attacks Antony in the famous temptations. Satan comes to Antony as a beautiful woman and as wild beasts, and tests him with gold and silver and with a physical assault that leaves Antony unconscious. Satan tempts Antony with pain (as he does Job), with physical appetites (as he does Jesus), and with the idols of Greek philosophy (as Paul experiences). According to Athanasius, Antony never seeks anything other than spiritual perfection—the fame that he receives as a result of his zeal is reported as a gift from God and is given after he has lived in solitude for twenty years. As he grows in age, he gains the powers of prophecy and healing; he is able to refute Greeks who come to question him, even though he is illiterate; and he attributes all of these abilities directly to God. Athanasius is emphatic: "It was clear to all that it was not he who did this, but the Lord bringing his benevolence to effect through Antony. Only the prayer was Antony's, and the discipline" (84). Athanasius emphasizes discipline rather than obedience, and he strips everything else from Antony but his discipline: Antony was heroic, but that heroism stemmed "neither from writings, nor from pagan wisdom, nor from some craft" (93). Though Antony wanted only to live in secret, God showed him "like a lamp to everyone," so that all might know the power of God.

Athanasius realizes the danger of Antony's discipline seeming to make him special in himself, and he carefully counters that tendency; but even so, Athanasius admires Antony the man, even as he ascribes the ultimate glory to God. Antony is described with certain heroic conventions. His every action is a battle, a struggle, a contest, or a fight; the whole work is laced with martial language describing Achillean invulnerability. His physical appearance is attractive and pleasant: even after 20 years of bread, water, extended fasts, and no bathing, he emerges healthy, and his countenance and movements reveal the stability and peace of his soul. He lived to the age of 105 with his eyesight and no cavities. His speech is gracious and civil, and he is irrefutable in argument. He founds a city of monks in the desert, and "administers" it with such wisdom and order that he is consulted by judges, military commanders, and emperors. And when he dies, the few things that he leaves behind are "great treasures" to their recipients, as memorials of the great man. These heroic conventions serve to fill out Antony's character so as to make him seem a worthy receptacle of this power of God.

As we began by saying, neither Judaism nor Christianity has traditionally viewed participation in God's greatness as a problem, and St. Antony can be seen as a supreme example of the combination of obedience and personal distinctiveness: the narrative can alternate between versions of *not Antony but God, Antony with God, God through Antony* without apparent discomfort. Antony becomes separable from Jesus only in the factual details of his life, not in the essence of his character or power. For Athanasius, Antony both possesses God's power through his obedient faith and has a personal distinctiveness. But Athanasius also reveals an awareness that some might be confused on that point, so he reaffirms relentlessly that the spectacular things about Antony were all from God. And at the same time, he treasures Antony's sheepskin and cloak like relics.

The test is a critical moment for understanding obedience and personal distinctiveness. Like the trial of Abraham, when Antony is tested by Satan, the attention shifts away from God and to the fitness of Antony as a vessel of God's power. According to Athanasius, Antony teaches that the question of divine victory is a closed one. God has all the power, Satan has none. The demons can only threaten; they are powerless to act; they are like actors on a stage, illusory (28).[18] In support of this Antony quotes from the book of Job, citing the permission God gives to Satan to test Job and the limitations of that permission. The only open questions concern Antony: will he manifest God's power over the devil, will his faith stand up to the challenge? However similar the trope of the test is, there are crucial differences between Genesis 22 and *The Life of St. Antony*. Abraham's test is an end in itself; Antony's tests are a means to greater perfection. Abraham's test comes near the end of his faith; Antony's tests come near the beginning of his. Abraham gives us nothing to imitate other than his obedience; Antony shows us steps to follow in his discipline. The account of Abraham is spare, even skeletal; Antony's is fleshed out and full. Athanasius does to Antony what Josephus does to Abraham: he fills him out with motivations, reasons, and personality. In the testing of Antony, Antony emerges as an individual progressing in his possession of God's power through his imitable discipline. He is more than self-emptying, more than mere obedience. For Athanasius, Antony appropriates the power of God—we all see, Athanasius implies, that Antony was godly because he lived an active, enacted, engaged life and obedience became his possession and his personality, unlike Genesis 22 and the obedience of Abraham. Athanasius' strategy is to have it both ways: ascetic self-denial is both an obedience and an achievement, both a possession and something imitable.

MILTON'S HERO OF ENDURANCE

John Milton is not so confident with Athanasius' strategy of personalizing obedience through a character and a life shaped by discipline, but he firmly believes in the importance of the test.[19] In a well-known passage in his *Areopagitica*, Milton requires the knowledge of sin for the true avoidance of sin:[20]

> I cannot praise a fugitive and cloistered virtue, unexercised and unbreathed, that never sallies out and sees her adversary, but slinks out of the race where that immortal garland is to be run for, not without dust and heat . . . . That virtue therefore which is but a youngling in the contemplation of evil, and knows not the utmost that vice promises to her followers, and rejects it, is but a blank virtue, not a pure; her whiteness is but an excremental whiteness.[21]

Untested virtue, which Milton deigns "fugitive and cloistered," is for him "blank"; enacted virtue, on the other hand, is "pure." The path between "blank" "white" and "pure" white is mediated through action, like the path between the infant Son of God celebrated in Milton's ode *On the Morning of Christ's Nativity* and the victorious Son of God hymned in the conclusion of *Paradise Regained.* A change takes place, though not in essence or quiddity — Milton does not suggest that unenacted virtue is not *virtue* — but in reality. Virtue unexercised through action is less strong, less substantial, less *itself* than realized, enacted virtue, like exposed but still undeveloped film. For Milton, like for Athanasius, enacted virtue is combatant, and he too uses martial language in describing victory over foes through conquest and warfare—but Milton applies this language to the single action of obedience.[22] Milton's virtue conquers in an enduring, not a destructive way. It participates in a footrace with evil; it does not fight it to the death or raze it to the ground.

This is true even in the greatest contest that the Christian world view imagines, that between Jesus and Satan. When in *Paradise Lost* the fallen Adam asks the archangel Michael for details about the promise of the "capital bruise" that the Serpent shall receive, "say when and where/Thir fight" (12.384-385), Michael responds clearly that violence is not the method of this victory, that it will not be "a Duel, or local wounds":

> Not by destroying Satan, but his works
> In thee and in thy Seed: nor can this be,
> But by fulfilling that which thou didst want,
> Obedience to the Law of God.
> (12.394-397)

Milton does not disagree with *The Life of St. Antony*: the contest is vital. However, by changing the terms of victory, and therefore of obedience, from the active resistance and repulsion of Satan to enduring and standing, Milton sets aside a straightforward use of the heroic tropes that Athanasius employs to fill out his description of Antony.[23] Milton rejects the location of personal significance in a progressive, imitable discipline. But Milton abandons neither the need for heroic achievement, which takes place in the context of the test, nor the need for recognizable human character.

Paradise Regained is Milton's great poem of testing. In it, Milton presents Jesus' victory and our participation in it; *Paradise Lost* explains our participation in our common human predicament. In fact, *Paradise Regained*, more than Milton's other poems, rejects the value of Greek and Roman literature straightforwardly, along with its picture of heroism. This rejection is explicit: when Satan offers Jesus the knowledge of the pagan cultures, Jesus refuses on the grounds that the philosophy, literature, and rhetoric of Greece and Rome are inferior to the Hebrew Scriptures because they lack "True wisdom" and have only "her false resemblance" (4.285-364). The role of the Scriptures is vital, as is the right use of them, because it is through them that Jesus knows who he is and that Satan knows who Jesus is. Of course, though their knowledge comes from the same source, it is not the same knowledge. Satan can conceive of heroism only in one way; it happens to be the way in which he understands himself. The Son cannot be understood in the same way; therefore, he cannot be understood by Satan. For the Son, what is heroic to Satan is not heroism. But Jesus must progress to the proper self-definition and, in so doing, reveal that definition to Satan, whether Satan understands it or not, and to the readers.[24] The Scriptures, and *right* knowledge of them, are an essential part of the test and of true heroism.

Satan tests Jesus in the wilderness, privately and secretly, as he tests Antony, and his temptations of Jesus share the forms of Antony's temptations, but not their substance. Satan first suggests turning stones to bread, "So shalt thou save thyself, and us relieve/ With Food"(1.344-345); that is, he tests Jesus not just with appetite, but with "false pity"[25] and good deeds. At an infernal council another demon, Belial, suggests the pleasure of sex, but Satan rejects that suggestion, of tempting Jesus with a woman, on the grounds that physical pleasure has been rejected by many and Jesus will require "manlier objects such as have more show/ Of worth, of honor, glory, and popular praise"(2.225-227). To Jesus himself, Satan claims to want to *see* his status as Son of God. He claims not to have lost the capacity

> To love, at least contemplate and admire
> What I see excellent in good, or fair
> Or virtuous; I should so have lost all sense.
> What can be then less in me than desire
> To see thee and approach thee, whom I know
> Declar'd the Son of God, to hear attent
> Thy wisdom, and behold thy Godlike deeds? (1.380-386).

What Satan offers and requests is, apart from himself, not inherently or obviously sinful. How could love, contemplation, and admiration of Jesus' divinity be wrong? When Jesus does nothing but refuse everything, Satan even questions the reality of his power: "A Kingdom they portend thee, but what Kingdom/ Real or Allegoric I discern not"(4.389-390). Satan wants

Jesus to use God's power to reveal himself; otherwise, Satan implies, he is invisible, and by remaining invisible the heroism of Jesus is blank rather than pure.

Satan argues that visibility comes through action, and as such it is an argument that Athanasius might not disagree with. We *see* Antony's discipline. What do we see of Jesus? Satan's power is equally and ultimately empty in both literary works. In words Antony might have said, Milton's Jesus tells Satan to "do as thou find'st/ Permission from above; thou canst not more"(1.495-496). But Jesus' faith and his fitness as a vessel of God's power are not the open questions that they are for Antony. In *Paradise Regained*, the test is entirely static, and the victory is static. Unlike Antony's, Jesus' progress is not easily identifiable, even though he emerges "By proof th' undoubted Son of God"(1.11). The testing is not a battle of deeds but of words and of understanding, of naming and claiming. Even so, Jesus and Satan are speaking different languages; on that score, they seem not to enter truly into conflict at all. Satan seems to make no real inroads into Jesus, but understandably so. Falsehood can no more make inroads into the truth than "unsubstantial" darkness and night can make inroads into the light of day.[26]

Milton declares in the prologue that the events of the temptation and the character of Jesus are "Above Heroic." By such he is not qualifying the results of the temptations. He is clear that they are real and significant—no less than "Paradise Recover'd"—and he is clear about the means of recovery: "by one man's firm obedience fully tried/ Through all Temptation." How this means, obedience fully tried, leads to that end, paradise recovered, is the problem. It is clear that Milton believes that there is something more in the wilderness test than revealing God's power and Jesus' worthiness. That would be conventional heroism with a Christian setting. In fact, that is what Satan *wants* the test to be. But for Jesus, being is the issue, not revealing, at least at the moment of the test. We, as readers neither entirely divine nor infernal, expect from the tests some account of Jesus' gradual becoming the Son of God. We never get it. Milton folds becoming into being; that is, by being the Son of God, Jesus becomes even more of what he is. Satan stresses an active revelation of that status. This is in essence Satan's one and only temptation of Jesus: act like the Son of God. Do something. Reveal yourself in true glory. Let the world see. Ironically, in the end the world does not see. Before his baptism, Jesus' life is "Private, unactive, calm, contemplative" (2.81); after his temptation he returns to his mother's home "unobserved . . . private"(4.638-639).

Jesus goes into the wilderness with unexercised faith and without exact knowledge. It is through the temptation that he gains the exercise and the knowledge. Yet Jesus' entire exercise is nothing more and nothing less than to obey:

> What if he [sc. God] hath decreed that I shall first
> Be tried in humble state, and things adverse,
> By tribulations, injuries, insults,
> Contempts, and scorns, and snares, and violence,
> Suffering, abstaining, quietly expecting,
> Without distrust and doubt, that he may know
> What I can suffer, how obey? Who best
> Can suffer, best can do; best reign, who first
> Hath well obeyed.
>
> (3.187-196)

The readers know that Jesus will suffer these things eventually, and Jesus knows, too. In *Paradise Regained*, however, there are no injuries, insults, contempts, or scorns, and no open violence. The more "heroic" fortitude that he will display in "due time"(3.182) through his public trial and crucifixion is no different from his fortitude in standing and waiting "without distrust and doubt" during the private temptations in the wilderness. The patient obedience in the desert is no less significant for our salvation than the patient endurance of the cross.[27]

Ultimately, Jesus does nothing in the *Paradise Regained* except withstand. Satan asks for good reason, after Jesus has refused everything (wealth, honor, arms, arts, kingdom, empire, glory, and fame): "What dost Thou in this world? The Wilderness/ For thee is fittest place" (4.372-373). It is hard not to ask this question along with Satan, as many readers have. Satan's final temptation of Jesus is to carry him[28] to the top of the temple in Jerusalem and challenge him to throw himself down. Jesus simply quotes the Hebrew Bible back: "'Tempt not the Lord thy God' he said and stood." (4.561) Milton's Jesus does absolutely nothing but stand, and his stasis is his obedience, his possession, his nature, and his heroism. Milton's Jesus goes from blank to pure by doing nothing, which is a different solution to the problems of possession and personal distinctiveness. By doing nothing but standing in God, there seems to be no danger that Jesus will float free and represent individual and distinctive heroism. At the same time, as a personal possession, standing may seem a spectral possession, a doing nothing at all.

To the degree that God is the true hero and source of heroism, Milton believes something completely opposite, that our active personal distinctiveness is specious, vain, and meaningless. In his other works, he offers us heroes who though active fail, who truly do nothing because they fail to obey. In contrast to these heroes, the standing of the Son of God does seem to be a real achievement, even a possession. Adam in *Paradise Lost* provides the best counter example. Adam's full humanity would have been expressed had he obeyed; but he did not, as the first line of the epic reveals: "Of man's first disobedience and the fruit of that forbidden tree . . . Sing heavenly Muse." Of course, Milton's song in *Paradise Lost* has a promissory component. His muse sings not only of man's Disobedience but of "one greater Man" who will "restore us" (1.4-5). The archangel Michael explains clearly how that greater Man will accomplish this: by obedience (*PL* 12.393-410). That greater man, for Milton, was Jesus. In his epic, Adam learns too late: "Henceforth I learn, that to obey is best" (12.561), to which Michael responds: "only add/ Deeds to thy knowledge answerable . . . then wilt thou not be loath/ To leave this Paradise, but shalt possess/ A paradise within thee, happier far" (12.581-2, 585-7). Adam's relation to heroic humanity is like his relation to faithful Christianity: he is a blank template, exposed but undeveloped film. He is belief without participation. The true hero of *Paradise Lost* is the Son of God, the warrior-hero in the fight against Satan and Death, and Michael's long prophecy in the twelfth book underscores that heroism. Milton's epic follows the pattern of the Hebrew Bible: the role of hero belongs to God and to God's Son in the *Paradise Lost*. *Paradise Lost* is about the heroism of God along the lines of the Hebrew Bible. *Paradise Regained* captures the moment of obedience, before the active heroism of God, when the Son, "quietly expecting," must wait for the right time and withstand the temptation to act otherwise.

THE DILEMMAS OF MODERN HEROISM

Milton is often seen as a precursor of the modern age in his views championing personal freedom and conscience. Both combine to shape a readily identifiable modern hero, a Henry David Thoreau who bucks social conventions in faithfulness to conscience or a Martin Luther King, Jr. who risks personal harm in the service of justice. Our American mythology is full of figures who stand up against corrupt authority or mindless collectivism. To a great extent, these heroes do fit Milton's pattern. However, when the lens is focused on the issues of heroic testing and obedience, we can see just how fragile is the balance which Milton strikes between a hero with enduring individuality and a heroism which is more than a mere expression of individuality. For in his answer to the problems of possession and personal significance, Milton is far closer to the narrator of Genesis 22 than to prevailing and popular assumptions about the unique and abiding significance of the individual person.

Obedient enduring is a heroic achievement because it allows us to participate in the greatness and glory of God. In this sense, Milton's Jesus does nothing more than articulate the logic of Abraham's laconic obedience. Yet, Milton's poetic genius lies in his ability to convince us that enduring is true heroic action and accomplishment. In the maelstrom of temptations, we attain height and breadth by standing strong. Against the enduring stability of biblical heroism, Milton is able to portray all the active, independent, creative figures of Hell as, finally, empty and futile. As for our personal significance, Milton declares not only that our enduring and obedient standing is a real achievement, in fact the only real achievement, but also that it is truly ours. In his "modern" works which champion freedom and conscience, such as the *Areopagitica*, Milton is arguing that Christians should always and everywhere be allowed to enter into the test of faith, since it is only in the test of faith that personal significance is found. As our faith moves from blank to pure we become heroically "thick" human beings. For Milton, obedient enduring is the one distinctive achievement that is not absorbed into God. To a great extent, modern heroes of conscience are patterned after Milton's Christ-hero. Their importance is not in their achievements or creations. Instead, they command our admiration because they have stood strong against a storm of temptation. Outwardly, Thoreau accomplished nothing by going to jail. Yet, his fortitude against the compelling powers of the state and the insidious pressure of social disapprobation makes him a great witness to the inviolability of conscience. Conscience is divine, and to endure in obedience to conscience consecrates modern life with dignity. To this Thoreau's life testifies. The modern mythic landscape is dotted with Thoreauian heroes of conscience. Even as the religious and moral certainties of premodern life crumble, the ideal of steadfast faithfulness to our inner sense of rectitude endures as an ideal.

Pressed too far, however, the equation of conscience with divinity undermines Milton's delicate solution to the problem of portraying obedience as heroic. We easily transform the obedience to conscience into obedience to self, and very quickly the narrow path of rectitude becomes a compulsive and scattered impulse to say and do whatever constitutes the "real me." The dignity of conscience descends into the banality of self-expression. The upshot is the most unhelpful of maxims: "Be yourself." This is a counsel of despair, and the high vocation of Milton's hero to possess the mark of divinity in the form of enduring obedience crashes to earth, as ordinary veniality is sanctified as "genuine" or "authentic." If we insist upon constituting our dignity through self-expression rather than inhabiting it through obedience to conscience, then we are left with the very thin heroism of individuality for its own sake. Far from heroically "thick" human beings, the achievements of modern individuality disappear into the thinnest vapors of feeling, the spectral and labyrinthine deceptions of the "real me."

Just this tendency in modern heroism, the relentless shift from personal fidelity to the divine to faithfulness to oneself, exposes a paradox as profound as the enigma of Abraham's obedience. Whereas the biblical ideal threatens to absorb our distinctiveness into the eternity and infinity of divine glory, the modern ideal seems to condemn us to the insignificance and mediocrity of our little corner of the cosmos. If we are the sole source and measure of the greatness and dignity of our heroic accomplishments, then can our lives be heroic?

Notes

[1] The literary forms of the biblical emphasis upon God's preeminent role are manifold. One particularly clear case is the way in which the biblical narrative presents armed conflict. As Leonard Greenspoon has shown, the conduct of warfare in biblical and post-biblical Jewish literature consistently subordinates human strength and power to divine strength and power, even to the point of entirely superseding human efforts. See "The Warrior God, or God, the Divine Warrior," in *Religion and Politics in the Modern World* (New York: New York University Press, 1983), 205-231.

[2] See *Genealogy of Morals* (New York: Random House, 1967), Essay Three. There, Nietzsche describes the discipline and obedience of faith as a vivisection of the soul (Section 9), as world-denying (Section 10), as self-inflicted pain (Section 11), as self-contempt and self-mockery (Section 12).

[3] See Nietzsche's account of the inverse relationship between divine dignity and human worth, *Genealogy of Morals*, Essay Two, Sections 19-21.

[4] We use the Revised Standard Version throughout the paper.

[5] Consider, for example, the way in which the Genesis story handles the scene of Abraham's military victory over the enemies of the King of Sodom. Abraham is portrayed as an adept strategist, but when the time comes for dividing the spoils of

victory, Abraham sets himself outside the framework of military greatness. Like Achilles, he turns down gifts. To the king of Sodom, he says, "I have sworn to the LORD, God most high, maker of heaven and earth, that I would not take a thread or a sandal-thong or anything that is yours, so that you might not say, 'I have made Abram rich'" (Gen 14:22-23). However, unlike Achilles, Abraham turns away entirely from the ambiance of military excellence. Abraham's greatness is not his prowess on the battlefield. His greatness flows from the fact that he owes all to God — a greatness highlighted by his refusal of the gifts of the king of Sodom, gifts which would have put him into the debt of someone other than the LORD.

[6] See Psalm 26 where the psalmist petitions for the opportunity to be tested. The petition need not presume that God is blind to the integrity of the psalmist and that the psalmist wishes for a test to bring his sanctity to the attention of God. Instead, the petition is for the opportunity to bring sanctity into its fullest form and development through enduring tests and trials. This petition for the opportunity to enact what is already possessed runs through the Christian literature of martyrdom like a red thread. Consider, for example, Ignatius of Antioch's *Letter to the Romans,* available in *Early Christian Fathers*, ed. and trans. Cyril C. Richardson (New York: Collier Books, 1970). There, Ignatius pleads with the Romans that they not interfere with his imprisonment and execution. He treats his trials as an opportunity to become more fully the faithful witness he hopes he already is ("if you quietly leave me alone, people will see in me God's Word" 2:1). Even further, as one who is to suffer and die for Christ, he anticipates a fuller form of discipleship ("Then I shall be a real disciple of Jesus Christ" 4:2) and that he will even come to inhabit the very glory and salvation of Christ ("If I suffer, I shall be emancipated by Jesus Christ; and united to him, I shall rise to freedom" 4:3). In no sense does Ignatius anticipate acquiring anything new. He already possesses Christ and salvation in faith. Yet, by enduring a trial on behalf of that faith, he hopes that he might become more completely and more visibly that which he already is.

[7] An ancient pseudoepigraphic retelling of Genesis, the book of Jubilees, suggests otherwise. (English translation in *The Old Testament Pseudoepigrapha*, ed. James H. Charlesworth [New York: Doubleday & Co., 1985].) As an introduction to the story of the testing of Abraham, Jubilees echoes Job by narrating a scene in which Satan comes before God to request a test of Abraham's faith (17:15-18). For the divine perspective, this test is unnecessary. Abraham has already been tested: "with his land, and with famine," "with the wealth of kings," "with his wife," "with circumcision," "with Ishmael and with Hagar." "And," concludes the text, "in everything which [God] tested him, he was found faithful." The reader senses that the writers of Jubilees were concerned that Abraham always be a worthy covenant partner, so concerned that they suggest rather strained readings of Abraham's flight to Egypt and the deceptions with his wife as acts of covenant faithfulness! Nonetheless, Satan's wish is granted, and Abraham is tested again, and the upshot is that the faithfulness which is obvious to God (and to the godly or "spiritual" reader of entire story of Abraham) is evident even to Satan (and the unholy or

"carnal" reader).

[8] See Targum Pseudo-Jonathan. An English translation is provided by J.W. Etheridge (New York: Katv Publishing House, 1968). This retelling of Genesis 22 begins with a dispute between Isaac and Ishmael in which Ishmael claims superiority over Isaac and, on that basis, lays a claim to Abraham's inheritance. Ishmael brags that he had been circumcised at the age of majority, while Isaac was circumcised as a newborn. Ishmael taunts Isaac, "If you had been aware, perhaps you would not have handed yourself over to be circumcised." Isaac rises to the challenge and says that his claim to his father's inheritance is entirely justified, for he is willing to give over his entire self to God. Following upon Ishmael's allusion to circumcision, Isaac seems to be saying, in effect, that he is willing to have his neck circumcised!

This introduction to Genesis 22 offers an extraordinarily fertile field for speculation. Targum Pseudo-Jonathan's elaboration of a debate between Ishmael and Isaac shifts the question forward one generation. How is Isaac rather than Ishmael a fitting recipient of the promise? This shift forward may suggest the influence of Christianity, which does not call into question Abraham's status as chosen but calls into question a Jewish understanding of who inherits that chosenness. Perhaps the Targum has in mind the Pauline claim that faith in Jesus circumcises the heart, a claim which, in the context of the Christian elevation of the martyrs, might be transformed into a boast. "See," we can imagine the early Christians saying to Jewish opponents, "circumcision of the heart is a far more powerful service to God than circumcision of flesh." The Targum writers then respond by interpolating a scene of martyrdom into Genesis 22, proving that circumcision of the flesh is vindicated by a courage and commitment as deep as any Christian might imagine.

In the end, these speculations are not as important as recognizing how the dominant question in the Targum is the same as that of the canonical text and, ultimately, the same as Christianity: what is the character of those who are chosen? This question is sufficiently basic to both Judaism and Christianity that it emerges on its own and not just in the context of engagement and polemic. A simple intra-textual question, "Why Isaac and not Ishmael?," is sufficient to motivate the kinds of interpolations one finds in the Targum.

[9] English translation is available in the Loeb edition: *Josephus IV: Jewish Antiquities Books I-IV*, trans. H. Thackery (Cambridge: Harvard University Press, 1930).

[10] Josephus has Abraham pronounce the pending sacrifice of Isaac a blessing. Isaac shall leave the world amidst prayer and ceremony rather than by the common way of sickness, war, and calamity. Further, by allowing himself to be sacrificed, reasons Abraham, Isaac will in fact fulfill the blessing of his birth by securing the protection of the blessing of God. On Josephus's portrayal of Abraham, see further Louis H. Feldman, "Abraham the General in Josephus," in *Nourished with Peace: Studies in Hellenistic Judaism in Memory of Samuel Sandmel*, ed.

Frederick E. Greenspahn, Earle Hilgert, and Burton L. Mack (Chico, California: Scholars Press, 1979), 43-49.

[11] For a discussion of each of these historical summaries and their role in identifying exemplary ancestors, see Pamela Michelle Eisenbaum, *The Jewish Heroes of Christian History* (Atlanta: Scholars Press, 1997), 20-35.

[12] See F. M. Cross, *Cannaanite Myth and Hebrew Epic* (Cambridge: Harvard University Press, 1973).

[13] English translations of 1 and 4 Maccabees are found in the NRSV Oxford Annotated Bible with Apocryphal/Deuterocanonical Books.

[14] Irenaeus also merges Abraham and Isaac, although not in the person of Jesus, but in obedient discipleship. In an extended demonstration of the fulfillment of Old Testament figures in Christian teaching and practice, Irenaeus observes, "Righteously also do we, possessing the same faith as Abraham, and taking the cross as Isaac did the wood, follow [Christ]" (*Adv. Haer.*IV.5.4). (English translations found in *The Ante-Nicene Fathers*, vol. 1, ed. Roberts and Donaldson (Grand Rapids: William B. Eerdmans Publishing, 1953).

[15] See, also, Romans 8:32: "He who did not spare his son but gave him up for us all." For a consideration of the role of Genesis 22 in the formation of both Jewish and Christian conceptions of atoning death, see Alan Segal, "Sacrifice of Isaac in Early Judaism and Christianity," in *The Other Judaisms of Late Antiquity,* ed. A. Segal (Atlanta: Scholars Press, 1987), 109-130.

[16] Cf. the preface to R. Gregg's translation of *The Life of St. Antony*, where W. Clebsch speaks of "the ladderlike quality of the saintly life, in which each higher step risked a harder fall" (New York: Paulist Press, 1980), xv.

[17] All quotations are taken from R. Gregg's translation of Athanasius, *The Life of Antony and The Letter to Marcellinus* (New York: Paulist Press, 1980).

[18] The same allusion to drama appears in John Milton's *Paradise Regained.* All quotations from Milton are taken from *John Milton: Complete Poems and Major Prose*, ed. Merritt Y. Hughes (Indianapolis: Odyssey Press, 1957). When Satan returns to the desert to tempt Jesus, he takes with him "a chosen band/ Of Spirits likest to himself in guile/ To be at hand, and at his beck appear/ If cause were to unfold some active scene/ Of various persons, each to know his part" (2.236-240). Cause does not occur in *Paradise Regained*, unless the "Infernal ghosts and hellish Furies" of the storm are parts played by these actors (cf. 4.419-431).

[19] There is no mention of St. Antony nor of Athanasius' *Life of Antony* in Milton. Milton read Athanasius and quotes several of his works, some approvingly, some disparagingly, in his anti-prelatical tract "On Reformation" and also in the *First Defense*, for example. Milton may have read Athanasius in the 1601 edition of his *Opera* by Nannius, published in Heidelberg (cf. *Complete Prose Works*, I, ed. Don M. Wolfe, p. 564, fn. 164). The possibility that Milton did *not* know of the *Life of Antony* seems quite remote, since it is generally regarded as the most influential text for the formation of Christian monasticism and is mentioned in other authors, such as Augustine, whom Milton also read and knew well. We

know of no attempt at a comparative study of Athanasius' *Life* and Milton's *Paradise Regained*; though Merritt Hughes, in his introduction to *Paradise Regained*, remarks that the Christ of *PR* is "a figure less like St. Anthony than he is like Ghandi."(1957:478). Some similarities are discussed throughout this paper, such as the dramatic nature of the demons mentioned at footnote 18 above, but for the purposes of this paper these similarities need not have been intentional. We are inclined to think, however, that they are not accidental or the inevitable result of Athanasius' approximation of Antony's temptations with Christ's. Milton knew what he was doing.

[20] For what Stanley Fish calls "the piecing together of the shattered image of truth . . . the recovery of the unified moral vision of Edenic innocence" (*Surprised by Sin: The Reader in Paradise Lost*, [Berkeley: University of California Press, 1967], 160).

[21] *Areopagitica*, 728.

[22] Fish's influential study discusses this "singleness" in Milton's mind: in Adam and Eve's sin were *all* sins; in the command to obey God was the entire Law; and "Faith, discipline, obedience— they are one, along with heroism and love; and none of them can be invoked to sanction a movement away from God"(1967:157-159).

[23] Cf. Fish's chapter 4, "Standing Only: Christian Heroism"(1967:158-207).

[24] It is important that Milton does conceive of stages in Jesus' self-realization, even though he obscures those stages in the course of the temptations. Milton's Jesus recalls his progressions up to his withdrawal to the desert in a meditation: first his childhood was marked by delight in the Law of God; then "victorious deeds/ Flamed in my heart, heroic acts"; then he determined "By winning words to conquer willing hearts." Mary then revealed to him the miracles and prophecies of his birth; he then realized that he was the Messiah and "that my way must lie/ Through many a hard assay even to the death." After his baptism by John, God "pronounc'd me his,/ Me his beloved Son, in whom alone/ He was well pleas'd." "The Spirit has led him into the desert, "to what intent/ I learn not yet; perhaps I need not know;/ For what concerns my knowledge God reveals"(1.196-294).

[25] Anthony Low, *The Georgic Revolution* (Princeton:Princeton University Press, 1984), 338: "Satan urges the Son to lift all the hardships from life."

[26] Milton makes this assessment of darkness and night himself, as "Privation mere of light and absent day" (4.397-400).

[27] For this reason, Anthony Low and others see the genre of *Paradise Regained* as "heroic georgic." Cf. Low (1984:351): "Like the *Georgics*, *Paradise Regained* does not describe a pastoral retreat from responsibility but instead dwells on small, recurrent actions, often trivial or inglorious in themselves, that nevertheless converge toward a turning-point in the world's history that will be truly apocalyptic."

[28] There is a suggestion of violence here, present in the temptations of Antony,

which is otherwise lacking from the temptations in *Paradise Regained*. Jesus' victory is one over violence. Milton's simile of Satan's fall compares his defeat of Antaeus, whom Hercules killed simply by lifting from the earth from which he drew strength. Milton probably knew the battle of Hercules and Antaeus primarily from Lucan, *Pharsalia* 4.588-660 (trans. J.D. Duff [Cambridge: Harvard University Press, 1928]). See also J.G. Frazer's translation and notes to Apollodorus, *The Library* 2.5.22 (Cambridge: Harvard University Press, 1921).

The Bible and Art at the End of the Millennium: Words, Ideas and Images

Ori Z. Soltes

I. WORDS AND THE *OTHER*

The notion of the power of the *Word* helps to account for the centrality of the Bible as an instrument of intermediation between humanity and Divinity. The *Word* which is the Bible is spoken by God through a range of prophets; *words* are the particular shape that each prophet accords to that Word. Words function as an instrument as well with respect to intra-human contact: they extend us and join us to each other; words offer us communication options that no other species on the planet apparently has. But they can also function, by paradox, to obstruct relationships, to obfuscate: we have the ability to speak words that don't say what we mean or that do not really express what we feel and which thus end up distancing us from each other rather than bringing us closer to each other.

Historically, then, humans have used words both poorly and well to explore our own reality—to try to express what it is that is around us and in a very fundamental and important way to try to explore and explain that Other reality, which either is out there (as traditionalists of all religions assume) or, because there is something in our brains that makes us humans, we believe is out there (as some secular psychologists would assert). We have used words as instruments in our attempt to understand that Other reality that we believe has created us and, we presume, has the power to destroy us — and that is, by definition, so unfathomable and ungraspable as to be *inaccessible* to words.

All questions pertaining to the issue of what sort of entity that Other might be are part of the province of religion, and religion makes use of words in order to explain that other and its relationship to us. Indeed, Judaism, Christianity, and Islam are three instance of religions which make particularly emphatic use of words to explore and explain. The Bible is one of *many* texts whose words have been used for millennia to try to understand the God that is, according to these traditions, the very source of the words within it.

An endless flow of words has sought to fathom the Divine Word. Thus, in the Jewish tradition there are angles of exploration that use words to dig beneath the surface of the Biblical words. The process which is referred to in Jewish terms as *midrash*—a term that derives from a root *(d-r-sh)* meaning "to dig," "to dig beneath the surface" of things—has been evolving for well over two thousand years.

But *Midrash* is not merely an aspect of *Jewish* textual thinking. It is found (if obviously not called by its Hebrew name) in Christianity and Islam as well, in their encounters with the stories and issues embedded in the Bible. Indeed if one looks at the Gospels one after the other, one realizes that they *are* a form of midrash: they offer four different ways of digging underneath the surface of the basic biographies of Jesus and those around him. The Qur'an, while it is not a sequential narrative, offers in part an interpretive digging beneath the surface of issues whose original verbal/written forms one finds in the Hebrew Bible and in the New Testament. In Christian, Muslim, and Jewish traditions, then, one observes continuous digging—layers of literature of interpretation—beneath and around the words of the Qur'an, the Gospels and the rest of the New Testament, the Torah and the Hebrew Bible, as we attempt to understand what it is that the God upon which all three faiths focus their attention has in mind for us as a purpose and meaning for our lives.

II. WORDS AND IMAGES: GENESIS' FIRST FAMILIES

Words (to repeat) are limited as instruments of exploring God: not only can they deliberately obfuscate, but they can only express and therefore intermediate up to a point. Thus religion has also made use of other means to grasp the Other. We have used images, as we have used music and dance, as concomitants of words to explore and to explain God. Images function *intrinsically* as a kind of midrash, digging *beneath the surface* of texts like the Bible to interpret their words and interpret the issues imbedded within the words. Visual midrash, like its verbal counterpart, is found across the panoply of human faiths generally, but it is a significant part of Judaism, Christianity, and Islam in particular, in their respective wrestling matches with meaning in the Hebrew Bible.

My primary focus in what follows is on Jewish images that have emerged during the past few decades to address the Bible and its questions. By "Jewish" I mean two things. First, most of the artists whose work I will consider are Jewish. Second, the text upon which I focus is what Jews regard as the totality of God's Word, the Hebrew Bible. I am not focusing on art that devotes itself to the New Testament, to the Qur'an, or for that matter to the Apocrypha or Pseudepigrapha. Nor should this discussion be taken as a definitive presentation of all the outstanding artists so engaged, but rather as an introduction to some of the range of engagement.

In focusing on the Hebrew Bible, one might start where it starts, with an image of *Adam and Eve* (Figure 1) by Bill Giacalone, an artist from New Jersey. With regard to his style, the first thing that one observes is the rich use of color; one can readily recognize how indebted the artist is to Marc Chagall, in his soft use of blue and green and red with a kind of general symbolic intention: blue the color of the sky and thus (for heaven is associated with God) the color of truth; green the color of the earth (of the grass, of the trees, of the spring), of birth and rebirth; and red the color of passion, the color (through its obvious association with blood) of sacrifice. One observes that

Figure 1 *Adam and Eve*

he focuses on Eve. Adam is reduced to a small black and white figure, a kind of shadow figure up under the crescent moon.

Eve dominates the painting in a form that, on the one hand, calls to mind any number of paintings that from the Renaissance to our own time focus on a woman lying on a couch: an *odalisque*—the kind of portrayal offered by Titian, Giorgione, Manet, Boucher, Pascin, and others through the last five centuries. Thus Giacalone, tongue perhaps ever-so-slightly in cheek, simply makes Eve part of that seductive sequence.

On the other hand, in considering such a sensuous style, one is perhaps not surprised to realize that this artist has worked successfully as an illustrator for *Penthouse* magazine. So his interest in women and his midrash that focuses primarily on Eve are all in part a function of his thinking about Eve both as the mother of humankind and as the one who initiates the seductive process which ultimately makes humankind possible. If Eve does not convince Adam to taste of the fruit of which she tastes, and if they aren't removed from the Garden of Eden, and if they don't grow up in sexual as well as other ways, then we wouldn't perhaps be here considering these matters. Part of the source of his Eve-focus, of course, may simply be Bill Giacalone's playfully salacious nature: what interests him he places in the foreground.

In a second *Adam and Eve* (Figure 2) by the same artist, once again we observe an emphasis that is far more on the erotic than on the sinful. This is clearly the moment after which the primordial couple have eaten from the famous fruit—which, with its missing bites, the artist has strategically placed

Figure 2 *Adam and Eve*

so that one's eye cannot help but move from the fruit up towards Eve by way of the inner thighs toward which Adam is also gradually working his way.

That the issue is the beginning of the propagation of humankind and that at the same time this is a delicate romantic moment—this is a first kiss, not original sin—we see through his midrashic eyes. Even the serpent weaves a rather lyrical encirclement of them, in sensibility far from the image of the Satanic bringer of the Fall from Grace that is the traditional Christian and sometime Jewish understanding of that creature. Here he is part and parcel of a picture that is positive and that is love-focused (or at least love-making focused) rather than sin-focused.

A rather different use of a biblical idea comes as one follows the biblical narrative forward from one generation to the next in a work by Catherine Kahn. In that narrative, no sooner are Adam and Eve out of the garden, no sooner have they come to know each other sexually, then they bear their first progeny, Cain and Abel. If the first human sin was the disobedience to God on the part of Adam and Eve, the second sin is the murder of Abel by Cain—although it is perhaps less the murder of Abel than Cain's failure to take responsibility for it that is the sin. One could argue that when he smashes his brother over the head—or whatever means he uses to act out his anger towards him— never having seen a dead person, never having seen an act of human killing before, he may not understand the consequences of what he is doing. But surely by the time God comes around and asks him what he did, Cain knows that Abel is not getting up again, and it is at that point perhaps that his failure to own up to what he has done places him in the arena of sin (and furthers the paradox of human existence: we are so creative and so destructive).

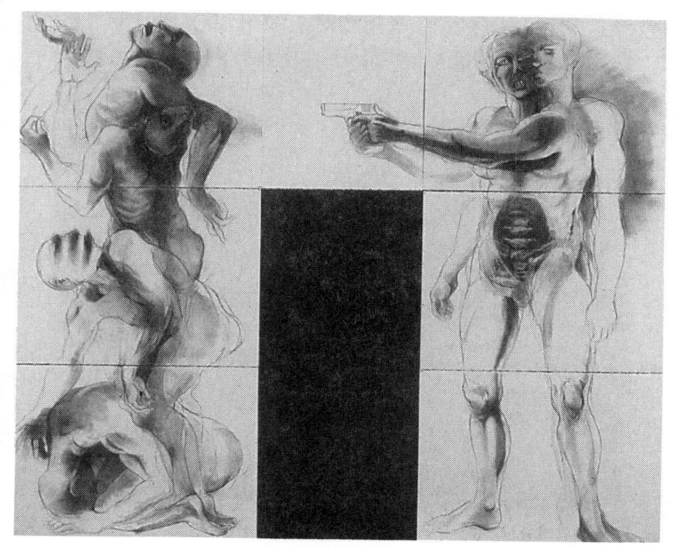

Figure 3 *Cain and Abel*

And that hasn't changed.

If Kahn has given us a painting of *Cain and Abel* (Figure 3), this is only the first part of the title; the subtitle is *The Assassination of Rabin*. She has taken the biblical subject and transformed the figure of Abel into the figure of Yitzhak Rabin conceptually—midrashically—by the imposition of words (the title) upon the image; she also thereby transforms the figure of Rabin's murderer into the figure of Cain. Again this is not by way of the details of the image, but by the intellectual reconception of who he is—because the artist *says* that this is who he is. It is a rather extraordinary use of words imposed on an image to clarify for us what we otherwise might not have understood. One recognizes in Kahn's *style* the tradition of the Renaissance: the twisting and turning of bodies, one of them facing away from us, one facing toward us, in order to give us a sense that we are not seeing pencil or charcoal on a flat piece of paper, but figures moving through volumetric space, with light and shadow falling upon them. This is as much a part of her concern as is her intention to make a political statement by allusion both to the world around her and to that most ancient of stories, in one fell swoop underscoring the timelessness of Cain's act.

A second work by Catherine Kahn also reflects her interests in the human form as it has been explored over the millennia in the Western tradition. The subject is *Jacob Wrestling the Angel* (Figure 4), moving us

Figure 4 *Jacob Wrestling the Angel*

several biblical generations forward. If on the one hand we see the imprint of Pollaiuolo (and of Michelangelo, Leonardo, and all those fifteenth and sixteenth century Italian artists who scrutinized and so effectively reproduced the human physiognomy on paper), on the other hand we also recognize the post-Freudian psychological approach to the tradition of Jacob wrestling an angel (that Jacob wrestles with his conscience and his anxiety dreams) and we ask the question: what *is*, after all, an angel? What is a *malach*, to use the Hebrew term that is rendered by way of Greek to Latin to English as "angel"? It is an emissary, something between God and ourselves, between heaven and earth. The problem with this is that if we were pagan Greeks or Romans or Egyptians, who worshiped many gods, and if accordingly our understanding of that Other reality were that it has many aspects to it, then an angel would pose no conceptual problem to our thinking. But the understanding that we have as Jews, Christians, and Muslims is that the Other is (inhabited by) a single entity called God. Such a pattern of understanding does not technically or logistically leave room for some kind of intermediary series of beings. Yet the Hebrew biblical text, the foundation stone of Judaism and Christianity as well as, albeit more indirectly, Islam, has ample references to such creatures. So we really cannot know who or what they are, can we? They are simply a contradiction in terms; they are a paradox perfectly appropriate to a paradox-filled text, perfectly appropriate to what the text wrestles to present (the ongoing wrestling match/relationship between God and ourselves), and perfectly appropriate to be wrestled with in the wrestling match represented by Kahn.

Indeed the artist responds to this issue by offering us a figure wrapped in a figure or a figure wrapped in itself; a figure that is not two but seems at one and the same time to be one, two, and multiple figures. This is the ultimate kind of visual statement of a psychological wrestling match, which is after all what Jacob surely would have had on the night before seeing his brother Esau after having been apart for twenty years. Having cheated his brother of the birthright, albeit so many years earlier, Jacob has no idea how Esau is going to behave when he sees him that next morning. Surely he is wrestling all night long with whatever memories, thoughts, fears, hopes, and concerns have emerged in the night. This is one among many passages in the Hebrew Bible that deal ultimately with the issue of relationship. In this case, the issue is that of relationship with one's self, with one's sibling, and with God — whereby Jacob's name will be transformed to *Israel*, "one who has striven with God."

III. FROM PATRIARCHS TO KINGS: THE ART OF MALE-FEMALE RELATIONS

The issue of relationship brings us, both narratively and visually, simultaneously backward and forward: back to the idea, begun with Adam and Eve, of the relationship between man and woman; forward in the biblical narrative to *David and Bathsheva* (Figure 5). Back again to an image by Bill Giacalone: once again the Chagallesque representation, once again the female as the dominating figure. Once more one notes how unique this is as far as the history of art is concerned because it is absolutely antithetical to the text of the Bible itself, and therefore to traditional representation, that Bathsheba be the primary focus. In the Bible she is barely mentioned as far as the importance of her role in the progression of history is concerned. The focus is on David, as it is in the usual midrashic traditions that follow. Giacalone has radically altered that "norm" and given us a much larger focus on the woman than on the man. Center stage belongs to the wife of a Hittite mercenary rather than to the king of Israel, who is the beginning point of Israelite greatness in the political sense, and the ancestor and descendant of so much of significance in the spiritual sense. For the artist, all of that significance shrinks before the figure of a woman. But she *is*, after all, the cause of it all: her desirability inspiring David to pile sin upon sin; and later, the mother of

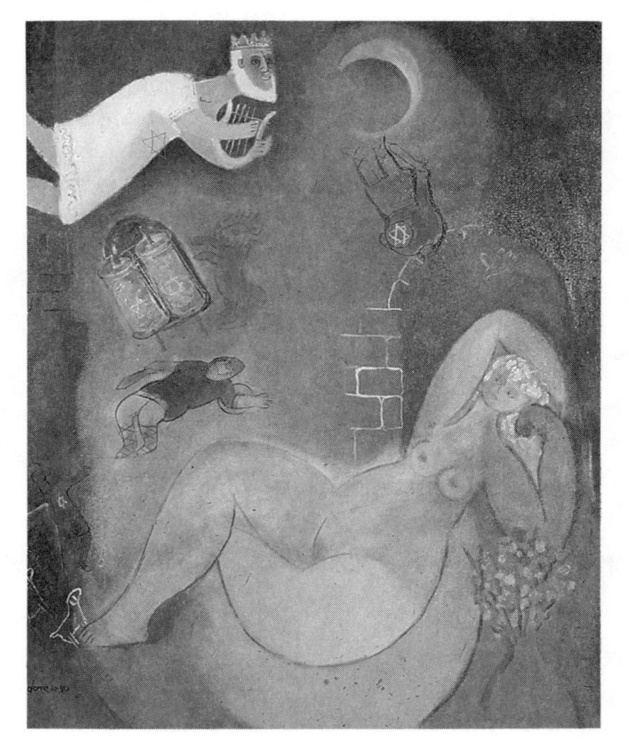

Figure 5 *David and Bathsheva*

Solomon, with all of the importance thereunto appertaining for Israelite—and human—history. The matter of representing relationships thus yields to the matter of representing women, as we move from one artist to the next and move once more backwards in subject, to Eve. *Eve* (Figure 6) we now see by way of Rachel Partnoy, an artist from Argentina whose parents were part of a large family group that emigrated from Eastern Europe to South America immediately prior to World War I. Partnoy's father was engaged in the *shmateh* (textile) trade, and her very interesting works are not really paintings, but reliefs made up of pieces of fabric. In the instance before us her subject is, as with previous artists' work, not viewed in precise accordance with the text, where Eve eats from the tree, shares the fruit with Adam, and is expelled from the garden of Eden. This is an Eve whom we see simultaneously reaching for the fruit and already swelling in pregnancy, as if the reaching for the fruit has already created that condition.

We recall myriad Medieval, Renaissance, and Baroque *Annunciation*s, where the Virgin Mary, that ultimate innocent, is shown with swollen belly even as she hears of her immanent pregnancy by Divine Grace though the Holy Spirit. And thus Eve's act and her fate, in Partnoy's re-vision, are not to be construed as a negative act and fate (that she is disobeying God and suffering the pangs of childbirth as a punishment), but as positive. She is fulfilling the plan of God in becoming the mother of humankind. Without this act of "disobedience," that part of the Divine plan (the proliferation of humanity) might not have been fulfilled

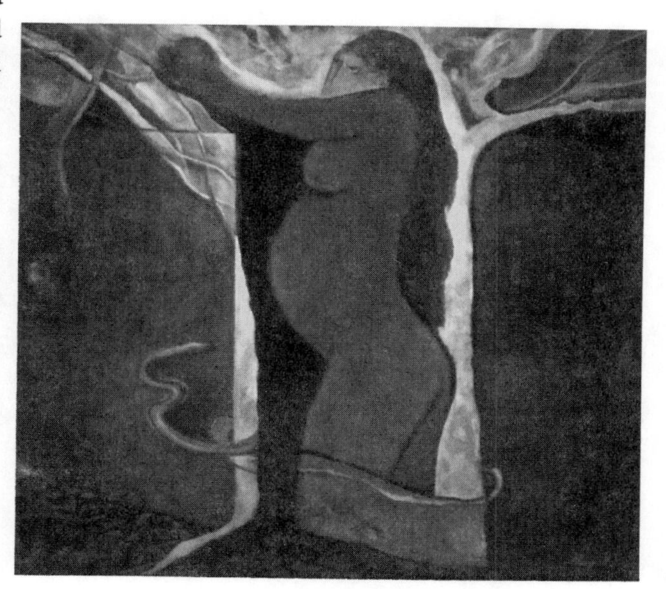

Figure 6 *Eve*

and humankind might not have moved forward. So the artist has captured Eve in a timeless manner, simultaneously reaching for the fruit and already swelling with pregnancy in a moment that defies normative chronological constraints.

Over the course of the last quarter of the twentieth century there have been many artists who have represented female figures of significance in the Hebrew Bible. Not only has Eve been depicted, and other heroines like Ruth and Esther, but even females who have less commonly been the focus of text or of art in the past, but whose position has come to the forefront in the minds of a good number of those focused on the Bible today. Again we view a

Figure 7 *Celebration in Israel: Miriam*

Rachel Partnoy fabric relief "painting," the subject of which is *Celebration in Israel: Miriam* (Figure 7). The sister of Moses is shown leading the women of Israel in a chant of rejoicing, praising God— "...he is my Lord and I shall praise and adorn Him..."—in the aftermath of passing through the Red Sea, of passing out of the servitude of Egypt and out into the wilderness toward the Promised Land. Miriam, like Bathsheva in the later text of the Book of Kings, is a relatively minor figure as the Torah presents her, but has recently been elevated by a number of women artists to a more major position in our thinking. This is accomplished not only in recalling her role through works such as Partnoy's unique visual presentation, which focuses so lushly upon her, but also through an extensive recent movement, which Partnoy in a sense anticipates, to create *Miriam Cups,* decorated goblets whose presence offers a genderal balance to the Elijah goblet on the Passover table—a *new* Jewish ritual object devoted to the story of Miriam as she leads the children of Israel in rejoicing after coming through the Red Sea. This new engagement of Miriam, then, has yielded another filament in the evolving web of Jewish ritual objects.

Among the artists who have created Miriam Cups is New Yorker Carol Hamoy, an artist whose family, like that of Rachel Partnoy, was involved in textiles. Hamoy's art is often a production of fabric fragments that recall her childhood and her mother using the sewing machine at home, doing piecework to make extra money so that the family might eat. One might ask what it is that we are examining other than a bunch of such fragments that the artist has put together in what looks like a giant pin cushion adorned here and there with breasts. We have moved forward biblically to *Vashti* (Figure 8), another woman of the Bible who has until quite recently received scant or negative attention. In the Book of Esther, Esther is the heroine, the hidden Jewess who becomes the queen of the Persian king Ahasuerus, to whom she also has to reveal herself to be a Jew (risking her life by the revelation and its process), in order to save her people and perhaps herself. It is the first text—biblical or otherwise—that deals with the situation of the Israelite-Judean-Jewish people as

Figure 8 *Vashti*

a minority religion dispersed within a majority population of questionable hospitality-hostility.

Esther was put in a position to be the heroine because Vashti, Ahasuerus' first queen, had refused to come dance before the king and his drunken friends, who had been feasting and drinking for days. Having so refused, she was put out of the way because this was not how the queen is supposed to behave when the King says "come, dance, let my fellow noblemen see you." The king is embarrassed when she refuses his order, and his advisors say that this is the wrong kind of woman to have at the royal side. She sets a bad example; she is not obedient. And Carol Hamoy grits her teeth at the idea that blind obedience is the proper role for Vashti or anyone else. So she has brought her out of the closet of the biblical text and given her, tongue-in-cheek, a kind of traditional role: darning those socks, putting the buttons on those shirts, cooking and cleaning, and doing everything her husband says. She has become a pin cushion, for goodness' sake, into whom everyone sticks their pins of need and request and desire. At the same time, the loss of her sexuality, because she has become everyone's mother but nobody's soul-mate or sexual partner, has been restored to her by the cupcake-like breasts that Hamoy adds, with a smile, to this gigantic pincushion.

In the course of her work, Hamoy focuses on a range of different women found in the Bible. Sometimes her interest is less in particular women than in Woman in a more generalized sense. In *Canaanite Goddess Ladder* (figure 9), for example, Hamoy's intention is to remind the viewer that the God of Israel, as that God has been understood over the course of Jewish, Christian, and Muslim history primarily by male commentators, is very much a male God-head. And thus the mother goddess concept, which was so important among the peoples where the Israelite religion developed, has been expunged. She has dropped out of our thinking, and it is in part Hamoy's intention to restore the goddess' importance to us, as we imagine a Divinity that includes compassion among its attributes well before Kabbalah (Jewish mysticism) invests God with a Shekinah. She offers not just a ladder, but a ladder overrun with various found objects that imply femaleness: a pubic triangle upside down, a bird's nest with eggs within it to remind us of the fertility and nurturing aspects of femaleness, for instance.

Of course, when one thinks of the biblical—the Hebrew-Israelite-Judean—context and one sees a ladder, one cannot help but come back to that figure whom we saw wrestling with his dreams and his God earlier. Jacob—not on the voyage back to see Esau, but on the twenty years' earlier voyage out, away from Esau—dreams that extraordinary dream of a ladder

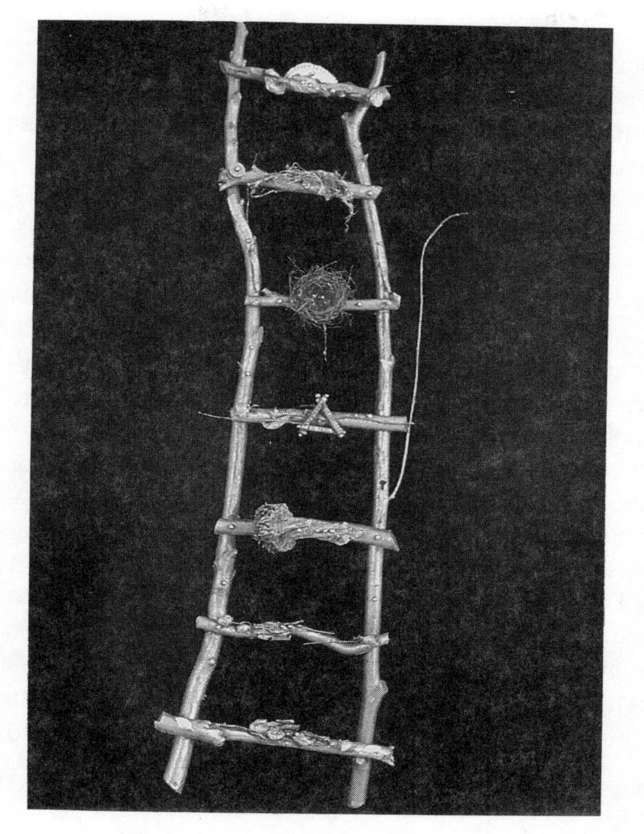

Figure 9 *Canaanite Goddess Ladder*

extending from earth to heaven and heaven to earth, with angels ascending and descending, intermediaries between realms. We see that vision here at the same time as we see the allusion to the Canaanite Ashtoret. Thus the artist offers a revision of our thinking in which the patriarchal narrative is fused with maternal imagery, and the God of Jacob-Israel is filled out as not one-gender-limited.

IV. BETWEEN PAST AND FUTURE

Among those who have focused on the subject of Jacob's ladder-dream is Rabbi Douglas Goldhammer, who brings a rabbi's eye to his primitivist artist's style. His *Jacob* we see dreaming a dream of a ladder with a patriarchal angel reaching down and hovering above. One thinks about the meaning of Jacob's dream, when he experiences an extraordinary connection to the Maker of heaven and earth, and realizes for the first time that the God of Abraham and Isaac, his grandfather and father, is to be found anywhere and everywhere and not just back home, the home which he has just left afraid for his life. If we consider the long-term ramifications, it is a dream that sets in motion the future not only for him, but for all of his descendents.

The entire history of Israel will follow the experience away from home in which the boy becomes a man; the return from home in which he wrestles with God and his own conscience; his later journey into Egypt and, for all his descendents, the journey out; the subsequent eras through which those descendents (including ourselves) live.

Goldhammer sees all of those descendents and all of that history as coming from this moment of Jacob's first Dream. He includes the unexpected image of a crucified Christ, and if one looks carefully, one realizes that this Christ wears a phylactery (a prayer box, one of the *t'filin*) across his brow. So he is very much a *Jewish* Christ. The idea of re-imposing Jewishness onto the image of Christ is one which was already being explored by Jewish artists in the late nineteenth century and exploded in its most stunning and complete representation by Marc Chagall in his *White Crucifixion* of 1938. In Chagall's work the image of Christ—the savior and redeemer in traditional Western (i.e. Christian) ideation and imagery—is transformed into a powerful and symbol-laden image of the suffering Jew. Goldhammer has picked up that theme and that experience of Jacob's descendents in this Dream that hinges both heaven to earth and past to future.

One sees this even more emphatically in Goldhammer's *Jacob's Kabbalistic Dream* (figure 10), where the figure of the crucified Christ has moved to the foreground, so that this part of the future past, the history to

Figure 10 *Jacob's Kabbalistic Dream*

come of Jacob's descendents and our ancestors, is central to the artist's and viewer's thoughts. On the other hand, he has turned the ladder into that *kind* of ladder that, in Jewish mysticism, specifically in the *Kabbalah*, connects to heaven to earth by way of a series of ten entities called *spherot*. The *spherot* represent one part of a way of understanding reality as comprised of layers of worlds and the deconstruction of both, in part, by way of Hebrew language designations for each *sphera*, each "rung"—up from earth to heaven and down from heaven to earth. This mystical midrashic tradition is one of trying to dig far beneath the surface of words and ideas to find the *mysterion*—the mysterious *hiddenness* of the God that has created us and has the power to further or to destroy us, the answer to the question how, why, for what purpose God created us, which answer holds the *secret* to our furtherance. In Goldhammer's hands, that digging becomes an intensely intellective kind of process by way of the combination of word (i.e., text) and image. His visual midrash is thus reinforced by specific kabbalistic texts within the painting that we are to contemplate—to meditate on—as much as we do their visual context.

This approach is antithetical to the approach of Morris Yarowsky, whose *Jacob's Dream (figure 11)* is not only limited to purely visual terms, but whose terms are completely abstract, built entirely on patterns of form and color. Indeed

Figure 11 *Jacob's Dream*

for this artist, color is a symbolic conveyor of *emotion*. Yarowsky's is thus an abstract expressionist style, meaning both that his visual vocabulary is abstract and that he uses bold color and/or dramatic line to express (and to engender within the viewer) intense feeling. More specifically, in this instance, emotion is expressed through the symbolic meaning traditionally associated with particular colors: thus within the darkness of the night that surrounds the dream-vision of a ladder, that ladder is expressed as a burst of yellow, a burst of light, a burst of illumination—of recognition of the relationship between heaven and earth and of the future to come. It emanates out of a blood-red head that is a head of ambition and hope, guilt and fear, a head of red fierceness of feeling, beginning to dream dreams.

Dream, ambition, problem, promise—all of these are part and parcel of the biblical text upon which an infinite range of visual approaches is focused. And that range of *visual* approaches parallels a range of different *textual* and *narrative* elements, from which we have been sampling only a few. Thus, as we turn to another medium (sculpture) and style (figuration), we also turn to another passage in the biblical saga. We face not the representation of an individual *person*, like Jacob, but follow the biblical narrative forward again to an *object* which nonetheless signifies another important moment in the meeting of heaven and earth, in the relationship between human and divine, and in the history that began with Abraham, Isaac, and Jacob, that moves forward from Jacob's transformation as Israel by way of his descendants, and which culminates at its next major stopping point after the dream sequences of Jacob and Joseph in the encounter that Moses has with the bush that burns but is not consumed.

This is what sculptor Bea Mitchell has given us: the *Burning Bush* (Figure 12), which, like an angel, is a paradox that suggests the un-fathomable and ineffable relationship between heaven and earth. It is a pure contradiction in terms in burning without being consumed, this medium through which God speaks to Moses and sets forth for the prophet both what he must do and the history which will follow what he must do. Yet *how* God speaks remains an unfathomable mystery.

Bea Mitchell's *Burning Bush* does double duty because it is actually a *Hanukiyyah* (Hanukah menorah); the Burning Bush is for her the paradigm for what is today perhaps the best—known ritual object/symbol of the convenantal relationship between God and Israel. It takes us from the redemption which we associate with Moses standing in the Burning Bush's sacred space to that other redemption thirteen centuries later, effected by

Figure 12 *Burning Bush*

Judah Maccabee and his brothers, when they lead the Judaean descendants of the Israelites out of the exigencies of Syrian Seleucid rule and away from the attempt to impose pagan spirituality on Judaean Faith. Mitchell's visual midrash connects the two salvational moments, recognizing that in God's time-beyond-our-time they are one.

Between these two historical moments—the moment of Moses and the Burning Bush, and the moment of Judah Maccabee and the miracle of the cruse of oil in the Temple—a good deal, to say the least, transpires. The central event, perhaps, is the rise and fall of the kingship that we associate with David's house. We saw David himself a moment ago in the context of Bathsheba; that is, in the context of an aspect of male and female relations. One might see him as well in the context of a different relationship: father and son. So a second Yarowsky painting, *David and Absalom* (Figure 13), offers another instance of abstraction. Absalom is that prodigal offspring who rebels against his father, yet never loses the love of his father—causing enormous grief to his father both *by* rebelling and by being *killed* by his father's lieutenants against the Israelite king's wishes. As earlier in Yarowsky's work, we see this figure as blocks of pure color—as the frustration, the anger, and furor of the son who plots against the father (who, he feels, is getting too old and should give up the rule to him—but David will not). We see Absalom hanging, as it were, by his brash coloristic anger as he hung by his hair (perhaps red, moreover, as his father's hair is specifically said to have been red in the biblical text) from the terebinth tree, whose branches caught Absalom by that source of his overweening pride as he rode through them in flight from his father's soldiers.

Father and son, husband and wife, mother and son, brother and brother, all of these are issues and ideas that one finds encompassed in the biblical text, and nothing in the Bible encompasses these relationships—both human and human, and human and Divine—more powerfully than does the story in Genesis 22 of the binding of Isaac, the *Akedah*. That chapter (which again moves us backwards in the biblical narrative, but forward to the culminating story of covenantal relationship and its transformation for *our* narrative) tells the story of the offering of Isaac by Abraham on Mt. Moriah, in a daring act of proving his faith *in* God and his faith *to* God. The narrative presents an Abraham who, with his rational faculties, must doubt the Divinity who, after having so recently promised him descendants as myriad as the sands on the seashore and the stars in the heavens, now demands the sacrifice of his beloved son. Abraham nonetheless responds not only in the affirmative to God's demand; he does so with apparently not a moment's hesitation. The text gives us no pause, there is no suggestion of a question, there is not even a true dialogue. Abraham simply does what is asked of him.

Figure 13 *David and Absalom*

Jews read this story every year at the time of the High Holy days because of its emphatic representation of faith. We also do so amidst all the expressions of continuity between old year and new because it offers such a stunning statement of continuity—of a trans-generational covenant which continues to be shaped during the time of Abraham, Isaac, Jacob, Moses, and David. For Isaac shares with his father a peculiar profundity of faith, as is clear when he asks Abraham where the animal to be slaughtered is, and Abraham responds simply that God will provide it. When his father trusses him up and lays him on the altar, when Abraham raises his right arm high, clutching the knife aimed at his son, Isaac's reason (regardless of how we might understand his age) cannot doubt his imminent death at his father's hand, and yet he utters not a single word of protest or opposition or question. Like Abraham's, the absoluteness of Isaac's faith overwhelms all rational doubt. This is the first moment, moreover, in which Isaac is personally and intimately connected to the faith—demanding God of his father; it is the supreme moment of transition and of transmission from one generation to another of the relationship between God and Its adherents who begin with Abraham. That moment is articulated in a covenant, a *brit,* which continues from Abraham to Isaac, from Isaac to Jacob, and from that early biblical period to our own time.

That reference to the moment on Mt Moriah as the *Akedah*, the *Binding*, is surely not only to the physical act of Isaac's being bound up by his father and placed on the altar. It is also a reference to the binding of Isaac to the covenant that is implied and that makes the narrative so significant to this time of year, the beginning of the spiritual year on the Jewish calendar. Isaac's extraordinary act of willingness to be bound to that relationship encompasses not only the promises that are symbolized by the reference to myriad descendants, but also the responsibilities that are symbolized and the problems that are suggested in works like those of Douglas Goldhammer, which we have just noted above. The problems and responsibilities symbolized by silence in the face of apparently outrageous and irrational Divine demands, a willingness to be silent that follows from Abraham to Isaac, both spiritually and genealogically from father to son, is the model, the ideal that we hold up to ourselves as we pass from one year to the next.

We see one mode of portraying Isaac and Abraham in a sculpture by Bea Mitchell, whose *Burning Bush* we saw earlier. Her second work is simply called *Yitzhak* (Figure 14). (Although we necessarily see it from one angle in a single photograph, its visual complexities are far greater in the three dimensional form than a photograph can offer.) There is no angel, there is no ram, there is no bush—just Abraham and Isaac, two human beings, father and son. Moreover, Isaac is stretched across Abraham's lap. Or, put another way, Isaac is being cradled in the manner in which, traditionally in Western art, we often see the figure of the adult Christ being cradled by his mother after his body has been taken down from the cross. Mitchell has given us a *Pieta Akedah*, an *Akedah Pieta*.

As an idea, this leads us in two important conceptual directions. First, we are looking at the work of a Jewish artist who, we might say, asks herself as she crafts such a rendition (as many Jewish artists in the twentieth century ask themselves): "Where do I as a Jewish artist fit into the history of Western art, which is after all *Christian* art?" Second, it reminds us that the importance of the *Akedah* narrative for the Jewish tradition—the transmission of the covenantal relationship—is related to, but different from, its significance for Christianity. The willingness of the father to offer his son and the willingness of the son to be offered are viewed in Christian terms as one of the most important moments in the Hebrew Bible in large part because it is viewed as the forerunner of a yet more significant, far-reaching moment in the New Testament.

The scene on Mt. Moriah is the ultimate prelude to the ultimate main act of God the Father offering his only-begotten Son, Jesus, as proof of his love for humankind. The *Akedah* demonstrates the unequivocal love of father and son for God; the Crucifixion, for which it is a forerunner, demonstrates the unequivocal love of divine Father and Son for humanity. The sacrifice of God the Son by God the Father atones on behalf of humankind for that act of disobedience against God by Adam and Eve (which we have seen visually explored earlier). The sin of God's *first* progeny, which led to their exile from the Garden of Eden and to consequent and subsequent human mortality, is the Original Sin,

Figure 14 *Yitzhak*

without normative means of being washed away and therefore requiring the extraordinary act of sacrifice which is the Crucifixion. That act of *universally*-focused sacrifice is the expanded sequel to the act of *personally*-focused sacrifice played out in Genesis. Moreover the issue of words, with which this discussion began, takes on a new directional meaning in the context of the *Akedah* as forerunner of the Crucifixion: for Christianity, the Crucifixion pertains to the culmination, in earthbound form, of the process (articulated at the outset of the Gospel According to John) of *word* becoming *flesh* to experience passion—to experience suffering and to atone for earthbound sin.

V. ART AND DIVERSITY OF PERSPECTIVE

Isaac then is the ultimate intermediary in a multiple sense. He is one in a series of go-betweens — a prophet with metaphorical feet in both human and divine realms (i.e., his being one of us and his direct contact with God) — and he is also a figure who is variously understood by (thus intermediating between) Judaism and Christianity, his significance similar yet radically different for the two traditions. And as he leads from path-breaking Abraham to path-breaking Jacob-Israel, he leads from past to future. More complicating: if Isaac is unequivocally the figure whom Jews and Christians understand to be offered on Mt. Moriah, for Islam this is by no means so clear. The allusion to the binding on Mt. Moriah, found in *sura* (chapter) 37 of the Qur'an, is ambiguous as to whether it is Isaac or Ishmael. Ali, the son-in-law and nephew of the prophet Muhammad, believed that it was Isaac, while most of his contemporaries among the Muslim leadership believed that it was Ishmael. I think it likely that nearly any Muslim today, even Shi'ite followers of the tradition that stems from Ali, would understand that it was Ishmael. The order of events as they are set forth in Genesis 21 and 22—whereby Ishmael is driven away and subsequently Isaac is brought by Abraham up to Mt. Moriah—is perceived by Islam as a corrupt version of history and the truth.

How, indeed, do we know which understanding is accurate? We know by means of *faith*. If we are Jews and Christians we simply *know* that it was Isaac. If we are Muslims we simply *know* that it was Ishmael. And since none of us was there at the time, we are hardly in a position to argue except from our faith, our beliefs. Bea Mitchell gives us a subset of the question of faith and belief by superimposing the image idea of the *Pieta* over that of the *Akedah*. Howard Lerner also superimposes one set of image ideas over another. He gives us a *Binding of Isaac* (Figure 15) in which we see Isaac rendered in a rather stylized and simple manner at the top of an altar. Now at the base of the altar is a ram which is derived, indeed precisely *inspired*, by a relief carved at the Chateau de Biron in Perigord, France, in the sixteenth century. Thus a Christian image is a direct part of what shapes his image. We observe, too, that there is a green tree that grows up through the altar and actually comes out, as it were, from Isaac's belly, so that Isaac has, emerging from his "womb," the tree of the future which is the *Tree of Life*. The Tree of Life, in the Jewish tradition, is the *Torah*—"a Tree of Life to them that hold fast to it." The Torah, record of covenantal development and transmission, is born and grows from Isaac's belly at the moment of the *Akedah*.

But Lerner is also playing on the Western (i.e., Christian) idea of the Tree of *Jesse*, growing out of the belly of a recumbent patriarch (David's father), that gives us, in its branches, a genealogy leading from the time of David to the time of Jesus. Lerner's tree, moreover, spreads its branches as outspread (the intervening angel's?) wings, which, extended as they are, may also be seen as outstretched arms—and therefore a crucificatory image rises into the future from that belly. This image (and its sacrificial concept) is not disconnectable from what we find in the altar

Figure 15 *Binding of Isaac*

itself, from the base of which that green tree grows. At the base one sees the kind of dark arched opening which is an image that anyone who has looked at photographs from Auschwitz or at art that reflects on the Holocaust at large will recognize: the image of the crematory ovens of Auschwitz. So what Lerner has done is to take that most excruciating of human, certainly of Jewish, experiences in the twentieth century and place it within the central context of Isaac's sacrifice. This is the sacrifice of his descendants for the very differences of *belief*—differences of *interpretation* of God's *word*, to which we alluded in the previous paragraphs—that have driven so much of human history, and certainly and ironically much of the history of the supposedly secular twentieth century. Thus, Lerner's image swallows Jewish and Christian history as it has been swallowed by such "midrashic" conflicts.

Yet again, on the other visual hand, Yarowsky offers *color—expression* indicated by color—even as his *Sacrifice of Isaac* (Figure 16) is more representational than his earlier images which we examined. In this work one gets an almost figurative sense of Abraham wrapping around Isaac. One also gets a color-based sense of the question, "*Who* is commanding the action," by the way in which a shining swath of white (which is the knife in Abraham's hand) is echoed in shape and color by a second swatch of white (which is the Angel of the Lord). If white is the color most fea-

Figure 16 *Sacrifice of Isaac*

sibly used to represent pure *light*—God's ordering instrument (Genesis I:3), here wielded to restore the order that Isaac's immanent death was about to upset—it is also, fundamentally, the *absence of color*. From a painter's perspective, one might say, as *non*-color, white can represent nothing—no-thingness, even as it is the *totality* of color. Which is to say both that, from a Jewish artist's perspective, it offers itself as a means of representing the unrepre-sentable (pure nothingness) God of intervention (who *is every* thing) and it eliminates the angel (reducing it to nothing)— leaving Abraham and Isaac, father and son, engaged alone in this difficult moment.

The issue of God's invisible presence or actual absence (something we know only by faith) raises the question of whether what Abraham does is impelled by a God who is after all a reasonable God, or whether It is an *irrational* god; whether Abraham is inspired by his faith in God that is expressed in the blood-red passion that envelops him, or whether it is the yellow of betrayal—that also, in Yarowsky's painting, embraces Abraham —that should be our central visual and conceptual focus. After all, what kind of father offers his son without so much as a question? That's betrayal! Yet, no, we counter-argue: that's *faith*, that's *passion* because even though Abraham knows rationally that he's going to lose his son, he knows in a way beyond normative knowledge that he *won't* lose him. Or *does* he know? Is Abraham a madman, or is Abraham a prophet? It depends on whether we accept what he does as something that is legitimate or not. If Abraham's name, for example, were David Koresh, and he prepared to offer his son or a whole slew of children to his belief in his relationship with that Other, perhaps we would find him a madman and not the prophetic genius that is otherwise our view of Abraham.

While Yarowsky suggests the possibility of such questions as he works within the abstract and semi-abstract style that dominates the second half of the twentieth century in western art, Jack Levine is one of the masters of twentieth century art who most often works within the figurative tradition that leads from the Renaissance forward. His *Sacrifice of Isaac* (Figure 17) could as well be a Dürer or a Rembrandt as a Jack Levine. Once again we see emotion and passion—but not conveyed by color as much as by line, light and shadow, and facial expression. Abraham's hands are thrown up in dismay either at what he is *about* to do or at what he almost *did* with that knife still glistening in his hand. Do we discern marks on the hands which, in their up and outward thrust, suggest a kind of crucificatory gesture, thus once again implying a questioning recognition of Abraham as the ancestor of

Figure 17 *Sacrifice of Isaac*

descendants who will suffer sacrifice, and Isaac as would-be sacrifice, a kind of forerunner of ultimate sacrifice? Except that, whereas Isaac is redeemed at the last moment (that's part of the point of the *Akedah*), there will be no redemption—no salvation through divinely-directed angelic intervention— for those descendants.

John Bradford also works very much within the classicizing stylistic tradition of the Renaissance and its aftermath. Moreover, while all of the artists whose work we have considered up to this point are Jewish, Bradford is Christian—so his view of the *Sacrifice of Isaac* (Figure 18) might be expected to reflect a Christian perspective. How might that affect his results? By and large the kinds of images that we have seen tend to eliminate angels and other supernatural elements, particularly when they are figurative representations, and limit the overt imagery to the humans involved: Abraham and Isaac—not necessarily even including the ram. The ram is present in Bradford's painting (and the angel is not). As in other works, the issue of composition is present: dynamic diagonals dominating the picture, *from* the ram in the lower left to the knife and upstretched left hand of Abraham in the upper *right* side of the painting. But one of the more fascinating features of this particular work is the way in which the artist has presented Isaac to the viewer *head on*, his upturned face toward us. Students of art history cannot help but be reminded of the wonderful Mantegna painting, done at Padua at the very beginning of the sixteenth century, of the *Dead Christ*, where for

Figure 18 *Sacrifice of Isaac*

the first time in Western art this kind of perspective was attempted, so that we see the figure from feet to face. Bradford's work reflects that lesson in creating the illusion of space on a flat surface, but it would also seem that Bradford has Mantegna's work in mind specifically to indicate that this moment is a conceptual forerunner of what Mantegna represented: the sacrifice of Isaac is the forerunner of the sacrifice of Christ, when God became man to participate in, empathize with, and atone for the human condition.

It is the intense issue of human relations within the layers of the human condition that we see so interestingly dealt with by Richard McBee, who grew up quite disconnected from the Jewish side of his parentage, but who in early adulthood turned to an Orthodox Jewish way of life. Over a twenty-year period, McBee has painted several dozen versions of the *Akedah*; the one I comment on here is entitled *After* (Figure 19). Let us again consider for a moment the poignant human aspects of the condition surrounding the moment on Mt Moriah. Abraham as a father acts in a very strange way, to say the least, even as Abraham as the prophet par excellence acts exactly as he should —in a manner reflecting what the philosopher Soren Kierkegaard refers to as the actions of the *Knight of Faith*. He offers his son to God without a scintilla of hesitation or questioning. In more down-to-earth, human terms, though, consider: Abraham never tells Sarah what he is going to do, and he never speaks to her again or perhaps even sees her again. The end of Genesis 22 tells us that he returns from Mt Moriah to dwell in Beersheba. Genesis 23 opens with the announcement that "the life of Sarah was 127 years"—and she died in Hebron—and that Abraham came there to mourn for his wife. He must never have seen her alive again after the *Akedah,* because in fully and simply human—as opposed to *sui generis* prophetic, heroic—terms, he could never face her with the account of what he almost did to their son. "You almost did *what*?" she surely would have screamed and beaten him with the Middle Bronze Age equivalent of a broom. So, afraid to return to tell her about the trip up Mt Moriah, perhaps, he moved on to Beersheba, rather than back home to Hebron, and never saw her again until he came up to mourn for and bury her.

If the Bible's purpose is the forward motion of the covenantal saga and not this small-scaled human dimension, and it never directly addresses this issue, it is also one of the extraordinarily beautiful qualities of the Bible that it *offers* us figures like Abraham and Sarah, who are human even *as* they are

Figure 19 *After*

heroic bigger-than-life. They are, in a sense, spiritual demi-gods to us, yet without eliminating from our sight what they also are: people like you and me, even in the *Akedah's* full, emotionally grueling context (which adds deep empathetic value to the narrative). If as bigger than life characters they provoke our awe, they also provoke our empathy for the foibles and stumblings that they share with us.

And after the *Akedah*, then, what *about* Isaac? What—in the human, not prophetic-heroic sense—will Abraham *say* to his son when the inspired aura of the moment wears off and they are alone in the silence of its aftermath? What *should* he say to the son whom he awakened early in the morning without a word, led up the mountainside, trussed up, placed on the altar, and whose throat he nearly slit? "Son, I...I...I was inspired by God, I...I...I did what I was supposed to do"? McBee gives us that moment; in his *After* we see Abraham reaching out to the son to whom he *must* reach out. He's not going to see Sarah again, and Ishmael is already gone—sent away by Abraham's own hand (ironically so, in the context of the larger situation). If he doesn't reach out to Isaac, he is alone until he dies. Isaac is the only link between him and the remnant of a family at the center of which he stands —not only in his role as father/husband, but as the prophet at the beginning of an enormous, bigger-than-life covenantal relationship. Indeed if there is no family, there is no covenantal relationship transmission, which was a key part of the *purpose* of the *Akedah* in the first place: to bring Isaac into Abraham's circle of Faith. So, he must deal with him.

Isaac doesn't look overly convinced at first, his back turned to his father, as it is toward us, the audience of this heart-rending scene. If the text tells us that Abraham and the young men who assisted him returned to Beersheba; we might infer that Isaac actually went back to his mother in Hebron, since that is where, the text continues, he would later receive Rebecca as a wife who would comfort him for the death of his mother. Of course we also note that Giotto-esque beginning of Renaissance thinking—seeing a figure with its back to us, to give the viewer the implied sense of the three-dimensional volumetric space into which the figure looks, as we do. We note the color yellow, the traditional (in western, Christian art) color of betrayal, richly enveloping both of them. Questions without answers—outside of faith— are being addressed by them, for them, and between them for *us*. One notes how, if Abraham is attired in what looks like biblical garb, Isaac is, to the extent that we can see his clothing, wearing a conventional pair of pants. It is difficult to gauge whether he wears a shirt or is bare-backed, but either way he is portrayed sartorially as one of *us*, from *our* era, reinforcing the timeless significance of this moment–not just the import of the Covenant, but the import of father-son relations within the compendium of the human experience.

Among the artists who have dealt with the complexity of this relationship in a most interesting manner is Carol Barsha. She offers a trio of images called *The Love that Binds* (Figure 20), in which each of the three elements presents a part of a human figure: parts of Isaac, feet or hands, floating among the clouds of a bright blue heaven, trussed up in sacrifice-symbolic blood red rope. Hovering thus, as a *triptych*, he is offered in the classic Western (i.e., Christian) form of visual self-expression. Disembodied as he is, he relates to the issue of the Christian/Jewish line between understanding God as incarnate and understanding God as intangible. The combination of form and the particulars of its visual content, used by a Jewish artist, expresses that struggle to understand where she fits into the Western visual tradition which we have earlier observed as a concern by any number of Jewish artists in our time.

Moreover, the image offers an Isaac "floating in a limbo of love and oblivion," as the artist herself has expressed it, tied to the process created

Figure 20 *The Love that Binds*

by his father's relationship with God. He is tied in trust of the oblivion of meaninglessness—of complete unreason—because, after all, what he is involved in is completely unreasonable, beyond normative meaning. And at the same time he is full of the meaning of faith, caught *between* heaven and earth, caught between love and faith: his father's faith in and love of God and his father's love for him, and his own love for and faith in his father. "Take your son, your only son, your son whom you love, Isaac, and take him to a place that I will show you and offer him unto me," the words read. Barsha's image is of an Isaac whom we don't really see. All we see are parts of him in parts of the triptych: here, feet; there, hands. Part of him is visible, most of him is invisible—like the text in which he is imbedded, like the text of the Torah, most of whose meanings are not immediately visible to us—hence the need for midrash (to come full circle back toward where we began), the need to dig beneath the surface of the text (*lidrosh*) with both words and images as our instruments.

VI. THE ART OF SYNTHESIS

One recognizes a human need both to dig into (*lidrosh*) and to encompass (*latour*) the possibilities for understanding the mysteries that simultaneously connect us to and separate us from that Divine Source of Creation. The Bible, as the primary text which explains to us creation and our role within it, *is* the center of a *circle* of diverse instruments which, as we have been seeing, wrestle with the relationship between Creator and Creation, as well as among the elements of Creation.

An appropriate image to lead to our conclusions, and an extraordinary visual and conceptual approach to exploring and explaining these relationships, is offered by Simonida Uth, a Christian artist originally from Serbia. Her diptych utilizes the instruments of various traditions. To the right, in gold and copper leaf, we see the figures of Sarah and Hagar; in other words, the two women—one of whom is virtually written out and the other completely written out of this story—have been to a certain extent restored to it by the artist. If they are side-placed *observers* of the main action, they are at least visually there as part of what *we see*. To the left, the central composition offers the figure of Abraham on the left and Isaac on the right, and we recognize that they have virtually the same face: mirror images of each other, they are emphatically father and son. Between them there is a third figure, also with the same face, so that these are three entities which partake of one entityship—one being, so to speak: they are *triune*.

The middle figure has blood-red protrusions rising from its back, as it were: they have the appearance of wings. To that extent this may be construed easily enough as the angel coming between Abraham and Isaac. At the same time this figure may be seen as the Ishmael who was between them (before being sent away), even as Ishmael is also represented by a kind of fourth figure, the half-invisible shadow behind Isaac. We recognize, too, that the protrusions rising from the central figure's back also form a kind of pomegranate-like crown shape: the crown that evokes King David. That crown leads, in the vocabulary of Christian genealogy, to Jesus, just as the trio of figures, while it is father, son, and angel between them, may obviously also be understood as a symbol of the ultimate Christian trio: Divine Father, Son, and Holy Spirit. The work is indeed inspired, in part, by the famous Russian icon of *The Holy Trinity* by Rublov, with its three angels.

Uth has entitled her diptych *The Cup of Hermes Trismegistus* (Figure 21, detail). She brings into this mixture of Christian and somewhat Jewish patterns of thinking yet another element, Egyptian Hellenistic thinking: Hermes of the three paths, Hermes of the crossroads, Hermes who stands between realms. The pomegranate crown that rises from the angel is also,

Figure 21 *The Cup of Hermes Trismegistus*

in form, one of the crowns of Egypt: the crown of Osiris. The artist brings the Egyptian god who presides over death and rebirth into the picture (literally, one might say)—Osiris who is the father torn apart by his enemies, who is reborn as his son Horus, who in turn is incarnate in every pharaoh in Hellenistic Egyptian (and not only Hellenistic, but the cult is especially strong during that era) thought, and whose "life cycle" story is one of the sources of inspiration for Christianity's understanding of an incarnate, dying, and resurrected God. Simonida brings to bear a wide range of different visual ideas, as the ram to be offered in lieu of Isaac, off to the left, yields part of its outline to that of a gigantic blue fish. The fish symbolizes Jesus as Redeemer, by virtue of the play on the Greek word for fish, *ichthys*, which, as an acronym, spells out the phrase "Jesus Christ Son of God Savior."

The entire composition, at the same time, combines to create a six-pointed star, which in medieval alchemy (as well, eventually, as elsewhere) is called the Star of David or the Shield of David, bringing us back to that biblical figure yet again by yet another path. Alchemy, a strong interest of the artist, abounds in instances of transformation: lead can become gold; oil and water can mix with each other. And transformation is very much what Simonida's thinking is about; she is well-versed in mysticism and alchemy, and in her painting she sees a transformation of separate strands of thinking with respect to the *Akedah* into a unified idea that incorporates a range of different perspectives.

Differences of perspective, which define the marvelous range of visual approaches to the Bible taken by artists within all three traditions that stem from Abraham, lead us finally to a modern traditionalist, Mohammed Zakariya, of Washington, DC. Zakariya's centuries' old Muslim approach is to glorify the Word visually by means of often spectacular calligraphy of the letters that *comprise* the words. As we might expect, Zakariya's primary textual focus in approaching the *Akedah*, for example, is actually not the biblical account, but that found in the Qur'an, which he calligraphizes (in Arabic writing) together with other passages in the Qur'an that refer to *Abraham, Isaac, and Ishmael* (Figure 22), respectively.

But among the Muslim equivalents of Jewish midrash and rabbinical commentary is that of Ath-tha'labi, in the 11th century. Zakariya calligraphizes, in an Andalusian Moorish style rarely seen today, a passage from Ath-tha'labi's *Stories of the Prophets*, where the Muslim theologian discusses the question of whether it *is* Isaac or Ishmael whom Abraham offers to God, arriving at the conclusion that we do not and cannot know. It is that enlightened perspective that Zakariya visually glorifies with ink, gold leaf, and grace of form.

There is so much—there is too much—that we do not and cannot know, as we have earlier noted; in fact we have arrived back to where we began. A sense of unfathomability applies to the text of the Bible, which not only connects the human creation to our Creator, but also connects the Creator to the entire created world in the center of which that text stands: the world of Jewish, Christian, Muslim—and, more simply, human—relations. Tied by love, redeemed and/or consumed by love, consumed or distorted by Faith, *unfathomability* defines the human state of *being*. The twentieth century, our own, is surely the most ambiguous and unfathomable of centuries, at least in *Western* history. We have created technology that can take us to the moon and even to Jupiter and beyond, and enjoy verbal, visual, and other arts at an unprecedented level. At the same time, the Holocaust, Hiroshima, Biafra, Cambodia, Rwanda, Yugoslavia—a list that goes endlessly on—demonstrate how deeply within us the destructive impulse remains imbedded and how readily and irrationally we sacrifice others to that impulse.

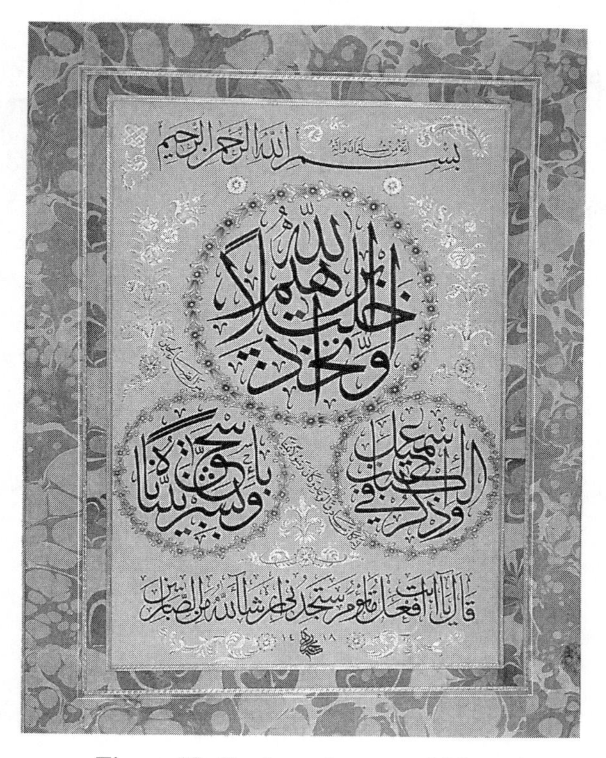

Figure 22 *Abraham, Isaac, and Ishmael*

All of this provokes our *need* to understand what we cannot. If with all of its unfathomability the Bible is still the beginning of understanding (at least for the monotheistic traditions), then the Bible also demands that we wrestle with it with as many words and images as we can throw into the fray — *because* it is a text which offers the beginnings of answers, even as those beginnings most often beget yet more questions than completed, simple answers. This process, in turn, is part of what provokes and necessitates not only the endless flow of human words which explore and explain, but also the images which re-vision words, questions, and would-be answers with color, line, and form—and which have the power, in digging beneath the surface of words, so richly to enrich our thinking and our lives.

Retrospecting Rape in Christian Commentaries of Genesis 34 and Forensic Medical Textbooks from Nineteenth-Century Germany

Susanne Scholz

1. INTRODUCTION

Recent biblical scholars have emphasized the significance of the Bible for Western culture. J. Cheryl Exum believes that "perhaps no other document has been so instrumental as the Bible in shaping Western culture and influencing ideas about the place of women and about the relationship of the sexes."[1] Vincent L. Wimbush maintains that the Bible has "profoundly affected the imagination of western culture."[2] A group of scholars calling themselves "The Bible and Culture Collective" argues that "the Bible has exerted more cultural influence on the West than any other single document."[3] The statements posit a relationship between the Bible and culture. My paper analyzes this relationship for the issue of rape in interpretations of Genesis 34 and forensic medicine. I propose that the ideas on rape in these literatures illustrate the extent to which academic scholarship, religious and secular, has contributed to (Western) misogynist culture.

Here is a summary of Genesis 34: Dinah, the daughter of Leah, is raped by Shechem, the prince of the land, when she goes out to visit women in her neighborhood. "Desiring" her after the rape, Shechem abducts Dinah and asks his father, Hamor, to assist him with his plan to marry her. In the meantime Dinah's father, Jacob, and her brothers hear about the rape. The brothers react strongly. When Shechem and Hamor negotiate the marriage, the brothers request that the Canaanite males of the town be circumcised.

While they lie in pain after the circumcision, Dinah's brothers attack the city and kill all the males, including Shechem and Hamor; they abduct the women and children of the city. When Jacob hears about these actions, he condemns his sons. They ask in return if their sister should be treated like a prostitute. With that question the story ends.

This chapter in the Bible is a straightforward report, or so it seems. A woman is raped by a man; her family seeks revenge. Her brothers kill the rapist, his father, and the male inhabitants of the town. Rape receives a clear, precise, and enormous punishment. The story cannot easily be forgotten — if one chooses to read it. Indeed, compared to other biblical narratives, Genesis 34 has not attracted much attention. Rape and violence have not appealed to theologians and religious scholars. The report of a rape and the events following the crime were uneasy topics. Often scholars maintained that the chapter was an independent later source that did not belong to the original Jacob cycle.[4] Even major publications of feminist biblical scholars did not include treatments of this narrative.[5]

When scholars read Genesis 34, the provocative and complex story line challenged them to disclose their views. This disclosure did not, however, happen consciously. Exegetes did not consult literature on the subject of rape before they interpreted Genesis 34. Rather, evaluations about the various characters and value judgments about the purpose of the narrative reflected their interpreters' views to a degree that a less provocative narrative might not have stimulated.

This essay describes the ideas on rape expressed by Christian biblical commentators of nineteenth-century Germany. Paralleled with forensic textbooks, the views on rape in biblical interpretations are related to a specific cultural context of nineteenth-century Germany. Although the juxtaposition of the commentaries with forensic medicine promotes intertextual reading strategies between different academic disciplines, the examination does not posit causal links. The analysis will not prove that biblical scholars interacted personally or intellectually with forensic researchers. Rather, the correlation provides a rationale to evaluate ideas on rape within a specific cultural context. The connection between textbooks and commentaries is therefore a cultural, not a causal, link.

2. IDEAS ON RAPE IN THE COMMENTARIES

The commentaries did not display their views on rape in a straightforward way. Scholars employed different approaches in their attempt to deal with the challenging content of the Dinah story.

a. MARGINALIZATION OF RAPE

Many commentators barely mentioned the rape, referring to it only in passing or focusing on other topics. The choice of titles, the actual content of the interpretations, and the way in which Dinah was blamed all accomplished this marginalization of the rape.

Of twenty commentaries examined, only three referred to the rape in the titles that prefaced the actual discussion. The term "rape" was, however, not used explicitly,[6] and so most titles did not mention the rape or indicate any violation of Dinah. For example, Johann S. Vater entitled his chapter simply: "Jacob's Events at Shechem and his move to Bethel."[7] Heinrich Holzinger used the ambiguous title: "Complications with Shechem because of Dinah."[8] Gottfried Hoberg focused only on Jacob: "Jacob's Stay in Shechem: Chapter 34."[9] Stressing the fraternal revenge, Franz Delitzsch chose the title: "Simeon's and Levi's Outrage at the Shechemites: 33:18-34."[10] Similarly, Michael Baumgarten opted for "Simeon's and Levi's Revenge against the Shechemites."[11] Hermann Strack combined two titles, one emphasizing Jacob and another stressing the fraternal revenge: "Jacob at Shechem; Simeon and Levi Revenge the Dishonoring of Dinah."[12] Johann Lange was satisfied with listing topics: "Jacob's Settlement at Shechem; At Succoth; Dinah; Simeon and Levi; The first manifestation of Jewish fanaticism; Jacob's rebuking and removal to Bethel (33:17-35:15)."[13] Each of these titles reflected the perspective of the interpreter. Ignoring or minimizing Dinah's situation, they concentrated on Shechem, Jacob, or the brothers.

What the titles suggested, the interpretations confirmed. Several mentioned the rape only to shift their attention to other topics. For August Dillmann, the fraternal response became the dominant issue. He explained that v. 2b referred to abduction and "rape." However, he connected it quickly to v. 26 and to "all statements about the anger and malice of Dinah's brothers in 5. 7. 13. 31."[14] Acknowledging the rape as the standpoint from which to discuss the fraternal response, Dillmann emphasized the activities of the brothers. Friedrich W. J. Schröder stressed the aristocratic and privileged position of Shechem. Calling Shechem a rapist, Schröder considered him as the most respected son of the tribal sovereign Hamor.[15] Hoberg equated the rape with seduction. He wrote that "Dinah was raped by Shechem, the son of Hamor (vs. 1-2). Shechem and his father make preparations for marriage ... but Jacob's sons (Simeon and Levi) killed the seducer...."[16] For Hoberg, the wedding preparations recast the rape as seduction, with Dinah as "the one who was seduced."[17] Hermann Gunkel applied yet another strategy. He recognized that a rape occurred in Genesis 34 but only in one source,[18] the late priestly source. Hence, Gunkel ignored the issue.

Some commentaries blamed Dinah for what happened and so marginalized the phenomenon of rape. Baumgarten stated: "It is Dinah's punishable curiosity that she goes out to see the daughters of the land because the daughters of Israel have nothing do with the daughters of Canaan."[19] Schröder blamed Dinah even more. In his opinion, it was wrong for Dinah "to visit them; a familiarity which is hardly appropriate for a daughter of Israel to do with the daughters of Canaan (2 Corinthians 6:17). The punishment therefore followed soon."[20] He supported his view with a reference from the New Testament and with his understanding about nature:

> Leaving the father's house, Dinah is dishonored violently because she roams about more freely than she should. She should have stayed at home, as the apostle orders (Titus 2:5) and nature recommends, because virgins, like wives, should be keepers of the house.[21]

Blaming Dinah, Schröder deferred attention from the rape. Lange argued similarly. He used the terms "rape"and "seduction" indiscriminately because "some measure of consent on the part of Dinah is altogether probable."[22] Consequently, "Dinah's history [is] a warning history for the daughters of Israel, and a foundation of the Old Testament's limitation of the freedom of the female sex."[23] Whereas Dinah's fate should warn all women, Lange did not consider Shechem's fate as a warning for all rapists. "Seduction" was Dinah's problem alone, and so Lange ignored the significance of the rape in his interpretation.

b. MALE BONDING: CONDEMNATION OF THE BROTHERS AND SIDING WITH THE RAPIST

Most interpreters bonded with the men of the story, so that they became the exclusive point of attention, both negative and positive. Judging the brothers, most Christian scholars condemned them for their violent revenge. For instance, Dillmann evaluated the brothers as "malicious," both for holding tribal honor above all else and for using circumcision as a trick to kill the Shechemites.[24] He characterized the fraternal reaction to Dinah's rape as "tribal pride" and dismissed their response for its narrowness. Delitzsch found the brothers deceitful despite their "energetic moral purity." They sinned because they used the "sacred sign of the covenant to so base a means of malice."[25] The whole story showed "the disgrace of the promised generation not hiding how Simeon and Levi abused the sacred sign of covenant for their private execrable revenge."[26] And his colleague C.F. Keil lamented simply, "The way the brothers rejected the Shechemites was wrong." The brothers deceived the Shechemites, abused the covenant sign of circumcision, and extended the revenge to the whole city. Jacob's "crafty character" degenerated "into malicious cunning in Simeon and Levi, and jealousy for the exalted vocation of their family, into actual sin." The last words of Jacob in Genesis 49:5-7 provided "sufficient proof that the wickedness of their conduct was also an object of deep abhorrence."[27]

Continuing the condemnation, O. Naumann judged the fraternal revenge "as a remarkable example of religious intolerance," Variations in the Fiat Pattern of Gensis"[28] and the "means of fighting" as immoral and full of "falsehood and deceit."[29] Christian C. Bunsen was disgusted by "the horrible and degrading revenge of the brothers."[30] Schräder characterized the brothers as cruel, greedy, crude, and carnal characters. They were "men of blood" and "robbers who broke the covenant."[31] He believed that Jacob's judgment in Genesis 49:5-7 gave condign punishment to his sons Simeon and Levi: "That is why their misdeed, in which Simeon and Levi focused only on their private revenge instead of leaving revenge to the Lord, is so severely punished."[32]

Lange evaluated negatively the brothers when he called them "fanatical." He believed that "their resort to subtle and fanatical conduct merits only a hearty condemnation."[33] For him, the story is even "the birthplace of Jewish fanaticism." He characterized "this narrative as the history of the origin and first original form of Jewish and Christian fanaticism" and presented examples from the Christian tradition for "this Shechemite carnage of blind and Jewish fanaticism." Therefore, their father Jacob "justly declares his condemnation of the iniquity of the brothers not only at once but also upon his deathbed (ch. XLIX)." Lange argued that Jacob rightly condemned his sons because they were "full of cunning, falsehood, and cruelty."

Lange appreciated the fact that the narrator did not hesitate to bring "into prominence whatever traits of excellence there were in the characters of Shechem and Hamor." His interpretation related the fraternal "guilt of fanaticism" to Jacob's task in Genesis 35, where the father needed to purify his house:

> As Jacob intends holding a feast of praise and thanksgiving at Bethel, he enjoins upon his household first a feast of purification.... But it is to be observed here that Jacob is first sealed after having purified his faith from any share in the guilt of fanaticism.[34]

Lange sympathized with Jacob, Shechem, and Shechem's father Hamor because the brothers exemplified fanaticism which "either discredit[s] Christianity in the moral estimate of the world, and imperil[s] its very existence by its unreasonable zeal, or...expose[s] it to the most severe persecutions."[35] Rejecting the brothers as carriers of fanaticism, Lange bonded with the father and the rapist.

Other commentators also bonded with the rapist after their dismissal of the brothers. Delitzsch commented:

> Shechem, the son of the ruler, sees her, causes her to fall, and is no longer able to leave from the loved one.... Because of his love toward Dinah, the young prince hurried to fulfill the conditions [of the brothers].[36]

Delitzsch liked that the rapist became the "lover" of Dinah. Love led Shechem to accept the condition of the "fanatic" brothers. Dillmann emphasized Shechem's love because Shechem "spoke to her heart and sought to comfort her with his love and with the future that emerged from the past events."[37] Gunkel wrote repeatedly about Shechem's love: "Because he loves Dinah, he soothes her, and promises to marry her"; and "because he loves her, he asks his father to court for her"; and "the enarmored Shechem accepts immediately the conditions."[38] Lange not only stated that "Shechem ... passionately loves and would marry the dishonored maiden and is ready to pay any sum as an atonement," but he also imagined that Dinah consented: "Judging from Dinah's levity, it [the rape] was not without her consent."[39] Imagining that Dinah consented and that Shechem was in love, Lange found the brothers truly despicable.

c. RAPE AND LOVE

Commentators declared that the deed of Shechem was an expression of love, and so "love" erased rape and its horror. For example, Delitzsch believed that "the young seducer only loved her whom he had seduced the more, soothed her with pleasant prospects of the future, and actually entreated his father to take him the damsel for a wife.... Shechem really loved Dinah."[40] Hence, Delitzsch proposed that Shechem hurried to fulfill the fraternal demand for circumcision because of his love for Dinah.[41] Dillmann saw no contradiction in his statement when he wrote that "after the violent act follows love for the weakened," that is, for Dinah.[42] His colleague Keil argued that "Shechem ... sought to comfort her by the promise of a happy marriage."[43] Hoberg considered the love of Shechem an "awakening" one which led Shechem to desire "legitimate marriage."[44]

Other scholars adopted this view that Shechem was really innocent and in love. For Lange, the expression "his soul clave unto Dinah" showed that Shechem's act was "not an act of pure, simple lust, which usually regards its subject with hatred...."[45] Lange defined rape according to the assumed feelings of the rapist. Shechem was absolved from the rape because he loved genuinely. Only "pure, simple lust" turned a man into a rapist. Love and the promise of an "honorable" marriage turned the sexual assault into an act of love. Gunkel explained that Shechem "started loving Dinah, soothed her, and promised to marry her."[46] So deeply in love with Dinah, Shechem immediately accepted the fraternal demands. Referring to Shechem's speech in verses 11-12, Gunkel said, "A listener likes to hear that such a noble Canaanite takes such pains over an Israelite girl." No criticism of the rapist emerged from these scholarly interpretations—only admiration and appreciation for Shechem's love.

3. IDEAS ON RAPE IN FORENSIC MEDICAL TEXTBOOKS

Forensic scholars disclosed comparable ideas on rape in their textbooks. These books were used to educate the next generation of forensic practitioners and served as guidelines for deciding forensic-medical cases.

a. RAPE AS ILLEGAL INTERCOURSE

Many textbooks discussed rape in chapters alongside other sexual matters. Not treated as a separate issue, rape was juxtaposed to "peder-asty,"[47] lesbianism, sodomy, bestiality, and necrophilia. All these issues were classified under the rubric "illegal intercourse." Even in textbooks that attempted to separate rape from other sexual issues,[48] chapter headings classified rape as one among other "devious" forms of intercourse. For instance, Adolph Chr. H. Henke presented a discussion on rape in the chapter entitled "Examinations about Unclear Sexual Conditions."[49] Christian F. L. Wildberg used the title "Examinations with Regard to Intercourse."[50] Johann D. Metzger proposed "Illegal Intercourse."[51] Franz von Ney wrote "On Rape and Other Cases of Vice."[52] Ferdinand Hauska entitled the chapter "Prohibited Ways to Satisfy the Sexual Urge."[53] J. Maschka treated rape in a chapter called "Signs of Virginity and Illegal Satisfaction of the Sexual Urge."[54]

A comparison of Henke's textbook in the first and last edition (the book had thirteen editions!) illuminates the continuous effort to merge rape with other forms of "illegal intercourse." In the first edition, Henke included a chapter on "Examinations Concerning Unclear Sexual Conditions." This chapter contained a section "About Illegal and Unnatural Intercourse, paragraphs 174-182."[55] Like many textbooks, this section discussed rape with "pederasty," sodomy, lesbianism, and bestiality. For Henke, rape was not an issue unto itself; it belonged to "unnatural intercourses." The last edition appeared to break this pattern. It treated rape as a single issue in a section entitled "About Rape, paragraphs 181-185" and offered a distinct section entitled "Unnatural Intercourse, paragraphs 186-188."[56] Both sections, however, belonged to one chapter called "About Illegal and Unnatural Intercourse." The issue of rape continued to be merged with other forms of "illegal intercourse." Many textbooks used this design. For example, G. H. Masius entitled a chapter "About Illegal Intercourse," in which he discussed virginity, rape, and then sodomy.[57] Hence, forensic textbooks did not consider rape as an issue unto itself. This approach is parallel to biblical interpretations that omitted explicit discussions of rape and focused on other topics.

b. RAPE AND DISTRUST

Distrusting a woman's testimony was another way forensic scientists handled the issue of rape. Henke wrote: "Because of frequently false accusations of rape, one asks above all: Is rape possible everywhere?"[58] Written with a detached tone of objectivity, this statement of profound distrust followed a discussion in which Henke doubted the ability of a strong man to rape an equally strong and healthy woman. Henke concluded that such a woman could not be raped. Similarly, Christian F. L. Wildberg argued:

A rape of a grown-up, equally strong, completely conscious, and

> especially virginal person [i.e.woman] done by a single man only through physical strength must indeed be considered as impossible according to almost all teachers of forensic medicine....[59]

Forensic investigators dismissed a rape accusation if they judged the woman as able to fight off her attacker. The perception of the expert was valued more than the testimony of the raped woman. Forensic scientists provided detailed instructions on a woman's method for resisting: with equal physical strength and with her "natural" weapons—her hands and especially her nails. Thus Johannes B. Friedreich proposed:

> If, therefore, a grown-up, healthy, and moderately strong woman claims to have been raped by a single man because of his physical strength, this statement does not deserve credence.[60]

The forensic world profoundly distrusted women who claimed that they had been raped. The assumption that "for every ten accusations of rape nine might easily be wrong"[61] fueled suspicion against raped women, but supported rapists. Read in this context, the suggestion of Carl G.L. Bergmann was not surprising:

> Complaints about such crimes are so often unfounded that it would be interesting to determine statistically the degree of doubt with which such a complaint should generally be evaluated.[62]

Bergmann proposed to introduce mathematical tools for evaluating a woman's complaint, so that forensic scholars would not have to rely on her word.

Lacking such measurements, some scholars offered alternatives to establish the truth of the accusation. The forensic doctor Adolph Lion recommended the following procedure:

> As with all sexual examinations, what is essential here is the way in which the forensic physician carries out his examination. He should be told the exact events of the rape. He should pay attention to the expressions, morality, and behavior both of the child and the relatives and of those others who are believed to have an interest. He should especially search for contradictions and improbable descriptions. Together with the physical finding, he will usually detect the truth. If

> teachers, directors of institutions, physicians, or officials in general are accused, he should be particularly on his guard.[63]

Forensic scholars proposed to look at the woman's personality, lifestyle, and educational background. Openly distrustful, they scrutinized not only the woman's body but also her whole personality and background. A raped woman could not project a trustworthy image during the examination. In the context of assumed scientific objectivity, the medical world was encouraged to doubt rape claims. This approach resembled biblical scholars. They distrusted Dinah, condemned those on Dinah's side, and sympathized with Shechem.

c. RAPE AS LIBIDO

Although most forensic scholars concluded that a strong man could not rape an equally strong woman, others rejected this view. Johann A. H. Nicolai, and Ignaz H. Schürmeyer claimed that a strong man could rape an equally strong and healthy woman.[64] Even Wildberg, who initially considered a rape between equally strong participants as impossible, admitted its possibility later:

> That a violent or fraudulent rape of a grown-up, healthy, conscious person can be completed by *one* man alone and that this makes possible conception and impregnation should not always be denied. Because it may be, when the male penis reaches at or in the vagina despite all female resistance, exactly at the time of the complete exhaustion of the woman's strength, that the lewd stimulation of the genitals done against the will of the person achieves its highest degree, paralyzing all her power of resistance and then making an impregnation possible.[65]

Physicians pondered whether the physical stimulation of a woman forced her psychologically to give in and consent to the forced sexual intercourse. They imagined that her libido took over so extensively that the woman was not raped physically. Her body supposedly enjoyed the physical manipulations, so that her willpower collapsed. Hence, she was raped psychologically. Even Friedreich, for whom an equally strong woman could not be raped by an equally strong man, stressed the force of the libido in overpowering the will of a woman. He wrote:

> It is possible that seduction and fondling arouse a woman's eroticism and libido, so that she will surrender to the man's embrace without further resistance although at first she really did not agree to the intercourse and seriously resisted any attempt. Based on a physical point of view, no rape seems to have been committed. However, physical coercion is replaced by psychological coercion, and the female individual is put into a passive and almost will-less condition because of strong arousal, and thus she is raped.[66]

Many scientists agreed that the movement of the penis sexually stimulated a woman despite her initial or continuous resistance. The forensic writer Johann A. Schmidtmüller thought that the libido of a resisting woman was aroused, if the "fiery lover" immediately raped her a second time.[67] Masius stated that a rapist could take advantage when the libido overwhelmed the woman, a situation thus complicating the medical decision as to whether the intercourse was voluntary.[68] Wolfgang F. W. Klose imagined that even a "fiery girl who is unexperienced in physical love will easily ... be enraptured by a certain degree of libido ... especially if the sight of the rapist is concealed in the darkness of the night."[69]

As these descriptions demonstrate, forensic scholars did not view rape as an attack on a woman's personhood. They saw it as a physically satisfying encounter between a man and a woman. Rape was seen on the continuum of libido. Similarly, biblical interpreters took refuge in textual ambiguity and defined rape as love.

4. CONCLUSION

Biblical commentators and forensic scholars of nineteenth-century Germany legitimized rape. Although biblical and forensic scholars did not explicitly acknowledge each other, the religious and the secular disciplines shared assumptions. First, both disciplines maintained that rape is not a topic in its own right. Biblical commentators omitted explicit references to the rape. Forensic scholars considered rape a subcategory of illegal intercourse. Second, both bonded with a male perspective. Biblical commentators sympathized with Shechem. Forensic physicians distrusted a raped woman. Men, whether the male characters of the biblical narrative or the male writers of the textbooks, stood in the center. Third, both characterized rape as an experience of love or libido both for the rapist and the woman.

The retrospection demonstrates that the religious and the secular disciplines participated in a common discourse grounded in androcentrism. Although this result is hardly surprising, the depth and the persistence of this perspective into all facets of life and scholarship continues to be amazing. The illumination of the relationship between the Bible and (Western) culture promises, therefore, further insights. Examining other issues, other biblical texts, and other cultural contexts will not only clarify the connection between the Bible and (Western) culture, but also renew the relevance of biblical narratives for people living on the brink of the twenty-first century.

Notes

[1] Cheryl Exum, "Feminist Criticism: Whose Interests Are Being Served?," in *Judges and Method: New Approaches in Biblical Studies*, ed. Gale A. Yee (Minneapolis: Fortress, 1995), 66.

[2] Vincent L. Wimbush, "Biblical-Historical Study as Liberation: Toward an Afro-Christian Hermeneutic," *Journal of Religious Thought* 42, no. 2 (Fall-Winter 1985-1986): 15.

[3] The Bible and Culture Collective, *The Postmodern Bible* (New Haven: Yale University Press, 1995), 1.

[4] Michael Fishbane, "Composition and Structure in the Jacob Cycle (Gen. 25:19-35:22)," *Journal of Jewish Studies* 26 (1975): 15-38.

[5] Note that the chapter is not interpreted in Phyllis Trible, *Texts of Terror* (Philadelphia: Fortress, 1984); Letty M. Russell, ed., *Feminist Interpretation of the Bible* (Philadephia: Westminster Press, 1985); Katheryn Pfisterer Darr, *Far More Precious Than Jewels: Perspectives on Biblical Women* (Louisville, KY: Westminster/Know Press, 1991); J. Cheryl Exum, *Fragmented Women: Feminist (Sub) Versions of Biblical Narratives* (Valley Forge, PA: Trinity Press International, 1993). For an analysis of interpretations on Genesis 34 by early Christian and medieval exegetes, see Lucille C. Thibodeau, "The Relation of Peter Abelard's 'Planctus Diane' to Biblical Sources and Exegete Tradition: A Historical and Textual Study" (Ph.D diss., Harvard University, 1990).

[6] Peter von Bohlen, *Die Genesis historisch-kritisch erläutert* (Königsberg: Gebrüder Bornträger, 1835), 324: "Schwächung der Dina und Blutbad an Sichem"; August Dillmann, *Die Genesis*, für die 3. Auflage nach Dr. August Knobel, Kurzgefasstes exegetisches Handbuch zum Alten Testament, Eilfte Lieferung, 3rd rev. ed. (Leipzig: Hirzel, 1875), 383: "Jacob bei Sikhem und die Entehrung der Dina"; Carl Friedrich Keil and Franz Delitzsch, eds., *The Pentateuch*, Biblical Commentary on the Old Testament, vol. 1, trans. James Martin (Grand Rapids, MI: Eerdmans, 1949), 311. For the original German see Carl Friedrich Keil, *Genesis und Exodus*, vol.

1, Biblischer Commentar über die Bücher Moses, ed. C. F. Keil and F. Delitzsch (Leipzig: Dörffling & Franke, 1861), 224: "Cap XXXIV: Schändung der Dina und Rache Simeon's und Levi's."

[7] Johann Severin Vater, *Commentar über den Pentateuch, mit Einleitung zu den einzelnen Abschnitten, der Eingeschalteten Uebersetzung von Dr. Alexander Geddes's Merkwürdigeren critischen und exegetischen Anmerkungen und einer Abhandlung über Moses und die Verfasser des Pentateuchs*, 3 vols., Erster Theil (Halle: Waisenhaus Buchhandlung, 1802), 279: "Begebenheiten Jacobs in der Gegend von Sichem, und sein Zug nach Bethel."

[8] Heinrich Holzinger, *Genesis*, Kurzer Hand-Commentar zum Alten Testament (Freiburg: Mohr, 1898), 213: "Die Verwicklungen mit Sichem wegen der Dina."

[9] Gottfried Hoberg, *Die Genesis nach dem Literalsinn erklärt* (Freiburg im Breisgau: Herder, 1899), 291: "Jakobs Aufenthalt bei Sichem. Kap. 34."

[10] Franz Delitzsch, *Die Genesis* (Leipzig: Dörffling & Franke, 1852), 339: "Simeons und Levi's Frevelthat an den Sichemiten XXXIII, 18. bis c. XXXIV." See also the title in the later edition of his *Neuer Commentar*, 1887, 411: "Der Aufenthalt in Sichem und Simeons und Levi's Rache wegen Dina's Entehrung XXXIII,18-c.XXXIV" (The Stay at Shechem and Simeon's and Levi's Revenge because of Dinah's Dishonoring).

[11] Michael Baumgarten, *Theologischer Commentar zum Pentateuch* (Kiel: Universitäts-Buchhandlung, 1843), 291: "Simeons und Levis Rache an den Sichemiten."

[12] Hermann L. Strack, *Die Bücher Genesis, Exodus, Leviticus und Numeri*, Kurzgefasster Kommentar zu den heiligen Schriften Alten und Neuen Testamentes sowie zu den Apokryphen, A. AT. 1. Abt., ed. H. Strack & Otto Zöckler (Munich: Beck, 1894), 109: "Jakob in Sikhem. Simeon und Levi rächen die Entehrung der Dina."

[13] Johann P. Lange, *Die Genesis*, Theologisches-homiletisches Bibelwerk: Altes Testament (Bielefeld: Velhagen und Klasing, 1864), 557.

[14] August Dillmann, *Die Genesis*, 4th ed. (Leipzig: Hirzel, 1882), 349: "alle die Aussagen über die Entrüstung und Tücke der Brüder der Dinah 5.7.13.31."

[15] Friedrich W. J. Schröder, *Das erste Buch Mose*, Das Alte Testament nach Dr. Martin Luther: Mit Einleitungen, berichtigter Uebersetzung und erklärenden Anmerkungen: Für Freunde des göttlichen Wortes, mit besonderer Rücksicht auf Lehrer in Kirchen und Schulen (Berlin: Wohlgemuth, 1846), 530: "Nothzüchtiger."

[16] Hoberg, *Genesis*, 291: "Dina wurde von Sichem, dem Sohne Hemors, vergewaltigt (V. 1-2). Sichem wie sein Vater trafen Veranstaltungen, eine legitime Ehe herbeizuführen ... aber Jakobs Söhne (Simeon und Levi) ermordeten den Verführer."

[17] Ibid., 292: "die Verführte."

[18] Hermann Gunkel, *Die Genesis*, Reihe Göttinger Handkommentar zum Alten Testament, 1st rev. ed. (Göttingen: Vandenhoeck & Rupprecht, 1901), 338.

[19] Baumgarten, *Genesis*, 292: "Es ist eine sträfliche Neugierde der Dina, daß sie ausgeht die Töchter des Landes zu besehen, denn die Töchter Israels haben mit den Töchtern Canaans nichts zu schaffen."

[20] Schröder, *Erste Buch Moses*, 530: "sie zu besuchen; eine Vertraulichkeit, wie sie der Tochter Israels mit den Töchtern Canaans schwerlich ziemt (2 Cor. 6, 17), daher auch die Strafe nicht ausbleibt."

[21] Ibid. For further examples, cf. O. Naumann, *Das Erste Buch der Bibel nach seiner inneren Einheit und Echtheit* (Gütersloh: Bertelsmann, 1890), 217: "So hat Sichem ... Dinah geschändet, wohl nicht ohne ihre Schuld, da der Lea Fleischeslust der Tochter Erbe wurde"; Heinrich W. J. Thiersch, *Die Genesis nach ihrer moralischen und prophetischen Bedeutung* (Basel: Schneider, 1870), 307: "Sie versäumte das, was in solchen Lagen der Jugend als Schutz notwendig ist. Es war bereits, ehe sie ausging, etwas in ihrem Herzen nicht richtig. Nur so war es möglich, daß es bei diesem Ausgang zu einem so tiefen Fall mit ihr kam."

[22] Johann P. Lange, *Genesis or the First Book of Moses together with a General Theological and Homiletical Introduction to the Old Testament*, trans. with additions by Taylor Lewis and A. Gosman, 5th rev. ed. (New York: Charles Scribner, 1884), 560.

[23] Ibid., 563f.

[24] Dillmann, *Genesis*, 1875, 373, 375; see also Holzinger, *Genesis*, 213, 216. For an examination of anti-Judaism in these interpretations, see Susanne Scholz, "Rape Plots: A Feminist Cultural Study of Genesis 34" (Ph.D. diss., Union Theological Seminary, NY, 1997), 70-73.

[25] Delitzsch, *New Commentary*, 1889, 225f.

[26] Delitzsch, *Genesis*, 1852, 341: "Die ganze Geschichte ... zeigt uns, die Schande des Verheissungsgeschlechts nicht bemäntelnd, wie das heilige Bundeszeichen von Simeon und Levi zum Trugmittel einer fluchwürdigen Privatrache gemissbraucht ward."

[27] Keil, *The Pentateuch*, 315.

[28] Bohlen, *Genesis*, 326.

[29] Naumann, *Erste Buch Moses*, 218.

[30] Christian C. Bunsen, *Die Bibel oder die Schriften des Alten und Neuen Bundes nach den überlieferten Grundtexten übersetzt und für die Gemeinde erklärt: Vollständiges Bibelwerk für die Gemeinde, in 3 Abtheilungen*, Erste Abtheilung: *Die Bibel: Uebersetzung und Erklärung*: Erster Theil: *Das Gesetz* (Leipzig: Brockhaus, 1858), 72: "die entsetzliche und unmenschliche Rache der Brüder."

[31] Schräder, *Erste Buch Mose*, 532.

[32] Ibid., 533.

[33] Lange, *Genesis*, 1884, 561. The following quotes are from his interpretation.

[34] Ibid., 565.

[35] Ibid., 564.

[36] Delitzsch, *Genesis*, 1852, 340.

[37] Dillmann, *Genesis*, 1875, 386: "[Er] redete ihr zu Herzen, suchte sie mit seiner Liebe und mit der Zukunft über das Geschehene zu beruhigen." See his other comments on p. 386: "An die Gewaltthat schliesst sich Liebe zu der Geschwächten"; on p. 388: "Weil Sikhem die Dinah so lieb hatte, zägerte er nicht,die Beschneidung anzunehmen."

[38] Gunkel, *Genesis*, 336. See also Schräder, *Genesis*, 531.

[39] Lange, *Genesis*, 1884, 564 and 567.

[40] Franz Delitzsch, *A New Commentary on Genesis*, trans. Sophia Taylor, 2 vols. (Edinburgh: Clark, 1889), 219, 222.

[41] Delitzsch, *Genesis*, 1852, 340.

[42] Dillmann, *Genesis*, 1875, 386.

[43] Keil, *The Pentateuch*, 312.

[44] Hoberg, *Genesis*, 291, 292.

[45] Lange, *Genesis*, 1884, 560.

[46] Gunkel, *Genesis*, 1901, 336: "Er [gewinnt] Dina lieb, beruhigt sie und erspricht ihr die Heirat." The following quotes are from his interpretation.

[47] Quotation marks are used with the term "pederasty" because at that time it covered what the term "homosexuality" describes today. For a history of the terminology see Jonathan Katz, *The Invention of Heterosexuality* (New York: Dutton, 1995).

[48] See Johann Valentin Müller, *Entwurf der gerichtlichen Arzneywissenschaft nach juristischen und medicinischen Grundsätzen, für Geistliche, Rechtsgelehrte und Aerzte,* vol. 1 (Frankfurt/Main: Andreäische Buchhandlung, 1796); Theodor G. A. Roose, *Grundriss medizinisch-gerichtlicher Vorlesungen* (Frankfurt/Main: Wilmans, 1802); Johann A. H. Nicolai, *Handbuch der gerichtlichen Medicin nach dem gegenwärtigen Standpunkt dieser Wissenschaft für Aerzte und Criminalisten* (Berlin: Hirschwald, 1841); Johannes B. Friedreich, *Handbuch der Gerichtsaerztlichen Praxis, mit Einschluss der gerichtlichen Veterinärkunde*, 2 vols. (Regensburg: Munz, 1843-1844).

[49] Adolph Chr. H. Henke, *Lehrbuch der gerichtlichen Medicin: Zum Behufe academischer Vorlesungen und zum Gebrauch für gerichtliche Ärzte und Rechtsgelehrte entworfen,* 13th ed. with additions by Carl Bergmann (Berlin: Dümmler, 1859), 133: "Untersuchungenüber weifelhafte Geschlechtsverhältnisse."

[50] Christian F. L. Wildberg, *Handbuch der gerichtlichen Arzneywissenschaft zur Grundlage bey akademischen Vorlesungen und zum Gebrauche für ausübende gerichtliche Aerzte* (Berlin: Dieterici, 1812), 102: "Von den Untersuchungen in Hinsicht des Beyschlafes."

[51] Johann D. Metzger, *Kurzgefasstes System der gerichtlichen Arzneywissenschaft*, nach dem Todte des Verfassers revidirt, verbessert, mit den nöthigen Zusätzen und einem Register versehen von Dr. Christian Gottfried Gruner,

4th rev. and enlarged ed. (Königsberg: Unzer, 1814), 457: "Gesetzwidriger Beyschlaf."

[52] Franz von Ney, *Systematisches Handbuch der gerichtsarzneilichen Wissenschaft mit besonderer Berücksichtigung der Erhebung des Thatbestandes im Straf- und Civilverfahren für Aerzte, Wundärzte, dann Justiz- und politische Beamte und Advokaten in den k.k. Staaten, nebst einem Anhange über den Geschäftsstyl* (Vienna: Mörschner's Witwe & W. Bianchi, 1845), 77: "Von der Nothzucht und anderen Unzuchtsfällen."

[53] For example, Ferdinand Hauska, *Compendium der gerichtlichen Arzneikunde*, 2nd rev. ed. (Wien: Braumüller, 1869), 11: "Verbotene Arten der Befriedigung des Geschlechtstriebes."

[54] J. Maschka, *Handbuch der Gerichtlichen Medicin*, vol. 3 (Tübingen: Laupp, 1882), 88: "Zeichen der Jungfrauschaft und gesetzwidrige Befriedigung des Geschlechtstriebes."

[55] Henke, *Lehrbuch,* 1812.

[56] Henke, *Lehrbuch,* 1859.

[57] G. H. Masius, *Lehrbuch der gerichtlichen Arzneikunde für Rechtsgelehrte*, Ersther Theil: *Propädeutik zur gerichtlichen Arzneikunde*, 2nd rev. and enlarged ed. (Altonau: Hammerich, 1812).

[58] Henke, *Lehrbuch,* 1859, 128.

[59] Wildberg, *Handbuch,* 115. See also Ernst Buchner, *Lehrbuch der Gerichtlichen Medicin für Aerzte und Juristen* (München: Finsterlin, 1867), 194; Johann F. Niemann, *Handbuch der Staats-Arzneywissenschaft und staatsärztlichen Veterinärkunde nach alphabetischer Ordnung für Aerzte, Medicinalpolizei-Beamte und Richter,* 2 vols. (Leipzig: Barth, 1813), 109f;

Casper Jacob E. von Siebold, *Lehrbuch der gerichtlichen Medicin: Zur Grundlage bei academischen Vorlesungen und zum Gebrauch für gerichtliche Aerzte und Rechtsgelehrte* (Berlin: Enslin, 1847), 108. For a different view, see Ludwig J. K. Mende, *Ausführliches Handbuch der gerichtlichen Medizin für Gesetzgeber, Rechtsgelehrte, Aerzte und Wundärzte*, vol. 4 (Leipzig: Dyk, 1826), 480f.

[60] Friedreich, *Handbuch,* vol. 2, 285.

[61] Henke, *Lehrbuch,* 1859, 129.

[62] Carl G. L. Ch. Bergmann, *Lehrbuch der Medicina forensis für Juristen* (Braunchweig: Vieweg, 1846), 370.

[63] Adolph Lion, *Taschenbuch der gerichtlichen Medicin nach dem neuesten Standpunkt der Wissenschaft und der Gesetzgebungen Deutschlands zum Gebrauche für Aerzte und Juristen.* (Erlangen: Ferndinand Enke, 1861), 132.

[64] Nicolai, *Handbuch*, 162; Ignaz H. Schürmayer, *Lehrbuch der Gerichtlichen Medicin: Mit Berücksichtigung der neueren Gesetzgebungen des In- und Auslandes insbesondere des Verfahrens bei Schwurgerichten. Für Ärzte und Juristen,* vol. 2, 2nd ed. (Erlangen: Ferdinand Enke, 1854), 332.

[65] Christian F. L. Wildberg, *Codex medico-forensis oder Inbegriff aller in gerichtlichen Fällen von den Gerichts-Aerzten zu beobachtenden Vorschriften* (Leipzig: Brockhaus, 1849), 41f.

[66] Friedreich, *Handbuch,* II, 1844, 287.

[67] Johann A. Schmidtmüller, *Handbuch der Staatsarzneykunde zu Vorlesungen und zum Gebrauche für Bezirksärzte, Polizei- und Justizbeamte* (Landshut: Krüll, 1804), 209. See also Ludwig J. K. Mende, *Ausführliches Handbuch der gerichtlichen Medizin für Gesetzgeber, Rechtsgelehrte, Aerzte und Wundärzte*, vol. 4 (Leipzig: Onk'sche Buchhandlung, 1826), 479; Müller, *Entwurf,* 129f.

[68] Georg H. Masius, *Handbuch der gerichtlichen Arzneiwissenschaft: Zum Gebrauche für gerichtliche Ärzte und Rechtsgelehrte,* vol. 1, part 1, 3rd ed. (Stendahl: Franzen und Grosse, 1821), 247f.

[69] Wolfgang F. W. Klose, *System der gerichtlichen Physik* (Breslau: Korn, 1814), 272-273.

Editor's note: This article is an abbreviated version of chapters three and four of *Rape Plots: A Feminist Cultural Study of Genesis 34* (New York: Peter Lang, 2000).

Surviving Genesis: Dangerous Worlds Both Narrative and Real

Mark McEntire

The past three or four decades have witnessed an explosion of attention to biblical narrative. With varying success, numerous critics and theoreticians have attempted to describe how biblical narrative, and narrative in general, operates. All of this exertion of effort is in part a backlash against the historical tendencies of the previous two centuries, which tended to devalue the stories found in the biblical text in favor of analysis of the events and transmission processes which lay behind them. This essay will begin with a discussion of the nature of biblical narrative, but I hope it will not be one which ultimately removes, or even obscures, a sense of mystery about how stories operate.

My end goal is to make some observations about violence in the book of Genesis and how the presence of violence in the Genesis narratives might affect readers of the book. In order to do this, I will adopt the concept of narrative worlds.[1] How narratives create a world for readers to enter is a subject of much dispute, but hardly anyone will deny that narratives, including those in Genesis, do create such worlds. Therefore, I propose to enter the world of Genesis and, without fully understanding how that world comes to be or how it draws me in, to ask some questions about violence such as: What is the effect of violent stories in Genesis on modern readers? How do readers' views of and experiences in their own real worlds influence their comprehension of the text?

The most prominent feature of the current debate over biblical narrative focuses on the problematic use of the term "realistic" to describe it. The term has been brought to the center of the debate by the influential work of Hans Frei. Frei defined "realistic narrative" as "that kind in which subject and social setting belong together, and characters and external circumstances fitly render each other."[2] Frei argued further that because of these qualities realistic narrative is very much like history. Therefore, he also labeled biblical narrative "history-like." Frei's conclusions, despite the problems which I will discuss below, have provided a great service for the field of biblical interpretation. He has been at the forefront of bringing narrative, or stories, back to the center of attention. Most importantly, he has reminded us that a story and its meaning are inseparable. Biblical stories do not illustrate meanings that can be extracted and stated as principles.[3] The way to their meanings is to enter the stories and hope to emerge transformed.

The shortcomings of Frei's understanding of narrative are best illustrated by examining the narrative theory of Paul Ricoeur. Extensive attempts to compare and contrast Frei and Ricoeur have been made by others,[4] so only a brief summary is called for here. Among other differences, Ricoeur's theory of narrative places greater emphasis on the role of the reader. While Frei's insistence on the realistic nature of biblical narrative led him to stress the autonomy of the text,[5] Ricoeur has argued for the importance of the reader's contribution to the determination of the meaning of biblical language.[6] Mark Ellingsen, a strong critic of Ricoeur, has correctly understood that "correlation" is vital to the hermeneutics of Ricoeur and others who take a similar view.[7] Correlation may be understood most simply as the need for some experience of correspondence between the world of the reader and the narrative world of the text in order for an experience of the narrative to take place. Ellingsen was incorrect, however, in supposing that meaningful reading of narrative can take place without correlation.[8] Somehow, the world of the text must fit together with the world of the reader. The text cannot remain completely autonomous and self-referential once the act of reading has begun. Lewis Mudge has aptly labeled Ricoeur's approach "anti-Cartesian."[9] Our pure, objective, and unaccompanied minds do not enter biblical narrative worlds.[10] Simplistic notions about readers inhabiting biblical narrative worlds and experiencing them as the real world do not stand up to close scrutiny. Amos N. Wilder stated that "the ancient rehearsals may be recognized in some sort as the archetypal molds of our own histories and fabulations." In plain terms, when contemporary readers travel through biblical narrative worlds they carry a great deal of baggage.

There are important issues at stake in this debate. Perhaps the most important is the Bible's ability to transform readers and the world they live in. For those who follow Frei, it is vital that the Bible be able to stand apart from human culture, in critique and judgement.[12] The supposed autonomous nature of Biblical narrative, which means that the text does not rely on the reader or the reader's culture and experience to determine its meaning, would seem to guarantee this critical position. This notion of how narrative operates, however, relies on a highly idealistic understanding of the reader and the reading process. This problem has been noted by many critics of Frei. Francis Watson, for example, has contended that "it is one thing to identify the role these texts outline for their implied reader, quite another to show how a real reader might be able to fill that role."[13] This gives rise to the key question of whether complete textual autonomy is the only situation which allows for reader transformation. Might readers' experiences of their own worlds interact with the world of the text within the reading process in a way which transforms both the text and the reader?[14]

A profound illustration of the effect readers' choices have on their experiences of biblical narratives can be observed in the African debate about the meaning of the Cain and Abel story in Genesis 4. The character with whom the reader chooses to identify, Abel (murdered herdsman) or Cain (dispossessed farmer who responds with violence), determines how the narrative world is experienced.[15] To illustrate the problem in a different context, we might pose the question, how can the story of the battle of Jericho in Joshua 6 operate autonomously when read by a contemporary Palestinian Christian, for whom this text is supposed to be the inspired word of God?

Mention of these two biblical stories brings us to the issue of violence in the Bible. This issue has received rapidly growing attention over the past two decades. The impetus can probably be attributed to the work of the literary critic René Girard, who has often applied his general literary and anthropological theories to biblical texts.[16] Studies of violence in the Bible have continued and multiplied in the work of Walter Wink, Robert Hamerton-Kelley, James G. Williams, Mieke Bal, Regina M. Schwartz, and many others.[17] What explains the sudden prominence of this issue? The texts have been there all along. Something has changed in the collective manner of reading. Surely, this has something to do with the increasing awareness of violence in our own world. Late twentieth century culture has produced readers who approach the Bible with a new set of questions, who find a stunning correspondence between their own violent world and that of the Bible. Those who enter the Bible with an awakened sensitivity find that it is filled with violence from beginning to end, and the book of Genesis establishes a pattern of violence.

The book of Genesis begins with the creation of the universe and ends with the death of Joseph in Egypt. For those who read the book from beginning to end, the shape of a funnel might be the best visual representation of the story line.[18] The narrowing of focus is a dominating narrative process. Traditionally, a clear line of division has been drawn between the Primeval Story in chapters 1-11 and the Patriarchal Narratives in 12-50. A number of recent interpreters have effectively emphasized both the narrative and theological continuity between these two sections and the somewhat arbitrary nature of the sharp divisions often drawn between them, including the chapter and verse divisions.[19] Regardless of one's conclusions about possible seams or divisions, the narrative is continuous. The world and humanity within it are created by God at the beginning of Genesis and by the end a family, the children of Jacob, has been separated out from all of the other peoples of the world to be the focal point of God's attention.

The setting of the book of Genesis is vague at the beginning, but becomes clearly focused as the book progresses. Genesis 1 has a universal scope, of course, and Genesis 2-3 has a deliberately ambiguous setting. According to 2:10-15, Eden is the place where the rivers of Mesopotamia, the northern and eastern boundary of the world known to Genesis, meet the rivers of Cush, the known southern and western boundary. Eden is both everywhere and nowhere at the same time. Once Adam and Eve leave the garden, the setting of the Cain and Abel story is unspecified. The text gives only a sense of eastward movement in 3:24 and 4:16.[20] The setting of the flood narrative is again universal, but beginning with the genealogies in chapter 9 and, more specifically, chapter 10, clear lines on the map finally appear. Geographical names familiar even to most modern readers arise, though they are sometimes listed as the names of the descendants of Shem, Ham, and Japheth. The wandering reader finally begins to get a sense of direction. That sense is delayed one last time by the ambiguous setting of the Tower of Babel incident in 11:1-9, but in the family of Terah the reader finds companions moving in a clear direction, through a known landscape.

At this point in the book of Genesis, characters come to the forefront. Adam, Eve, Cain, and Noah are personages about whom we discover some traits, but Abram/Abraham and Sarai/Sarah are the first three-dimensional characters in the book. We learn of their hopes and dreams, their successes and failures, their strengths and weaknesses of character. Indeed, this is one place where the reader, carrying his or her own cultural norms for human behavior, may be invited to participate in the story. The book of Genesis is notorious for refusing to pass judgment on the actions of Abraham and Sarah. Is it inappropriate for modern readers to condemn the behavior of Abram in 12:10-20 when he passes Sarai off as his sister, thus threatening her life, bringing undeserved punishment onto Pharaoh, and enriching himself? Is it wrong to pass judgement on both Abraham and Sarah for their treatment of Hagar and Ishmael? The world of Genesis becomes a world of moral ambiguity at these points, but contemporary readers have no problems evaluating these actions as wrong.

The most difficult test for modern readers lies in the Akedah story of Genesis 22. Here the biblical text clearly commends Abraham for an act modern readers find repugnant, the near sacrifice of his son Isaac. The moral ambiguity of the narrative reaches its high point in the beautifully developed character of Jacob, who lies and schemes his way through his entire life, without explicit disapproval from the narrator. Indeed, one can argue that there is implicit approval of his behavior because he continues to be the object of God's covenant affections.

Finally, in Joseph, the modern reader finds a nearly ideal character. Throughout the ups and downs of his life, Joseph remains steadfastly virtuous and God is with him. [21] He is eventually rewarded for his virtue and finds himself in a position to save his brothers from famine, which he does despite their past mistreatment of him. The book of Genesis ends with a note on the embalming of Joseph. His dead body and the faithful promise he demands from his family point forward to the Exodus and the Promised Land. [22]

The plot of Genesis receives its structure from genealogies. [23] They often carry the reader through hundreds and thousands of years very rapidly. At the same time, their roots and branches present an understanding of Israelite identity. Here is a place where the modern reader must make clear choices about how to interact with the narrative. The most common choice is probably to skip over the genealogies. They are exceedingly dull and repetitive. The genealogies told ancient Israelite readers who they were and how they fit into the story, but modern readers are left to position themselves. Frei's autonomous, self-referential text fails here. Modern readers must find some sense of correspondence between their lives and the world of the story because the attempt by the text to tell the reader how to read falls on deaf ears, or blind eyes. A simple example of this occurs in the narratives about Jacob stealing the birthright (25:29-34) and the blessing (27:1-40) of Esau. Surely, Israelites were to associate themselves with Jacob, the one receiving the blessing, no matter what the circumstances. Modern readers, however, are quite prone to empathize with Esau, the cheated one. Is this way of reading improper? I suppose that Frei and his followers would have to say that it is. Such readers are imposing their own set of values, which are seemingly foreign to the text. Nevertheless, this is the reading experience that many, if not most contemporary readers have.

The other components of Genesis, the stories,[24] hang on the skeletal framework of the genealogies. These more lengthy narratives function like a zoom lens, giving the reader a close-up view of specific events. These stories often provide detailed accounts of the lives of those who are chosen to receive God's blessing, the winners of the genealogical contest. In telling us these stories the text depicts a stunningly violent and dangerous world. The recent work of Regina M. Schwartz has drawn significant attention to some of the foundational understandings behind these stories. Schwartz's underlying thesis is that biblical thought is dominated by an "assumption of scarcity."[25] Abel and Jacob are blessed while Cain and Esau are not because there are not enough resources in the world for everyone to be blessed. This assumption sets up a world where chosenness and rejection, blessing and curse, and possession and dispossession are determined by violent means.

The first narratives of Genesis are of utmost importance. Genesis 1-3 is the portal through which we enter the world of this book. What kind of world is it? According to the first story of creation in Genesis 1, it is unmistakably an ordered world. Every aspect of the account exhibits this sense of order, from the numbered days to the increasing complexity of the life forms which appear. Not only is creation ordered, it is designed to maintain this order, each plant producing seeds "according to its kind"(1:12), and human beings "having dominion" over the other life forms (1:28). This feeling of order creates in readers expectations about the nature of the world. Ricoeur, in dialogue with Hans-Heinrich Schmidt and Jon Levenson, links this expectation of order with a desire for justice.[26]

Some sense of order remains throughout the second story of creation in Genesis 2. Order is brought from the cosmic dimensions of Genesis 1 down to the scale of a man and a woman and a garden. The world of Genesis does not remain idealistic for long, however. In Genesis 3 things begin to fall apart. The orderly world is disrupted by the disobedience of the man and the woman in 3:1-7 and, thus, requires some reordering by God in 3:14-24. This establishes a pattern for the following chapters. Things go wrong when Cain kills Abel (4:8), when all of humanity becomes consumed by wickedness (6:5), and when the entire human race attempts to stay together in one place and build a great city (11:1-4). These problems force God to revise creation by banishing Cain further to the east (4:11-16), by flooding the earth (6:7), and by scattering the builders of the tower so that they have no choice but to fill the earth (11:8-9).[27] The disorder in creation is caused by actions that are frequently violent, but God's corrective measures are at least equally violent.

Once the scattering is accomplished, God chooses one man, Abram, through whom to work his purpose in the world. The purpose is rather vague in the beginning. God will bless Abram and through him all the families of the earth (12:2-3). Tension arises in the plan immediately, however, because God also says, "I will curse the one who curses you" (12:3). The remainder of the book of Genesis is a series of stories of selective blessing. It turns out that not all can be blessed. The potential for violent competition within creation has erupted earlier. When God regards Abel but not Cain (4:4-5), the result is murder (4:8) and cursing (4:11). Noah finds favor in the sight of God (6:8) and God blots out all life on earth (6:7) except for those persons and animals which find refuge with Noah. The positive side of God's choosing of Abraham, Isaac, and Jacob is shadowed by the rejection of Lot, Ishmael, and Esau.

In Genesis 12-50, God is actively producing Israel, but this production is accomplished at a price. The cities of Sodom and Gamorah and their inhabitants are destroyed. Abraham struggles to be a blessing to them (18:22-33) but he fails. Hagar and Ishmael are expelled into the wilderness in order to secure the place of Isaac (21:14). They nearly die before God helps Hagar to find water (21:15-19). The "blessing" they receive is minimal at best. Jacob steals the birthright and blessing of Esau and the two brothers are thrown into conflict. Esau is prosperous, but he and Jacob are unable to live peacefully in proximity to one another (36:6-8). The defining of Israel is accomplished by means which are violent and destructive. Even the naming of Israel and the working out of its relationship to God are represented as a violent wrestling match which causes permanent physical injury (32:22-33).

The pattern of conflict does not end once Israel is clearly defined as the twelve sons of Jacob and their families. They continue to fight with their neighbors (34:25-31) and quarrel amongst themselves (37:18-24). The song of Jacob in Genesis 49 points to differing degrees of blessing. Simeon and Levi are characterized by violent anger and God will ultimately "divide" them because of it (49:5-7). On the other end of the scale of blessing is the tribe of Judah, which will receive the praise of all the other tribes and will rule over them (49:8-12). Joseph's success in Egypt reunites the family, and the book of Genesis ends with Joseph struggling to maintain family unity in the future through the oath to carry his bones out of Egypt (50:24-26), but the internal and external conflicts of the future are already foretold.

In Western traditions of interpretation, Genesis has most often been conceived as a story of Creation, Fall, and Redemption. My reading of Genesis is not inconsistent with this picture, but emphasizes other aspects. Perhaps this doctrinal scheme has been extracted too neatly from the disturbing narrative world of Genesis. When the violent and destructive nature of the story is repressed, two diverging movements often appear. One is a tendency to see the world as hopelessly fallen and lost. Those who view the world in this way long for the order of Genesis 1 and sometimes attempt to reproduce it in small, encapsulated spaces. This tendency extends at least from Qumran in the first century to Waco in the twentieth.[28]

A second movement tends to understand the order of Genesis 1 as still present and often ignores the chaotic nature of the world. Those who assume this understanding commonly explain and accept every event as part of God's will or design. The book of Genesis certainly encourages this tendency, especially in the Joseph narratives (e. g. 45:4-15). For both views, the world depicted in Genesis 2-50 is a frightening place to live. When the real world corresponds to the world of Genesis in its violent capacities, as it all too often does, they must isolate themselves with walls of brick or ignorant bliss. Both of these approaches to surviving in the world frequently idealize the characters of Genesis, isolating certain traits such Noah's obedience, Abraham's faithfulness, or Jacob's strength, for emulation. This ignores the complexity of the stories which Genesis uses to develop these characters, who are rarely models of virtue.

When we enter the world of Genesis, we discover that violence is an inevitable part of human character and existence. It is inextricably woven into our patterns of identification and material production. In this world, human beings must struggle to find hope. Moral choices are not clear. Creation is not typically characterized by justice. Yet the world of Genesis is not without hope. Finding and holding onto the thread of hope throughout the long journey from creation to the embalming of Joseph require honesty, diligence, and tenacity. But this final scene points forward to continued existence, blessing, and even deliverance (50:26).[29] Is it appropriate for us to add our own modern sensitivities and try to extend this hope to all persons, and not just chosen groups? The impact of Genesis on the modern world has too often come from the reading of individual texts. Genesis 1 and 2 provide visions of order and harmony which characterized the world in its infancy. These visions alternately cause feelings of unrealistic hope and total despair, giving rise to Utopians and prophets of doom. Such counterproductive readings result from a disjointed, non-corresponding experience of the first two chapters of Genesis as narrative worlds in and of themselves, rather than as portals to a fuller world developed in the whole book.

Genesis 3 offers an explanation for the difficult (fallen?) nature of the world. Strong traditions of interpretation have focused specifically on sexual sin as the legacy of this "fall."[30] Whether the Western world's preoccupation with sexual sin is to be blamed more on the text of Genesis 3 or on St. Augustine's reading of it is debatable, but this is certainly a place where readers' assumptions and expectations play a large role in determining their narrative experiences and the impact that these narrative experiences have on their lives.

If one reads on from Genesis 4 to 50, however, it becomes evident that violence, not sex, is the sin which does so easily beset humankind. Bad habits of fragmentary reading, for which lectionaries and devotional guides are partly to blame, form this misconception. In following Ricoeur more closely than Frei, I must conclude that it is not the Bible which shapes and transforms our world, but our reading of it. Narrative experiences are not uni-directional. Reader and text interact, both bringing something to the table, and this interaction is most productive when a sense of correspondence is found between our experience and the fully developed narrative world of the text.

It would appear that our increased awareness of violence in our own world can create a sense of correspondence between our world and the narrative world of Genesis. We then become more aware of the violent nature of the text. This interplay between the world of the text and the world of the reader may explain the intensified interest in the issue of violence in the Bible at the end of the twentieth century. A transformed reading offers possibilities for transforming our own world. The difficulty of such a reading creates barriers, but there are signs in contemporary hermeneutics and in a renewed interest in the book of Genesis that such barriers might be overcome.

Notes

[1]The origin of this concept is difficult to trace. Its application to biblical studies is perhaps best credited to Amos N. Wilder in "Story and Story-World." This article, originally published in 1983 in *Interpretation,* is most easily accessible in *The Bible and the Literary Critic* (Minneapolis: Fortress, 1991), 132-148.

[2] Hans Frei, *The Eclipse of Biblical Narrative: A Study in Eighteenth and Nineteenth Century Hermeneutics* (New Haven: Yale University Press, 1974), 13. Frei acknowledged the influence on his own understanding of narrative of the work of Erich Auerbach. Most significant is Auerbach's discussion of the Akedah story of Genesis 22 in *Mimesis: The Representation of Reality in Western Literature* (Princeton: Princeton University Press, 1953), 7-23.

[3] *The Eclipse of Biblical Narrative*, 280.

[4] The most balanced and informative of such analyses has come in a pair of related articles by Gary Comstock. See "Truth or Meaning: Ricoeur versus Frei on Biblical Narrative," *Journal of Religion* 66 (1986): 117-140; and "Two Types of Narrative Theology," *Journal of the American Academy of Religion* 55 (1987): 687-717. In the end, Comstock gives much credit to Frei, but positions himself closer to Ricoeur. A somewhat polemical attempt to analyze Frei and Ricoeur has been made by Mark Ellingsen, who follows Frei closely and rejects Ricoeur's views entirely. See *The Integrity of Biblical Narrative: Story in Theology and Proclamation* (Minneapolis: Fortress, 1990).

[5] Hans Frei, *The Identity of Jesus Christ: The Hermeneutical Bases of Dogmatic Theology* (Philadelphia: Fortress, 1975), xiii-xvii.

[6] Paul Ricoeur, *Time and Narrative,* vol. I (Chicago: University of Chicago Press, 1984), 77-82.

[7] Ellingsen, *The Integrity of Biblical Narrative,* 13.

[8] Ibid., 43-52. Here in a sample of Ellingsen's own narrative interpretation he relies on correlation. Comstock has also noted a "tacit" need for correlation in the interpretations of Frei. See "Truth or Meaning," 124-127.

[9] See Lewis Mudge, "Paul Ricoeur on Biblical Interpretation," in *Paul Ricoeur, Essays on Biblical Interpretation*, ed. Lewis Mudge (Philadelphia: Fortress, 1980), 8-10.

[10] Note that this idea is very close to Hans Gerge Gadamer's influential description of a "fusion of horizons" as a model for the hermeneutical process. See Gadamer, *Truth and Method* (London: Sheed and Ward, 1975), 269-278.

[11] Amos N. Wilder, "The World Story: Biblical Version," in *Jesus' Parables and the War of Myths: Essays on Imagination in the Scriptures* (Philadelphia: Fortress, 1982), 52. Note also that Wilder's description of biblical narrative raises problems with notions of realism: "The human actions [in the Bible] burst the wonted course of affairs and explode, as it were, into the hyperbolic. They go over

the limits of human scale, in heroism or immolation, in ecstacy or horror" (p. 58).

[12] See, for example, Ellingsen, *The Integrity of biblical Narrative*, 27; or George Lindbeck, *The Nature of Doctrine: Religion and Theology in a Postliberal Age* (Philadelphia: Westminster, 1984), 117-118.

[13] Francis Watson, *Text and Truth: Redefining Biblical Theology* (Grand Rapids: Eerdmans, 1997), 36-37. In addition, it relies on an unclear notion of how narratives are related to history. This problem has been described by a number of critics. See Watson, *Text and Truth,* 39, and Stephen Prickett, Words and the *Word: Language Poetics and Biblical Interpretation* (Cambridge: Cambridge University Press, 1986), 194-195.

[14] For a highly developed hermeneutic which may point in this direction, see Anthony C. Thiselton, *New Horizons in Hemeneutics: The Theory and Practice of Transforming Bible Reading* (Grand Rapids: Zondervan, 1992), 8-29.

[15] For a more complete discussion of the competing understandings of Genesis 4 in Africa, see Mark McEntire, "Cain and Abel in Africa: Using Competing Hermeneutics as a Pedagogical Method with Ethiopian Students," in *The Bible in Africa*, ed. Gerald West (Leiden: Brill, forthcoming).

[16] Girard's first extended application of his theory of violence to biblical texts came with the publication of *La Violence et la sacre* in 1972. This work was published in English as *Violence and the Sacred* (Baltimore: John Hopkins University Press, 1977).

[17] The works of the authors listed here include Walter Wink, *Engaging the Powers: Discernment and Resistance in a World of Domination* (Minneapolis: Fortress, 1992); Robert Hamerton-Kelly, *Sacred Violence: Paul's Hermeneutic of the Cross* (San Francisco: Harper Collins, 1991); Mieke Bal, L*ethal Love: Feminist Literary Readings of Biblical Love Stories* (Bloomington: Indiana University Press, 1987); and Regina M. Schwartz, *The Curse of Cain: The Violent Legacy of Monotheism* (Chicago, University of Chicago, 1997).

[18] One problem with the entering of narrative worlds is that repeated readings may make the text too familiar. It may sometimes lose its power to draw us in and to surprise us because of this familiarity. For those who want to experience a new sense of freshness in reading the book a Genesis, the new translation by Robert Alter may prove helpful. This translation is a unique and daring attempt to reproduce in English the literary effect of the Hebrew text. This guiding principle provides Alter's translation with a different feel from many traditional English translations. See Robert Alter, *Genesis: Translation and Commentary* (New York: Norton, 1996).

[19] See the discussion of John J. Scullion, "The Narrative of Genesis," in T*he Anchor Bible Dictionary,* vol. 2, ed. David Noel Freedman (New York: Doubleday, 1992), 949. The separation of these two blocks of material also involves a supposed shift in theological theme from creation to salvation. See the critique of this easy separation by André Lacoque and Paul Ricoeur, *Thinking Biblically: Exegetical and Hermeneutical Studies,* trans. David Pellauer (Chicago: University of Chicago

Press, 1998), 3-8 and 31-34.

[20] For an insightful discussion of all the eastward movements in the book of Genesis, see Devora Steinmetz, *From Father to Son: Kinship, Conflict and Continuity in Genesis* (Louisville: Westminster, 1991), 143-144.

[21] The nature of God's presence has changed, however. Unlike the face to face contact enjoyed by Abraham and Jacob, Joseph receives only symbolic dreams and the reader is merely informed of God's presence in colorless statements (39:2,21). On this issue in the Joseph narratives, see Claus Westermann, *Joseph* (Minneapolis: Fortress, 1996). For more comprehensive discussions of the progressive withdrawal of God's presence throughout the course of the Bible, see Jack Miles, *God: A Biography* (New York: Knopf, 1995), and Richard Elliott Friedman, *The Disappearance of God: A Divine Mystery* (Boston: Little, Brown, 1995).

[22] Friedman has discussed in significant detail the progressive changes in character development in Genesis. See *The Disappearance of God,* 31-35.

[23] For a thorough discussion of how the lists of descendents form the literary framework of the book, see Joseph Blenkinsopp, *The Pentateuch: An Introduction* (New York: Doubleday, 1989), 58-60, 98-100.

[24] Labeling the non-genealogical material in Genesis is problematic. The designation I have chosen, "story," is not entirely fair. The genealogies themselves are stories, in a way, and the non-genealogical material contains other forms of literature, such as songs and poems.

[25] Regina M. Schwartz, *The Curse of Cain,* 19.

[26] See La Cocque and Ricoeur, *Thinking Biblically*, 54-61.

[27] This movement in the book of Genesis has been described as "cracks in the wall" by La Cocque. See *Thinking Biblically,* 3-29. La Cocque has also noted the tendency of readers to recognize themselves in the characters of these stories and the powerful results of this sense of correspondence (p. 29).

[28] From the Dead Sea Scrolls, we know that the community associated with these documents isolated itself from first-century Judaism, lived a regimented lifestyle, and looked forward to a future war of righteous vindication. They were likely destroyed when the Roman army rolled over Palestine in the late first century. The Branch Davidians in Waco, Texas, also isolated themselves, lived a regimented life, and heavily armed themselves. They were destroyed in a conflict with American authorities in 1993.

[29] In a recent book, Gareth Lloyd Jones has used the "bones of Joseph" as a metaphor for tradition. This metaphor symbolizes the very act of carrying something from the past into the uncertain future. See *The Bones of Joseph: From the Ancient Texts to the Modern Church* (Grand Rapids: Eerdmans, 1997).

[30] See Elaine Pagels, *Adam, Eve, and the Serpent* (New York: Vintage, 1989), xvii-xxviii.

Portrayals of Power in the Stories of Delilah and Bathsheba: Seduction in Song

Helen Leneman

This paper explores commonalities and differences between the stories of Delilah and Bathsheba and discusses the gaps in plot that have led to a wide variety of interpretations of these stories. After a review of these interpretations, there will be an overview of Talmudic and other post-biblical interpretations, including current biblical scholarship. Following this will be a discussion of literature and music from the sixteenth century up to the present inspired by the stories of Delilah and Bathsheba.

Although the songs referred to in the title of this paper depict seduction, the thesis of this paper is that these were not true seductions but only misrepresented as such by the popular media; this was due largely to post-biblical interpretations of the stories beginning in Talmudic times and continuing through twentieth century literature. In addition to character and plot similarities, there is also a theme common to both stories. A sexual act between the most powerful man of his time and a "seductive" woman is at the center of both stories, and this brings up the theme of rape and seduction as acts of power. Temptation and the male response to it are part of this theme. *Who has the real power in these stories?* is the question posed to the reader.

Though both Delilah and Bathsheba have been commonly portrayed and perceived as seductresses, a review of the literature does not reveal sustained discussion of parallels between their stories. Yet parallels do exist: both are assumed to be beautiful, virtually irresistible women; though in a sense both could be seen as victors, this paper will attempt to show they were both victims and pawns of men. As elsewhere in the Bible, motives and responses in both stories are ambiguous, leaving the reader unclear even as to who the hero is. This ambiguity has led to a great deal of interpretation and midrashic emendation, most at the expense of Delilah's and Bathsheba's reputations. Ultimately both these women are denigrated in order to elevate the men with whom they are involved, so the men can remain the focal point and hero of their respective sagas.

There are obvious differences between the stories as well. Bathsheba's story is part of the Davidic chronicles, believed to be fairly historical; the story of Samson and Delilah has a folk tale tone and is likely to be more myth than history. Yet in both cases the writer's agenda was to elevate the male hero, so ultimately it may not matter to which genre of biblical literature the stories belong.

Taken simply as two stories, the most obvious difference is in the type of woman involved: one reputable (Bathsheba), the other disreputable (Delilah). This distinction was crucial to the biblical writers, who took any opportunity to warn men of the dangers of disreputable women. And clearly Delilah posed a greater danger to Samson than did Bathsheba to David. The other major distinction between the stories is in the conclusion: Bathsheba resurfaces to become a much more well-rounded and important character in the ongoing story of David's reign, while Delilah simply vanishes. The fact that he was tempted by a reputable woman rather than by a Delilah was an advantage not only to David but also to Bathsheba herself.

The story of Samson and Delilah (Book of Judges, chapter 16 verses 4-30) is too well known to warrant a lengthy introduction: Samson falls in love with Delilah, who is paid by the Philistines to find out the source of his great strength; she nags him until he tells her the secret, which is his hair. She has it cut off, Samson is captured, blinded and imprisoned. When his hair grows back and he is put on display in the Philistines' temple, in a final show of superhuman strength Samson brings down the whole temple.

Prior to the episode with Delilah, Samson had been involved with other women, none of them Israelites. Most significant are the opening three verses of chapter 16, wherein Samson meets and has sex with a prostitute in Gaza. He escapes a planned ambush, then grasps the posts of the town gate and carries them off on his shoulders. The story continues:

After that, he fell in love with a woman in the Wadi Sorek, named Delilah. The lords of the Philistines went up to her and said, "Coax him and find out what makes him so strong."[1]

The placement of the meeting with Delilah immediately after the episode with the prostitute is significant. Is it not possible, as some scholars have suggested, that some of the attitude towards the prostitute could wash over Delilah? Possibly because of this association with the previous verses, Delilah has often been considered a prostitute herself, but nowhere is she thus identified. Contrary to common misconceptions and unlike Bathsheba, there is actually no description of Delilah at all.

The story of Bathsheba to be treated here is from 2 Samuel 11 and 12: 1-25, in which David spots Bathsheba bathing, has her brought to him, sleeps with her and makes her pregnant. David then orders her husband Uriah, a soldier in his army, home from the front and strongly encourages him to visit his wife. Uriah refuses several times, leaving David with only one option, namely, to arrange to have Uriah killed in battle. After this deed has been accomplished, he marries Bathsheba. The prophet Nathan then comes to David and, by use of a parable, makes it clear that God is displeased with David's actions and that David will be punished. The punishment is the death of their firstborn child. The fact that this is at least as much punishment for the mother, Bathsheba, as for David is never mentioned by the writer. David mourns and then another child, Solomon, is subsequently born to them, destined to succeed his father as king. (According to 1 Chronicles 3:5, Bathsheba had four sons: Shimea, Shebab, Nathan and Solomon.) It is quite possible that the account of David and Bathsheba is a case of layering a story on top of a historical reality, whereas that of Samson and Delilah is the opposite, an attempt to historicize a folk tale.

Unlike Delilah, who is never described, Bathsheba is described as "very beautiful." In addition, she is identified by her relationship to males: "She is Bathsheba daughter of Eliam, wife of Uriah the Hittite" (2 Samuel 11:4). However, her reactions and point of view are not revealed by the writer any more than are Delilah's.

Delilah is arguably the most famous woman in the Book of Judges, her name a synonym for the mature seductive woman. Though not identified as a prostitute, she was obviously a woman available outside marriage, overtly using sexual attraction to entice Samson. Delilah, the only woman named in Samson's story, is identified not by the name of any male relatives (as was common when introducing an Israelite woman such as Bathsheba), nor even by her home town, but rather by a whole region, the *nahal sorek. Nahal* means wadi, a gully which becomes a virtual torrent after a rain; and *sorek* alludes to a choice wine grape. Thus the place name itself, Lillian Klein suggests, could imply passion and loss of control. Even more importantly, Delilah is identified as an unattached woman, whom biblical writers often depicted as seductively leading men astray. [2]

The great importance of names in biblical tradition has led some to stretch for meaning in explicating both Delilah's and Bathsheba's names. The name Delilah itself may derive from *dalal*, which as a Hebrew root means to be weak or to hang, to let low. The Arabic root *dalla* means to behave amorously. So the name could mean "falling curls" or "flirtatious." It might also mean "one of the night" (Hebrew *de-laila),* since her name in Hebrew *(de-laila)* could be based on the Hebrew root *laila*, meaning "night" (although it is pronounced as *de-leela*). Interpreted this way, Delilah would be the night who extinguishes "one of the sun" (*Shimshon,* the Hebrew for Samson, from the Hebrew word, sun).[3]

The name Bathsheba *(bat*=daughter, *sheba*=oath or a name) might refer to uncertain parentage (though her father's name is known) or an oath. Yet she is rarely even called by her name after her initial identification in 2 Samuel 11:3. Her name is uttered only after her infant dies (12:24), and only here is she called "David's wife"; otherwise she is always called "Uriah's wife" or simply "the woman."

Bathsheba's feelings are not relayed to the reader. In fact, the delineation of her character is so sketchy that it leaves virtually everything open to the imagination. In the early scenes, Bathsheba is a nonperson, merely part of the plot. Adele Berlin points out that she is not even a "type," but rather an "agent," an Aristotelian term which describes the performer of an action necessary to the plot. Where the plot called for adultery, Bathsheba became the agent. Berlin claims that Bathsheba is not considered guilty of adultery because she was only the means whereby it was achieved. [4]

Similarly one could claim that Delilah is also an "agent," since the Philistine leaders are acting through her. Partly because these Philistines come to her, it has commonly been assumed that Delilah is herself a Philistine, although it is not stated in the biblical account. But why would an Israelite woman betray her people's hero? Lillian Klein admits that there is only the "suggestion" that she is Philistine.[5] Tikva Frymer-Kensky, on the other hand, sees no compelling reason to assume this. The text, she points out, "never tells us that Delilah was a foreigner. The valley of Sorek is only thirteen miles west-southwest of Jerusalem...Danite territory, still occupied by Israelites. It was a border area that may not even have been under Philistine control.... Since the text does not mention that Delilah was a Philistine, there is no reason to assume it." [6]

Delilah is often assumed to have been a Philistine in order to make the lesson of the story one of a warning against foreign women. For example, Cheryl Exum writes: "The lesson of this text is to teach the Israelite male a lesson about the dangers of foreign women; nationalism reinforces gender ideology." [7] Lillian Klein adds: "Delilah may not be a prostitute; the text is ambiguous, showing that the Israelite male cannot comprehend foreign women's words, values, or allegiances." [8] But the warning could just as well be against any independent, unattached woman, regardless of nationality. Part of the androcentric agenda of biblical writers was to portray women as powerful and dangerous, yet still subject to control by men. The narrator of this story seems to attach the blame for Samson's downfall to women, who are themselves victims of exploitation, since the Philistine men act through Delilah (rather than the usual reverse).

Cheryl Exum has called this story a "variation of a traditional folk tale whose latent meaning discloses male fear of women." [9] In a more recent interpretation, Exum coins the phrase "Samson complex," by which she means "the man's desire to surrender to the woman and his fear that he will be destroyed by her....Samson yielded, and look what happened to him, says our story. If even an apparently invincible man like Samson can be undone by a woman, how much more so should the ordinary man be on his guard. Such is the fear the woman inspires."[10] The point is that Delilah does not betray Samson so much as he betrays himself by revealing his secrets to her.

In a similar interpretation, Betsy Merideth points out that this story "is at least as much about Samson's pride and pretensions to immortality as it is about Delilah's harm to him." Merideth's thesis is that "betrayal" is not the appropriate term for Delilah's actions, since Samson is depicted as knowing what is going on. As an active participant in the events, he is not merely a victim. [11]

Whoever was the guiltier party in the story of Samson and Delilah, both paid a price in the end. Samson dies as a hero, destroying himself along with the Temple of the Philistine god Dagon. Delilah dies a textual death, vanishing from the story with her fate unknown to the reader.

Bathsheba, on the other hand, is notable as the only woman in David's life who participates in the ongoing story of his reign, for she vanishes from the text only to resurface later (in the Book of Kings) as a much stronger person, the queen mother. As Alice Bach points out, the length of a female's textual life seems connected with the extent of sexual pleasure she provides her male creators (or the males in the story) [12]—or, of course, how many sons she provides!

There are many disturbing aspects to the account of Bathsheba and David's initial encounter, as well as gaps in the narrative. The ambiguity has led to a wide range of interpretations around the simple issue of Bathsheba's role: Was the act of bathing innocent or intentionally provocative? If innocent, then surely she is blameless. The text and later commentaries never blame her for adultery, implying she was coerced, if not actually raped. Yet virtually all painters of later eras depicted Bathsheba as a seductress, fully in control of the situation. And these paintings had their impact on the public imagination, leading to popular songs and stories that have continued to perpetuate this idea. Most people today cannot separate the artistic renditions of the story from the biblical account.

The reason so many have felt the need to fill in the blanks in this story is that it is one of the briefest and most abrupt passages to relate such events. One and a half cold, stark verses (11:26-27a) sum up the condition of a woman who has had an adulterous affair, become pregnant, lost her husband, married her lover, the King of Israel, and borne his child. Only five actions —three on David's part, two on Bathsheba's—are minimally described. David sent, he took, he lay—verbs signifying control and acquisition, as Cheryl Exum points out. By contrast, Bathsheba "came" and "returned."[13] Meir Sternberg notes that the suppression of essentials, the narrator's pseudo-objectivity, and the rendering of horror as an everyday matter, all create an extreme ironic discordance between the mode of presentation and the action itself. [14] Stylistically this differs from the story of Samson and Delilah, probably because of the difference in genre.

The sexual act itself is reported very rapidly, with minimal dialogue; as Robert Alter points out, the elaborate scheme involving Uriah is much longer and has much more dialogue. Alter thinks this implies that the writer is directing our attention to the murder, not the sex act, as the major crime. [15] The male writer (or reader, for that matter) would probably not have found fault with the sexual encounter.

The sex act between Samson and Delilah is not reported at all. It is assumed to be the means by which Delilah enticed Samson's secret from him. But the reader does not know if, how, or when the act takes place. The text says only, "She lulled him to sleep on her lap," and this presumably would follow sexual intercourse.

Delilah's motives are never stated. Her primary motive could have been patriotism. The fact is, she betrays Samson for a price. If she loved him, this would show a lack of ethics and morality; yet nowhere in the text does she ever claim to love him. As Mieke Bal rightly points out, the fact that Delilah is given a name of her own, possesses her own house, and associates with high-placed people places her in the category of a successful and independent woman. [16] So Delilah is not in dire need of money; she simply engages in a business transaction, either out of patriotism or simple practicality. To call it greed would be an unwarranted value judgment.

Delilah's goal might be to aid her people by eliminating an outside threat, while at the same time taking care of her own financial security. It is the *men* who direct Delilah in how to learn Samson's secret. She is not paid for sexual services, only for information.

Just how much money was she offered? This is of some importance in determining motive. In the text, the five "rulers" or "princes" (Hebrew *seren)* of the Philistines tell Delilah, "we'll each give you eleven hundred shekels of silver" (Judges 16:5). Assuming there were five men involved, this amounts to a bribe of 5,500 shekels, an incredible figure when it is recalled that Abraham had paid only 400 shekels for a family burial place (Genesis 24:15, 19), Jeremiah paid seventeen shekels for a piece of property (Jeremiah 32:9), and thirty shekels is the value of a slave according to the covenant code (Exodus 21:32). Robert Boling suggests that the source for the figure of eleven hundred could be the story that opens the following chapter, where Micah's mother budgets "eleven hundred of silver" for the manufacture of a metal sculpture (Judges 17).[17] David Noel Freedman suggests that the term "elef," translated here as a thousand, can also be understood as a term for the military district of which each tyrant was leader.[18] George Foot Moore points out that the number 1100 is unusual and is meant to seem enormous. [19] So the financial motivation to follow the Philistines' order would have been high. In addition, coercion could have played a part: How much choice did Delilah really have? When all five leaders of the surrounding territory approached her, what would the consequences of refusing them have been? She was as much the victim or pawn of these men as Bathsheba was of King David.

Once she has agreed to do the job, Delilah is not devious; she says exactly what she wants. She never says she loves Samson; she uses his emotions without compromising her own. In Lillian Klein's words, "she uses a man's love to bring him down—an age-old ruse."[20] Delilah's point of view is never given.

Determining Bathsheba's motives is still more difficult, since the author consistently withholds her point of view, creating an ambiguous portrayal. In the crucial scene, the initial sex encounter with David, neither she nor David has a voice. The question of Bathsheba's guilt or innocence in this encounter has preoccupied many commentators. Rabbis writing in the Talmud were much more concerned with the question of David's guilt, yet closer to modern times Bathsheba became the focus. Some male commentators believe the text hints that "she asked for it." Two commentators, H. W. Hertzberg and

Randall Bailey, argue for Bathsheba's complicity. Hertzberg feels Bathsheba knew the place she was exposing herself was overlooked by the palace, implying a possible element of "feminine flirtation."[21] Bailey argues for Bathsheba as a "prime mover, a willing and equal partner to the events which transpire," and he turns the whole David-Bathsheba narrative into a "tale of political deal-making and intrigue."[22] These are both prime examples of "blaming the victim."

Cheryl Exum's response to such male commentators is that they are too quick to blame Bathsheba. She points instead to the responsibility of the narrator, who after all was the one who decided to portray Bathsheba in the act of bathing. The narrator, using David as his agent, "makes Bathsheba the object of the male gaze." Since the narrator chose to portray her bathing naked, how can we blame her or assume she might have known she would be seen? Readers of this text are watching a man watching a woman touch herself (purifying herself after her period, implying where she was touching). Looking at the female body is a cultural preoccupation and an accepted expression of male sexuality. [23] By contrast, when David had exposed himself publicly (2 Samuel 6:14), he aroused anger, not desire, in his wife Michal.

Trevor Dennis points to Bathsheba's vulnerability. The narrator chooses to show Bathsheba bathing naked, which the reader could view as provocative behavior. But if she did not know David was watching, then she is vulnerable and actually humiliated. [24] As J.P. Fokkelman points out, the story puts David "in the position of a despot who is able to survey and choose as he pleases."[25]

Tikva Frymer-Kensky points out that Bathsheba was not out to get anything by using her beauty. The Bible in general, she notes, "does not consider beauty a power or strategy of women." In fact, Bathsheba's beauty is her vulnerability, not her power. Beauty only begins to be seen as a power of women in the post- bibilical period. [26]

The issue of love between these two people is never raised. Whereas Delilah is introduced as the woman with whom Samson fell in love, the question of whether David ever loves Bathsheba (or vice versa) is left unanswered. The minute she announces her pregnancy, his interest is in the paternity of the child, conceding her to Uriah from the start. This does not suggest great love. Once pregnant, Bathsheba is de-sexualized—this is how patriarchy severs the relationship between eroticism and procreation to render a mother's sexuality non-threatening. [27] Delilah, of course, is not destined to become a mother because that is not her purpose. Therefore she remains a threat to the very end and must disappear from the story.

A close reading of the story of Samson and Delilah still leaves obvious gaps. Mieke Bal highlights three unanswered questions: Why doesn't

Samson reproach Delilah for her betrayal? Why does he accept her reproaches without giving his own view? And, most vital of all, why does he finally give her the crucial information? [28]

Two opposing viewpoints have been offered to explain most of these gaps. Samson was either incredibly stupid, in which case the story could be read as an indictment against the institution of both Judges and Nazirites (since he was considered a Judge and a Nazirite); or he was too smart for his own good, and thought he could play games with Delilah and still come out ahead.

Both of these stories were interpreted by post-biblical commentators including rabbis in the Talmud. Later interpreters generally chose to keep Samson as a hero by in some way denigrating Delilah, a pattern that can also be seen in interpretations of the David/Bathsheba story. Pseudo-Philo, probably writing in the first century CE, was one of the first to retell the Samson and Delilah story. He combined the first four verses of chapter 16 with the subsequent verses:

> Then Samson went down to Gerar, a city of the Philistines, and he saw there a harlot whose name was Delilah, and he was led astray after her and took her to himself for a wife. And God said, "Behold now Samson has been led astray through his eyes...and he has mingled with the daughters of the Philistines....Samson's lust will be a stumbling block for him, and his mingling a ruin"....And his wife was pressuring him and kept saying to him, "Show me your power and in what your strength lies, and so I will know that you love me" ....the fourth time he revealed to her his heart. And she got him drunk, and while he slept, she called a barber and he cut the seven locks of his head. [29]

The notion of making Delilah a respectable woman by marrying her off to Samson was probably motivated more by a need to make *Samson* more respectable and settled. This idea, plus that of getting Samson drunk, was picked up by much later writers who might have been familiar with this text.

Similarly with the David and Bathsheba story, the rabbis' preoccupation was with exonerating David. Thus in Ketubot 9b, they explain: "Everyone who goes into the war of the House of David writes for his wife a deed of divorce (so if he falls in battle his wife can be free to marry without 'halitza')."[30] The divorce was conditional, in the sense that it became retrospectively valid only if the husband died. Thus, since Uriah died, Bathsheba was a free woman from the time he went out, and she was not married when David took her. This typically ingenious rabbinic exegesis essentially absolves David (and Bathsheba) of adultery.

Other passages go even further. Sanhedrin 107a contains this elaborate midrashic retelling:[31]

> R. Johanan said...David forgot there is a small organ in man which satisfies him in his hunger but makes him hunger when satisfied....Now Bathsheba was cleansing her hair behind a screen, when Satan came to him, appearing in the shape of a bird. He shot an arrow at him, which broke the screen, thus she stood revealed, and he saw her.

This interesting retelling exonerates both Bathsheba (of immodesty) and David (of lust—"the Devil made me do it!" excuse).[32]

Other attempts to exonerate David utilize extensive quotes from Psalms (supposedly composed by David) to prove he could not be guilty.[33] The rabbis used numerous means to exonerate David of guilt; never do they deal with the issue of Bathsheba's guilt or innocence.

Commentaries on both these stories continued through the centuries. In a much later period and different place, Baroque Europe, Delilah was seen as a heroine. In 1671, John Milton wrote *Samson Agonistes,* in which Delilah acts out of patriotism and even tries to be reconciled with Samson. Seeing her as simply motivated by greed was unconvincing. Like many other later writers, Milton saw Delilah's love for Samson as conflicting with her patriotic duty.

Samson Agonistes opens in prison, that is, near the end of the biblical story. Some 700 verses into the epic poem, Delilah enters, announced thus:

> Some rich Philistian matron she may seem;
> And now, at nearer view, no other certain
> Than Dalila thy wife.

To which Samson replies: "My wife! my traitress! let her not come near me." A dialogue ensues in which Delilah entreats Samson's forgiveness:

> With doubtful feet and wavering resolution
> I came, still dreading thy displeasure, Samson;
> Which to have merited, without excuse,
> I cannot but acknowledge.[34]

To which Samson replies,

> Out, out Hyena! These are thy wonted arts,

And arts of every woman false like thee--
To break all faith, all vows, deceive, betray;
Then, as repentant, to submit, beseech ,
Ane reconcilement move with feigned remorse.

Milton offers a new motive for Delilah's actions, namely, to gain power over him in order not to lose him. [35] Samson asks her why she revealed his secret to the Philistines, and Delilah replies that they had reassured her no harm would come to him. Further on she also implies that great pressure was applied to force her to betray him.

William Blake (1757-1827) wrote a short poetical sketch called Samson which opens:

Samson, the strongest of the children of men, I sing:
how he was foiled by women's arts, by a false wife brought to the gates of death!
For Delila's fair arts have long been tried in vain; in vain
she wept in many a treacherous tears.[36]

Altogether this is not a very flattering portrait of Delilah, it has influenced modern views of Delilah more than the biblical story itself by its use of prejudicial adjectives such as "false" and "treacherous." The biblical account, like the Bible in general, has virtually no descriptive adjectives.

Attempts at humanizing the characters and filling in the gaps were copied by several later writers. Eugene Moore wrote *Delilah, A Tale of Olden Times* in 1888.[37] In this version Delilah is not only in love with Samson, but also is impressed with his God. Her priest tries to convince her to betray Samson, but she never agrees.[38] Samson rebels against the Nazirite vows made for him by his mother, gets drunk deliberately, and when drunk reveals his secret. Delilah never means to betray him at all, but she cuts his hair in a sort of trance, wondering if he spoke the truth in his stupor.[39]

Moore suggests the same motive for Delilah as did Milton: Weakening Samson, she can hold him to herself by making him dependent. Woman here is depicted as manipulator rather than betrayer. It now becomes a struggle for power. Delilah tries to save Samson from the Philistines, follows him to prison and ultimately to the Temple of Dagon, to die by his side.

In 1931 Austrian writer Felix Salten (of *Bambi* fame) based his novel, *Samson and Delilah: A Novel,* on the biblical tale.[40] He makes numerous interesting changes, qualifying the novel as true modern midrash. Delilah was "a girl, untouched, who had never as yet known a man's kiss"—until meeting

Samson. She lives with her parents and comes to believe in Samson's God. Her unsavory mother makes a deal and acts as go-between to bribe Delilah. In a subplot her sister is lusted after by the Philistine leader, giving her a motive to side with their mother and persuade Delilah to betray her lover. She cleverly asks Delilah, "How would you find out if someone loved you?" When Delilah starts asking Samson questions about his strength, he first tells her his secret is too "holy" to reveal. But when he does finally reveal it, the sister is eavesdropping, and it is she who cuts his hair! Delilah remains by Samson's side to the very end. The novel is vividly written, particularly the blinding sequence, in which the red hot points coming toward Samson's eyes are described as the last things he would ever see.[41]

The story of David has also been retold in many ways through the centuries, but the encounter with Bathsheba is more often than not simply omitted. Not having Talmudic means of discourse at their disposal, later writers utilized a simpler technique: whitewash. The goal was to make David into a hero, albeit a complex one, and it was too difficult to integrate the incident with Bathsheba into this picture.

One interesting exception is *David and His Wives*, a 1923 novel, originally in Yiddish, by David Pinski.[42] The final chapter deals with Bathsheba. It opens with Nathan confronting David, telling him the parable as a warning. When Bathsheba is then brought to David, she refuses his advances, even reciting some of his own psalms as part of her argument! Nathan sends Uriah into the room. Bathsheba tries to convince Uriah to take her away from the palace, but he insists he must follow his king's orders. Exasperated, Bathsheba rips open the message delivered to Uriah, which he was to take back to the front. Even after she has proved David's evil intentions, Uriah still will not disobey his king's orders. Finally Bathsheba sends him away with the words, "I have loved a slave! Now I shall love a king!"[43] Just as in the modern retellings of Delilah's story, this modern midrash makes Bathsheba into much more of a real person and turns many preconceptions on their head.

Composers, too, have found inspiration from these stories in every era. The two most famous musical renditions of the story of Samson and Delilah are by Handel and Saint Saens. The libretto for the Handel opera of 1735 is by Hamilton Newburgh, based on his play, which is based more on Milton than the Bible. Most of the opera takes place in the prison, and Delilah, "Samson's wife," appears only briefly in Act II to sing two successive arias (one is traditionally cut) in which she pretends to be penitent and submissive.

The music itself does not convince the listener of Delilah's duplicitous nature, however, and in this sense may not have achieved the librettist's goal.

The libretto for the Saint Saens opera of 1877 is by Ferdinand Lemaire, who makes Delilah a cold, calculating seductress. This is an important point because Lemaire's portrayal has probably molded modern views of Delilah's character far more than the biblical account did. The story has been altered somewhat. In her first appearance Delilah, in the company of other Philistine women, greets Samson in a public place. In the first of her three arias, "Printemps Qui Commence," she reminds Samson of their earlier liaison as her compatriots dance sinuously. Praising spring, she sings to Samson of how eagerly she awaits the renewal of their relationship. The listener is hard pressed not to feel some empathy for her. The music paints a softer portrait of Delilah than the librettist probably intended! However, in her second aria, "Amour, Viens Aider Ma Faiblesse," the only one not sung for Samson's benefit, Delilah "shows her true colors." Such is the power of music to move the listener that even in Delilah's famous seduction aria, "Mon Coeur S'Ouvre à Ta Voix," the music is so lush and seductive that the listener simply has to empathize with poor Samson. Who could resist such music? The fact that the biblical Delilah nags and cajoles rather than seducing is immaterial to composers: seduction music is far more appealing than nagging music, so Delilah became imprinted in all opera lovers' minds as the temptress par excellence. And no amount of scholarship or commentary can undo the power of music. The arts have done a great deal to popularize biblical stories, but this popularization has not resolved the ambiguities of the original stories in a favorable way for the female characters.

This is even truer in more popular renditions of the Samson story. In all of these, Samson is the poor sap and Delilah the temptress. Three such versions are "Delilah Done Me Wrong," or "The No Haircut Song," written by Gerard Calvi with words by Harold Rome for the 1963 musical *La Grosse Valise*; the 1957 song "Samson, Mighty Samson," by Hamilton Henry (Terry) Gilkyson, popular singer, songwriter, and guitarist of the 40s and 50s; and the 1974 mini-epic oratorio *Samson and Delilah,* by Sam Pottle, who also composed the *Muppet Theme Song.*[44]

Musically, Bathsheba has fared no better than in most artists' representations, generally being depicted in popular songs as the temptress who brought David down. Numerous operas and oratorios titled *David* completely ignore Bathsheba. Several examples are operas by Alessandro Scarlatti, Arthur Honegger, and many lesser known composers. One notable exception is Darius Milhaud's *David*, with text by Armand Lunel in French and Hebrew.[45] This work was commissioned by the Koussevitzky Foundation of the Library of Congress. Milhaud dedicated the work to "the people of Israel, on the occasion of the 3000 year anniversary of the founding of Jerusalem." It was written in 1952 and received its world premiere at La Scala in 1955. The initial encounter between David and Bathsheba is not depicted, but is referred to in a duet which takes place after their firstborn has died. Both express sadness and regret at what happened between them.

There is also a popular rendition, in which the lyrics show total ignorance of the story but use it as a vehicle to warn men of the dangers of women's charms, much as the popular Delilah songs do. This song, "David and Bathsheba," is a true product of the 50s, written in 1951 with words and music by Gordon Jenkins, Robert Allen, and Allan Roberts, who have their roots in vaudeville.[46] This song is both a wonderful and horrible example of how biblical women have fared in popular interpretations that unfortunately have always been more accessible to the general public than scholarly papers.

The fascination of these modern retellings, whether through drama, poetry, novels, or music, is the way they illustrate the prismatic quality of the original story. The biblical writers left so many ambiguities and unanswered questions that the story may be understood any number of different ways without contradicting the actual text. Artists, writers, and composers all felt the need not only to fill in the gaps, but to make their version the most emotionally compelling one. Each viewed the light through a different angle of the original prism. And each has opened new windows which illuminate the texts for readers of every generation.

Notes

[1] All Bible translations are from the JPS *Torah* (Philadelphia:Jewish Publication Society, 1962).

[2] Lillian Klein, "The Book of Judges: Paradigm and Deviation in Images of Women," in *A Feminist Companion to Judges* (Sheffield: Sheffield Academic Press, 1993), 62.

[3] Ibid.

[4] Adele Berlin, *Poetics and Interpretation of Biblical Narrative (*Indiana: Eisenbrauns, 1994*),*26.

[5] Klein, *A Feminist Companion to Judges*, 62 (footnote 1).

[6] Tikva Frymer-Kensky, *In The Wake of the Goddesses* (New York: Fawcett

Columbine, 1992), 260.

[7] Cheryl Exum, *Fragmented Women: Feminist (Sub)versions of Biblical Narrative* (Valley Forge: Trinity Press International, 1993), 87.

[8] Klein, *A Feminist Companion to Judges*, 63.

[9] Exum, *Fragmented Women*, 82.

[10] Cheryl Exum, *Plotted, Shot and Painted: Cultural Representations of Biblical Women* (Sheffield: Sheffield Academic Press, 1996), 221.

[11] Betsy Merideth, "Desire and Danger: The Drama of Betrayal in Judges and Judith," in Mieke Bal, *Anti-Covenant: Counter-Reading Women's Lives in the Hebrew Bible* (Sheffield: Almond Press, 1989), 72.

[12] Alice Bach, *The Pleasure of Her Text: Feminist Readings of Biblical and Historical Texts* (Philadelphia: Trinity Press International, 1990), 36.

[13] Exum, *Plotted, Shot and Painted*, 21.

[14] Meir Sternberg, *The Poetics of Biblical Narrative* (Bloomington: Indiana University Press, 1987), 191.

[15] Robert Alter, *The Art of Biblical Narrative* (Basic Books, 1981), 182.

[16] Mieke Bal, *Lethal Love: Feminist Literary Readings of Biblical Love Stories* (Bloomington: Indiana University Press, 1987), 50.

[17] Robert Boling, *Anchor Bible: Judges (*New York: Doubleday, 1975), note 249.

[18] Ibid.

[19] G.F. Moore, *Judges: International Critical Commentary* (Edinburgh: T&T Clark, 1949), 352.

[20] Klein, *A Feminist Companion to Judges*, 63.

[21] H.W. Hertzberg, *I & II Samuel: A Commentary,* Old Testament Library (London: LCM Press, 1964), 309.

[22] Randall Bailey, *David in Love and War: The Pursuit of Power in II Samuel 10-12* (Sheffield: JSOT Press, 1990), 85.

[23] Exum, *Fragmented Women*, 187-9.

[24] Trevor Dennis, *Sarah Laughed: Women's Voices in the Old Test-ament* (Nashville: Abingdon Press, 1994), 145.

[25] J.P. Fokkelman, *King David (II Samuel 9-20 & I Kings 1-2)*, vol. 1 of *Narrative Art and Poetry in the Books of Samuel* (Assen: Van Gorcum, 1981), 51.

[26] Frymer-Kensky, *In the Wake of the Goddesses*, 140, and 262 (note 132).

[27] Exum, *Fragmented Women*, 191.

[28] Bal, *Lethal Love*, 40

[29] Pseudo-Philo 43:5-7, in James H. Charlesworth, *The Old Testament Pseudepigrapha* (New York: Doubleday, 1983), 357.

[30] All Talmud quotes are from the Soncino Talmud. Another example can be found in tractate Shabbat 56a: "R. Samuel b. Nahmani said in R. Jonathan's name: Everyone who went out in the wars of the house of David wrote a bill of divorcement for his wife."

[31] This lengthy passage opens with: "One should never intentionally bring himself to the test, since David king of Israel did so, and fell...(David said) 'Sovereign of the Universe, examine and try me' — as it is written, 'Examine me, O Lord, and try me' (Psalms). (God) answered 'I will test thee, and yet grant thee a special privilege, for I inform thee that I will try thee in a matter of adultery.'"

[32] The passage goes still further: "Bath Sheba, the daughter of Eliam, was predestined for David from the six days of Creation... the school of R. Ishmael taught likewise: She was worthy (i.e., predestined) for David from the six days of Creation, but he enjoyed her before she was ripe [before she was his legitimate wife]."

[33] For example, Avodah Zarah 5a contains the following:"David was not the kind of man to do that act, as it is written, 'My heart is slain within me' (meaning, David's inclinations had been completely conquered by himself)." Similarly in tractate Shabbat 56a, "R. Samuel b. Nahmani said in R. Jonathan's name: Whoever says that David sinned is merely erring, for it is said, 'And David behaved himself wisely in all his ways, and the Lord was with him.'" (Ps. 18:14)

[34] John Milton, Samson Agonistes, (London: University Tutorial Press, 1974).

Delilah continues: "If aught in my ability may serve
To lighten what thou suffer'st, and appease
Thy mind with what amends is in my power —
Though late, yet in some part to recompense
My rash but more unfortunate misdeed."

[35] Delilah's words are:
I saw thee mutable of fancy;
feared lest one day thou would'st leave me
As her at Timna; sought by all means, therefore,
How to endear, and hold thee to me firmest;
No better way I saw than by importuning
To learn thy secrets, get into my power
Thy key of strength and safety.

[36] William Blake, in *The Works of William Blake* (New York: A.M.S. Press, 1979).

[37] Published by Press of T. McGill & Co., Washington D.C.

[38] Delilah's words to the Priest are:
Priest! Fool! A pliant tool thou thought'st to have
Wherewith to work thy will; but there's one page
Which thou with all thy craft hast failed to read —
That page whereon is writ in letters large —
'The love that woman giveth unto man
Is stronger than the fear she hath of gods.'

[39] She says:
Yes, I this hair will shear away, and thus
My will may have and hold him at my side.
If truth to me he told, if he grows weak,
He'll here abide..
While he's weak, upon my arms he'll lean,
And for a space dependent be on me.

[40] Published in 1931 by Simon & Schuster, New York.

[41] In a particularly poignant and humanizing touch, Salten invents a pet dog who comes to visit Samson and Delilah in prison every night and who ultimately dies, trustfully, by their side. (Well, what can you expect from the writer of *Bambi*?)

[42] David Pinski, *King David and His Wives,* translated from the Yiddish by Isaac Goldberg (New York, 1930).

[43] Ibid.

[44] Words by Grace Hawthorne, ASCAP; Copyright 1974 by Trigon Music, Inc., Nashville, TN.

[45] Published in 1953 by Leeds Music Corp.

[46] Copyright 1951, Twentieth Century Music Corp., New York.

Shukr Kuhayl II Reads the Bible

Harris Lenowitz

I. THE NAMES AND ACCOUNTS OF MESSIAHS

Among nonacademic Jews, knowledge of the received text of the Hebrew Bible has fallen into a sort of languor in our time. Something similar occurred in the early modern period. In the *heder*s (schoolrooms) of Europe before the Second World War, the Bible was the first text children studied after they learned their prayers. But its status was that of a stepping-stone to higher studies, so much so that this status was enshrined in a joke. When asked, "Where does it say *bereshis boro elokim eis ha-shomayim ve'eis ho-oretz*?" the *talmid hokhem* answered, "In *Hagiga* and also in *Tamid*."[1] Religious Jews did study the Torah and did attend its public readings; but in spite of the fact that Jewish interest in the Hebrew Bible itself underwent a renaissance with the Haskalah (the Jewish Enlightenment movement of the eighteenth-nineteenth centuries), it remained captive to the spirit of that movement, one which promoted analysis over simple anamnesis.

In some few communities, however, *ve-hagita bo ("You* shall study it," Josh. 1.8*)*, "keep [this Torah] in mind day and night," was taken literally, and the exercise of one's memory as the essential first step towards all further study began with the memorization of the Bible; this attribute and this text, then, existed as a common possession and served as the very custodian of identity proclaimed in the book of Joshua. The Yemenite community retained this characteristic well into the present century.[2] A conversation among Yemenite males, or equally a sermon, could rely on this common store of recollection. The oral quotation of a few words took the listener back immediately to the entire context from which they were plucked and to other related biblical passages as well, as surely as if they were linked in hypertext.

In the following pages I will show with what great art and effect this collective intimacy with the Hebrew Bible was employed on one crucial occasion in the last quarter of the nineteenth century to establish the relationship between a Yemenite messiah of the time and his followers and antagonists.[3]

In my work with the accounts of Jewish messiahs,[4] I have found that several different kinds of stories may be told in order to substantiate a messiah's claim to be the messiah, whether he makes it himself or others make it for him. In such stories as the miraculous birth of the messiah and the messiah's miracle working, it is common to find a comparison with a text from the Bible which is brought in to serve as a witness. This proof-text supports the claim that this figure is the messiah. Most frequently the Biblical passage has a long history of repeated use in discussions of the attributes of the *true* messiah and his times, but there is always scope for the new reading of a passage. If the passage is brought forward skillfully enough, novelty contributes significantly to the impact of the claim. A famous example of a similar process has to do with the name of the messiah, Shabtai Zvi (fl. 1665-6, Izmir). No other messiah has used the name Shabtai (related to the word Shabbat, "Sabbath") as his messianic name. Shabtai Zvi used the name he was given at birth because it related him to the seventh day of the week and the peace and freedom of that day in Judaism. Likewise, he made use of the fact that he had been born on the fast day of the Ninth of Av (the fast commemorates a number of disastrous events) to promote his program to release the Jews from the strictures of history and Jewish law.[5] The world had been waiting, it appeared, for the double coincidence of his birth and name.

The given (or appropriated) name of the messiah, like the title messiah itself, makes an essential statement about the individual and how he will interact with his community, and how his community and others are expected to relate to him. Though he was not a Jewish messiah, David Koresh of the Branch Davidians recognized how crucial a name is and, in addition to his given name — David, one of the hoariest messiah-names — took another messiah name: *Koresh* (the name of the Persian king Cyrus as it appears in Hebrew), which is the name of the only non-"Jew" specifically referred to as messiah and the redeemer of Israel in the Hebrew Bible. In Isaiah 45.1 we read, *ko amar adonai limshicho, lekhoresh,* "This is what the Lord said to his anointed one, to Cyrus," at the beginning of a passage composed by the prophet in order to define the identities of God and his anointed redeemer as well as their relationship. David Koresh knew his Bible; he taught it to others, and they became his followers. (The sect name, *Branch Davidians*, also contains biblical references: Zechariah 3.8 and Jeremiah 23.5, and other passages. Many readers of the Bible in Hebrew were surprised by David Koresh's revelation, but as far as I know none took his claim to heart.)

This matter of name and title is but one aspect of one sort of messiah account. The accounts themselves are the defining complement of a messiah event and constitute the most important source of information we have about the Jewish messiahs. Later accounts of an event, constructed after the event ends, can have an impact only on subsequent events, and their force is sufficiently weakened that the elements of these *secondary* accounts fall into a large category of optional symbolic components that may be incorporated into accounts of later messiahs in order to reference symbols that are generally associated with the messiah. The later accounts contend with current, magically meaningful dates, gematria (the numerical decoding of the Hebrew alphabet), symbols of the millennium and of the messiah, weather phenomena, socio-psychological stresses, and so forth. On the other hand, those accounts that are *primary*—accounts made of the messiah by himself or by those among his contemporaries who are concerned with his acts—reveal the most about a messiah event. Such accounts clearly illustrate the interdependence of historiography and events; they not only recapitulate the event of a messiah and so participate in later messiah events (and in their accounts), but these accounts are also important structural constituents of the typical event, involving themselves in developments of which they would seem at first glance merely descriptive. They are not at all optional. Without the tales told by followers and messiahs to convince others to join them, or by antagonists to dissuade others from joining, no event can be said to occur, just as no messiah event can occur without a messiah and no messiah, to come full circle, can be usefully spoken of who does not account for himself or allow others to account for him in one way or another as *a* messiah or *the* messiah in that very term.

The accounts are assuredly constitutive to any understanding of the individual movements, events, performances, rituals. They are often naive witnesses, unaware of the display they make of themselves as they make their cases for or against what their authors or others are doing or failing to do. Several familiar genres appear in the accounts: the call vision, for example; the birth tale; and miracle tales of various sorts. Some genres are peculiar to messiah accounts, such as the tale of the messiah's insertion into the society, and have their own histories of inheritance from earlier examples. Nevertheless, the accounts are themselves all different from each other. The messiahs in them are all different from each other, and their followers, as they appear in the accounts, are also all different from each other. The contribution that the accounts make towards our understanding of a particular messiah event is far more substantial than is the modest subvention they provide towards a model of the typical messiah event as the result of a typical set or sets of causes. The accounts put on display the un-understandability of each event and the un-predictability of the phenomenon in all its resplendent complexity.

II. THE YEMENITE MESSIAH, SHUKR KUHAYL II, AND HIS BODY

The author of the account I will examine here is Yehuda bar Shalom, who called himself Shukr Kuhayl (hereafter, Shukr II), adopting the name of his immediate predecessor. Shukr II began his career as messiah in 1868 in San'a', the capital of Yemen, and died a sad death there in 1877 or 1878. In his own story, this was but the second stage of his life and career. In the first stage, he had appeared as the messiah in 1861, likewise in San'a', and had been "killed" and decapitated in 1865. The man who had in fact appeared in 1861, and been murdered as he climbed the lonely mountain of the Bani Jabr, to the south of San'a', his head brought down to be displayed on the wall of the capital, was Shukr ben Salaam Kuhayl. His sister kept alive the tradition that this Shukr had said that he would rise again and did not mourn him. Taking advantage of his predecessor's claim that he would return from the dead, our protagonist called himself Shukr Kuhayl. The (divorced) wife and the son of the first Shukr Kuhayl even recognized this second man as their husband and father.

Shukr II attracted adherents and brought in donations through what was the largest self-publishing public relations activity of any of the messiahs until the most recent times. We see him become present in his letters and papers. His flesh is made word in them, however far away from him they may be. Papers emerging from beneath his hand become him; they are not to be threatened or harmed, and they possess the power to carry out his desires.[6] His written demands could not be denied or disclaimed as mere words written on paper. They carried his signature, his seal impressions, and his very physical presence. As we shall see, they may in fact have been made of his name.

ERRATUM

The illustration on page 249 is upside down.
The production department regrets the error.

This is a letter written by Shukr Kuhayl II to Moshe Hanoch:[7]

The historian D. S. Sasson, who published this letter, describes it as follows (pp. 164-5):

> The letter was found among our family papers in Bombay a few months ago. It is preceded by five Biblical verses of a messianic character which the writer obviously applies to himself. These messianic pretensions also explain the words, "May his glory be high and his kingdom be exalted" [referring to himself in the body of the letter], and also the letters *qof shin* on his seal, which cannot mean anything but *qadish shmaya* "the holy of the heavens." According to [Jacob] Saphir [the nineteenth century traveler and author who gathered information and reported to the Jewish world on Shukr's messiahship], he called himself *mashiah ben david.*
>
> The letter itself begins with a few rhymed sentences in Aramaic, probably owing to cabbalistic influence. The letter is addressed to Moses Hanoch ha-Levi, in reply to a letter which the messianic pretender received from him. He states that he answers this letter only out of consideration for the writer; but he will not pay any attention to the other people who, in reply to his petitions for money, wrote asking him to perform miracles, and also to send the replies by a bird, things which he could not do then, having no permission from his lord Elijah, and being altogether forbidden by God to perform miracles. It seems he had previously written a letter to Moses Hanoch ha-Levi asking him for money to build the Temple at Jerusalem. He asks for a loan of 1,000 "Reals," and begs to be informed how much money had been collected previously by his representatives in India. At the end of the letter there are three seals: one on the right, with the words *[qadish shemaya]*; the second one, on the left, is in Arabic but illegible; and the one in the centre has a "Magen David" surrounded by some mystical letters.

III. THE LETTER OF LETTERS, TO SAGES AND RABBIS OF JERUSALEM

Now let me describe another letter before looking closely at its opening passages.[8] It is one of several letters written by the messiah himself, the first of which was sent to the rabbis and sages of Jerusalem after Shukr II had been informed of Saphir's arguments against him and had become aware of widespread rabbinic support for Saphir. His letters to other communities used this one as a model (a sentence or two from it appears in the Sasson letter reproduced above). This letter was sent on to Saphir by R. Hayim Faraj Mizrahi, who copied it out, as it was contained in another letter sent by Moshe Hanoch of Aden, himself the addressee of the Sasson letter and a central figure in Shukr's propaganda network, to Rafael Suares in Alexandria, Egypt, in the early spring of 1870.

This long letter flows from subject to subject in a single argument on Shukr's own behalf, justifying his deeds and non-deeds. It begins with Shukr's promise of the Redemption, presenting a mosaic of biblical texts that are traditionally associated with the messiah's coming. Shukr praises the virtue of patience, making reference to his followers' demands for him to work wonders; then he lauds the rabbis and sages for their discernment and says that all true Jews rely upon them. At the same time, he puts them in their place and moves on to his own role as spokesman for the Lord, emphasizing the sufferings he has undergone in order to fulfill his obligations (actually the sufferings of Shukr I). At this point he introduces the narrative of his call vision, followed by an updated history of himself as Shukr I, killed at the mountain of Al-Tiyal and resurrected by Elijah. Elijah orders him to set aside his Torah study and turn to preaching. Shukr II then recounts his own adventures and says in conclusion that all his wonders and miraculous rescues were the work of God through Elijah; he pleads with his audience to act properly and speed the Redemption thereby. In a codicil addressed to Yahya Mizrahi, Shukr encourages him to remain faithful in the face of the opposition of Shukr's enemies, some of whom are community leaders, and in spite of the spreading rumors that accuse Shukr of witchcraft.

Turning now to a close exploration of the opening passage of the letter — the introduction to his history, as it were — I hope to show with what genius Shukr II wrote and in particular how greatly he depended on the verbatim-and-more memory of the Hebrew Bible common to his readers (or listeners) to perfect his rhetorical purpose, drawing them together with him, under his control.

The letter contains no notes; the punctuation marks are added (cf. the Sasson letter described and discussed above). This text is as laconic as any biblical text. It is replete with possibilities, and the reader is led to actualize the right ones. In the translation that follows, I use italics to indicate Shukr's own "additions" (words that are not in the biblical text; in one case, I use bold italics to signal that Shukr is using a biblical word but in a different way than does the Bible). The "deletions" are just as important, but I have explained them in my commentary rather reinserting them into the text, as it were:

The letter which that man sent to the sages
and rabbis of the holy city of Jerusalem

How beautiful upon the hills are the feet of the harbinger sounding forth salvation, sounding forth peace, saying unto Zion, Your God has become king [Isaiah 52.7], Behold them the very first of Zion and I will give a harbinger to Jerusalem [Isa. 41.27], Israel is saved an eternal salvation by the Lord, they shall not be ashamed nor embarrassed to the end of time [Isa. 45.17].

Hear this, House of Jacob, those who are named Israel [Isa. 48.1] *who receive upon themselves the yoke of Exile and heed the voice of their authorities* ***for*** they are summoned from the holy city and by the God of Israel have they been ordained [Isa. 48.2], *the one who will raise up for them a savior,* the Lord of Hosts is his name [Isa. 48.2]. Recall this and be strengthened [Isa. 46.8], turn unto me and be saved [Isa. 45.22], speak it and proffer it [Isa. 45.21], gather and come [Isa. 45.20], I have not said it in secret or in the dust, I have not said to the seed of Jacob, Seek me out in chaos [Isa. 45.19]. Who said this aforehand [Isa. 45.21], that [even] before the harvest (when) the flower is perfect [Isa. 18.5]? The watchman said, The morning has come [Isa. 21.12], and those whose spirit is misguided shall know discernment [Isa. 29.24], and the ears of those who listen will heed [Isa. 32.3], and the light of the moon will be as the light of the sun [Isa. 30.26]. The first things I have spoken aforetimes and from my mouth they have come forth [Isa. 48.3], I have made heard that which was created and done so recently [Isa. 48.7], neither have you heard nor have you known [Isa. 48.8]. Rejoice, o Jerusalem, and take joy in her all her lovers [Isa. 66.10]. The Lord has repented of this[Amos 7.3], call it out among the Gentiles [Joel 4.9], Who has heard such a thing as this, Who has seen things such as these [Isa. 66.8]? Shall one of you rise to kill? My people has been destroyed for unknowing [Hosea 4.6]. Hear [this], peoples, all, [1Kings 22.28]. Sun [and] moon stood still in its habitation [Habakkuk 3.11]. The Lord is righteous, he will not commit a misdeed [Zephaniah 3.5], this too has come forth from the Lord of Hosts, o dove-like Ephraim [Hosca 7.11]. He has advised/determined/ planned wondrously, he has multiplied skill [Isa. 28.29]. Be not afraid, o earth [Joel 2.21]. Sanctify the flock [/a fast], proclaim a gathering [Joel 1.14], above all seek out the book of the Lord and proclaim it: not one of these has failed [Isa. 34.16]. The spirit of the Lord is upon me, thus he has anointed me to call out the captives to freedom [Isa. 61.1], to summon the imprisoned, Come forth, to him who is in darkness, Come out [Isa. 49.9], to replace the dust [on the heads of] the Mourners of Zion with glory [Isa. 61.3]. Who believed what was heard of us [Isa. 53.1]? Drip, sky, from above, the heavens will flow with righteousness [Isa. 45.8], rejoice, sky, for the Lord has done, sound forth, o depths of the earth, burst forth in joy, o hills, for the Lord has redeemed and will be glorified in Israel [Isa. 44.23], [he] gives strength to the weary and magnifies the power of the helpless [Isa. 40.29], for a day of vengeance it is unto the Lord, a year of repayment unto Zion [Isa. 34.8], for the Lord is our judge, the Lord is our lawgiver, the Lord is our king, he will save us [Isa. 33.22].

Do you not know, have you not heard, has it not been said from the first unto you [Isa. 40.21], weak hands grasp each other and stumbling knees gather strength [Isa. 35.3] for there the mighty one, the Lord, is ours [Isa. 33.21], bend your ears and come to me, pay heed and may your soul revive [Isa. 55.3], *just as it is for me so is it for you. And this is my good advice for you, the Lord of Hosts will do it,* for in only a brief time his anger will be ended [Isa. 10.25], therefore wait for me [Zephaniah 3.8], the Lord of Hosts, sanctify him [Isa. 8.13], therefore the Lord will give you a sign [Isa. 7.14]. Why should you be despondent, my people [Isa. 3.15], *for I have not yet permission to make use of any doing, for the Lord has bound me not to make use of the Torah, for first Israel must gather together and thereafter the Lord will do wonders,* this determination concerns the whole earth [Isa. 14.26]. For the Lord of Hosts has determined and who shall annul it and it is his hand stretched out so who shall withdraw it [Isa. 14.27]? The Lord of Hosts has sworn, shall it not be as I have said and come to be as I have determined [Isa. 14.24]? The Lord has made it heard to the end of the Earth, Say to daughter Zion, See your savior comes, See his repayment is with him/attends him and his endeavor before him [Isa. 62.11] and they have never attended [Isa. 64.3]. See, the hand of the Lord is not too short to deliver, but you will not come forth hastily nor go forward fleeing [Isa. 52.12], Burst out, rejoice together, ruins of Jerusalem, for the Lord has comforted his people, He has redeemed Jerusalem [Isa. 52.9] *and in this has been fulfilled the scripture*, And those the Lord has ransomed will return and come to Jerusalem in happiness and eternal joy, they will attain gladness and rejoicing, suffering and moaning will have fled [Isa. 51.11]. Happy is he who waits and reaches [the Land of Israel; the end of tribulation] [Daniel. 12.12], and a redeemer shall come to Zion [Isa. 59.20]. Amen, may it be his will.

1. How beautiful upon the hills are the feet of the harbinger sounding forth

salvation, sounding forth peace,

2. saying unto Zion, Your God has become king [Isa. 52.7], Behold them the very first of Zion and I will give a harbinger to Jerusalem [Isa. 41.27],

3. Israel is saved an eternal salvation by the Lord, they shall not be ashamed nor embarrassed to the end of time [Isa. 45.17].

My focus, in the following analysis, is on how the passages selected from the Bible have been arranged, how material from within the verses or from between the verses has been deleted, how material from other verses or material the author has written himself has been added—by insertion, usually. I will use the results of this in order to show how Shukr II's arrangement of the verses, or bits of verses, and his rhetorical aims operate together. The devices used to accomplish the perfection of the structure—rhymes, rhythms, sound-plays, wordplays—and the ways they operate—naturally, artfully—unite the creation decoratively.

The first three lines (translated above) in the printed version form a paragraph,[9] one that is distinguished from the second paragraph by Shukr's turn to address the rabbis and sages in the second person (the imperative plural) and by its attention to a single thought or topic: the identification of the recipients and the writer in terms of the tidings of their common destiny, redemption. In this preamble,[10] Shukr brings together three verses from the book of Isaiah: 52.7, 41.27 and 45.17 in that order. As they stand here, the first two verses are joined together by a lovely frame structure, an envelope: the first part of 52.7 is linked to the last part of 41.27 by the repetition of the key word identifying Shukr: mevaser ("harbinger"). Within this frame, the last part of 52.7 is linked to the first part of 41.27 by the repetition of the key word identifying the recipients, the sages and rabbis of the holy city of Jerusalem, tsiyon (Zion). This structure connects the two verses and brings them to a conclusion by joining the first verse-part to the last verse-part. The suspension of their juncture intervenes as the middle parts construct a central unity. The third verse, 45.17, stands apart from this structure and concludes the three-verse unit. It restates in plain words and in a single verse from the Bible what the composition of this whole opening passage itself has set out to do. It repeats the message that determines all identity, "Israel is saved," defining the readership as a saved people; it says that Shukr II is not a false prophet but a true one, "they will not be embarrassed"; and it does this in response to the rabbis and sages whose opinion upon the matter is different.

The most precious title of the Jerusalemite establishment is rishon le-tsiyon, the first [one] of Zion, the leadership of the religious community of the land of Israel; but Shukr is the mevaser, the harbinger, and one is reminded by the counterposition of the terms that Shukr II is under attack by the men he is addressing and that even though they are powerful, he is, after all, the messiah. This third verse, then, constitutes the kernel of the unit and the conclusion of the argument, the message of the messenger to the recipients. It has two parts: the good tidings themselves and a second in which Shukr turns to the rabbis and sages in the third person, places them within the larger framework of Israel (removing them from their position of authority over Israel), and asserts that his message is a true one that will redeem Israel from its past shame and embarrassment. The composite is quite typical of the style of classical biblical poetry. Noticing that the tidings of the messenger present in the first verse are absent in the second, one's expectation is immediately met by the third verse, which fulfills the promise of the ritual cry, malakh elohayikh (Your God has become King), and fleshes out the meaning of God's coronation. This time Israel's salvation is to be eternal and never again will the people falter, be punished, and put to shame. Lest we forget, however, Shukr has a point to make against the sages of Jerusalem, and even though the verses are cited here just as they appear in the Bible, each of them has its own context. The second of the two verses that make up the body of the argument that precedes the summary (the tidings of the third verse) is taken from a passage (beginning six verses earlier in chapter 41, with verse 21) that is extremely critical of rulers and their vaunted wisdom and insight. Moreover, the biblical verse that follows our verse immediately is another that describes the rulers as "nobodies," eyn ish, and "know-nothings," eyn yo'etz. This label clings to the "first men of Zion" as tightly as plastic wrap.

We have seen that Shukr II's reconstruction of biblical material at times involves linking verses together on the basis of repeated terms; other operations — leaving biblical material out and inserting material within and between verses — are equally simple. The quoted passage may lack material from within itself or may leave out what immediately precedes or follows it, with or without the insertion of new material. The inserted material, if there is any, may be from other biblical verses or may be newly written.

4. Hear this, House of Jacob, those who are named Israel [Isa. 48.1] *who receive upon themselves*

5. *the yoke of Exile and heed the voice of their authorities for* they are summoned from the holy city and by the God

6. of Israel have they been ordained [Isa. 48.2], *the one who will raise up for them a savior,* the Lord of Hosts is his name [Isa. 48.2]. Recall this

and be strengthened [Isa. 46.8],

7a. turn unto me and be saved [Isa. 45.22], speak it and proffer it [Isa. 45.21], gather and come [Isa. 45.20],

The first sentence of the next section of the address exhibits a typical, if complex, sample of these rhetorical maneuvers. Line 4 of the printed letter begins, "Hear this, House of Jacob, those who are named Israel"; these words constitute the first part of Isa. 48.1, which goes on to say in the Bible, "and are come forth out of the fountain of Judah; who swear by the name of the Lord, and make mention of the God of Israel, but not in truth, nor in righteousness." Verse 48.2 follows, "For they call themselves of the holy city, and stay themselves upon the God of Israel, the Lord of hosts is his name."[11]

Shukr II deletes the second part of verse 1 and inserts his own words, "who receive upon themselves the yoke of exile and heed the voice of their authorities," before returning to verse 2. The material is inserted between two forms of the verb *niqra'* which has the basic meaning of "call," both "summon" and "name"; the interruption is not then a disjuncture. Shukr II makes use of the particle *ki* (***for*** in the translation) which begins verse 2 in the Bible, in order to establish a causative link between the material he has written and the biblical material which follows. The result is a very natural, biblical, composition. Of course, Shukr has entirely changed the meaning of the verses.

The pericope which these verses open in the Bible accuses the Jewish authorities in Jerusalem of treason against YHWH; this is brought to a sharp point by the end of verse 1, "but not in truth, nor in righteousness." The particle *ki* originally introduced the explanation for the accusation against the leadership, its unrighteous claim to speak to and for the people of Israel and God. In Shukr's construction, it joins his inserted phrase, "who receive upon themselves the yoke of exile and heed the voice of their authorities," to the opening of verse 2. Since the insertion is one of pity and praise for those who suffer the loss of their homeland and yet continue to obey those figures of authority who reside there, verse 2 now reads as a justification of that authority. The authorities are now "righteously called" rather than "unrighteously presumptuous" and have been "properly ordained" as opposed to "ordaining themselves unrighteously." When we turn to Shukr's insertion, immediately recognizable as post-biblical Hebrew,[12] we find that the praise for those in authority has been made to depend on their "calling" to the position, and that voluntary and conative act on the part of God has kept them bound to his authority.

Now, according to Shukr's verses, that authority which ordained them has the power to ordain another leader over them. The excised conclusion to verse 1 hovers over the Jerusalem-based leadership like a sword about to fall on their heads: if they do not acknowledge God as "[that authority] who will raise up for them a savior," they not only deny the ancient dream of redemption but also their own authority to act in the name of the people of that vision and in their behalf. This last phrase has been inserted into verse 2 without deleting any material. It, too, is post-biblical Hebrew.[13] The full name and title of the almighty author, "the Lord of hosts is his name," serves to ratify the newly composed verse and authorize its biblicity. Anna Deavere Smith described the language she found and used among those she interviewed and re-presented in her play about the Crown Heights incident as "the American character [that] lives in broken sentences—not in perfect syntax, but in the place where it breaks down."[14] What we see here in our letter is that Shukr's passionate message is to be found there too, where the expected perfection of the biblical text breaks down and the "natural" expressions of the common Hebrew style of his own time appear. These two inserted passages have converted the discourse that lies about them.

It seems clear that Shukr is addressing not only the authorities in Jerusalem, but also all those who read his letter to them. His topic is not only the requirement that the authorities join with him in the work of salvation, but also that all those who read the letter do so and urge his cause against his adversaries. His phrase "who heed the voice of their authorities" addresses both the rabbis and sages of Jerusalem and all Jews everywhere; it directs the reader to consider how such a figure controls his following, a daily problem for the messiah. If he is absolutely in charge and something goes wrong, he must explain that it was intended to go wrong or he will lose his adherents. Shukr's biggest problem in this regard is always a difficulty for messiahs—the constant demand that they perform miracles.[15]

Shukr directly answers the question about why he isn't working any miracles, but he has begun to spin an atmosphere surrounding this response in which his audience will embrace his answer. Since he cannot accomplish all he needs to by commanding and directing people and events from an insuperable height, he makes himself one with them, one of them under the authority of Heaven. Before turning to the opening sentence of the third paragraph—one whose argument and atmosphere support Shukr's explanation, that he doesn't have permission from God yet to work wonders —it is worth dwelling on the artistic construction of the material that intervenes, lines 7-23, and suspends the conclusion.

7b. I have not said it in secret or in

8. the dust, I have not said to the seed of Jacob, Seek me out in chaos [Isa. 45.19]. Who said this aforehand [Isa. 45.21], that [even]

9. before the harvest (when) the flower is perfect [Isa. 18.5]? The watchman said, The morning has come [Isa. 21.12], and those whose spirit is misguided shall know discernment [Isa. 29.24],

10. and the ears of those who listen will heed [Isa. 32.3], and the light of the moon will be as the light of the sun [Isa. 30.26]. The first things

11. I have spoken aforetimes and from my mouth they have come forth [Isa. 48.3], I have made heard that which was created and done so recently [Isa. 48.7],

12. neither have you heard nor have you known [Isa. 48.8]. Rejoice, o Jerusalem, and take joy in her all her lovers [Isa. 66.10]. The Lord has repented of this[Amos 7.3],

13. Call it out among the Gentiles [Joel 4.9], Who has heard such a thing as this, Who has seen things such as these [Isa. 66.8]? Shall one of you rise to kill?

14. My people has been destroyed for unknowing [Hos. 4.6]. Hear [this], peoples, all [1K. 22.28]. Sun [and] moon stood still in its habitation [Hab. 3.11]. The Lord is righteous,

15. he will not commit a misdeed [Zeph. 3.5], this too has come forth from the Lord of Hosts, o dove-like Ephraim [Hos. 7.11]. He has advised/ determined/planned

16. wondrously, he has multiplied skill [Isa. 28.29]. Be not afraid, o earth [Joel 2.21]. Sanctify the flock [/a fast], proclaim a gathering [Joel 1.14], above all seek out

17. the book of the Lord and proclaim it: not one of these has failed [Isa. 34.16]. The spirit of the Lord is upon me, thus he has anointed me to call out the captives to freedom [Isa. 61.1], to summon

18. the imprisoned, Come forth, to him who is in darkness, Come out [Isa. 49.9], to replace the dust [on the heads of] the Mourners of Zion

19. with glory [Isa. 61.3]. Who believed what was heard of us [Isa. 53.1]? Drip, sky, from above, the heavens

20. will flow with righteousness [Isa. 45.8], rejoice, sky, for the Lord has done, sound forth, o depths of the earth, burst forth in joy, o hills,

21. for the Lord has redeemed and will be glorified in Israel [Isa. 44.23], [he] gives strength to the weary and magnifies the power of the helpless [Isa. 40.29],

22. for a day of vengeance it is unto the Lord, a year of repayment unto

Zion [Isa. 34.8], for the Lord is our judge, the Lord is our lawgiver,

23. the Lord is our king, he will save us [Isa. 33.22].

Following the tidings that have determined the roles of the rabbis and the role of the savior, Shukr joins together several verse parts by repeating pairs of masculine, plural imperatives. (An imperative opened the passage following the preamble—"Hear!"—And it is to that verb form Shukr returns.) The series begins, "Recall and be strengthened," "Turn and be saved," "Speak it and proffer it ," and concludes, "Gather and come." The set enrolls a sequence of actions, from interior recognition and encouragement through the physical manifestation (turning towards the stimulus) of that emotion, through sharing it with others (speaking), and then—with the reciprocal/reflexive nif'al verb *(hiqqabsu)* and its modal adverb *(bo'u),* the phrase "be continuously gathering together"—all the acts are literally gathered together.

From the end of line 8 to the middle of line 12, Shukr argues that his tidings are true and easy to grasp if his listeners will only be attentive and believe what they hear. He assures the truth of the message that he brings by identifying himself with God. Following the phrase, "I have not said 'Seek me out in chaos,'" Isa. 45.19 goes on to say, "I the Lord am a righteous speaker and tell the straight truth." Shukr deletes this part of the verse, in order to avoid ascribing the speech to God and to substitute himself, the harbinger, in the role. With great daring, he even refers to what he has just done by asking, "Who was it that said this?" The answer he supplies is the prophet, the messenger: the "watchman." By stripping Isa. 18.5 of its continuation, one which describes the untimely ruin of the perfect flower by the hands of a retributive gardener, Shukr once again converts a negative passage into a positive one of promise. What has been deleted explicitly still remains complicit, a promise and a threat together, as in so many biblical passages. The watchman calls forth the dawn, and even the misguided will know it. Those who doubt Shukr (like the rabbis and sages of the preamble) will first hear his message and then see it. Shukr has deleted the beginning of Isa. 32.3 which speaks of seeing; by doing so he achieves a unity of the senses, a synesthetic effect, mentioning audition first and then returning to the visual, miraculous world where the moon burns bright as the sun "and the sun's light will be seventy times that of the sun at creation." "The first things" in the letter actually makes reference to this continuation of Isa 30.26 and links the visual image to the Creator's speaking the world into being, making what has been created audible, as "recently" as Shukr's re-voicing it.[16] But the deaf and dubious need more proof and are summoned again. They have failed to hear and heed.

Ingeniously, Shukr deletes the accusative marker from his version of Isa. 66.10. The original says something like "Make a rejoicing of Jerusalem"; Shukr's craft makes "Jerusalem" into a vocative that is addressed by the imperative. The balance of the verse is unharmed. Shukr quotes Amos 7.3 (or 7.6) and ties it across the "call" verse (Joel 4.9) to the passage from Isa. 66.8 by repeating the word "this." In lines 13-17a, Shukr refreshes the earlier theme — that the sages lack belief and the courage necessary to act on what the Bible clearly says, and bring on redemption. In 17b Shukr returns to his own role in all this, quoting Isa. 61.1ab. He deletes 61.1cd and almost completes his use of the verse with 61.1e, but not quite; f, the sixth of the half-lines of verse one, reads, "and to the imprisoned, 'Be free.'" Shukr uses this unmentioned fragment to tie the quotation he has made to the next quotation, where Isa. 49.9 picks up with the word "imprisoned." Isa. 61.1bc have been deleted because they speak of comfort rather than redemption, but the elipsis goes unnoticed.

The last word Shukr quotes from Isa. 49.9b, *higgalu*, is a nif'al imperative from the root *gly* and has a middle voice, between the reflexive and the passive: "reveal yourself/ be revealed." The word that is the nif'al imperative plural of the root *g'l*, "be redeemed," *higg'alu*, sounds very similar to this one. I believe that the confusion is intentional. There is really no space here to go into all the sound play Shukr employs, though, like the deletions-and-insertions, the sound play adds to the unification of the verse-parts and the unity of the message. The repetition of the word "this" in lines 12-13 has such a function and when the word occurs once again in line 15, it does so to say that all the preceding promises have been fulfilled as it concludes the passage. In line 19, Shukr exactly repeats the word play "glory [*pe'er*] will replace dust [*'efer*]" from Isa. 61.3. He picks up the play again in line 21 and attains the conclusion of this part of the "speech" before beginning the coda. The theme of redemption ends with the word *yitpa'er*, "will be glorified," and the theme of vengeance begins immediately afterwards. The verb complex "he has redeemed" occurs two words before "he will be glorified," completing the sound play begun in line 18 (*nigg[']alu*) just before the *pe'er/'efer* pun, and the two patterns of repetition coincide at the end of the pericope as they had done at its beginning.

In the center of this stands the term "mourners of Zion" from Isa. 61.3. Extra-biblical tradition speaks of a sect, called by this name, that arose following 70 CE. Babylonian Talmud, Tractate Sotah 60b, says that R. Ishamel b. Elisha proposed that Jews should stop having children, and R.

Yehoshua added abstinence from bread and water to a Pharisaic proposal to cease from eating meat and drinking wine. A sixth-century midrash (*pesiqta rabbati*, 34.2) calls the members of this sect "Mourners of Zion" and adds that they were accustomed to rise early and mourn all day long, supplicating God to return to his house.[17] Benjamin of Tudela encountered them in Yemen in the twelfth century, noting that in addition to abstinence from meat and wine "they wear black clothes and live in caves or concealed houses and torment themselves their entire lives, excluding Sabbaths and holidays."[18] The first Shukr Kuhayl was well known for his humble ways and for the wanderings to which he committed himself after divorcing his wife (ll. 93-96 of the same letter).

The argument of the last paragraph preceding the opening of Shukr I+II's biography is that one must not be impatient Although Shukr is indeed the messiah, the Lord employs him, and the Lord is waiting for a unified Jewry to gather behind him before he rolls out the marvels. So, in the argument, Shukr is no different from his recruits; they're waiting for him and he's waiting for the Lord, but the bare, cold demonstration needs to be fleshed out and warmed up with sympathy. Even though Shukr II has stated that he is the messiah—"The spirit of the Lord is upon me, thus he has anointed me to call out the captives to freedom" (Isa. 61.1)—he meets this felt need with pronouns and friendly counsel.

24. Do you not know, have you not heard, has it not been said from the first unto you [Isa. 40.21], weak hands

25. grasp each other and stumbling knees gather strength [Isa. 35.3] for there the mighty one, the Lord, is ours [Isa. 33.21], bend your ears and come to me,

26. pay heed and may your soul revive [Isa. 55.3], *just as it is for me so is it for you. And this is my good advice for you, the Lord*

27. *of Hosts will do it,* for in only a brief time his anger will be ended [Isa. 10.25], therefore wait for me [Zeph. 3.8], the Lord of Hosts,

28. sanctify him [Isa. 8.13], therefore the Lord will give you a sign [Isa. 7.14]. Why should you be despondent, my people [Isa. 3.15],

29. *for I have not yet permission to make use of any doing, for the Lord has bound me not to make use of the Torah,*

30. *for first Israel must gather together and thereafter the Lord will do wonders,* this determination concerns the whole

31. earth [Isa. 14.26]. For the Lord of Hosts has determined and who shall annul it and it is his hand stretched out so who shall withdraw it [Isa. 14.27]? The Lord

32. of Hosts has sworn, shall it not be as I have said and come to be as I have determined [Isa. 14.24]?

33. The Lord has made it heard to the end of the Earth, Say to daughter Zion, See your savior comes, See

34. his repayment is with him and his endeavor before him [Isa. 62.11] and they have never attended [Isa. 64.3]. See, the hand of the Lord is not too short to deliver,

35. but you will not come forth hastily nor go forward fleeing [Isa. 52.12], Burst out, rejoice together, ruins of Jerusalem,

36. for the Lord has comforted his people, He has redeemed Jerusalem [Isa. 52.9] *and in this has been fulfilled the scripture*, And those the Lord has ransomed

37. will return and come to Jerusalem in happiness and eternal joy, they will attain gladness and rejoicing,

38. suffering and moaning will have fled [Isa. 51.11]. Happy is he who waits and reaches [the Land of Israel; the end of tribulation] [Dan. 12.12], and a redeemer shall come to Zion [Isa. 59.20]. Amen, may it be his will.

The first phrase from Isa. 40.21 is brought in with a kindly question, "Is it perhaps that you don't know or just haven't heard?" and continues into a phrase from Isa.35.3 which leaves it unclear whether the "weak hands...and stumbling knees" belong to those who doubt him or to him as well. After all, perhaps he is their helper and they are his helpers too, since the "weak hands [are to] grasp each other" in the presence of the Lord, "who is *ours*" yours and mine together. "Attend to me" [Isa. 55.3], he says, because we're in the same boat: "just as it is for me so is it for you." Lines 24-26a are bound to the theme of speaker-speech-audience by the imperative for "listen" followed by the passive "it has been told," the image of attendant ears, and at last — just before the phrase Shukr himself creates (*kamoni kemokhem*, just as it is for me, so it is for you) — a return to the imperative, "Listen." Shukr has made this phrase to order, distinguishing the listeners ("you") from the speaker ("me") and relating them through their common desire for miraculous redemption. We can be sure, in fact, that he has been choosing his pronouns with care all along. While the Bible has three instances of *kamoni kamokha*[19] (the suffix to the second word is 2nd person, masculine singular), there are none where the speaker is identified as different from and yet one with a whole group of others (*-khem*, the 2nd person, masculine plural suffix). He is one of them now, and it is in order for him to give a little advice, not an order and not avoiding their questions; it's just an *eytsa tova*, but actually it's a *haeytsa tova*, and the structure returns to the familiar world of post-biblical

Hebrew where the phrase "good advice" has so often been tendered that it has become a single noun and one definite article will serve both its words.[20]

After Shukr says that it will just be a short wait, he enriches the conglomeration of himself with his listeners that he has introduced by his pronouns and proceeds to identify himselfboth with God and with the messiah who waits on God's instructions. The good advice is *lakhen haku li* (therefore wait for me) *[Zeph. 3.8] et adonai tsevao't, oto takdishu (the Lord of Hosts, sanctify him) [Isa. 8.13], lakhen yiten adonai hu lakhem* (therefore the Lord himself will give you a sign) *ot [Isa. 7.14]*. The first partial verse in the original actually does not refer to the coming of the messiah nor even to the coming of the Lord, but to the coming of a sign. The original phrase in the back of Zephaniah has the imperative in the singular, *hake* as opposed to plural *haku,* and the object awaited is "the Lord." What he will do to avenge Israel upon the nations when he does arrive is included in the following words, deleted in Shukr's version, all the more present as the listeners' familiarity provides it, "A speech of the Lord, [wait for] the unending day of my rising up." But if the prepositional phrase *li* means only wait *for me* (i.e., the Lord), the following grammatical particle makes it all unclear again. Shukr chooses to follow the verse from Zephanaiah with another from Isaiah that begins with the direct object marker *et*, so that we have two objects for the verb *hake*. In such a situation the first object (the one with the lamed) is the dative and the second (with *et*), the accusative, and with this structure Shukr has produced another moment of broken-down speech. The passage now means "Wait with me for the Lord of hosts, sanctify him" or "Please, for me, wait for the Lord of hosts, sanctify him," or also, "Wait for me. Sanctify the Lord of hosts." Although I think the last is the one Shukr intended his audience to hear most clearly in all these cases, what follows is the promise, "[having done this] the Lord will give you a sign." The remainder of the well-known verse says that the promised sign is a child, the famous Imanuel, the messiah. From here we tumble quickly into post-biblical Hebrew, as Shukr explains that he doesn't yet have permission to make use of any *pe'ula*, "deed," perhaps, "magic deed," or "miraculous act." Shukr makes this phrase, *lehishtamesh beshum peu'la* (to make use of any deed) parallel with *la'asok batorah* (to make use/engage in the Torah) implying that the messiah makes use of the Torah like others study it, which is the conventional meaning of the phrase, "to engage in Torah study." He then returns to biblical citations and assures his listeners that the Lord's acts at the right time will be through him: "See your savior comes, See his repayment is with him, and his endeavor is before him/attends him" (Isa.

62.11). With this, Shukr steps out from among those he has been advising to become the messiah and not someone waiting for the messiah. The *pe'ula* will come up again, as will be seen below, but in the meanwhile Shukr returns twice to the theme of the "advice" in lines 31 and 32.

There is a famous moment in Shukr I's story (though perhaps it is actually about Shukr II) and his reading of the classics. He is said to have corrected misreadings in the Zohar (the basic work of the mystical tradition in Judaism) and made the text clear thereby. He is moreover said to have corrected a biblical passage, saying that it was a scribal error. The passage is Isaiah 45.1, *ko amar adonai limshicho, le-koresh*, "Thus has the Lord said to his messiah, to Cyrus." One of the Shukrs said: "That is a scribal error; the letters are scrambled and one should read, not "*kaf-vav-resh-shin*" but "*shin-vav-kaf-resh*," not "to Koresh" but "to Shukr." If, as a result of their traditions of Bible study, Yemenite listeners were able to understand without difficulty what we have so much trouble in working out today, then could any of them, raptly attentive, have missed Shukr's point in this last verse? *hine adonai hishmi'a el ktse ha-aretz*, "Behold the Lord has made it heard to the ends of the earth"; *imru le-vat tsiyon, 'hine yishekh ba,'* "Say to Daughter Zion, [i.e., the people of Jerusalem] 'Behold your salvation comes'"; *hine skharo ito*, "Behold his repayment is with him/before him." Do not read *'skharo'* but its anagram, *'shukr'*: Would the listeners not have heard rather and been amazed, "Behold, Shukr is with him." "And his deed (*pe'ulato*)"—the word Shukr has used for "miracle"in line 30—"is before him."

In lines 34b-38, the epilogue that follows this utterly convincing textual demonstration, Shukr returns in despair to the rabbis and sages who wait, ever unlistening, in Jerusalem. Although he does not remove his attention from the recalcitrants for another twenty lines, he concludes the paragraph with the triumphant announcement from Isaiah 59.20 that "a redeemer will be coming to Zion." "Amen, May it be his will."

In his management of the traditional language and its argumentive assemblage, Shukr has merited our adoration along with that of his listeners; no messiah should really be expected to do more. Few have done as much.

Notes

[1] The verse is famous as Gen. 1.1; the learned scholar *(talmid hokhem)*, ignoring the biblical verse, recalls it instead from two talmudic tractates in which the

verse appears.

[2] See, among many studies, Sh. Garidi, "The education of children in Yemen," in *From Yemen to Zion*; and *The Teaching of Torah in Yemen* (Tel-Aviv, 1970)(in Hebrew).

[3] The most recent study of Yemenite messianism is B-Z. Eraqi Klorman, *Messianism and Messiahs: The Jews of Yemen in the 19th Century* (Tel-Aviv, 1995) (in Hebrew). This analytic work does not replace the source documents, but does provide excellent bibliographic guidance. The most important sources are Yakov Sapir, *The Sapphire* (vol. 1, Lyck, 1866; vol. 2, Mainz, 1874), *The Epistle to Yemen* (Mainz, 1869), and *The Second Epistle to Yemen* (Vilna, 1873) (all in Hebrew). Without intending to, Sapir, an opponent ultimately of Shukr II, provided him with a good deal of publicity then as now.

[4] One outcome of my work on this topic is *The Jewish Messiahs* (Oxford: Oxford University Press, 1998), in which fuller consideration of some of the matters raised here may be found.

[5] See the discussion in G. Scholem, *Sabbatai Sevi* (Princeton, 1973), 104 ff.

[6] In one tale, messengers carrying his letters are miraculously preserved from death; in another, released from prison; in a third, his words slay a distant prince and the qadi who had advised him to kill the messengers.

[7] D.S. Sasson, "An Autograph Letter of a Pseudo-Messiah,"JQR (1907): 162-70.

[8] The letter is from Saphir, *The Second Letter to Yemen*, 14-20. The translation is mine; more of the text appears in *The Jewish Messiahs* (fn.4).

[9] Lines 1-3 of the letter are laid out as a paragraph in Saphir's printed version. Saphir used the "rashi" script here rather than the "square" script he used in other works, presumably to give the work an appropriately rabbinic air. In the Sasson holograph the greeting is separated from the body of the letter; the opening poem, the epigraph, is in a super-section above the greeting while its parallel, Shukr's signature and the seals, is in a final section. Even though there are other groups of lines between these that have a single purpose and theme and that might have been divided up as paragraphs in the Sasson letter, only these four are set apart. One might suggest, then, that one or more of the transmitters of our letter, probably Saphir, have put it into sections that might not have existed in the original, in order to bring it into line with other conventions, and added punctuation as well.

[10] There might once have been an address like the one in the Sasson letter, but Saphir has replaced it in order to set the letter in the surrounding narrative.

[11] The translation is from the JPS version and reflects one common Jewish interpretation.

[12] q*abbel 'ol* (receive the yoke) is not a biblical idiom nor is '*ol ha-galut* (the yoke of exile); the hif'il of the root *nhg* (in the word *manhigim,* authorities) does not occur in the Bible.

[13] The relative particle *she-* is mostly post- biblical, particularly when followed

by the future tense as the expression of a wish; *'amd* (stand, in a verbal form meaning to make stand, appoint) is not the verb root that occurs biblically with *moshi'a* (savior), though it is close to the biblical Hebrew idiom (i.e., a verbal form of the root *qwm,* stand).

[14] Anna Deavere Smith, "Broken Dreams," *New Yorker* (Feb. 26, 1996): 158.

[15] In the Sasson letter, Shukr is expected to respond to the questions of his correspondents and send his replies by flying birds.

[16] The image of the sun of redemption shining bright over the newly redeemed world is familiar in descriptions of the eschaton; see Babylonian Talmud, Tractate Pesahim 68a and Tractate Sanhedrin 91b.

[17] See Y. Even-Shmuel, *Midreshei geulah*, (Tel-Aviv, 1954), 36 and the note to the articles by Mann there.

[18] See Klorman, 5 and note 3; 21-22 and notes 11 and 12.

[19] 1K 22.4, 2K 3.7, 2Ch 18.3.

[20] One might reasonably ask, "Who would give any other kind of advice?" Is there anywhere in human speech a proposal, "Let me give you a little bad advice?" Actually, and perhaps of some relevance to the discussion here, an *eytsa ra'a* is one which emanates from the Adversary.

Miami and the Babylonian Captivity

Miguel A. De La Torre

Cuba is the fantasy Island of dreams, an illusion, a construction of outsiders' imaginations. Thus envisioned, Cuba spans centuries. This imaginary space, superimposed on the Island, is a new way of comprehending the object by projecting oneself into the object. As such, representations of Cuba are but the product of an arbitrary choice made by the outside thinker. Alan West, the Exilic Cuban linguist, illustrates how Cuba has been visualized:

> From other shores, the island has been imagined and expressed in a series of more familiar discourses with a plethora of images: Pearl of the Antilles, tropical paradise, whorehouse of the Caribbean, Cuba as gold mine, cane field (slave trade), military outpost (strategic location/geopolitical pawn), tourist haven/exotic folkloric locale (flesh depot, fun in the sun, shed your inhibitions), investment opportunity (source of cheap labor), or revolutionary menace/ terrorist haven (as U.S. nightmare). Cuba's images of "otherness" come from outside observers or covetous foreign powers. [1]

If we define history as the memory of a people, at times intoxicated with false memories, how do we Cubans recall our history apart from the imagery imposed upon us by the colonial gaze? How can we create an enduring identity while living separated from the land which defines us?

Theologians who operate from a liberationist perspective have usually focused on the Exodus as a source of hope for their existential situation. The story of a God who hears the cries of an oppressed people and personally leads them toward liberation is a powerful motif.[2] The Exodus, however, is not the rubric I believe Exilic Cubans use to read the scriptures. It is the second exodus, narrating the Babylonian Captivity, that resonates within our very being. Like the Psalmist (Psalm 137) we sit by the streams of this country, singing about our inability to sing God's songs.

BESIDE THE MIAMI RIVER WE SAT AND WEPT AT THE MEMORY OF LA HABANA, LEAVING OUR CONGA DRUMS BY THE PALM TREES

The danger of exile is the end of history, for a people without land will eventually cease to exist as they assimilate to the dominant culture. Hence, we construct *el exilio* (the Exile). *El exilio* is the phrase constantly used among Exilic Cubans within the social milieu of Miami to name our collective identity. In our newspapers, television shows, radio programs, and our everyday conversation, we refer to our identity and social location as *el exilio*. This term connotes the involuntary nature of displacement and constructs us as sojourners in a foreign land. It is an in-between place, a place to wait and hope for a return to our homeland. Exile is more than geographic separation; it encompasses dis-connection, dis-placement, dis-embodiment. *El exilio* is existence in a reality apart from what one loves. *Exilio* becomes a structured reality for those of us who were forced to wave goodby to our homeland and love ones, as well for the resident Cubans who watched us leave.

El exilio, besides being a geographic reality, is a culturally constructed artifact imagined as a land-less nation complete with its own history and values. As travel writer David Rieff observes, "The country of which Miami is the capital is an imaginary one, that of *el exilio.*"[3] Dis-membered Miami becomes re-membered La Habana. We construct a socio-political space in which we cease being victims of the Anglo dominant culture by striving to become the new oppressors. In Miami, longing for Cuba or the "rhetoric of return" becomes the unifying substance of our existential being; however, this hope is being replaced with a stronger desire to adapt and capitalize on our presence in this country. *El exilio* becomes a sacred space making morality synonymous with nationality. Living in exile is a sacrifice constituting a civic duty representing a grander moral basis.

History is constructed from the Miami experience. I reread my story as one who escaped. Dictator Fulgencio Batista's departure from Cuba on New Year's Eve, 1959 triggered panic as party goers rushed to their houses to collect their sleeping children, moneys, and anything of value. Batista's children and money were already out of the country. Those who were able to leave arrived in this country still in their tuxedos and dress uniforms, their wives in formal gowns and high heels. These first refugees arrived with "class"—not so much in the elegance of their attire, but in their high economic social stratum. Unlike other contemporary examples of refugees, both the Babylonian-bound Jews and the United States-bound Cubans belonged to the privileged upper social class. The biblical account tells us that Nebuchadnezzar carried off *"all* Jerusalem into exile." "All" is defined as the officers, the mighty men of valor, craftsmen, and the blacksmiths. Those left behind were the "poorest of the land" (2 Kings 24:14). Exilic Cubans, like their Jewish counterparts, were not necessarily numerous. Yet they represented the top echelons of their country's governmental and business community, facilitating our reestablishment in a foreign land while creating a "brain-drain" that literally emptied the resident community of trained personnel indispensable for the socioeconomic development of the country.

The surreal scene at the Miami airport of well-dressed refugees was caused by the same forces that brought about the Babylonian exile. In both cases, the hegemonic northern power was responsible for the circumstances that lead to refugee status. Cuba's political system (especially the Batista regime) was designed to protect the commercial interests and assets of the United States.[4] As vassals, both Cuba and Judea were desirable prizes: Judah as a buffer zone between the powers of the north and south, and Cuba as a key to the entire hemisphere. While Judah's exile was triggered by the physical invasion of Babylon, Cuba's revolution was a backlash to the hegemony of the United States.

This first wave (1959-1962) brought 215,000 refugees to these shores who could be considered "political exiles." Demographically, these new Cuban refugees were quite homogeneous. The vast majority composed an elite of former notables who were mostly white (94 percent), middle-aged (about thirty-eight years old), educated (about fourteen years of schooling), urban (principally La Habana) and literate in English.[5] Unity existed in their bitterness at lost status and their commitments to overthrow Castro in order to regain their assets. The second wave (1962-1973) brought 414,000 refugees who were predominately white, educated, middle class and willing to work below minimum wages.

While all strata of Cuban society were represented in these first two waves, it was obvious the vast majority consisted of those from the upper echelons and middle class who most benefitted from the pre-Castro regime. Pierre Bourdieu's concept of the *habitus* illuminates how these Exilic Cubans ascended the socioeconomic institutions of Miami.[6] Being born into a position of privilege in Cuba, our socially constructed lifestyle facilitated our rise to the echelons of Miami's power structures. We merely had to assert what we were in order to become what we are, an effort done with the unselfconsciousness that marks our so-called "nature."

"SING," THEY SAID, "SOME MAMBO." HOW CAN WE SING OUR RUMBA IN A PAGAN LAND? MI HABANA, IF I FORGET YOU MAY MY RIGHT HAND WITHER

We call ourselves Cubans because we were born on that Caribbean Island. If the Island of Cuba never existed, then there would be no such thing as Cubans. But what happens when the land of your birth is no longer available to you? How do we forge an identity in exile? What if your love for La Habana remains stronger than your allegiance to Babylon? How can we continue to be Cubans without a Cuba? These questions go to the heart of understanding why we "cannot sing our rumba in a pagan land."

Those of us who arrived in Babylon from Cuba as infants or small children struggle with the realization that we do not belong to the mythical Cuba of our parents. In spite of our determination not to forget "*mi Habana*" lest "my right-hand withers," the paradoxical space we find ourselves in loudly asks, "How can we remember that which we have never seen?" As I look at my two children, born in the early 1990s, I realize that in spite of my efforts to raise them as Cubans (a term I struggle daily to define for myself) their blond hair and blue eyes allow them to "pass" for Anglos. In 2030, when my children are my age, will they define themselves as Cubans? The pain that prevents me from singing my rumba is the knowledge that while my parents, my children, and myself belong to the same biological family, we live in separate cultural families. Names like Ashly Gomez or Jordan Perez betrays the extent of our assimilation, an assimilation understood by the Exiled Jews. The name of the returning Jew who led emancipated compatriots to the homeland (Ezr 2:2), directed the building of the alter and temple (Hag. 1:12-14), and appointed Levites to inaugurate the finished Temple was Zerubbabel, "shoot of Babylon." Regardless of any role our children may partake in a post-Castro Cuba, they will always be "shoots of the U.S.A."

The disparity between the children of Exilic Cubans and other United States Latino/a groups is evident. For our children, becoming an "American" (United States definition) is desired. To become an "American" is a choice made by the individual but also accepted by the national community if the child is "white" enough and has sufficient middle-class status. Therefore, our children face an entirely different set of circumstances contributing to a rapid assimilation into the dominant culture. Alejando Portes and Rubén G. Rumbaut's 1992 study on segmented assimilation showed that while Exilic Cubans, have in common with other Hispanics the exilic experience, the next generation will share little if nothing in common with other Hispanics.[7]

While Exilic Cuban theologians construct a supposedly seemless Latina/o perspective, that effort is not beyond criticism. Our approach to reading the Bible, according to Justo González, is from the perspective of marginality, poverty, *mestizaje/mulatez*, exiles/aliens, and solidarity.[8] While such a perspective may appear normative to the overall Hispanic experience, I insist it does not properly represent the Exilic Cuban experience. Few of us address the Exilic Cuban theological location from within our context of power in the Miami community. When the Exilic Cuban perspective is discussed, it is usually done within the pre-1980s rubric of being an alien. To contribute to the overall Hispanic liberationist discourse, we have tended to speak either within a pan-ethnic space (which in fact does not exist) or within some other Latino/a tradition. Within the Mexican and/or Puerto Rican communities are Mexican and Puerto Rican theologians who construct their theology exclusively from their own social location in order to enrich the overall dialogue.[9] My suggestion is that we Exilic Cubans do the same.

Why are so few Exilic Cuban theologians willing to speak from our own constructed space in Miami? We generally ignore this space because of the obvious difficulty of "doing theology as an oppressed people" when in fact the overall Exilic Cuban community is economically well established, has a most effective United States lobbying group, and is the center of the political, economic and social power in Dade County, Florida. It is difficult to cry "oppression" once middle-class status is achieved.

Every Exilic Cuban has heard Celia Cruz sing the popular tear-jerker "*Cuando salí de Cuba* (When I left Cuba)." No other song better summarizes the pain of our existential location. "Never can I die, my heart is not *here*. Over *there* it is waiting for me, it is waiting for me to return *there*. When I left Cuba, I left my life, I left my love. When I left Cuba, I left my heart buried." This popular Cuban ballad, written by a Chilean and sung as a hymn of the faith, illustrates the denial of accepting the reality of being, living, and most likely dying on foreign soil. Lourdes Casal writes that "exile is living where no house holds the memories of our childhood."[10]

Both Exilic Jews and Cubans were forced to deal with this incomprehensible pain. Judaism was constructed in Babylon through the pain of questioning the sovereignty of a God who would tear God's people from their homes and plant them in an alien land. A major concern for those in Exile was their status as deportees. Did removal from the "promised land," by which their identity as Jews was constructed, indicate a divine rejection voiding any future participation as God's chosen? Ezekiel (11:14-25) addresses the Exilic Jews' anxiety by attempting to construct a new covenant upon "a single heart" and "a new spirit." Moreover, with the fall of Jerusalem and the devastation of the Temple, questions were again raised concerning an everlasting rejection by God, or worse, an inability of God to prevent these destructive forces. For Ezekiel (chaps. 8-11) the fall of the city was not a result of God's powerlessness but of God's deliberate desertion containing the hope of restoration. Additionally, Ezekiel stresses the continuation of God's fidelity to Jerusalem and to the Exiles. While comforting, Ezekiel (chap. 18) words failed to initiate the overall repentance among those in Exile. Instead, Exile forged the construction of a new Judaic expression. Likewise, we Exilic Cubans subconsciously reconstructed ourselves to deal with our landlessness. We internalize and naturalize our structured image so we can begin to shape outside structures, always masking our drive toward mastering them. This reconstruction took the form as *la Cuba de ayer* (the Cuba of yesteryear).

La Cuba de ayer on Miami's soil created a land-less Cuban territory with its distinct cultural milieu and idiosyncrasies that served to protect us from the pain of the initial economic and psychological difficulties caused by our uprooting. Cuba became more than just the old country; it was the mythological world of our origins. Cuba is an ethereal place where every conceivable item *es mejor* (is better), where the sky is bluer, the sugar sweeter, the bugs less pesky, and life richer. Everything *aquí* (here), when contrasted with *allá* (there), is found lacking. Unlike the stereotypes of other immigrant groups who left painful memories of the old country behind, joyfully anticipating what they perceived was a new country where "the streets were paved with gold," Cubans did not want to come to what we perceived to be an inferior culture. Like the Babylon Jews, we rejoice every time someone says, "Let us go to our house" (Ps 122). In our attempt to avoid our pain, we construct a mythical Cuba where every *guajiro/a* (country bumpkin) had class and wealth, where no racism existed, and where Eden was preserved until the serpent (Fidel) beguiled Eve (the weakest elements of society: blacks, poor, etc.) and brought an end to paradise.

Is it any wonder that when Exilic Cubans read Psalm 137 we are stirred to the core of our souls? We fully comprehend the tragic pain of sitting by the rivers of an alien land unable to sing to a God the Psalter secretly holds responsible. Landlessness, which comes with the ninety-mile crossing of the Florida Straits, radically disenfranchises us. The hope of returning to one's land becomes a foundational building block for the construction of our Exilic Cuban ethnicity. Yet, with the passing of each year, the cemeteries of Miami increase with headstones engraved with Cuban surnames. Rather than proclaiming, "next year in Jerusalem," we tell each other, "this year Castro will fall," as though this one person is the only thing that prevents us from "going home."

In reality, the hope of returning home has been replaced with a private desire to adapt and capitalize on our presence in this country. Bright documents the success of the Exilic Jews by pointing out that their names frequently appear in business documents from Nippur (437 and afterwards). He also quotes Josephus (Ant. XI, 1, 3) as stating, " they were not willing to leave their possessions," to be their excuse for not returning to Jerusalem.[11]

Jeremiah writes a letter to the Exilic Jews to forget about their hope for a speedy return. He tells them (29:5-9): "to build houses, live, plant gardens and eat their fruits; . . . [they are to] seek the peace of the city [to which exiled] . . . and pray to Yahweh for its peace, for in its peace there will be for you peace." Like the Jews, Exilic Cubans are forced to relinquish the old world and deal with the realities of the new space they occupy. Our adherence to Jeremiah's dictates was facilitated through our former contacts with elites in other Latin American countries, the possession of the necessary language skills and cultural links to deal with these contacts, our confidence to succeed due to our *habitus*, and our connections with United States corporations developed when we were their representatives back in the homeland.

These advantages created a space allowing us to bring new businesses to Miami and gain positions of power within the banking industry. We established "character loans" as a way of providing entrepreneurs the seed money required to start up businesses. This action helped create an ethnic enclave.[12] Labor was easily obtained from both family members and other more recent refugees. With time, Exilic Cubans with business acumen acquired in La Habana filled an economic space in Miami. Exilic Cuban Guillermo Grenier, head of Florida International University's Sociology Department states, "As the Western Hemisphere becomes more Hispanic, Miami has become the frontier city between 'America' and Latin America."[13] We Exilic Cubans took advantage of this emerging "frontier" space.

Exile can bring some levels of success. In the closing chapter of 2 Kings (25:27-30) the disgraced king of Judah, Jehoiachin, is allotted a seat at the Babylonian king's table "above those of the other kings." From the former Judean elite arose leaders like Nehemiah who occupied the post of "cupbearer" for the Persian king Artaxerxes. The cupbearer was more than an individual who tasted the king's wine to thwart assassination attempts. The cupbearer was a confidant of the royal entourage who exercised influence upon king's policies, as was the case with Nehemiah. While life in exile contained numerous hardships, the Exilic Jews possessed the necessary *habitus* and resources to overcome their predicament. In Babylon, Exilic Jews constructed a community whose legacy is still felt to this day. This independent and powerful community participated in the life of post-Exilic Israel by providing financial support to the Palestinian community until the Roman destruction of the Second Temple. The importance of the Babylonian Jews to the construction of Judaism is evident by the monumental development of the Babylonian Talmud in subsequent centuries.

Like the Exilic Jews, Cubans suffered no unusual physical hardship. On the contrary, life in Exile opened up opportunities never existing in the homeland. Exilic Cuban sociologist Lisando Pérez, who heads the Cuban Research Institute at Florida International University states, "In Miami there is no pressure to be American. People can make a living perfectly well in an enclave that speaks Spanish."[14] As a unilingual Exilic woman told me, "Even though I hate Fidel, I thank him every day. In Cuba I had nothing, living in a dirt floor hut. But now, look at me. My two sons went to college and have good jobs, and I own a house with Italian tiles." Like the Babylonian Jews, Cubans entered trade and grew rich, with some, like Nehemiah, ascending the political structures to hold power over those who did not go into Exile. The United States became the space where Exilic Cubans placed their hope.

While Jerusalem was falling, Jeremiah bought a plot of land (32:9-11). His message juxtaposes God's judgement with deliverance. The true hope for Jerusalem did not lie in Babylon; rather, it was rooted in the homeland. Similarly, Exilic Cubans, especially YUCAS, see their exilic experience as positive due to their individual economic advancements.[15] While we look toward the United States to define the future of Cuba, we also look toward Cuba to define our present reality in this country. The historical activity of remembering *la Cuba de ayer* protects us from the apocalyptic danger of having our history come to an end. The greatest danger of landlessness is the ushering in of the end of history for a people. Separated from our land, *la Cuba de ayer* protects us from extermination, and creates the hope of one day returning to the "promised land."

Self-deception and denial are manifested in the construction of our ethnic identity. Identity as an Exilic Cuban is a social construction created from the pain of living in *el exilio*. A foundational tenet of this construction claims we are victims who "fled" tyranny. In the 1960s, the United States lost Cuba to the communists (assuming Cuba had belonged to the United States and thus could be lost) and was defeated at *Playa Girón*. These were major setbacks in the ideological struggle against the Soviet Union. But the image of Cubans getting off rafts and kissing United States' soil provided powerful propaganda showing the superiority and desirability of capitalism over communism.

YAHWEH, REMEMBER WHAT THE COMMUNIST DID— A BLESSING ON HIM WHO TAKES AND DASHES THEIR BABIES AGAINST THE ROCK!

The psalmist prayed for the enemy's babies to be dashed against the rocks. The pain of Exile fuels dreams of revenge toward those perceived to be responsible for one's expatriation. *En el noventa, Fidel revienta* (In 1990, Fidel will take off) was proudly worn on the T-shirts of Exilic Cubans in 1990. After the fall of the Sandinistas government of Daniel Ortega in Nicaragua and the United States' invasion of Panama, which led to the imprisonment of Manuel Noriega, crowds in Miami chanted, "*Ayer Daniel, hoy Manuel, mañana Fidel*" (Yesterday Daniel, today Manuel, tomorrow Fidel). Even though the Cold War against communism has ended, Miami remains the only place in the United States where Cold War hatred and fervor have not abated. Mimicking the psalmist, the Exilic Cuban United States Congressman Diaz-Balat (ironically a nephew of Castro) called for a post-Castro Cuba to launch a campaign of retribution against anyone who participated in "collaborationism with tyranny." Ten years in prison will not be enough for those who are guilty. The Congressman even called for the abduction of foreign investors presently doing business with Cuba, to be brought to the Island for punishment.[16]

Hatred is not limited to one side of the Florida Straits. While the Exilic community calls its critics "Castro agents" for suggesting any deviation from the tenets of *el exilio*, the resident community calls each Exilic Cuban a *gusano* (worm) for leaving the Island in the first place. Each Cuba sees itself as the true remnant. Resident Cubans, see themselves as the true Cubans, just as King Zedekiah's nobles who remained in Judah saw themselves as true Jews (Ezek 11:14, 33:24). Similarly Exilic Cubans see themselves as God's "good basket of figs," as opposed to the "bad basket of figs" with which Jeremiah (chapter 24) represents King Zedekiah and all those who remain behind. Resident Cubans are seen as pseudo-Cubans in need of being educated in the ways of capitalism and democracy.

Before we Exiles attempt paternalistically to educate resident Cubans, we of *el exilio* must first recover from our amnesia. Jeremiah (chaps. 4-5) strives to overcome the Babylonian Jews' attempt to displace blame. He explains that their condemnation is partially due to the oppression of the powerless by the powerful elite (Jer. 2:33-24; 5: 26-27). Babylon was not the culprit, it was only a designated agent used by God to punish Judah for their unfaithfulness to justice. Jeremiah explains that their condemnation is due to their ignorance of God in spite of their cleverness to do wrong (Jer. 4:22).

Our own sins, and the sins of those to whom we have become vassals, are the causes of our exile. Our reconstruction of the *Cuba de ayer* ignores the reality that La Habana was an exotic space constructed by the United States, where the repressed libidinous appetites of the Anglos could be satisfied. The commercialization of vice afforded North Americans the opportunity to experience life outside of their accustomed moral space.[17]

As a playground for North Americans, Cuba developed an unequal distribution of wealth and violated basic human rights. Jeremiah's condemnation of King Jehoiakim also applies to Cuba's elite who profited from this arrangement. They built their house through the oppression of people (Jer. 22:13-17). No communal covenant based on justice and compassion existed between the elite and the masses. By continuing to scapegoat the communist, we deflect attention from our own responsibility. Castro is not the one responsible for our landlessness. The Cuban elite who profited from the United States' neo-colonial venture is responsible. Today, many of those responsible consist of today's Exilic Cuban elite.

Maintaining *la Cuba de ayer* insures the condemnation of our perceived enemies today, while it mythically creates the Cuba of tomorrow, a Post-Castro Cuba based on horizontal oppression, where resident Cubans will be subjected to Exilic Cubans. The overwhelming support of the embargo by Exilic Cubans denies resident Cubans basic medical supplies and causes death among the sick, the elderly and infants. From a sanitizing distance, we are dashing the "enemy's" babies against rocks when we deny insulin to those born diabetic.

Forms of punishment like the embargo lead Exilic Cubans toward horizontal oppression. Most Exilic Cubans have no desire to move physically to Cuba. Any type of physical return would mean a tremendous economic sacrifice. Like the Exilic Jews, we have become well-to-do, taking away motivation for any possible rush back to the homeland. The hardships required in nation-building do not outweigh the luxuries of living in Miami. While a willingness to financially support the venture may exist (Ezra 1:4,6), polls suggest that few are willing personally to participate.[18]

From the periphery of the Jewish Exilic community's epicenter of power, a prophet arose who became a subversive yet redemptive voice. While we do not know his name, his work is found in the later chapters of Isaiah. Appealing to the community's old memories, he plots a new trajectory to discern reality, a reality that conflicts with the self-deception of the exiles. Second Isaiah's vision is inclusive (49:6; 56: 1-8; 66: 18-21), calling the Exilic community to become "a light to the nations, that [God's] salvation [reconciliation] may reach to the end of the earth." The focus is on a God who acts on the side of the afflicted. Such a God opposes the partisan politics rampant in the post-exilic Jewish community. Consciously rejecting this prophetic voice, Exilic Cubans are aggressively taking the opposite role, that of the Zadokite priestly party.[19] The inclusiveness of Second Isaiah's community is met with accusations of being "communist dupes or agents."

Biblical scholar Paul Hanson points out that the Zadokites: 1) moved away from Second Isaiah's (60:21; 61:6) egalitarian call for a nation of priests by firmly holding power in their own hands; 2) replaced Isaiah's (Is 56:3-7) mission to the nations with a pragmatic and parochial strategy of domestic consolidation; and 3) confused the sovereignty of God with that of the Persian emperor, even to the point of proclaiming that God elected a pagan, Cyrus, to be His messiah (anointed). Thus the Zadokite hierarchy struggled against those who embraced Second Isaiah's egalitarian vision. The failure to pursue Isaiah's vision can be traced to the Persian Court's self-serving support of the Zadokites (255).[20] The construction of a post-exilic Judah was possible because it contributed to Persia's international goal of creating a buffer between them and their enemies, the Egyptians (Bright, 362). As such, Judah's existence depended on Persia's good will (Ezra 7:11-18). The nation was rebuilt at the price of being a vassal (583 to 332 B.C.E.) to its more powerful northern neighbor. The parallels to modern Cuba are striking.

Ezra (7:25-26), with legal and financial support from Persia, was sent to create this buffer zone where the inhabitants would strictly obey the "laws of your God *and the law of the [Persian] king*" (italics mine). Absent was any negotiation for land. Instead, land was controlled by the returning Jews. Like Ezra's approach, Exilic Cubans are preparing to demand that resident

Cubans "put away their foreign wives."[21] Some of those "wives," however, may be worth keeping (such as high literacy rates, a 100 percent social security system, a high doctor per patient ratio, a low infant mortality rate, and a long life expectancy).[22] Ignoring Second Isaiah's egalitarian call, the post-exilic community soon found itself weakened by internal economic abuses. Exilic Jews benefited from the economic misfortunes of the resident Jews, while concealing their profiteering in piety (Isa 58: 1-12; 59: 1-8). The resident poor found themselves enslaved as they lost their lands to the returning Exile (Ne 5:1-5), and they were cheated from wages by returning Jews who set up new business (Mal 3:5). The book of Ruth, written during this period, becomes an alternative voice to the imposition of the Zadokite power structure and captures the spirit of Second Isaiah. Here, God uses a "foreign wife," a Moabite, similar to the ones put away by Ezra, to represent society's most vulnerable members. Ruth is saved by the egalitarian laws that the exilic leaders aborted, and through her, King David arises to save Israel.[23]

This biblical paradigm of domination will repeat itself. The planned post-Castro community will lead to the subjugation of resident Cubans by Exilic Cubans, who in turn will be subjugated to the United States hegemony. The options available to us Exilic Cubans are similar to those faced by the Babylonian Exilic Jews. We can follow the example of Ezra, forcing resident Cubans to "put away their foreign wives," establishing a vassal political system that enriches the Exilic community elite to the detriment of the resident community. Or we can follow Second Isaiah's egalitarian vision which attempts to construct a reconciled and just community.

As long as we Exilic Cubans maintain our constructed ethnic identity, along with participating in the false religion of *el exilio*, and as long as Exilic Cubans theologians define our theological location in terms of some general Hispanic perspective "from the margins," reconciliation between the two Cubas remains impossible. I propose we construct our identity based on our socio-historical reality, unmasking the power and privilege held by Exilic Cubans and debunking our ethnic construction which prevents dialogue between us and our Other. A liberationist approach to theology liberates the oppressed as well as the oppressors. As present oppressors in Miami, and as future oppressors in a post-Castro Cuba, we Exilic Cubans are in need of liberation and reconciliation.

Notes

[1] Alan West, *Tropics of History: Cuba Imagined* (Westport: Bergin & Garvey, 1997), 2.

[2] The liberation of the Jewish slaves from Egypt is a fertile biblical theme informing the construction of Liberation Theology in Latin America. For example, see Segunda Conferencia General Del Episcopado Latinamericano, *La iglesia en la actual transformacion de america latina a la luz del concilio* [known as Medellín Documents], 3rd edicion (Bogotá: Secretariado general del CELAM. 1969), introducctión 6; Gustavo Gutiérrez, *A Theology of Libration,* new and rev. ed., trans. and ed. Sister Caridad Inda and John Eagleson (Maryknoll: Orbis Books, 1993), 87-91; International Theological Commisson, "Declaration on Human Deveopment and Christian Salvation," in *Liberation Theology: A Documentary History*, ed. Alfred T. Hennelly (Maryknoll: Orbis Books, 1995), 209.

[3] David Rieff, *Going to Miami: Exiles, Tourists, and Refugees in the New America* (Boston: Little, Brown, 1987), 149.

[4] Batista's utility to the United States was best expressed by William Wieland, Cuban desk officer at the State Department, who said, "I know Batista is considered by many as a son of a bitch . . . but American interests come first . . . at least he is *our* son of a bitch, he is not playing ball with the Communists." See Hugh Thomas, *Cuba: The Pursuit of Freedom* (New York: Harper & Row, 1971), 971.

[5] Richard R. Fagan, Richard A. Brody, and Thomas J. O'Leary, *Cubans in Exile: Disaffection and the Revolution* (Stanford: Stanford University Press, 1968), 19-28.

[6] *Habitus* is defined "abstractly as the system of internalized dispositions that mediates between social structures and practical activities, being shaped by the former and regulating the latter." See Rogers Brubaker, "Rethinking Classical Theory: The Sociological Vision of Pierre Bourdieu," *Theory and Society* 14 (1985): 758.

[7] Alejandro Portes and Rubén G. Rumbaut, *Immigrant America: A Portrait,* 2nd ed. (Berkeley: University of California Press, 1996), 232-68.

[8] Justo González, *Santa Biblia: The Bible Through Hispanic Eyes* (Nashville: Abingdon Press, 1996).

[9] It is common for non-Cuban theologians to construct their theology as a Hispanic national within the United States' context. For example, Puerto Ricans like Edwin Aponte, Yamina Apolinaris, or Sandra Mangual-Rodríguez ground their theological thinking within the Puerto Rican community. Moreover, those of Mexican descent like Virgil Elizondo, Luis Leon, or Michael Mata construct a theological perspective from the Mexican perspective.

[10] As quoted by Sonia Rivera-Valdés, "Grandmother's Night," in *Bridges to Cuba*, ed. Ruth Behar (Ann Arbor: University of Michigan Press, 1995), 226. Rivera-Valdés adds the postscript ". . . and where we cannot visit our

grandmother's grave." I would add, ". . . nor view picture albums of her life."

[11] John Bright. *A History of Israel*, 3rd ed. (Philadelphia: Westminster Press, 1959).

[12] The flight of capital from Latin America to the economic and political security of the United States provided an economic space for Exilic Cubans to manage said funds, leading to the creation and growth of banks. Once secured in banking positions, they provided "character loans" to their compatriots to encourage business. It mattered little if the borrower had any standing within Anglo banks, little collateral, or spoke English. Loans (usually from $10,000 to $35,000) were provided based on the reputation of the borrower in Cuba. This policy was discontinued in 1973 because the new refugees, who were not from the more elite first wave, were unknown to the lenders. This practice contributed to the development of an economic enclave. Alejandro Portes and Alex Stepick, *City on the Edge: The Transformation of Miami* (Berkeley: University of California Press, 1993), 132-35.

[13] Cathy Booth, "The Capital of Latin America: Miami," *Time Special Issue: The New Face of America, How Immigrants are Shaping the World's First Multicultural Society,* Vol. 142, No. 21 (Autumn 1993): 82-85.

[14] Booth, "Miami," 84.

[15] Yucca is an indigenous Cuban root, often tall and stout-stemmed, that when boiled or fried becomes a standard staple to most Cuban meals. They are brown on the outside yet white on the inside. We eat them as frequently as North Americans eat potatoes. The word YUCA stands for Young Upwardly-mobile Cuban Americans. Usually, this individual is first or second generation, between twenty-five and forty-five years old, and educated in North American schools.

[16] Patrick J. Kiger, *Squeeze Play: The United States, Cuba, and the Helms-Burton Act* (Washington, DC: The Center for Public Integrity, 1996), 57.

[17] La Habana was more than just North America's center for sexual high jinks. It was a cosmopolitan city of high culture and glamour. Rieff reminds us that for the Anglo Miami oligarchy, La Habana was the New York or Paris of the Caribbean, while for the Cuban oligarchy, Miami was a bucolic retreat to recuperate from La Habana's rigorous social life. The ferry transporting passengers across the Florida Straits was called the *City of Havana*, not the *City of Miami*, revealing the cultural pecking order in force in those days. Hence, Cubans always felt superior to the provincial city of Miami. Ironically, coming to the United States decosmopolitanized us. See David Rieff, *The Exile: Cuba in the Heart of Miami* (New York: Simon & Schuster, 1993), 29-31, 39.

[18] A 1997 poll revealed that 23 percent would be likely or somewhat likely to return to Cuba if the country's economy significantly improves, while 29 percent would be likely or somewhat likely to return if Cuba adopts a democratic form of government. However, 49 percent would be likely or somewhat likely to return if both the economy and government change for the better. This poll showed later

emigres more likely to express a desire to return then those of the first two waves. See Guillermo J. Grenier and Hugh Gladwin, *FIU 1997 CUBA POLL*, Institute of Public Opinion Research (IPOR) of Florida International University, questions 33-34A.

[19] The descendants of the priest Zadok, who served under King David (2 Sam. 20:25) and supported Solomon during the succession struggle (1 King 1:8, 32), controlled the Jerusalem priesthood from the reign of Solomon (ca. 965 BCE) until the Exile (586 BCE) Hence, the Zadokite priesthood was responsible for administering the reforms made during the reign of King Josiah in 622 BCE. They held exclusive responsibility for the temple cult, facilitating their leadership status within the Exilic Jewish community. Ezekiel (40:46; 43:19; 48:11) dictates that only Zadokite priests can minister within a rebuilt Temple. Their leadership expanded to civic matters with the mysterious disappearance of the Davidic prince Zerubbabel. The Zadokites were also officially sponsored by the Persian court and given the task of restoring Judea as vassal to Persia. Service in the high-priesthood continued until 171 BCE, when the line first passed to the Hellenizers and then to the Hasmonean house. See Lawrence H. Schiffman, "Zadok," in *Haper's Bible Dictionary*, ed. Paul J. Achtemeir (San Franciso: Harper & Row, 1985), 1155.

[20] Paul D. Hanson, *The People Called: The Growth of Community in the Bible* (San Francisco: Harper & Row, 1986), 255. I am aware that Hanson's clear dichotomy does not exist between the Zadokites and Second Isaiah. In an attempt to read the biblical passage with Cuban eyes, we confess the Bible does not occupy an intrinsic space within the Cuban experience. Because most Exilic Cubans seldom read the text, we end up emphasizing our religiosity with customs and traditions. Reading the Bible with Cuban eyes also means popularizing versions of the biblical stories, as in the case of mixing it with African traditions for the purpose of making a spiritual point. In an attempt to make a spiritual point, I overly stress the Second Isaiah/Zadokite dichotomy in order to illustrate two possible paradigms facing Exilic Cubans, who mainly look at returning to the Island as a form of acquiring financial and political gain.

[21] Ezra was appalled by marriages between Jewish men and non-Jewish women, specially the intermingling by the community's leaders. This was a clear violation of the Pentateuchal law which forbade the union of Canaanites with Jews lest, "their daughters, prostituting themselves to their own gods, may induce [Israel's] sons to do the same" (Ex. 34:14-16). Ezra's solution was for the men to divorce their foreign wives.

[22] Prior to the revolution, Cuba placed among the top three Latin American countries in the delivery of social services. However, these social service facilities were concentrated in La Habana and other urban areas while the rural areas lacked basic services. Rural peasants lived in thatched-roof shacks with no indoor utilities, no security of land ownership, no medical facilities, and no schools. The average peasant could expect to earn "91 a year as opposed to the nationwide

average of" 374. Castro's reforms have diminished the income gap between the agricultural and urban sector. Even Castro's detractors admit that the social service accomplishments (many of which were corroborated by UNESCO), specifically free education and public heath systems, rank among the best of the Two-Thirds world and are on par with many industrial nations. See David Barkin, "La redistribución del consumo," in *Cuba: Camino abierto*, ed. David Barkin and Nita R. Manitzas (Mexico City: Siglo XXI, 1973), 191-96.

[23] The book of Ruth provides a radical alternative to the societal construction advocated by the Zadokites, an alternative based on the classical form of Yahwism of the premonarchic period. If the Pentateuchal laws were legalistically followed — as advocated by the Zadokite priesthood — during the time of Ruth, then the story of Ruth would not have occurred. To begin with, the marriage of Ruth, the Moabite, to the Jewish son of Naomi was contrary to Ex. 34:14-16, which forbade mixed marriages. Notwithstanding, once this foreign woman entered the religious community through marriage, she could not be denied the right and protection to remain within the community. Boaz becomes a model for the Zadokites on how to demonstrate compassion and justice to aliens.

Weaving of a Humanistic Vision: Reading the Hebrew Bible in Asian Religio-Cultural Context

Archie C. C. Lee

I. INTRODUCTION

Whether the Hebrew Scripture or the Old Testament of the Christian Bible has any significant contribution to the weaving of a humanistic vision in the Asian context is the central question raised in this paper. Having read and taught the Hebrew Scripture in Hong Kong for the last 18 years, I can definitely respond to the question positively.

There are scholars who share similar ideas in dealing with the role of the Bible in the intellectual as well as cultural milieu of a society. Hans D. Betz of the University of Chicago has briefly summarized the twofold function of the Bible in the following words: "First, the Bible is recognized as a piece of world literature with a wide range of references to many disciplines. Second, the Bible is recognized sociologically as the holy scripture of living religious communities and traditions which exercise great influence in the contemporary society."[1] The "contemporary society" Betz refers to is of course set in the Western world context, where the Bible has exercised paramount impact on the intellectual tradition and the formation of socio-religio-cultural ethos, although increasingly so-called secularization has succeeded in substantially eroding the role of the Bible.

The situation in the East, with its multi-scriptural setting, is not comparable to the mono-scriptural status enjoyed by a single text in Western culture. My thesis is that bringing to Asia a text that originated in Western Asia and subsequently found its "home" in the interpretative traditions of the Western world is a formidable, but rewarding challenge to religious studies in Asia. The study of the Bible not only helps us to acquire the skills and practices of historical-critical approach and literary studies, but also enlightens us in grasping religious attitudes towards human life and the vision of the future of humanity and the divine-human relationship as they have been worked out in historical human experiences of both the Jewish as well as the Christian communities. Affirming the humanistic concern expressed in Asian religious heritage, I propose that the "otherness" of the Hebrew Scripture contributes to the weaving of a humanistic vision through a cross-textual reading of the Hebrew Scripture and our Asian scriptures.[2]

II. HUMANISTIC VISIONS OF THE HEBREW SCRIPTURE

It is widely recognized that the Hebrew Scripture, itself acknowledged and justified as part of the legacy of ancient Near East and the "canon" of Western civilization, has contributed to the significant development of social values and political thought in ancient as well as contemporary Western culture. Having given rise to different interpretations in Jewish studies and Christian theology, the Bible is taken as a basic text for the search for a humanistic vision that values human life and entails trust in humanity. It also functions as a foundation for the practice of critical inquiry in western society.[3] Since the Enlightenment the application of historical-critical investigation into the history of the text and the history of interpretation has not only testified to the diversity of tradition and plurality of perception of reality in the Hebrew Scripture, but has also refuted the claim to a monopoly on truth by any religious community, be it Jewish, Catholic, or Protestant. The Hebrew Scripture becomes a shared object of critical study. Baruch Levine thus states: "The study of the Hebrew Bible, known by Christians as the Old Testament, is a shared field of knowledge in universities and other open institutions of higher learning."[4] Its study of has been integrated into general education programs of university curricula.

If the Hebrew Scripture is studied in comparative or interdisciplinary perspective in the context of appreciation for world cultures rather than from any specific religious affiliation or identity, a humanistic understanding of reverence for life and notions of justice and compassion for humanity can be formulated and deduced from the text. This is not easy, and sometimes not possible, to do, since no interpretations are without preconceptions. What can be aimed at is to free the study of the Hebrew Scripture from anti-Semitism and missionary zeal.

A humanistic concern for human life, which is a common feature of ancient Near Eastern culture, is expressively found in the Torah tradition, the prophetic vision, and the wisdom literature. Biblical scholars have long recognized the Book of Deuteronomy as displaying a strong humanistic character.[5]

The phrase "remember that you were aliens" is a key to opening up the articulation of a humanistic vision in the Hebrew Scripture.[6] The Israelites were to consider themselves a dispossessed and underprivileged people, being politically oppressed, economically deprived, and culturally marginalized when they were in the Egyptian empire of the Pharaoh (Exodus 1-2). The God of justice and compassion worked miracles and wonders to dismantle the oppressive power structure, to free his people from slavery, and to give them a piece of land to possess (Exodus 3-15; Deuteronomy 26:5-9).

This Torah story entails an ethical humanistic attitude towards the poor, the alien, the weak, and the powerless. The following passages help to illustrate this attitude towards human life succinctly:

> You shall not wrong or oppress a resident alien, for you were aliens in the land of Egypt. You shall not abuse any widow or orphan. If you do abuse them, when they cry out to me, I will surely heed their cry. (Exodus 22:21-23)

> You shall not oppress a resident alien; you know the heart of an alien, for you were aliens in the land of Egypt. (Exodus 23:9)

> You shall not cheat in measuring length, weight, or quality. You shall have honest balances, and an honest ephah, and an honest hin. I am the Lord your God, who brought you out of the land of Egypt. (Leviticus 19:35-36)

> You shall not deprive a resident alien or an orphan of justice; you shall not take a widow's garment in pledge. Remember that you were a slave in Egypt and the Lord your God redeemed you from there; therefore I command you to do this. (Deuteronomy 24:17-18)

> When you gather the grapes of your vineyard, do not glean what is left; it shall be for the alien, the orphan, and the widow. Remember that you were a slave in the land of Egypt; there I am commanding you to do this. (Deuteronomy 24: 21-22)

One cannot, even by casually reading these passages, miss the interpretative power of the Exodus event as a mode to understand how the divine involves itself in history and how human beings should relate to one another in community and solidarity. These passages function to substantiate the claim, from the perspective of liberation theology, that the biblical God is one who exercises preferential options for the poor.[7] Biblical scholars have endeavored to present the complex historical critical issues of these passages; it is not the intention of this article, with a limited scope, to go into the different points and views.[8]

In the context of Asia, the Minjung theology of Korea, the Dalit theology of India, and the theology of struggle formulated in the Philippines can all trace their inspiration to the religiosity and spirituality of these and many other passages rooted in the Exodus event of the Torah.[9] It is very pleasing for me to detect efforts at contextualization in these theological constructions of Christianity in Asia. The transformative power of reading has contributed to the formation of a new context in which Asian Christians locate and define their identity.

The prophets dwell on this Torah tradition to constantly remind their audience of the ethical living demanded of them and to call them to humanistic concerns that take the values of human life seriously together with divine compassion and mercy. The Hebrew prophets articulate the divine word in the context of history and in human society. When commenting on the prophetic critiques of the biblical text, Michael Fishbane writes: "The Bible itself, with its own pretension to present a humanly conditioned divine voice, would also be radically transcended."[10]

In this respect Biblical humanism has a transcendent aspect, and humanity is defined in terms of divine-human encounter. Human beings can stand before the divine to challenge the ways things are and to transform as well as change the present order. In dialogue with the divine, humanity can also shape the mind of God (Genesis 18); it is the response of human beings that determines the course of history (Jeremiah 18). The psalmist articulates this prime position of humanity in these words:

> What are human beings that you are mindful of them, mortals that you care for them?
> Yet you have made them a little lower than God, and crowned them with glory and honor.
> You have given them dominion over the works of your hands;
> You have put all things under their feet. (Psalm 8:4-6)

Martin Buber, an influential Jewish thinker, proposes the dialogical I-thou model of the divine human relationship, thus characterizing the humanism of the Hebrew Scripture in terms of humanity living in the sight of God and being constantly spoken to by the divine.[11] Grete Schaeder sums up Buber's approach to humanism as follows: "His humanism, like every genuine humanism, is imbued with a strong faith in man's undamaged integrity and in his capacity to share God's wisdom, a venture some claim that runs counter to the Christian conception of fallen man."[12]

III. HUMANISTIC ORIENTATION AND THE CRITICAL SPIRIT OF WISDOM

The often neglected treasure of the Hebrew Scripture is found in the Wisdom Literature, which puts great emphasis on human experience and concern with the well-being of human life. Traditional wisdom in the ancient Near East and the Hebrew Bible is oriented towards humanity without the concept of election and the notion of a chosen people. A universalistic-humanistic base for human understanding and knowledge is characteristic of Wisdom Literature. It is generally assumed that creation theology is the framework through which wisdom ideas are formulated.[13]

Wisdom thought pursues and intends to establish "order." Knowledge of the cosmic order in divine creation can be obtained through observation and experience. Social order needs to correspond to creation order, and human beings, through the acquisition of wisdom and understanding, learn to cope with life and to order it accordingly.

Wisdom does not always present itself as a stabilizing factor, however. Some of the wise and the sages are open to new human experience that contradicts and challenges the conventional wisdom. A critical spirit of reform and re-evaluation is expressed in the radical wisdom presented in the Book of Job and the Book of Koheleth, which questions the validity and applicability of accepted concepts. This wisdom knows of its own limitation and looks beyond itself to the transcendental dimension in the conception of "fear of the Lord" as being the beginning of wisdom (Proverbs I:7 etc.). Some scholars refer to this development of wisdom as a gradual Israelization of the ancient Near Eastern wisdom tradition.[14]

In fact, the openness of the wisdom tradition and its spirit of self-criticism and self-transformation must be praised as one of the characteristic features of the humanistic vision of Hebrew Wisdom. It is one of the most valuable legacies of the Hebrew Scripture and its contribution to a comprehensive humanistic vision that incorporates the dynamic relationship of humanity to the divine realm.

IV. CROSS-TEXTUAL READING OF THE HEBREW SCRIPTURE IN MULTI-SCRIPTURAL ASIA

In order to enlarge and enrich the humanistic visions anticipated in the Hebrew Scripture, the rich scriptural traditions of Asia should be brought in to enhance the cross-fertilization process. The process is inevitable in the encounter of Eastern and Western culture in the global context. Furthermore, one can bear witness to these phenomena in Asia when the Bible was introduced to and accepted by Asian converts to the Christian faith. These new converts adopt the Bible along with their ancient scriptures and religio-cultural classics.[15]

It can be very enlightening to look into the process by which they tried to make multiple "crossings" from the Hebrew text to Asian texts and vice versa. The conventional comparative approach that locates the similarities and differences between two worlds of thought or two religious modes of perceiving reality is simply not very satisfactory, as it does not respect the contribution of the readers in reading a text. The interaction between a reader and a text in the reading process involves the pre-understanding, the religio-cultural legacy, and the social location of the reader. Asian readers of the Hebrew Scripture do not enter the world of the text from a vacuity or with a vacuous and blank mind.[16] Into their understanding of the Hebrew Scripture they bring with them their own religio-cultural texts and socio-political texts. This can be a creative integration that engages the human imagination and results in the fusion of different horizons, be they religio-cultural or socio-political. I propose a cross-textual reading of scriptures in Asian Christianity and cultural-religious studies in Asia.

Both Western and Asian scholars have done recent work in this respect. Martin Buber made some contributions in his reading of Chuang Tzu (Zhuangzi) and the Tao (Dao) alongside Jewish texts.[17] Sinologist John B. Henderson has also compared Confucian and Western methods of commentary and interpretation.[18] The present writer has attempted to cultivate new areas by reading the creation stories in Genesis 1-11 together with Chinese Creation stories of Pan Ku and Nu Kua.[19]

With respect to the five Confucian Classics (jing/ching), although they have been accorded scriptural status by Confucianism, they have not been seen as embodying any significant religious concepts. Traditions of interpretation have it that these writings are humanistic in outlook and concern mainly ethical teachings and cultivation of the self. Religious elements have been denied to them in the long history of development. This trend intensified since the beginning of this century when China was humiliated by the Western imperial powers. The striving for modernization and nation-building in the May-Fourth New Literary Movement and the Anti-Christian movement placed tremendous importance on democracy and science at the expense of religion. Anti-foreign, anti-imperialism sentiment and the victory of communism in the past decades have furthered the marginalization of religion in academic circles as well as in the public domain.

While on the one hand religion in traditional Chinese writings has been explained away, religion in society has been redefined as mere superstition. But field studies done in recent years in various locations in China help to illustrate the vitality and persistent impact of religion on social structure and public life.[20]

Religious concepts in the ancient classics can be recovered and revealed when they are studied side by side with religious texts that have been read continuously in religious communities and recognized as such both in academic pursuit and by the general public. The Hebrew Bible, among other texts, may play such a significant role in the process of redefinition of the notion and idea of religion embedded in the Chinese Classics. A clear case in point is the investigation into the contribution of the liturgical texts of the Psalms to the re-reading of the influential Book of Poetry (Shijing) in Chinese Classics. Some of the poems in the Shijing originated from cultic and ritual contexts, but they have been decontextualized in the hands of literary scholars of Confucianism. The present writer presented a paper on this topic at the recent Confucian-Christian Dialogue Conference held at the Chinese University of Hong Kong. In it the cross-textual reading of the laments in both the Hebrew Psalter and the Chinese Shijing is introduced.[21]

Since the royal dynasty in ancient China was thought to be sanctioned by heaven and the mandate of heaven was believed to be in the possession of the "Son of Heaven," the common people had no one to turn to in the face of hardship and suffering brought about by the imperial power. In the laments of Shijing, people's complaints and petitions to heaven were categorized by subsequent interpreters as only admonitions of the servants of the emperor to their overlord, the powerful earthly ruler. It has been commonly accepted that the people did not dare to provoke and enrage the ruler by approaching him directly with petitions. They had to hide their afflictions and grievances under the cover of cries to heaven, hoping that after hearing these cries the ruler would comprehend the underlying motive and intention and take the necessary steps to improve the condition of the suffering people.

With such a view, it is reckoned that the ruler and heaven are close allies possessing absolute power. The two united to form one supreme authority. Opinions or admonitions directed to the ruler are discouraged, not to speak of opposition and rebellious ideas. The religious dimension of a transcendental divine being, to whom lament is directed and petitions are brought, is non-existent. As a result, the religious world of the Chinese is inevitably impoverished. The dividing line between addressing Shangdi, which is the Chinese name for the Supreme Lord of Heaven, and the king is not clear-cut. Indictment and imputation against the ruler can easily be adopted to form inculcation against Shangdi. The shift from accusing Shangdi to bitter lamentation directed to the king and vice versa comes without any traces of transition. The use of Shangdi and that of Heaven are also similar, and these two concepts are, to the poet, transferable and interchangeable:

> Shangdi has reversed the regular course,
> And the people below are in complete distress.
> Speeches are not meant to be fulfilled
> Policies do not have any duration
> As there is no sagely way
> You have no truth in your sincerity.
> Because your policies do not endure
> I therefore make this strong remonstration.
> As Heaven now causes calamities
> Do not be so contended.
> As Heaven now causes unrest,
> Do not be so talkative.

The poem begins with the grievance to Shangdi for the reversal of the normal, usual course of operation, bringing distress and misery to the people below. Then ambiguity sets in in lines 3-4. The identity of the maker of the speeches and policies is not clear. Shangdi can be referred to, but the lines are equally relevant if they point to the earthly ruler. In lines 5-7 we find it more likely that not Shangdi but the latter is in the mind of the poet. Line 8 confirms this, as the poet talks about making strong remonstration. The last four lines then portray the accusation as directed towards Heaven, which causes calamities and turmoil. Restraint from delight and scarcity of words are then called for.

When we read the laments in the Hebrew Psalter, we find that psalms often allude to the theme of the involvement of God in human affairs.[22] The enemies or the wicked manipulate "a certain kind of social world in which the powerful are free to do what they want for their own interest." By dismissing God as an effective player and active agent in that social world, the wicked can inscribe their rules of the game and deal violently with the weaker party. Psalm 10 provides a good example of the ideology of the wicked, who claim that "there is no god" (v.4)—and even if there is God, they will not be called to account for their wickedness (v.13). They happily affirm: "I shall not be moved" and "I shall not meet adversity" (v.6). To them, the world consist of only two unequal parties: the strong and powerful versus the weak and vulnerable.

When this self-serving ideology is left unchallenged, there is no hope for the poor. It is even worse if the poor and innocent are coerced into accepting the dominant ideology. The statement of the mourner, that "God has forgotten, God has hidden God's face, God will never see it" (Psalm 10:11), is alarming, as it conveys a cry of desperation. On the other hand, lament is a powerful means to achieve a counter-reality. Its petition initiates a redefinition of undesirable social relations and political power structures. In lament we see the vulnerability of human life in the face of oppression and imbalance of power. Unless the power structure is redressed, life is hurt and lament persists. In this sense, Walter Brueggemann considers lament as contributing to "the redistribution of power."[23]

In a way, the Hebrew Bible can be instrumental in the process of reviving the religious scenes in the Shijing. It also contributes to the reconstruction of the religious world of ancient China, within which the precious tradition of humanistic vision can be perceived in a new perspective Until now, such a vision has been mostly formed in a rather reductionist way.

It is not only false, but altogether unhealthy, to rest humanistic concerns of a culture on the elimination and suppression of religion. In the case of Chinese culture, resistance to religion is successfully achieved only in the isolated intellectual tradition of the elite and aristocracy. Syncretistic folk religious traditions, with their rich rites and elaborate rituals, flourish in the life of the people at various social levels. Even intellectuals and scholars from the gentry observe certain religious practices and quest for religious meanings at various stages of their lives, especially when they advance in age. The influence of Buddhist thought and Taoist concepts can be discerned in some of their writings.[24] Government officials, who come to their positions through public civil examinations in which the classics take up the whole syllabus, participate in religious rites in festivals celebrated at the national, regional, and local levels.

Cross-textual reading cannot be said to be properly carried out if it is done only lopsidedly. Chinese texts also have a lot to offer to the reading process. They can enrich and enlighten our understanding of the Hebrew Bible. The uncompromising trust in and respect for the greatness of humanity, which stands between heaven and earth, come out loud and clear. Through a disciplined effort of cultivation, humanity can achieve righteousness, virtue, and harmony in human community. This stress on the role of humanity in the union between heaven and earth may invite us to reflect on the seemingly unbridgeable gap between the divine and the human in the Hebrew tradition. It is meaningful to reflect on the Chinese perception of the divine-human continuum in parallel with the Hebrew conceptions of God and humanity in the Bible.

This issue is central to the theological construction of a Chinese Christianity that has to reconcile these two different views of reality. The way Chinese Christians deal with this issue will in large part constitute the definition of their identity at the place where both cultures meet and where one challenges the other. The cross-textual reading of the Hebrew Bible and the Chinese Classics is part of the process through which Chinese Christians negotiate for an integrated religious and cultural identity.

In sum, the cross-textual hermeneutics that I have been putting into operation in my work on Asian Classics (Text A) and Biblical Scripture (Text B) not only elicits a better understanding of the texts under study in their cross-fertilizing potentiality, but also addresses the religio-cultural identity of Asians who have been converted to a non-Asian religion.Cross-textual reading of two texts thus enables us to weave together the understandings of humanity and conceptions of divinity in the two different traditions and at the same time to provide a platform for positive and meaningful wrestling with our identities in pluriformity.

Lastly, a crucial reminder for critical study of religious classics and scriptures: There are obviously both negative as well as positive, oppressive as well as liberating, and enslaving as well as affirming elements in all scriptural traditions and their history of interpretation. In order to draw out a balanced view on their notions of humanistic vision, the Hebrew Scripture and the Asian religious classics require critical examination. Any idealizing tendency or downgrading attitude must be excluded from both academic pursuit and the lived experience of a people.

Notes

[1]Hans Dieter Betz, ed., The *Bible as a Document of the University* (Chico. CA: Scholars Press, 1981), 2.

[2] On the notion of "otherness" and its contribution to comparative studies, see Lee H. Yearley, *Mencius and Aquinas. Theories of virtue and conceptions of courage* (New York: State University of New York, 1990), and Francis X. Clooney, S. J., *Theology After Vedanta, An Experiment in Comparative Theology* (New York: State University of New York Press, 1993).

[3] David Sidorsky, "Remembering the Answers: Jewish Studies in the Contemporary University," in *Teaching Jewish Civilization, A Global Approach to Higher Education*, ed. Moshe Davis (New York: New York University Press, 1995), 31-33.

[4] Baruch A. Levine, "Tanakh: A Shared Field," in *Teaching Jewish Civilization, A Global Approach to Higher Education*, ed. Moshe Davis (New York: New York University Press, 1995), 96.

[5] Moshe Weinfeld, *Deuteronomy and Deuteronomic School* (Oxford: Oxford University Press, 1972), 282-97.

[6] Christiana de Groot van Houten, "Remember That You Were Aliens: A Tradition-Historical Study," in *Priests Prophets and Scribes, Essays on the Formation and Heritage of Second Temple Jerusalem in Honour of Joseph Blenkinsopp,* ed. Eugene Ulrich, et al (Sheffield: JSOT, 1992), 224-40.

[7] There are many scholarly works on the Exodus pattern and its ethical implications. See recent writings of Walter Bruggemann collected in *A Social Reading of the Old Testament, Prophetic Approaches to Israel's Communal Life,* ed. Patrick D. Miller (Minneapolis: Fortress Press, 1994) and *Old Testament Theology, Essays on Structure, Theme, and Text*, ed. Patrick D. Miller (Mineapolis: Fortress Press, 1992).

[8] A recent scholarly work on the complexity of the historical traditions and the influence of the socio-political attitude of scholars on their work is very instructive: K.W. Whitelam, *The Invention of Ancient Israel* (London: 1996).

[9] Cyris H. S. Moon, *A Korean Minjung Theology: An Old Testament Perspective* (Maryknoll, N.Y.: Orbis Books, 1985); Kim Yong Bock, *Minjung Theology, People as Subject of History* (Singapore: The Christian Conference of Asia, 1981); Noriel C. Capulong, "Land, Power and Peoples' Rights in the Old Testament: from a Filipino Theological Perspective," *East Asia Journal of Theology* 2 (1984): 233-250; V. Devasahayam, *Outside the Camp: Bible Studies in Dalit Perspective* (Madras, India: Gurukul Lutheran Theological College and Research Institute, 1994); Aloysuis Pieris, S. J., *An Asian Theology of Liberation* (Maryknoll, N.Y., Orbis Books, 1990).

[10] Michael Fishbane, "The Notion of a Sacred Text," in *The Garments of Torah,*

Essays in Biblical Hermeneutics (Bloomington & Indianapolis: Indiana University Press, 1989), 131.

[11] Martin Buber, *On the Bible, Eighteen Studies*, ed. Nahum Glatzer (New York: Schocken Books, 1982), 213-15.

[12] Grete Schaeder, *The Hebrew Humanism of Martin Buber* (Detroit: Wayne State University Press, 1973), 366.

[13] Walter Zimmerli, "The Place and Limit of Wisdom in the Framework of Old Testament Theology," in *Studies in Ancient Israelite Wisdom* (New York: KTAV, 1976), 314-28; H.J. Hermission, "Observations on the Creation Theology in Wisdom," in *Israelite Wisdom: Theological and Literary Essays in Honor of Samuel Terrien*, ed. J. Gammie (Missoula: Scholars Press, 1978), 43-57.

[14] See James L. Crenshaw, *Old Testament Wisdom: An Introduction* (Atlanta: John Knox Press, 1981), 55-65, 190-211.

[15] S. J. Samartha.

[16] Au Kwok Pui-lan, *Discovering the Bible in the Non-Biblical World* (New York: Orbis Books, 1995); and R. S. Sugirtharajah, ed., *Voices from the Margin: Interpreting the Bible in the Third World* (Maryknoll, N.Y.: Orbis Books, 1991).

[17] Martin Buber, *Reden und Gleichnisse des Tschuang-tze* (Zürich: Manesse Verlag, 1951); "The Spirit of the Orient and Judaism,"in *On Judaism* (New York: Schocken Books), 56-78; "The Teaching of the Tao,"in *Pointing the Way* (New York: Harper and Brothers, 1957), 31-58; and *Chinese Tales, Atlantic Highlands* (Humanities Press International, 1991). Jonathan Roy Herman has done a doctoral dissertation on Martin Buber and Chuang Tzu: *The Text of "Chuang Tzu" and the Problem of Interpretation: A Critical Study of Martin Buber's Translation and Commentary* (Harvard University, 1992).

[18] John B. Henderson, *Scripture, Canon, and Commentary: A Comparison of Confucian and Western Exegesis* (Princeton: Princeton University Press, 1991).

[19] Archie Lee, "Genesis 1 from the Perspective of a Chinese Creation Myth," in *Understanding Poets and Prophets*, ed. Graeme Auld, (Sheffield: Sheffield Academic Press, 1993), 186-98, and "The Chinese Creation Myth of Nu Kua and the Biblical Narrative in Genesis 1-11," *Biblical Interpretation* 2 (1994): 312-24.

[20] Kenneth Dean, *Taoist Ritual and Popular Cults of Southeast China* (Princeton, N.J: Princeton University Press, 1993), and *Lord of the Three in One: The Spread of a Cult in Southeast China* (Princeton, N.J: Princeton University Press, 1998); John Lagerwey, *Taoist Ritual in Chinese Society and History* (New York : Macmillan, 1987). The Department of Religion of the Chinese University of Hong Kong has launched an extended field study project in South China under the leadership of John Lagerwey and Wai Lun Tam.

[21] Archie C. C. Lee, "Crossing Boundaries: Reimaging Humanity in the Hebrew Psalter and the Chinese Shijing."

[22] Walter Brueggemann, *The Psalms and the Life of Faith* (Minneapolis: Fortress Press), 227.

[23] Walter Brueggeman, "The Costly Loss of Lament," *Journal for the Study of the Old Testament* 36 (1986): 59.

[24] Judith Berling, *The Syncretic Religion of Lin Chao-en* (New York: Columbia University Press, 1980); Kai-wing Chow, *The Rise of Confucian Ritualism in Late Imperial China* (Stanford: Stanford University Press, 1994).